LANDSCAPE ARCHITECTURE AND ENVIRONMENTAL SUSTAINABILITY

Bloomsbury Visual Arts
An imprint of Bloomsbury Publishing Plc

Imprint previously known as AVA Publishing

50 Bedford Square	1385 Broadway
London	New York
WC1B 3DP	NY 10018
UK	USA

www.bloomsbury.com

British Library Cataloguing-in-Publication Data
A catalogue record for this book is available from the British Library.

ISBN: PB: 978-1-4725-9062-6
ePDF: 978-1-4725-9063-3

Library of Congress Cataloging-in-Publication Data

Names: Zeunert, Joshua.
Title: Landscape architecture and environmental sustainability : creating positive change through design / Joshua Zeunert.
Description: London ; New York : Bloomsbury Visual Arts, 2016. | Series: Required reading range | Includes bibliographical references and index.
Identifiers: LCCN 2015044114| ISBN 9781472590626 (pbk. : alk. paper) | ISBN 9781472590633 (epdf : alk. paper)
Subjects: LCSH: Landscape architecture| Sustainable architecture| Sustainable development.
Classification: LCC SB472 .Z48 2016 | DDC 712--dc23 LC record available at http://lccn.loc.gov/2015044114
Series: Required Reading Range

Cover design: Louise Dugdale
Cover image © www.jordisurroca.com

Typeset by Hoop Design
Printed and bound in China

Companion Website: www.bloomsbury.com/zeunert-landscape-architecture

LANDSCAPE ARCHITECTURE AND ENVIRONMENTAL SUSTAINABILITY
Creating Positive Change through Design

JOSHUA ZEUNERT

BLOOMSBURY VISUAL ARTS
AN IMPRINT OF BLOOMSBURY PUBLISHING PLC

B L O O M S B U R Y

LONDON · OXFORD · NEW YORK · NEW DELHI · SYDNEY

CONTENTS

CHAPTER 7 SOCIAL SUSTAINABILITY: INFLUENCE BEYOND SITE

CHAPTER 8 LESS IS MORE: A LIGHTER TOUCH

CHAPTER 9 LANDSCAPE AND PERFORMANCE

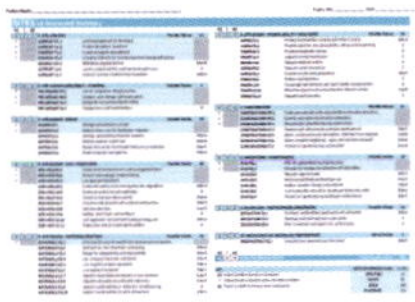

CHAPTER 10 SCENARIOS, CHALLENGES AND REFRAMING LAND(SCAPE)

This book explores and aims to demonstrate landscape architecture's potential for multidimensional sustainability through realized projects and initiatives to early to mid-level higher education students and a wider interested audience. It is intended to provoke and inspire discussion, further research and offer design solutions through a selected array of thought-provoking quotes, pertinent images, over 200 projects and works, study and discussion questions, interviews with noted professionals and further readings.

> "The thing itself is one; the images are many. What leads to a perceptive understanding of the thing is not the focus on one image, but the viewing of many images together."
> Rudolf Steiner, Goethe's World View (1897)

Designed to mirror the multifaceted, interdisciplinary, integrated nature of landscape sustainability, the book's aim is one of breadth, and it intentionally encompasses a wide cross-section of topics. Such broad-scale, systems-thinking is crucial for effective conception of the theory and practice of both sustainability and landscape architecture. Depth is therefore sacrificed in favor of presenting a wide spectrum encouraging the reader to seek additional knowledge through suggested further readings, quoted works and project examples. Further readings intentionally combine old and new, as many current sustainability trends and theories are rebadged classics.

The various textual and image components are threaded together through the framework of a discussion structured into chapter topics, each representing a key thematic area of multidimensional sustainable landscape architecture: ecology; pollution; infrastructure; food; art and aesthetics; social sustainability; light touch; and performance. These chapter topics are divided into a series of sub-themes and supported by (predominantly) realized projects, images and interviews, which have been positioned to reflect chapter focus.

Chapter 1 begins with a brief overview of historic environmental events. Chapter 2 examines ecological landscape topics with a focus on multidimensional, progressive and emerging areas for planning and landscape architecture. Chapter 3 demonstrates landscape's ability to remediate, mitigate and heal terrestrial and aquatic environments from industrialism's ongoing toxic legacy, through designed natural processes and ecosystem service provision. Chapter 4 explores possibilities to increase sustainability of transport and energy infrastructure networks through expanding disciplinary scale. Chapter 5 presents multifarious dimensions of landscape and food, aiming to convey their importance for landscape practice. Chapter 6 explores activist environmental possibilities in landscape, and sustainability's relationship with aesthetic and immersive experiences of nature and beauty. Chapter 7 touches on a wide range of social sustainability concerns and possible expanded territories including ethical, strategic, educational, health, economic and political dimensions. Chapter 8 showcases natural and cultural place concerns, highly attuned, 'light-touch', and sensitive work and in an increasingly globalized and homogeneous world, such practice is as important as it has ever been. Chapter 9 explores how ratings and performance approaches can capture and quantify landscape's capacity as a productive agent rather than merely consumptive, distinguishing landscape architecture from other design disciplines. The final chapter explores, questions and defines possible future scope for landscape architecture.

As this book is focused on completed projects and works bridging theory and practice, some unrealized and emerging theories have received little attention. Project text and imagery aims to unpack hidden subtleties often invisible in completed landscape architectural photographs. Where possible, 'before' or time-lapse imagery as well as drawings and diagrams have been included to clarify environmental processes, strategies and components, and to assist perception of the landscape architect's sometimes invisible guiding hand. A glossary defines terms and concepts used throughout (these may differ depending on regional variances, design jargon, or trends). Interviews are presented in the interviewees' own words and have not been edited. Consequently, length has been cut and the complete interviews are available online at the companion website, www.bloomsbury.com/zeunert-landscape-architecture.

Further resources are suggested and available online. The greatest of care has been taken to ensure that all project details and attributions are up to date at the time of writing.

Joshua Zeunert
February 2016

1.1a
Buried machinery, Dallas, South Dakota, 1936

I
AN INTRODUCTION

It is crucial to grasp the underlying factors affecting sustainability in order to conceive effective design solutions. This chapter briefly introduces some of the deep-seated practices and actions that have adversely impacted the environment (with a particular focus on industrialization), as well as the responses to this problematic phenomenon.

1.1a
1.1b

North Great Plains Shelterbelt (Toronto, Canada to Abilene, Texas), 1934

Early 20th-century agricultural practices like native vegetation clearance led to crippling frequent dust storms in the USA's Great Plains. This harsh, semi-arid environment became known as the 'Dust Bowl'. President Franklin Roosevelt and the US Forest Service coordinated a 100 mile (160km) wide 'shelterbelt zone' from Toronto in Canada to the Brazos River, Texas. Despite the substantial challenges and complexities of this continental-scale project (such as high capital cost and multiple jurisdictions), the Civilian Conservation Corps, aided by paid farmers, began planting 220 million trees in 1934. These shelterbelts would reduce the harmful effects of prevailing dry winds, protect fields and livestock; reduce evaporation through holding water and snow in the soil; reduce soil erosion by holding soil in place; and ultimately, eliminate large dust storms. Even today, the project perhaps represents the largest and most focused effort of the US government to address an environmental problem. Image 1.1b shows part of the planned shelterbelt zone.

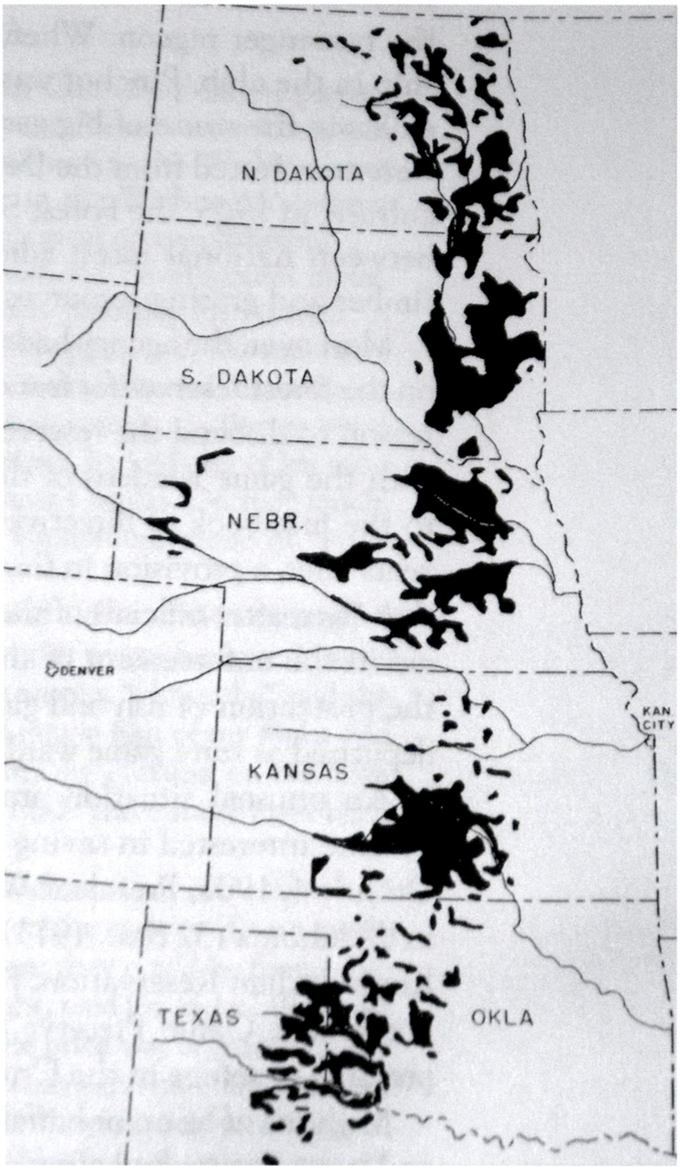
N. DAKOTA
S. DAKOTA
NEBR.
DENVER
KANSAS
KAN CITY
TEXAS
OKLA

1.1b

"Anthropocene is an apt and provocative term with which to describe the age and the world in which we now live. Thanks to this concept we can better place many observations about human influence on natural processes. Around the world there are more trees in parks, nurseries and other human settings than in the primeval forest. Humans are capable, in 500 years, of burning up the biomass produced in 500 million years, and of altering the climate with the greenhouse gases released. A single project for tar sand extraction requires as much soil displacement as the sediment carried off by all the rivers in the world ... The advance of humanity is coupled with an avalanche of species facing extinction."
DIRK SIJMONS, WAKING UP IN THE ANTHROPOCENE (2014)

"Could the stability achieved over aeons of geological time be destroyed within a few generations, with no guarantee that any new balance would offer our descendants an ecological niche?"
DAVID REID, SUSTAINABLE DEVELOPMENT (1995)

MESOZOIC ERA
TRIASSIC PERIOD
JURASSIC PERIOD
CRETACEOUS PERIOD
251 MILLION YEARS AGO
200 M.Y.
65 MILLION YEARS AGO
Paleocene Epoch
Eocene Epoch
Oligocene Epoch
Miocene Epoch
Pliocene Epoch
Pleistocene Epoch
Holocene Epoch
TERTIARY PERIOD
QUATERNARY PERIOD
CENOZOIC ERA
56 M.Y.
34 M.Y.
5 M.Y.
2 M.Y.
11,500 YR.
PERMIAN PERIOD
PENNSYLVANIAN PERIOD
MISSISSIPPIAN PERIOD
DEVONIAN PERIOD
SILURIAN PERIOD
ORDOVICIAN PERIOD
CAMBRIAN PERIOD
542 M.Y. AGO
PALEOZOIC ERA
PRECAMBRIAN
1 BILLION YEARS AGO
2 BILLION YEARS AGO
3 BILLION YEARS AGO
EARLIEST ORGANIC STRUCTURES
4.5 BILLION YEARS AGO

1.2

A BRIEF ENVIRONMENTAL HISTORY

1.2
Geologic Time
Since Paul Crutzen and Eugene Stoermer coined the term 'Anthropocene' in 2000 to reflect the evidence of substantial impact of humanity upon the Earth's systems, 'official' recognition of this new era to replace the existing 'Holocene' on the geological time scale (shown here) has gained significant momentum.

Before civilization

Prior to settlements and civilization, largely nomadic human populations were attuned to and constrained by seasonal rhythms and flows, yet still incrementally altered and reshaped the natural composition of environments (such as through the use of fire and targeting specific plants and animals for food). Low global human population reduced the extent of anthropogenic (human-generated) environmental impacts and roaming populations were more conducive to ecological recovery.

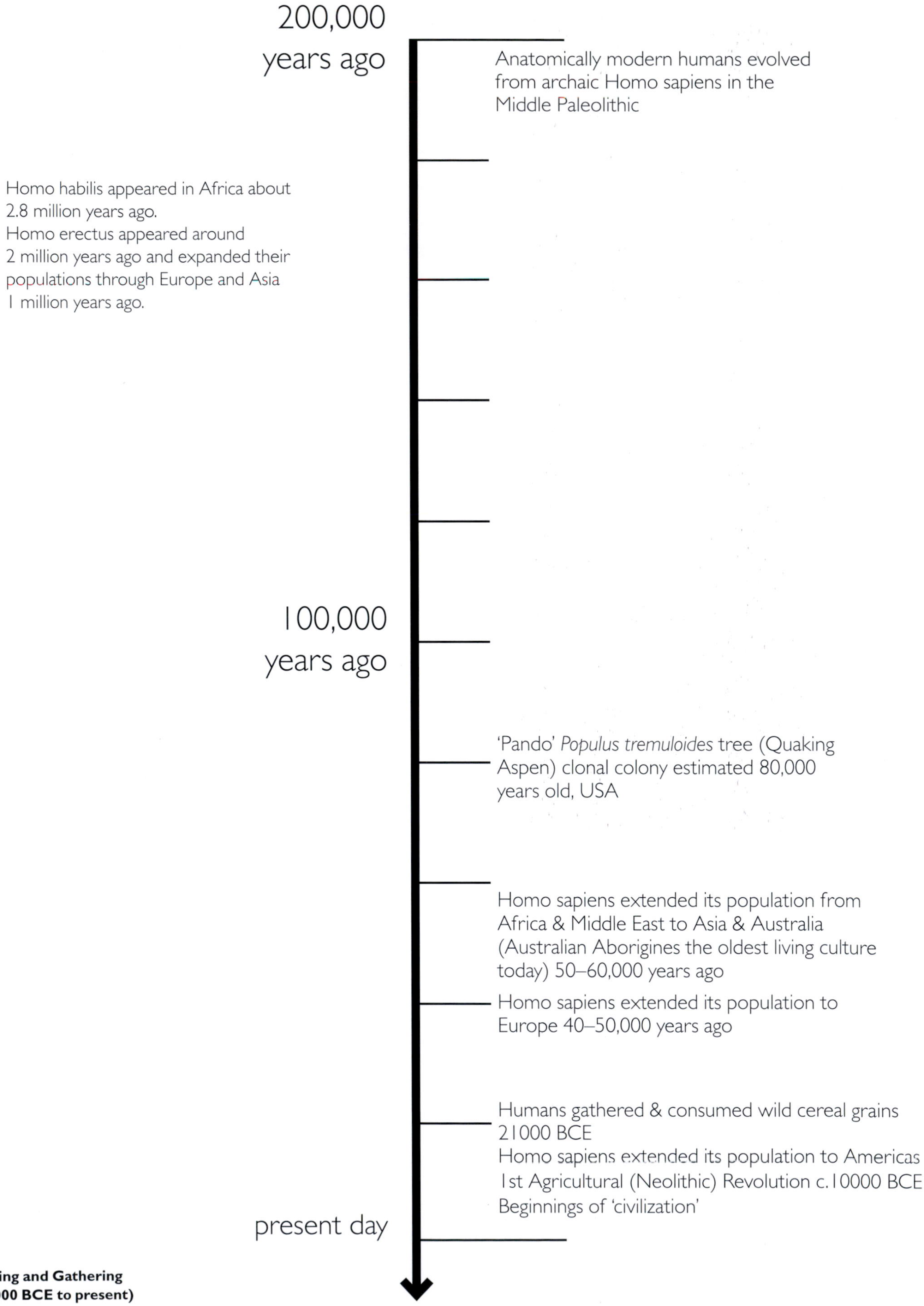
200,000 years ago
Anatomically modern humans evolved from archaic Homo sapiens in the Middle Paleolithic
Homo habilis appeared in Africa about 2.8 million years ago.
Homo erectus appeared around 2 million years ago and expanded their populations through Europe and Asia 1 million years ago.
100,000 years ago
'Pando' *Populus tremuloides* tree (Quaking Aspen) clonal colony estimated 80,000 years old, USA
Homo sapiens extended its population from Africa & Middle East to Asia & Australia (Australian Aborigines the oldest living culture today) 50–60,000 years ago
Homo sapiens extended its population to Europe 40–50,000 years ago
Humans gathered & consumed wild cereal grains 21000 BCE
Homo sapiens extended its population to Americas
1st Agricultural (Neolithic) Revolution c.10000 BCE
Beginnings of 'civilization'
present day

1.3
Hunting and Gathering (200000 BCE to present)

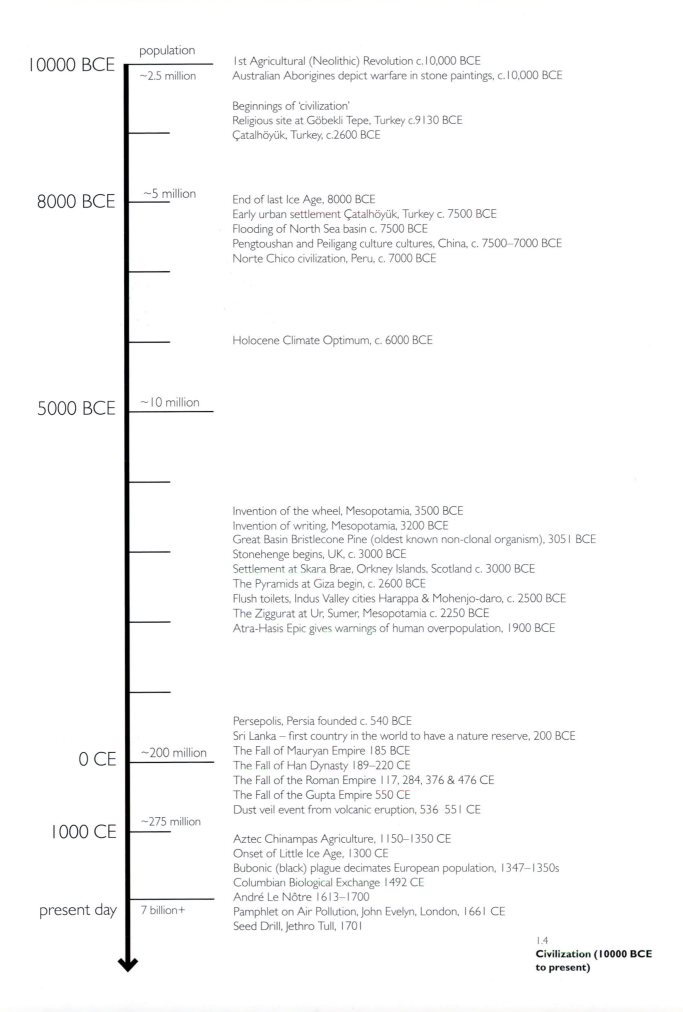

Date	Population	Events
10000 BCE	~2.5 million	1st Agricultural (Neolithic) Revolution c.10,000 BCE Australian Aborigines depict warfare in stone paintings, c.10,000 BCE Beginnings of 'civilization' Religious site at Göbekli Tepe, Turkey c.9130 BCE Çatalhöyük, Turkey, c.2600 BCE
8000 BCE	~5 million	End of last Ice Age, 8000 BCE Early urban settlement Çatalhöyük, Turkey c. 7500 BCE Flooding of North Sea basin c. 7500 BCE Pengtoushan and Peiligang culture cultures, China, c. 7500–7000 BCE Norte Chico civilization, Peru, c. 7000 BCE Holocene Climate Optimum, c. 6000 BCE
5000 BCE	~10 million	Invention of the wheel, Mesopotamia, 3500 BCE Invention of writing, Mesopotamia, 3200 BCE Great Basin Bristlecone Pine (oldest known non-clonal organism), 3051 BCE Stonehenge begins, UK, c. 3000 BCE Settlement at Skara Brae, Orkney Islands, Scotland c. 3000 BCE The Pyramids at Giza begin, c. 2600 BCE Flush toilets, Indus Valley cities Harappa & Mohenjo-daro, c. 2500 BCE The Ziggurat at Ur, Sumer, Mesopotamia c. 2250 BCE Atra-Hasis Epic gives warnings of human overpopulation, 1900 BCE Persepolis, Persia founded c. 540 BCE Sri Lanka – first country in the world to have a nature reserve, 200 BCE The Fall of Mauryan Empire 185 BCE
0 CE	~200 million	The Fall of Han Dynasty 189–220 CE The Fall of the Roman Empire 117, 284, 376 & 476 CE The Fall of the Gupta Empire 550 CE Dust veil event from volcanic eruption, 536 551 CE
1000 CE	~275 million	Aztec Chinampas Agriculture, 1150–1350 CE Onset of Little Ice Age, 1300 CE Bubonic (black) plague decimates European population, 1347–1350s Columbian Biological Exchange 1492 CE André Le Nôtre 1613–1700
present day	7 billion+	Pamphlet on Air Pollution, John Evelyn, London, 1661 CE Seed Drill, Jethro Tull, 1701

1.4
Civilization (10000 BCE to present)

1.5
Easter Island
Easter Island was once home to a range of plant and animal species including 21 tree species. By European arrival in 1722, the island's Polynesian population had dropped from its peak of 15,000 to 2,000–3,000 due to environmental mismanagement and mass tree clearing. Jared Diamond terms this process "ecocide" and the "clearest example of a society that destroyed itself by overexploiting its own resources."

1.5

Sedentary civilization

The development of agriculture around 10000 BCE (Before the Common/ Christian Era) facilitated establishment of permanent settlements. Such communities (hamlets, villages, towns, cities) created cumulative degradative impacts, heightening environmental pressures on fixed regions and greatly reducing the capacity for ecological recovery. Tree felling, vegetation clearance, grazing and agriculture in the Middle East's 'fertile crescent', for example, significantly altered its environment leading to considerable increases of marginal land. These smaller, relatively separated human populations, however, largely contained their ecological consequences to their immediate region for thousands of years—rendering them local and not yet global issues.

Civilization collapse

Civilization collapse has occurred throughout human history. Aside from societal conflicts, it can be caused by a failure to recognize, respond and adapt to the challenges of degraded environments, shrinking natural resources or a changing climate. Key factors include population, climate, water, agriculture, and energy. Given our dependence on natural systems for resources and ecosystem services, awareness of environmental health, resilience, carrying capacity and social structures is exceptionally important for sustainable management and anticipating future scenarios.

"The more you know, the less you need."
AUSTRALIAN ABORIGINAL SAYING

"Nothing perishes in this vast universe, but all varies, and changes its figure. I think that nothing endures long under the same appearance. What was solid earth has become sea, and solid ground has issued from the bosom of the waters."
OVID, METAMORPHOSES (8 CE)

population

1750 CE

Horse drawn 'Seed drill', Jethro Tull, 1701
Lancelot 'Capability' Brown, 1716–83
Humphry Repton, 1752–1818
'Enclosure' in agriculture became widespread in Britain, 1700s–

Britain's First Canal, 1757
Industrial Revolution, c.1760 CE

Spinning Jenny machine, James Hargreaves, 1764

Improvement of Steam Engine, James Watt, 1770
Spinning Mule developed, 1775
American Revolution, 1775–83

Steam powered mills, 1779
Selective breeding of livestock in British agriculture, 1780s–
John Claudius Loudon, 1783–1843

French Revolution, 1789–99
Coal gas home lighting, William Murdock, 1792

1800 CE

>1 billion

Steam locomotive demonstrated, Robert Trevithick, 1801
Ralph Waldo Emerson, 1803–82

Successful steamboat, Robert Fulton, 1807

Luddite Riots: laborers attack machines in factories, 1811–15

Andrew Jackson Downing, 1815–52
Henry David Thoreau, 1817–62

Frederick Law Olmsted, 1822–1903
Calvert Vaux, 1824–95
First subaqueous tunnel, London, Marc Brunel, 1826–42
On The Landscape Architecture of the Great Painters of Italy (Book), 1828

A Treatise on the Theory and Practice of Landscape Gardening (Book), 1841
Birkenhead Park, Britain's first publically funded civic park, 1847
Communist Manifesto (Pamphlet) Karl Marx & Friedrich Engels (Book), 1848
Ebenezer Howard 1850–1928
Superphosphate fertilizers emerge

1850 CE

Central Park, New York, 1857–
Central Park Competition won by Vaux & Olmsted, 1858
On the Origin of Species (Book) Charles Darwin, 1859
First mechanical (steam) oil well, Titusville, Pennsylvania, 1859
Jens Jensen, 1860–1951
Thomas Hayton Mawson, 1861–1933
Olmsted and Vaux adopted 'landscape architect' as professional title, 1863
U.S. Civil War, 1861–65
Completion of Suez Canal, 1869
Yellowstone National Park (1st in world & USA), 1872
Beatrix Jones Farrand 1872–1959
First patent of a living organism, 1873
Progress and Poverty (Book), Henry George, 1879
Royal National Park (1st in Australia), 1879
US Geological Survey established, 1879
Banff National Park (1st in Canada), 1885
New Zealand Tongariro National Park (1st in New Zealand) 1887
How the Other Half Lives (Book), Jacob Riis, 1880
Sierra Club founded, 1892
American Society of Landscape Architects (ASLA), founded 1899
Mass destruction mining (open pit), 1899
Thomas Church, 1902–78
Garden Cities of Tomorrow (Book), Ebenezer Howard, 1902
Sweden National Parks (1st in Europe), 1909

1900 CE

Lakeview Gusher Oil Spill, USA, 1910
Henry Ford Assembly Line, 1913
Federation of German Landscape Architects founded, 1913
Synthetic Nitrogen Ammonia fertilizers emerge
World War I, 1914–18
Cities in Evolution (Book), Patrick Geddes, 1915
American City Planning Institute founded, 1917
Mine Asbestos Contamination, Libby, Montana, 1919–
Ian L. McHarg, 1920–2001
The League of Nations founded, 1920
Council of Educators in Landscape Architecture founded, 1920
Netherlands Landscape Architecture (BNT) founded, 1922
Rudolph Steiner Biodynamic Agriculture, c.1925
Virunga National Park, Congo (1st in Africa), 1925
Japanese Institute of Landscape Architecture founded, 1925

2 billion

Landscape Institute (UK) founded, 1929
Plant Patent Act, USA, 1930
First National Parks in Japan, 1931
Canadian Society of Landscape Architects founded, 1934
American Society of Planning Officials founded, 1934
'Dirty Thirties' Dust Storms, USA, 1930s
Hoover Dam on the Colorado River completed, 1936
World War II, 1939–45
Emergence of Modern Organic Agriculture, 1940s
Love Canal toxic landfill, New York, 1942

1950 CE

2.5 billion

Green (Agricultural) Revolution, c.1943
Agricultural chemical pesticides widely emerge, 1940s
International Federation of Landscape Architects (IFLA) founded, 1948

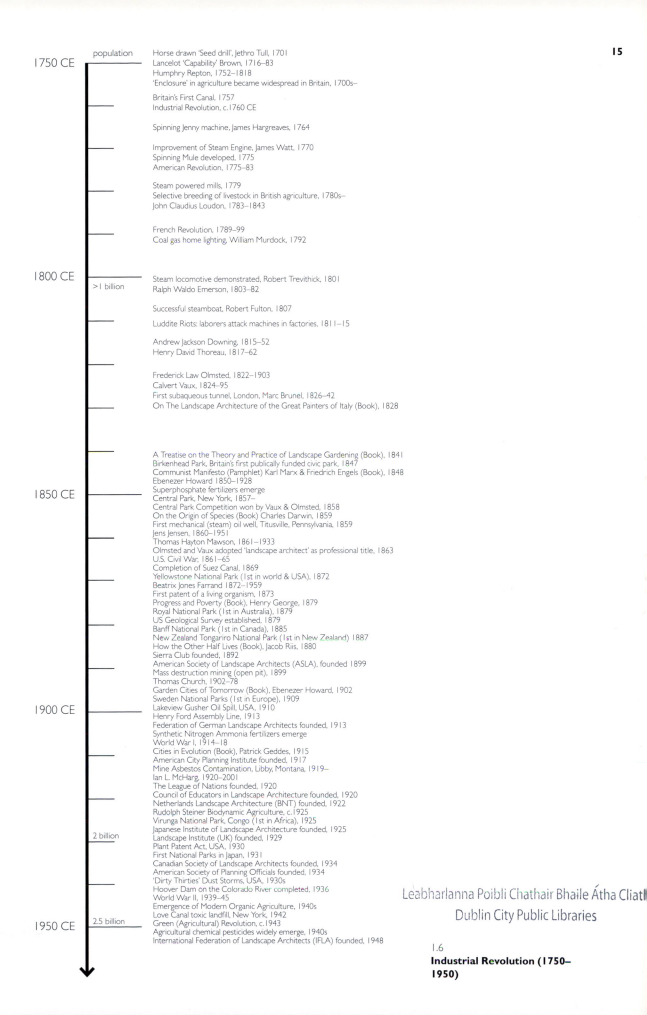

1.6
Industrial Revolution (1750–1950)

1.7

"You would make a ship sail against the winds and currents by lighting a bonfire under her deck? I have no time for such nonsense."
NAPOLEON I, ON ROBERT FULTON'S STEAMSHIP (CIRCA 1800)

LAND of the
ESKIMAUX's or LABRADOR
ATLANTIC OCEAN
NOVA SCOTIA
Newfoundland
VIRGINIA
NORTH CAROLINA
SOUTH CAROLINA
GEORGIA
WEST FLORIDA
PART OF THE GULF OF MEXICO
ATLANTIC OCEAN
CHART of The GULF STREAM

1.8

1.7
Coalbrookdale by Night, Philip James de Loutherbourg, 1801
Coalbrookdale is a village in Shropshire, England, where iron ore was first smelted through the use of locally mined 'coking coal'—a major factor in Britain's industrialization and the beginnings of the Industrial Revolution.

1.8
1770 map of the Gulf Stream
The earliest known chart of the Gulf Stream produced by Benjamin Franklin, was published in 1770 in England and mostly ignored for some time. Once the British heeded the chart they were able to gain two weeks in sailing time by following ocean current patterns.

1.9a
1.9b
Native vegetation clearance and modification, Victoria, Australia
Native vegetation clearance since the colonization of regions such as United States, Canada, Australia, New Zealand, Pacific and Africa has been dramatic. British and European settlers sought to reshape and familiarize claimed lands, resulting in often brutal clearance of native and indigenous vegetation communities and the displacement of indigenous cultures who managed them. The result today is a series of hybrid novel environments and vegetation types, neither native nor exotic. The maps show the extent of native vegetation types by bioregions within the Australian State of Victoria, before colonization in 1750 and after colonization in 2004.

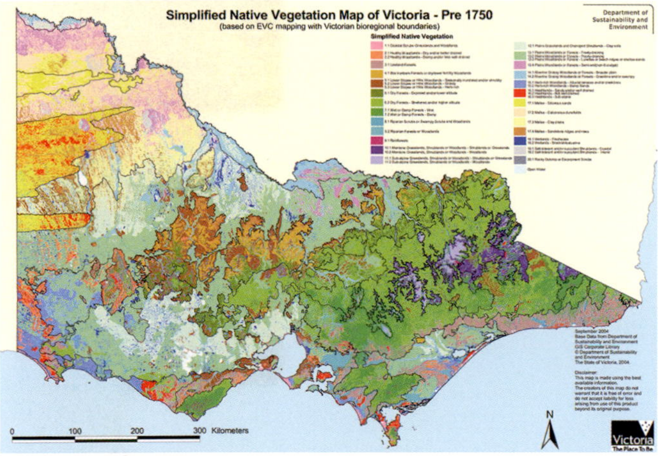
Simplified Native Vegetation Map of Victoria - Pre 1750
(based on EVC mapping with Victorian bioregional boundaries)
Department of Sustainability and Environment
Simplified Native Vegetation
0 100 200 300 Kilometers
N
Victoria
The Place To Be

1.9a

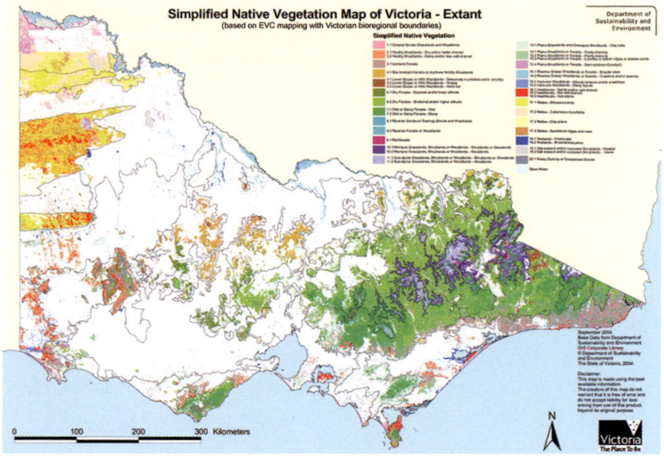
Simplified Native Vegetation Map of Victoria - Extant
(based on EVC mapping with Victorian bioregional boundaries)
Department of Sustainability and Environment
Simplified Native Vegetation
0 100 200 300 Kilometers
N
Victoria
The Place To Be

1.9b

1.10

1.10

Dingo Fence, Australia

The world's longest fence is an example of direct, sub-continental scale landscape intervention. Stretching 3,488 miles (5,614km), it was built in the 1880s to protect grazing sheep from dingoes in South eastern Australia. The fence has altered landscape dynamics by largely excluding the apex terrestrial predator from a large region. It is worth noting that dingoes themselves are a relatively recent introduction into Australia (approximately 3,000–4,000 years ago, compared to around 50,000 years of Aboriginal inhabitancy).

"I don't understand why when we destroy something created by man we call it vandalism, but when we destroy something created by nature we call it progress."
ED BEGLEY, JR

"Such is the ignorance of nature in large city's that are nothing less than overgrown prisons that shut out the world and all its beautys."
JOHN CLARE (1793–1864)

Industrial Revolution

The Industrial Revolution (c. 1760) marks a significant turning point in environmental history, shifting traditional agrarian, rural 'cottage industry' production methods to mechanized, urbanized mass production. Fueled by concentrated finite resources (initially coal), machinery replaced human labor at an inconceivable rate—a single spinner in 1812, for example, could complete the outputs of 200 workers in the British textile industry in 1770. Steamship and railroad transport covered large distances in record times, no longer restricted by winds, currents and landscape features. Industrialization's resultant population shift from rural to urban areas significantly altered town planning, with early urban parks intended as antidotes to new environmental problems such as air pollution from burning coal (see Birkenhead Park, Chapter 7).

Labor methods

Exploitative colonial-era slavery (prior to abolition in the UK and its colonies c. 1833 and USA 1865) and convict labor assisted mass development and urbanization in many colonial regions. Social reforms, regulations and philanthropic organizations (such as the Salvation Army, Social Gospel and YMCA) attempted to resolve associated urban growth problems such as slums, hunger and poor health. Unethical human labor systems found their substitutes: coal, natural gas and oil.

Hyper acceleration

Harnessing the fossil fuel trilogy of coal, natural gas and oil facilitated spectacular 20th-century global transformations. Cities became illuminated at night, facilitating 24/7 human activities, using kerosene (paraffin), natural gas and later, electricity from large power plants (Chapter 4). Abundant and therefore cheap coal became the central means for electricity production. Hydrological infrastructures (Chapter 3) could readily defy gravity through electrified pumping for filtration and distribution. Internal combustion engines in vehicles proliferated, fueled by crude oil distillates, with waste products from refining creating the smooth road surfaces on which to travel with newfound speed (Chapter 4). The assembly line became the norm for production of now uniform goods, rapidly increasing output and availability. The newfound access to wealth and increased consumption directly correlates with augmented environmental impacts. Industrialization continues to increase, with manufacturing centers largely outsourced to growing 'developing' nations.

1.11

1.11

Soil salinity in SW Australia

Colonization's imprint on world landscapes is substantial. In Australia, British and European settlers imposed their landscape and agricultural practices as well as aesthetic preferences in many unsuitable and fragile conditions. In south west Western Australia, one of the world's fragile and unique biodiversity hotspots, existing 'scrubby' vegetation was cleared at immense scales for pasture crops (and European hard-hoofed animals that further damage soil). This has resulted in a rising water table, creating catastrophic soil salinity and erosion-prone land. Farmers manage around 70% of the Australian landscape. Farming practices, driven by consumer trends, hugely impact the island continent. It has been estimated that for every kilogram of bread produced in Australia, seven kilograms of topsoil are lost. Decorated Australian Tim Flannery states that:

"The southwest region's few areas of natural vegetation (90% has been cleared) are threatened by salination, with no solution in view. Over 850 unique plant species are threatened … Two and a half million hectares of agricultural land are salt affected, 1.8 million of which are in the south west of Western Australia (WA). A further 10 million hectares are at risk nationally, 6 million of which are in the south west of WA."

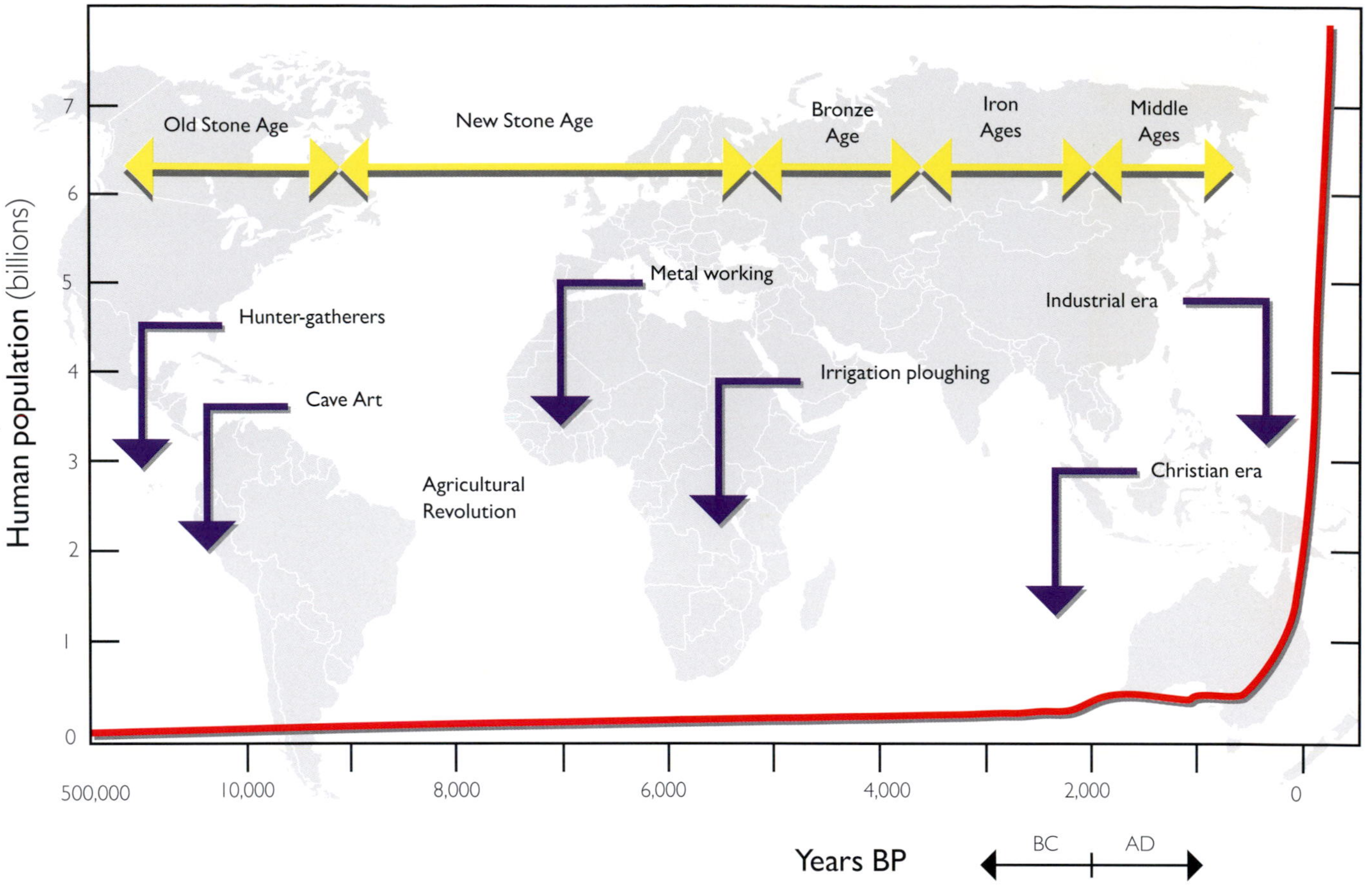

Human population (billions)
7
6
5
4
3
2
1
0
Old Stone Age
New Stone Age
Bronze Age
Iron Ages
Middle Ages
Metal working
Hunter-gatherers
Industrial era
Irrigation ploughing
Cave Art
Christian era
Agricultural Revolution
500,000
10,000
8,000
6,000
4,000
2,000
0
Years BP
BC
AD

1.12

1.12
World population graph
The spectacular evolutionary success of humanity has resulted in the recent phenomenon of billions of humans on the Earth.

Population growth

Industrialized production, hydrological infrastructures (Chapter 3), transport (Chapter 4) and food systems (Chapter 5) combined with medical advancements, continue to facilitate rapid population growth. In a single century, global population increased from just over 1 billion in 1900 CE to almost 7 billion in 2000 CE, with global life expectancy more than doubling in this time (being only 31 years of age in 1900).

"A population can sometimes increase so quickly that it overshoots carrying capacity before negative feedback arrests the growth and brings the population size to below carrying capacity once more."
GERRY MARTEN, HUMAN ECOLOGY: BASIC CONCEPTS FOR SUSTAINABLE DEVELOPMENT (2001)

1.13

CONSERVATION, ENVIRONMENT AND SUSTAINABILITY MOVEMENTS

1.13
A Sassafras Gully, Gippsland, Australia, c. 1870, Isaac Whitehead
Extensive land clearance for forestry and agriculture was seen as a civilizing process against an immensely scaled, wild 'nature'. This land clearance—shown here in what is now understood to be the most carbon dense forest in the world (*Eucalyptus regnans*)—continues today in Gippsland and Tasmania in Australia, despite enduring protests and public opposition.

Conservation, preservation and wilderness movements surfaced from the 17th century in response to rapid global change, reaching prominence in the 19th and 20th centuries. Key figures such as Ralph Waldo Emerson, Henry David Thoreau, Theodore Roosevelt, Gifford Pinchot, John Muir and Aldo Leopold created a strong foundation for the impactful 1960s environment movement. A broad agenda encompassed beauty, quality of life and political activism, helping to raise consciousness on a range of issues facing a collective, global human community. Influential figures included Rachel Carson (chemical pollution), Paul Ehrlich (overpopulation) and Ian McHarg (in landscape architecture). The continued development of the ecological movement placed the environment as central to life (ecocentrism), advocating for fundamental changes to ideology, ethics and practices from the dominant, Western human-centered (anthropocentrism) paradigm.

1.14

Explosion (1945–present)

"A thing is right when it tends to preserve the integrity, stability, and beauty of the biotic community. It is wrong when it tends otherwise."
ALDO LEOPOLD, A SAND COUNTY ALMANAC (1949)

"A wilderness, in contrast with those areas where man and his own works dominate the landscape, is hereby recognized as an area where the earth and its community of life are untrammeled by man, where man himself is a visitor who does not remain."
HOWARD ZAHNISER, THE WILDERNESS ACT (1964)

"We travel together, passengers on a little space ship, dependent on its vulnerable reserves of air and soil."
ADLAI STEVENSON, SPEECH TO THE UNITED NATIONS (1965)

"The most influential environmental photograph ever taken."
(EARTHRISE) GALEN ROWELL, ABC

"… provided that we are not so foolish as to continue to exhaust in a split second of astronomical history the orderly energy savings of billions of years' energy conservation aboard our Spaceship Earth".
BUCKMINSTER FULLER, OPERATING MANUAL FOR SPACESHIP EARTH (1969)

"We Do Not Inherit the Earth from Our Ancestors; We Borrow It from Our Children."
ANCIENT INDIAN PROVERB / MOSES HENRY CASS (1974)

"The urban eco-system is the most elaborate geographic control-system or integrated resource-management system in human experience."
IAN DOUGLAS, THE URBAN ENVIRONMENT (1983)

"Sustainable development is development that meets the needs of the present without compromising the ability of future generations to meet their own needs."
BRUNDTLAND REPORT (1987)

"The thing that has, at least in modern times, defined nature for us [is] its separation from human society."
BILL MCKIBBEN, THE END OF NATURE (1989)

"Travel is now the world's largest industry. The irony of tourism is that it often destroys some of the very places tourists travel to see."
JONI SEAGER, THE STATE OF THE ENVIRONMENT ATLAS (1995)

1945 CE — population

Atomic bombing of Japan by USA in World War II, 1945
United Nations Food and Agriculture Organization founded, 1945
First supermarket in USA, 1946
First images of Earth from beyond the atmosphere, 1946
Hydraulic fracturing (fracking) commences, 1947
International Union for Conservation of Nature established, 1948

1950 CE — 2.5 billion, Urban 29%

A Sand County Almanac (Book), Aldo Leopold, 1949
Peak District National Park (1st in UK), 1951
Great Smog, London, 1952
Nuclear accident, Chalk River, Ontario, Canada, 1952
First nuclear power plant for electricity in USSR, 1954
Castle Bravo US thermonuclear hydrogen bomb, Bikini Atoll, 1954
Peak Oil Theory presented (paper), M. King Hubbert, 1956
Minamata mercury wastewater dumping, Japan, 1956
Windscale Fire nuclear accident, UK, 1957
First urban growth boundary, Lexington, Kentucky, 1958
Kyshtym nuclear disaster, Soviet Union, 1959
Image of the City (Book), Kevin Lynch, 1960

3 billion, Urban 34%

The Death and Life of Great American Cities (Book), Jane Jacobs, 1961
World Wildlife Fund (WWF) founded, 1961
Silent Spring (Book), Rachel Carson, 1962
Ecocide by US Troops, Vietnam, 1965
International Society of City and Regional Planners founded, 1965
Australian Institute of Landscape Architects (AILA) founded, 1966
The Population Bomb (Book), Paul Ehrlich, 1968
Earthrise image captured, 1968
Lucens partial nuclear meltdown, Switzerland, 1969
Environmental impact statement (USA), 1969
Design With Nature (Book), Ian McHarg, 1969
New Zealand Institute of Landscape Architects (NZILA) founded, 1969
First 'Earth Day' (USA) January 1, 1970
'Door to Hell' methane reservoir, Turkmenistan, 1971
Greenpeace founded, 1971
First full-view photo of Earth, 'The Blue Marble', 1972
The Limits to Growth (Book), Club of Rome, 1972
United Nations Stockholm Conference & UNEP founded, 1972

1975 CE — 4 billion, Urban 37%

Endangered Species Act (USA), 1973
Energy crises and world oil shocks, 1970s
History of Landscape Architecture (Book), George B. Tobey, 1973
Richard Register founds 'Urban Ecology', 1975
The Landscape of Man (Book), Geoffrey and Susan Jellicoe, 1975
Seveso explosion disaster, Italy, 1976
The Gaia Hypothesis (Theory), James Lovelock, 1970s
American Planning Association (APA) founded from merger, 1978
Amoco Cadiz oil spill, France, 1978
Three Mile Island nuclear meltdown, USA, 1979
Ixtoc I oil spill, Gulf of Mexico, 1979–1980
World Conservation Strategy, 1980

5 billion

Rocky Mountain Institute founded, 1982
Bhopal gas disaster, India, 1984
French sink Greenpeace boat 'Rainbow Warrior', 1985
Chernobyl Nuclear Meltdown, Ukraine, 1986
Brundtland Commission, Our Common Future (Report), 1987
Dr James Hansen Greenhouse Effect US senate testimony, 1988
Intergovernmental Panel on Climate Change formed, 1988
Exxon Valdez oil spill, Alaska, 1989
Kuwait oil fires, Iraq, 1991
UN 'Rio' Earth Summit, 1992
Agenda 21, United Nations (Program), 1992
The Geography of Nowhere (Book), James Kunstler, 1993
The Trouble with Wilderness (Essay) William Cronon, 1995
Emergence of Landscape Urbanism, (mid 1990s)
Kyoto Protocol adopted, 1997
WWF Living Planet (Report), 1998
Cyanide spill, Baia Mare, Romania, 2000
Anthropocene term coined, Paul Crutzen & Eugene Stoermer, 2000

2000 CE — 6 billion, Urban 47%

UN World Summit on Sustainable Development, 2002
Al-Mishraq sulphur fire, Iraq, 2003
The Death of Environmentalism (Essay), 2004
Limits to Growth: The 30-Year Update (Book), 2004
Millennium Ecosystem Assessment (Report), 2005
Jilin chemical plant explosions, China, 2005
Southeast Asian Haze Air Pollution, 2006
Sidoarjo mud flow, Indonesia, 2006
'An Inconvenient Truth' (Documentary), Al Gore, 2006
'The Story of Stuff' (Online Animation), 2007
TVA Kingston Fossil Plant coal fly ash slurry spill, USA, 2008
Deepwater Horizon BP oil spill, Gulf of Mexico, 2010

7 billion

Cities for People (Book), Jan Gehl, 2010
Fukushima Daiichi nuclear meltdown, Japan, 2011
Hurricane Sandy eastern North America, 2012
Supertyphoon Haiyan, central Philippines, 2013
IPCC Fifth Assessment Report, 2014
Aliso Canyon gas leak, USA, 2015
Paris Agreement on Climate Change, 2015

Urban 55%

2025 CE — ?8 billion, ?Urban 60%

"Never waste a crisis."
UNKNOWN

"But man is a part of nature, and his war against nature is inevitably a war against himself."
RACHEL CARSON, CBS DOCUMENTARY (1964)

"We stand now where two roads diverge … The road we have long been traveling is deceptively easy, a smooth superhighway on which we progress with great speed, but at its end lies disaster. The other fork of the road—the one less traveled by—offers our last, our only chance to reach a destination that assures the preservation of the earth."
RACHEL CARSON, SILENT SPRING (1962)

Anthropocentricism

Based on a Judeo-Christian tradition (Genesis 1:26–28, 9:2–3, and Psalm 8:5–8), anthropocentricism is the view that humans, as Earth's central, most important species, have the right of dominion and control of other species and the land, which can be viewed as utilizable human resources. Anthropocentricism is considered to be implicit in environmental exploitation. Environmental scholars have suggested that this leads to nature being viewed as a limitless resource bank rather than a series of interconnected and interdependent finite systems.

1.15a
1.15b
1.15c
'Earthrise', 'The Blue Marble' and the thin atmosphere of the earth
'Earthrise' (1968) (1.15a) has been described as the most influential environmental photograph ever taken.

'The Blue Marble' (1972) (1.15b) captured the first unshaded image of the earth.

The thin line of Earth's atmosphere (1.15c) is visible against the setting last quarter crescent moon (2010).

1.15a

1.15b

"Man is a blind, witless, low brow, anthropocentric clod who inflicts lesions upon the earth."
IAN MCHARG, LIFE (15 AUG 1969)

"Anthropocentrism—human centredness—is a misguided way of seeing things … we need to develop a less dominating and aggressive posture towards the planet if we and the earth are to survive."
MICHAEL ZIMMERMAN, INTERVIEW (1989)

"Human domination over nature is quite simply an illusion, a passing dream by a naïve species. It is an illusion that has cost us much, ensnared us in our own designs, given us a few boasts to make about our courage and genius, but all the same it is an illusion."
DONALD WORSTER, UNDER WESTERN SKIES (1992)

"The field cannot be well seen from within the field."
RALPH WALDO EMERSON, CIRCLES (1841)

Gaia

The mid 20th- century space programs captured revolutionary imagery at a considerable distance from the Earth's surface. For the first time, people were able to see the Earth as a whole, interconnected entity. James Lovelock and Lynn Margulis' 1970s Gaia hypothesis (the Earth being an interconnected, self-regulating global superorganism) contributed to a growing movement advocating a holistic planetary view. Subsequent lobbying to establish global and collective environmental action in key works such as the Club of Rome's Limits to Growth (1972) were assisted by the 1970s energy crises—where major industrial countries faced substantial petroleum shortages. These tangibly demonstrated the extent of dependency on non-renewable energy resources. Such events, however, resulted in divided views on how natural resources should be managed, obtained and consumed at local and national scales, yet alone as one interconnected, cooperative community on Earth.

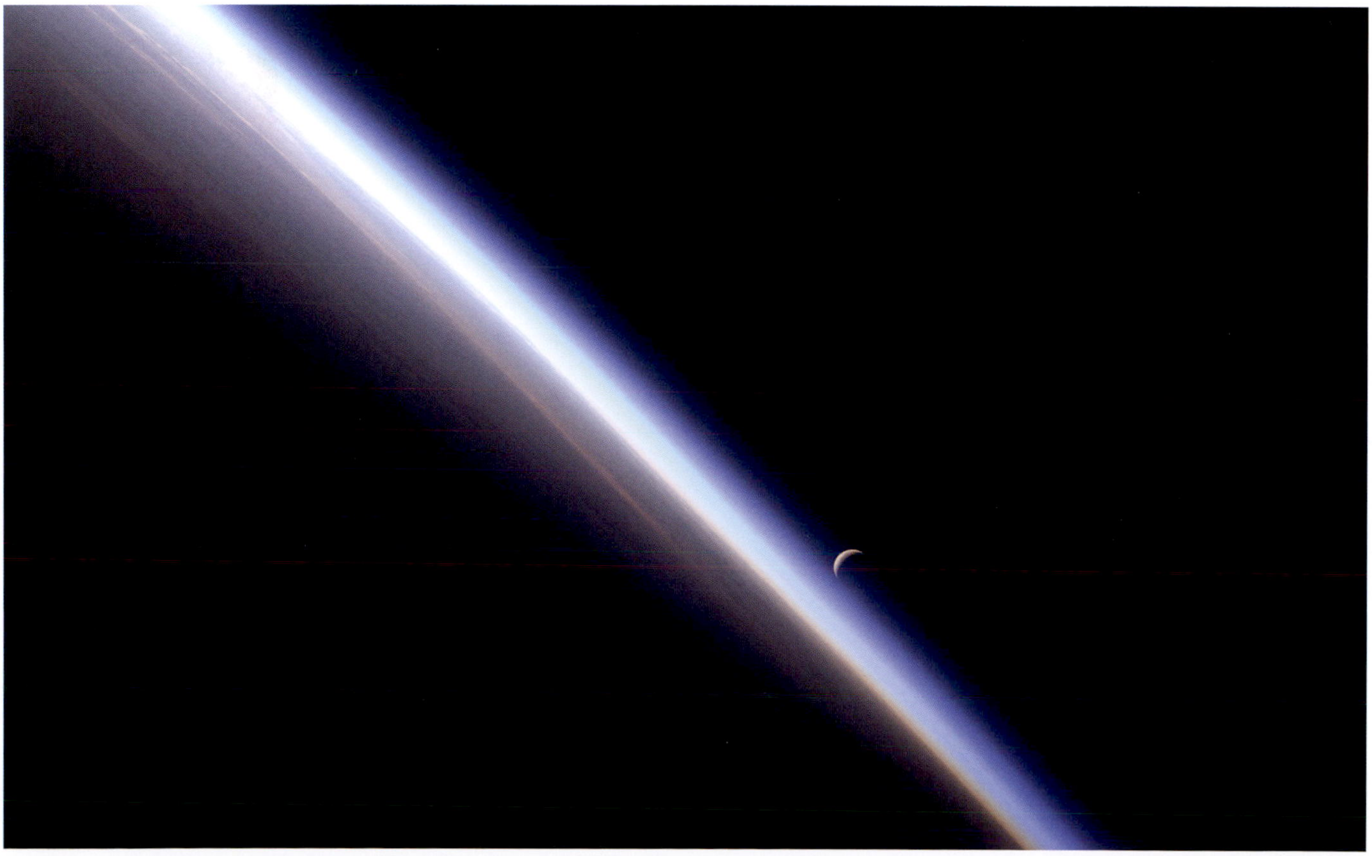

1.15c

"The opposite of nature is impossible."
BUCKMINSTER FULLER, LECTURE: COLUMBIA UNIVERSITY (1965)

"Scientific and technological 'solutions' which poison the environment or degrade the social structure and man himself are of no benefit, no matter how brilliantly conceived or how great their superficial attraction."
E. F. SCHUMACHER, SMALL IS BEAUTIFUL: ECONOMICS AS IF PEOPLE MATTERED (1973)

Sustainability

Ecological consciousness nevertheless gained widespread favor in the 1960s and 1970s, later fragmenting into a broad array of iterations. Together with countless sustainability works, the Brundtland Commission's (1987) landmark definition of sustainable development ("development that meets the needs of the present without compromising the ability of future generations to meet their own needs") heralded a period whereby multiple government, commercial and non-governmental organizations (NGOs such as the Sierra Club) sought to formalize civilizational and environmental longevity.

Failure to implement

While such international sustainability communications have continued over several decades (for example, various United Nations initiatives, Earth and World Summits, the Kyoto Protocol and the Intergovernmental Panel on Climate Change), agreement, vision and leadership, especially from world superpowers, has been slow, rare or non-existent. Even when agreements are reached—which can be vague or hopeful policy statements—action to match promises is often unforthcoming.

Ecological crisis

During the late 20th century, an increasing consensus in global scientific discourse and research emerged stating that the Earth has entered a biodiversity extinction crisis due to the cumulative effects of anthropogenic impacts on the environment. Since the 1990s, the broad discipline of ecology—with its roots in nature preservation and conservation and subscribing to empirical science—has perhaps emerged as the most powerful and influential force in modern environmentalism (Chapter 2). It is largely concerned with the plight of non-human species and ecosystems. Much discourse and practice in ecology, biological diversity and ecosystem services is focused on trying to halt and, if possible, reverse this crisis.

"Answering the question 'how can we live well within the means of one planet?' is the main research challenge of the 21st century."
MATHIS WACKERNAGEL, LIVING PLANET REPORT 2006 – GLOBAL FOOTPRINT NETWORK

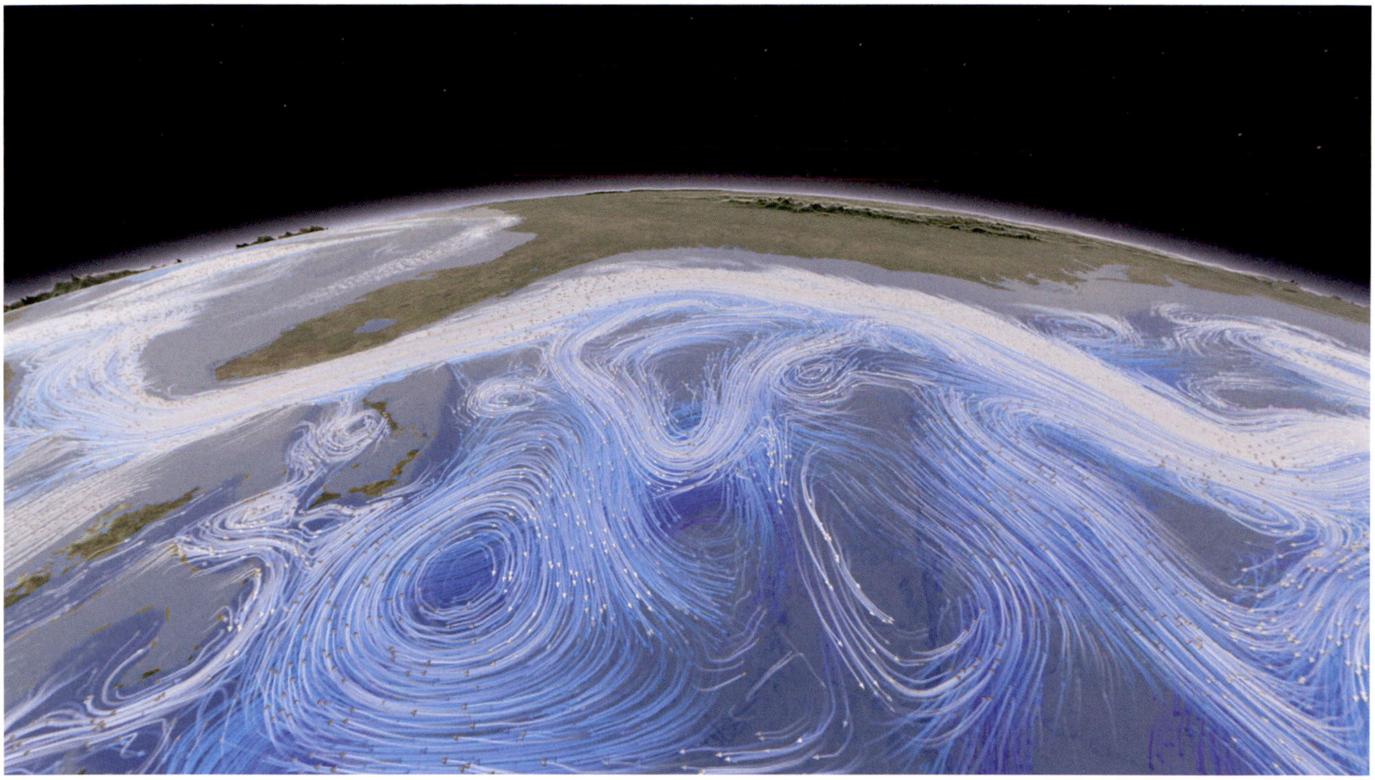

1.16

21st CENTURY CE

1.16
Ocean currents of the Gulf Stream
The Gulf Stream is responsible for bringing milder weather to important regions including North America and Europe. Climate change is altering the patterns of the natural systems such as the Gulf Stream's ocean patterns (driven by surface wind patterns and differences in water density), with significant potential impacts.

Human induced climate change

Human induced climate change occupies significant focus in sustainability discourse. For the first time in history, human activity is significantly altering how the Earth's climatic systems function, creating accelerated global warming, rising sea levels, manifesting changes in arable and agriculturally viable land, and increased incidence of extreme weather events. Emissions already released into the atmosphere are forecast to result in considerable planetary impacts, however, if the considerable deposits of low-grade fossil fuels (coal, shale gas, tar sands oil) are but partially utilized, climate scientists warn that apocalyptic climate change scenarios will result.

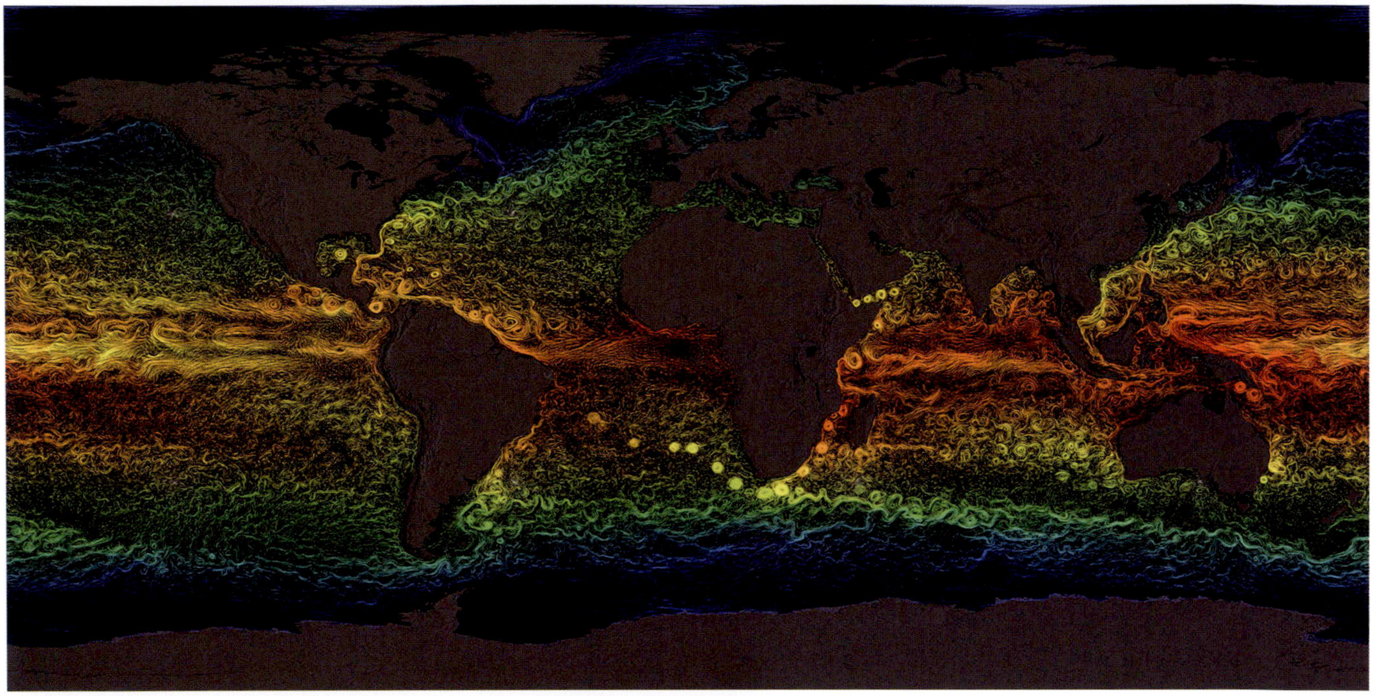

1.17

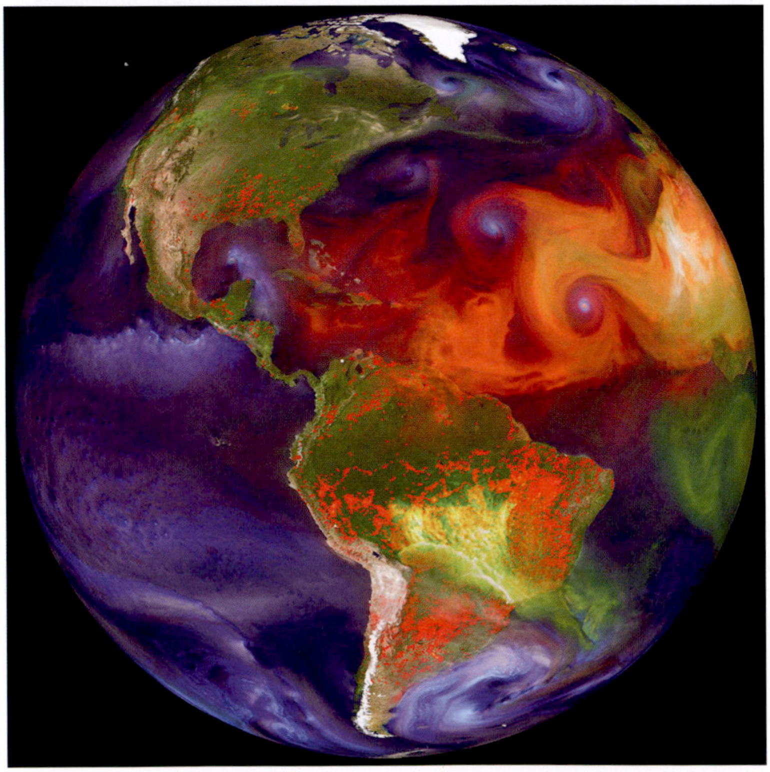

1.18

1.17

Sea surface current flows

The earth is a dynamic system—a discarded plastic bottle may travel thousands of miles on ocean currents before joining one of the various garbage patches suspended in the sea.

1.18

Global travel of aerosols and smoke

A fire or smokestack mixes with air currents, travelling across the globe to another continent. Winds disperse vast quantities of dust (orange), sea salt (blue), organic/black carbon (green), and sulfates (white) around the world. Examples of this include the regular southeast Asian haze from land clearance in Indonesia; wildfires in Australia, Africa, the USA and Mediterranean; and dust storms in the Sahara Desert that can reach many distant regions including Europe, the UK and the Amazon.

"A century ago, petroleum—what we call oil—was just an obscure commodity; today it is almost as vital to human existence as water."
JAMES BUCHAN (2006)

Fossil fuel addiction

Contemporary society's hyper-pace requires finite resources that are now becoming increasingly scarce, as we push further into the Earth's outreaches—squeezing tar sands and scouring extreme environments for oil (such as in the arctic and deep water locations), while destructively fracking terrestrial geologies to extract natural gas. Oil and natural gas products and their derivatives make up the majority of the modern world's manufacturing, processing, packaging and fertilizers, encompassing everything from transportation to our industrialized food system (Chapter 5), to underpinning digital and technological society. These uses are not always visible. Though natural gas is a well-recognized heating source and cooking fuel, for example, it is less known that half of the world's population survives on food calories produced by its synthetic nitrogen derivate used in agricultural systems. Synthetic nitrogen problematically accumulates in soils resulting in high acidity with the United Nations Food and Agricultural Organization (FAO) estimating that around one third of global arable land is so acidic it cannot support high-yielding crops.

1.19

1.19
'Tar Sands: Steam and Smoke Rise From Upgrading Facility at Syncrude Mildred Lake Mine', Alberta, Canada, 2014
Canada's tar sands are one of the world's largest industrial projects, producing around 1.5–2 million barrels of oil a day (in 2014). The tar sands deposits are distributed over an area larger than England—140,000km². Accomplished aerial photographer Alex MacLean's series of images paradoxically reverse the toxic project to stills of almost sublime awe (in the tradition of the *sublime* engendering a sense of terror and beauty (see Chapter 6). His image of the Upgrading Facility at Syncrude Mildred Lake Mine in Alberta is a more accurate depiction of the project, albeit, a spatial tip of the iceberg). MacLean stated that, "the scale of the oil sands area and the devastation to the landscape was overwhelming."

1.20

1.21

1.20
BAO Steel #10
China has industrialized on an unprecedented scale. Canadian photographer Edward Burtynsky states of his image showing immense iron ore stockpiles:
"Mass consumerism … and the resulting degradation of our environment intrinsic to the process of making things to keep us happy and fulfilled frightens me. I no longer see my world as delineated by countries, with borders, or language, but as 7 billion humans living off a single, finite planet."

1.21
CAFO, USA
Livestock consume around 40% of the world's grain production and in wealthy countries this is as high as 70%. Concentrated animal feeding operations (CAFOs) have significant effects on the global and local environment. Globally, livestock account for around 20% of greenhouse gas emissions, which is more than the transport sector. Locally, soil and aquatic systems are not adequately engineered to cope with vast amounts of animal wastes. Socially, the concentrated odor can destroy land values and communities within proximity to these factory farms. Here a vast corn stockpile is prepared for a CAFO in Nebraska with livestock contained in pens.

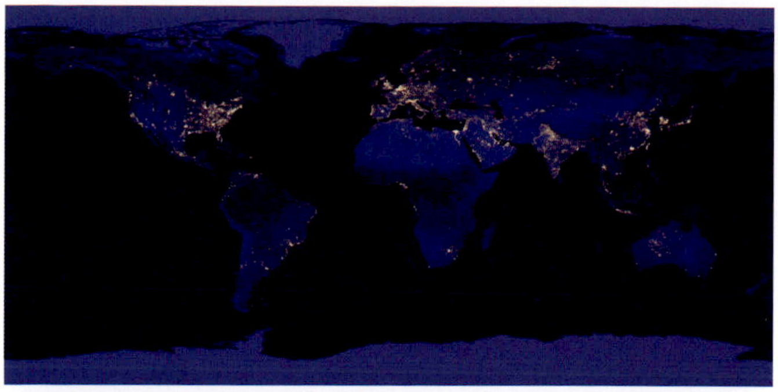

1.22a

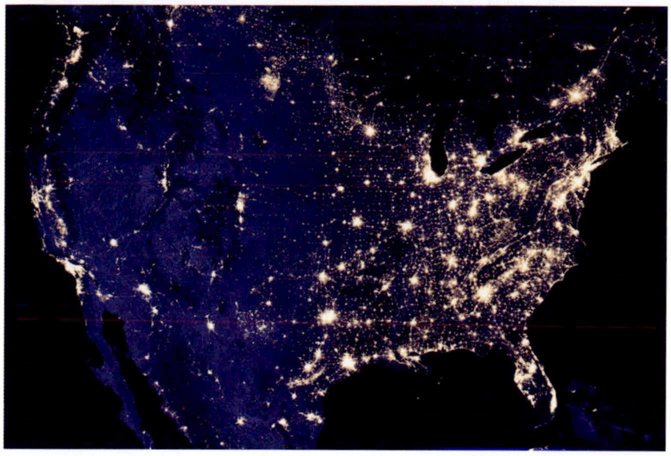

1.22b

1.22

1.22a
1.22b
1.22
Satellite images of Earth/USA/ Europe at night
Composite images of the earth flattened from space at night. Settlements give the appearance of a Christmas tree, especially in densely populated regions like Europe.

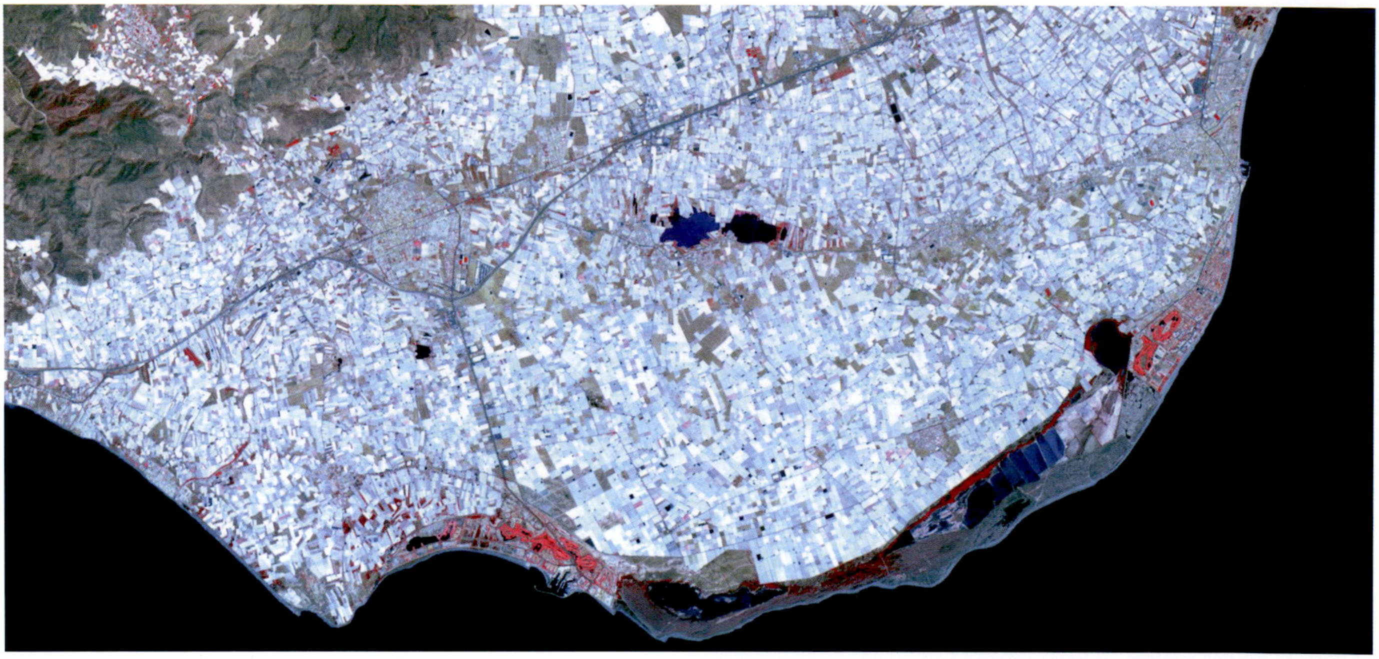

1.23a

1.23b

1.24
Desalination
Desalination and power plants (here in the United Arab Emirates) utilize the unparalleled energy source of crude oil. Large oil reserves in the Middle East have enabled the transformation of deserts into megalopolises and have been deployed to transform seawater into drinking water. In Sydney, Australia, which receives 47 inches (1,200mm) of balanced annual rainfall (thus with ample opportunity for rain and stormwater harvesting), a desalination plant was nonetheless constructed with a 50-year, A$2.3 billion lease (around $1.7 billion). Its intensive energy requirements are however being exceeded through construction of a purpose built 67 turbine wind farm. It has proved to be a white elephant.

1.24

"If there were a billion people living on the planet, we could do whatever we please. But there are nearly seven billion. At this scale, life as we know it today is not sustainable."
JAMES LOVELOCK, HOW TO COOL THE PLANET (2010)

"I sincerely believe... that banking establishments are more dangerous than standing armies."
THOMAS JEFFERSON, LETTER (1816)

1.23a
1.23b
Almeria greenhouses, Spain
Today's required scale of food production is immense. Near the town of El Ejido (Campo de Dalías, Almeria Province, Spain) is an urban region in its own right: 100,000 acres (40,000 hectares—equivalent to a large national park in Spain or Sweden's capital and largest city, Stockholm) of greenhouses in the greatest concentration in the world. The shimmering polythene covering the greenhouses creates an immense urban heat island effect. Over 2.7 million tons of produce is grown equating to over €1.2 billion in economic activity. Around 90% of the greenhouses use an artificial soil called enarenado (the remainder hydroponically) and a seawater desalination plant is used to defy the 200mm of annual rainfall the region receives. The aerial image is from 2008 and covers an area of 11.8 x 19 miles (19 x 30.5km). Yet the vegetable and fruit crops grown in the greenhouses are spatially efficient compared to world staple crops (rice, maize and wheat) that consume immense production areas.

Freshwater or energy water?

The extraction of the Earth's limited freshwater resources has placed immense pressures on both surface and underground supplies. Reports like the 2012 US Intelligence Community Assessment have warned of an increased likelihood for conflicts over freshwater reserves, with some organizations (such as the Pacific Institute) reporting a recent fourfold increase in water-related conflict. Although desalination (converting seawater into potable water) is being increasingly implemented to bypass traditional freshwater reserves and thus facilitating settlement growth and new urban regions, it uses immense amounts of energy/electricity (and high construction costs can accrue significant infrastructure debt). Over 80% of world energy is generated through fossil fuel usage, meaning that desalinated water becomes an industrial, finite energy by-product with an associated emissions footprint. Yet there are a range of environmental water management alternatives (Chapter 3).

Overpopulation, carrying capacity

Overpopulation is the 'elephant in the room' of sustainability discourse. Decades ago, authors like Ehrlich (1968) and Catton (1980) warned of population growth exceeding planetary carrying capacity. Similarly, 'ecological footprint' modelling convincingly demonstrates the likelihood that the human population—at some point in the future—will enter decline due to the over exhaustion of ecosystem services (see for example, the Global Footprint Network). Despite mounting global pressures, the problematic and delicate topic of population growth continues to remain largely unchecked, even being encouraged by the neoliberal economic and political model seeking continual growth (Chapter 7).

Economy first

In spite of widespread environmental consciousness, anthropocentrism has become increasingly entrenched through the global financial system where national and collective economies compete for financial dominance (Chapter 7). This means that few nations take serious endeavors to reverse 'business as usual' (BAU) practices and resultant emissions, overconsumption, population growth and environmental degradation, pressing forward with little serious environmental action for the decades and centuries ahead.

New wing 'environmentalism'

Environmentalist offshoots over recent decades (such as *ecopragmatism* and *ecomodernism*) have departed from a previously relatively unified approach into new areas. Though generally seeking to shrink the impact of humanity, they embrace technological and intensive pseudo 'green' approaches to achieve this, such as nuclear power, geoengineering and bioengineering. Understandably, 'horizontal hostility' is continuing between the old and new wing environmentalism factions.

What is forthcoming?

To mitigate the potentially devastating future scenarios predicted by climate change and sustainability crises experts (see further readings, particularly Chapters 1, 2, 7 and 10), it is essential that we seek collective and multifaceted global environmental solutions for a post-carbon era. It is crucial that these transcend local, national and international identities, histories, races, customs and beliefs. Though compelling, major environmental reform challenges chief economic and political power structures and hence is difficult to instigate. Many scholars (including several interviewed in this book) believe that current 'neoliberal' economic and political systems are incapable of accommodating environmental and social sustainability without a complete paradigm shift. Others suggest that the term 'sustainability' has been over-used, corrupted and has lost its original meaning (such as readings by Cronon, 1995; Nordhaus & Shellenberger, 2004; Freyfogle, 2006; Jensen & McBay, 2009). At the least, we must redress and redesign our local practices to adapt to future challenges in an environmentally and socially ethical way, or risk undermining democratic and cultural systems through unjust future scenarios (Chapters 7 and 10).

"Through their stories, institutions, and policies, environmentalists constantly reinforce the sense that nature is something separate from, and victimized by, humans. This paradigm defines ecological problems as the inevitable consequence of humans violating nature. Think of the verbs associated with environmentalism and conservation: 'stop,' 'restrict,' 'reverse,' 'prevent,' 'regulate,' and 'constrain.' All of them direct our thinking to stopping the bad, not creating the good."
TED NORDHAUS AND MICHAEL SHELLENBERGER, THE DEATH OF ENVIRONMENTALISM (2004)

"Design is basic to all human activities – the placing and patterning of any act towards a desired goal constitutes a design process."
VICTOR PAPANEK, DESIGN FOR THE REAL WORLD: HUMAN ECOLOGY AND SOCIAL CHANGE (1971)

"Design is a formal response to a strategic question."
MARIONA LOPEZ, TWITTER (2015)

"It is not about the world of design … it is about the design of the world."
BRUCE MAU, MASSIVE CHANGE (2004)

WHAT DOES THIS MEAN FOR LANDSCAPE ARCHITECTURE?

Where are we at?

Following 50 years of active sustainability discourse, have discussions (or sentiment) peaked? At what point will mounting environmental pressures such as finite resource exhaustion and climate change force dialogue (and perhaps action) to move from that of *sustainability* to one of *survival*? (Chapter 10).

Solving problems

There is an overwhelming amount of material focused on environmental destruction, what we shouldn't be doing, how it is not enough, which species we have lost and why change is too slow. Environmental discourse can therefore be embedded with what Nordhaus and Shellenberger articulates as a problematic psychology of fear, denial and guilt, engendering pessimism or inertion. Design, on the other hand, is often referred to as 'creative problem solving', offering constructive outcomes through a lateral yet formalized process that transcends rhetoric and seeks implementation.

Where do we need to go?

What can landscape architects do in the face of seemingly insurmountable environmental challenges? While landscape architecture and its associated disciplines are not in and of themselves a sole environmental solution, they can surely contribute more substantially. Implementing actions creating net environmental good can be challenging given our dependence on unsustainable finite resources. When combined with skillful execution and the intent of providing more ecosystem services than needed for use, the landscape medium provides a rare opportunity to contribute more environmental good than harm. Key to realizing this vision with impact and substance requires expanding the scale of the profession beyond the individual site to reclaim and reintegrate planning and practice at regional scales (as consistent with early landscape architecture in the tradition of Frederick Law Olmsted).

Multidimensional

Recent industry popularization of the term '*multifunctional landscapes*' makes inroads by stacking multiple functions, though its use of 'function' may fail to encourage less tangible, artistic and social design aspects (Chapters 6 and 7). Sustainable design requires even broader scope and comprehension—a *multidimensional* perspective and outlook. Multidimensional sustainability captures a broad spectrum of considerations, expanding traditional triple bottom line sustainability (encompassing the environment, the economy, and society) with performance and transformative aesthetics. The landscape medium has a unique capacity to harness the Earth's generative, abundant and healing natural systems, manifesting positive change, creating outstanding outcomes and demonstrating what we as a profession can collectively achieve.

Landscape what?

Unfortunately, landscape architecture suffers from a general lack of public awareness (including confusion with landscape gardening) and industry scope, commonly relegated to surface treatments and decorative art. The profession's influence is, however, increasing. Productive, participatory, substantive landscape architecture offers big-picture planning, broad-thinking strategy, large-scale projects and integrative responses with deeper impact for democratically engaged communities, living ethical, fulfilling lives based on environmentally sustainable practices. This book aims to document the breadth of landscape's potential by capturing an array of practice-based implementable and replicable design solutions with a call to expand this work to new scales. In addition to what is achievable within an expanded notion of our professional boundary (Chapters 4, 5, 6, 7, 9 and 10)—asking ourselves what we shouldn't do is just as relevant (Chapter 7).

Benson, J. and Roe, M. (2007) *Landscape and sustainability:* Second Edition, London: Taylor & Francis.

Carson, R. (1962) *Silent Spring*, USA: Houghton Mifflin.

Catton, W. (1980) *Overshoot: the ecological basis of revolutionary change*, Urbana a.o: University of Illinois Press.

Cooley, J. (1994) *Earthly words: essays on contemporary American nature and environmental writers*, Ann Arbor: University of Michigan Press.

Corner, J. (ed.) (1999) *Recovering Landscape: Essays in Contemporary Landscape Theory*, New York: Princeton Architectural Press.

Cronon, W. (ed.) (1995) *Uncommon ground: toward reinventing nature*, New York: W.W. Norton & Co.

Diamond, J. (2005) *Collapse: How Societies Choose to Fail or Survive*, London: Penguin.

Jensen, D. & McBay, A. (2009) *What we leave behind*, New York: Seven Stories Press.

Kunstler, J. (2006) *The Long Emergency*, USA: Atlantic Books.

McHarg, I. (1969) *Design with Nature*, Garden City, NY: Natural History Press.

MacLean, A. (2008) *Over: The American Landscape at the Tipping Point*, NY: Abrams.

Meadows, D.H., Randers, J. and Meadows, D. L. (2004) *The limits to growth: the 30-year update*. White River Junction VT: Chelsea Green Pub. Co.

Nikiforuk, A. (2012) *The energy of slaves: oil and the new servitude*, Vancouver, BC: Greystone Books.

Nordhaus, T. and Shellenberger, M. (2004) *The Death of Environmentalism*, www.thebreakthrough.org/images/Death_of_Environmentalism.pdf [accessed 13 December 2013].

Odum, H. and Odum, E. (2008) *A prosperous way down: principles and policies*, Boulder: University Press of Colorado.

Pretty, J. (2007) *The SAGE handbook of environment and society*, Los Angeles: SAGE.

Seager, J., Read, C. and Stott, P. (1995) *The state of the environment atlas*, London: Penguin Books.

Swaffield, S. (ed.) (2002) *Theory in Landscape Architecture*, Philadelphia: University of Pennsylvania Press.

Trimble, S. (1988) *Words from the land: encounters with natural history writing*, Salt Lake City: Peregrine Smith Books.

Wilson, E. (2002) *The future of life*, New York: Alfred A. Knopf.

2008

2009

2011

2014

2.1
Hart Road Wetland
These images demonstrate human-initiated and managed successional landscape transformation from barren and denuded agricultural pasture in 2008 to a restoring landscape in 2014—part of the wider change facilitated by this ecological restoration and wetlands project. The photographs show the landscape in (top to bottom): April 2008, October 2009, July 2011 and November 2014.

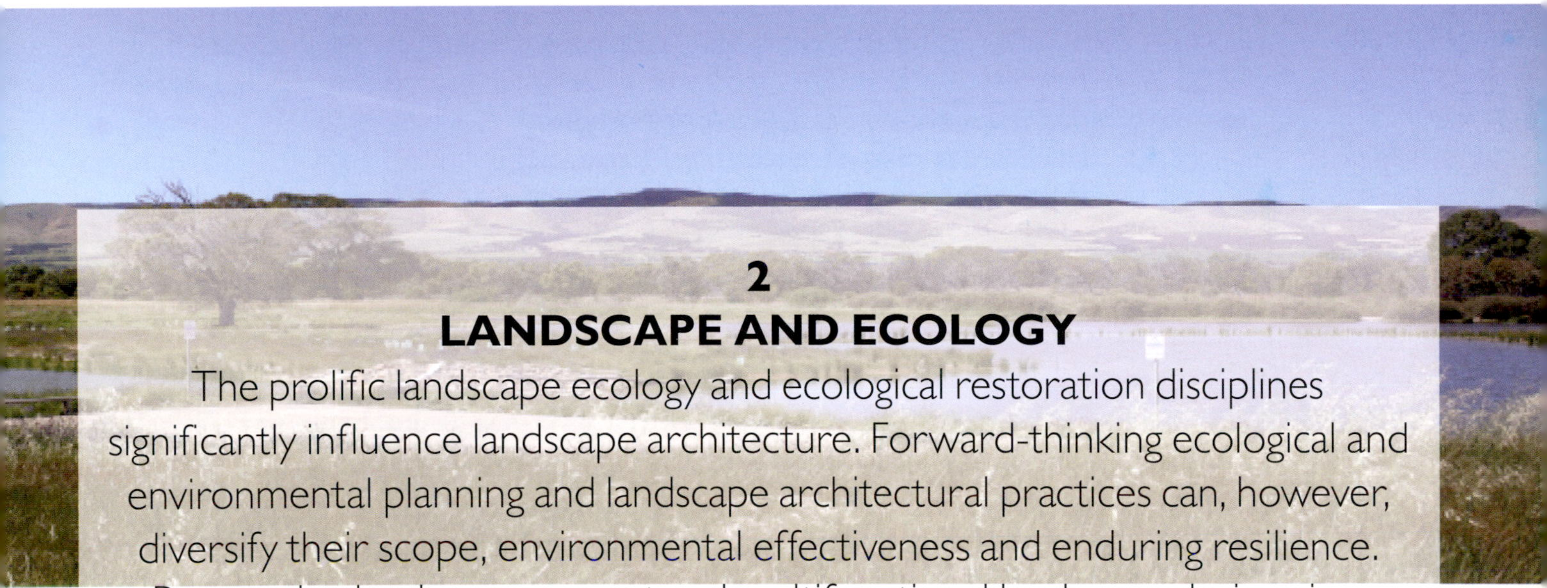

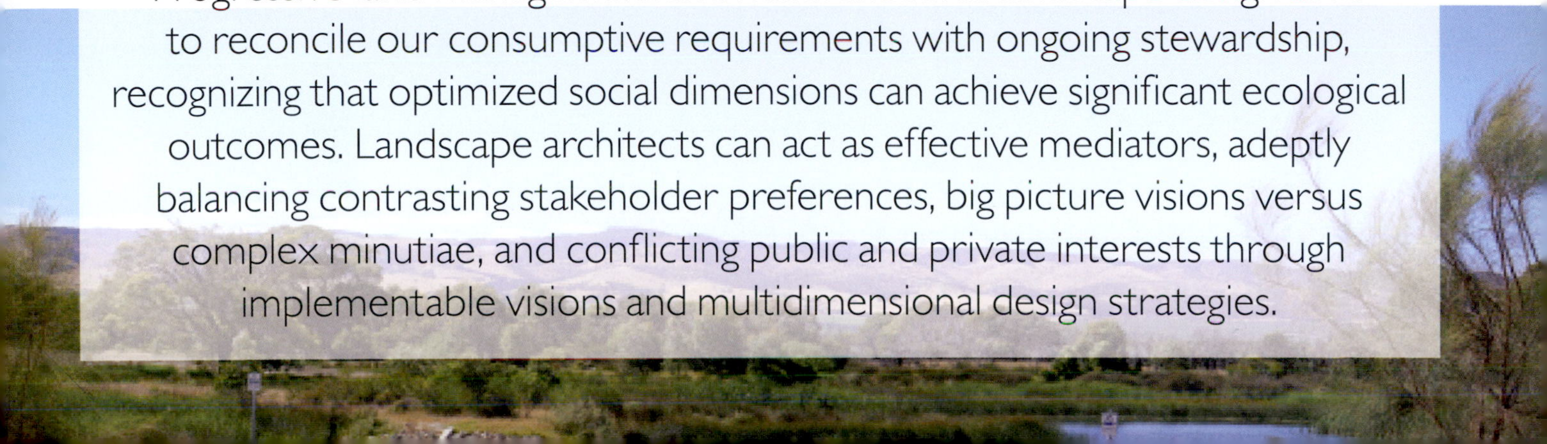

2
LANDSCAPE AND ECOLOGY

The prolific landscape ecology and ecological restoration disciplines significantly influence landscape architecture. Forward-thinking ecological and environmental planning and landscape architectural practices can, however, diversify their scope, environmental effectiveness and enduring resilience. Progressive land management and multifunctional landscape design aims to reconcile our consumptive requirements with ongoing stewardship, recognizing that optimized social dimensions can achieve significant ecological outcomes. Landscape architects can act as effective mediators, adeptly balancing contrasting stakeholder preferences, big picture visions versus complex minutiae, and conflicting public and private interests through implementable visions and multidimensional design strategies.

"When we try to pick out anything by itself, we find it hitched to everything else in the Universe."
JOHN MUIR, MY FIRST SUMMER IN THE SIERRA (1869)

"Let us resolve to green the earth, to restore the earth, to heal the earth."
IAN MCHARG, ECOLOGY AND DESIGN (1997)

"At a time when threats to the physical environment have never been greater, it may be tempting to believe that people need to be mounting the barricades rather than asking abstract questions about the human place in nature. Yet without confronting such questions, it will be hard to know which barricades to mount, and harder still to persuade large numbers of people to mount them with us. To protect the nature that is all around us, we must think long and hard about the nature we carry inside our heads."
WILLIAM CRONON, UNCOMMON GROUND: RETHINKING THE HUMAN PLACE IN NATURE (1995)

LANDSCAPE ECOLOGY AND ECOLOGICAL RESTORATION

Landscape ecology studies and aims to understand and improve relationships, such as composition, structure and function, in ecological processes and landscape systems. Ecological restoration (also known as 'ecosystem restoration', 'restoration ecology', 'biodiversity restoration') is the process of assisting the recovery of damaged, degraded or destroyed ecosystems. Both are focused on reversing the biodiversity extinction crisis (Chapter 1).

Theory or practice?

Ecological theory, landscape ecology and urban ecology are constantly evolving. Subsequently, it is challenging to capture and define the shifting movements and their subsets of varying beliefs, theories, practices and term reinventions (such as: *rewilding*; *ecosystem services*; *ecological urbanism*; *novel ecosystems*; *eco-pragmatism*; *multifunctional landscapes*; *social ecology*; *biomimicry*; *eco-revelatory design*; *biophilic design* and many others). An expansive breadth of ecological theory therefore influences landscape architecture. Much ecological theory and discourse is just that—and it remains to be seen how it will translate into action. Conversely, realized landscape projects can tangibly implement ecological principles in areas as diverse as high conservation to inner-urban brownfields, and from large scale planning to small park and aquatic environments.

Legacy

Landscape architects have long worked in sensitive ecological environments (such as national parks and nature reserves), including through management and master planning, restoration projects, circulation systems, and visitor infrastructure (such as lookouts, carparks, signage and interpretation; see Chapter 8). Additionally, many practitioners are involved in expanding ecological zones creating interlinking vegetation corridors often referred to as '*green infrastructure*' and more specifically, using indigenous plants to improve ecological (and reduced water use) outcomes.

Restoration

By the latter part of the 20th century, it became clear that protecting remnant ecosystems would simply not be enough to stem anthropogenic ecological impacts (Chapter 1). Ecology accordingly expanded to encompass restoration and later, ecosystem services and green infrastructure projects, linking remnant ecosystems' often small and isolated areas. Much ecological practice now seeks to rebuild and

"A considerable part of what we call natural landscape has the same kind of history. It is the product of human design and human labour, and in admiring it as natural it matters very much whether we suppress that fact of labour or acknowledge it."
RAYMOND WILLIAMS, IDEAS OF NATURE (1980)

"Restoring degraded ecosystems—or creating new ones—has become a huge global business. China, for instance, is planting 90 million acres of forest in a swath across its northern provinces. And in North America, just in the past two decades, restoration projects costing $70 billion have attempted to restore or recreate 7.4 million acres of marsh, peatland, floodplain, mangrove, and other wetlands."
RICHARD CONNIFF, REBUILDING THE NATURAL WORLD: A SHIFT IN ECOLOGICAL RESTORATION (2014)

reinstate destroyed ecosystems (see Hart Road Wetland). Ecological restoration practices have gained traction to become an international and commercial force, with millions of annual projects. Participating countries of the 2010 Convention on Biological Diversity have committed to restoring 15% of degraded ecosystems worldwide by 2020.

Restoration process

Landscape architects frequently adopt restoration principles while potentially working in tandem with environmental science trained ecologists. A scientific paradigm therefore dominates ecological restoration. The process focuses on flora and fauna (rather than human elements) and is generally as follows: interpretation of a site's historical 'baseline' condition (for example, prior to settlement/human intervention); condition analysis (whether damaged/severely degraded or completely destroyed); study, protection and recovery of any precious remnant ecologies; and recreation of baseline vegetation communities (and in theory, fauna). Indigenous planting is the simplest form of restoration but more involved techniques like fauna transplantation can also occur (see Queen Elizabeth Olympic Park, Chapter 4). The 'naturalistic' approach may effectively disguise human intervention to appear 'natural' once established.

Biodiversity offsetting

Where development or projects occur in locations with remnant and important ecosystems, ecologists and landscape architects may have input on the site's layout to protect features considered most valuable. If development proposes destroying/clearing existing ecosystems, some jurisdictions initiate biodiversity offsetting/mitigation/banking and species banking, whereby ecological restoration is employed on an alternative site to 'replace' destroyed ecosystems (usually at increased size and calculated through a nominal ratio). While certainly better than taking no action at all, offsetting is generally not considered to be an effective system, as unfortunately restoration is frequently a poor substitute for the diverse and complex plant, animal and microbiology interconnections developed over time from stability in existing ecologies.

"If there is one thing we know about ecosystems, and we know it more the more we discover about them, it's that you cannot safely disaggregate their functions without destroying the whole thing. Ecosystems function as coherent holistic systems, in which the different elements depend upon each other. The moment you start to unbundle them and to trade them separately you create a formula for disaster."
GEORGE MONBIOT, THE PRICING OF EVERYTHING (2014)

2.2a

2.2b

2.2a
2.2b
Hart Road Wetland, City of Onkaparinga, Adelaide, Australia, 2003–2008
The 642 acre (260ha) Hart Road Wetlands lie on the northern boundary of the Aldinga Scrub Conservation Park, which is the last significant vestige of indigenous coastal ecosystem on the Adelaide metropolitan coastline. Land around the site had been cleared and drained for cropping and grazing except for the Conservation Park. The wetlands were constructed by the City of Onkaparinga in 2007 as part of the 2003 council designed Aldinga Beach Drainage Scheme. Agricultural drainage lines (some eroded into deep channels) did not allow for ponding of water and aquifer recharge, resulting in remnant vegetation in the Conservation Park suffering. Hart Road Wetlands are designed to mitigate stormwater runoff from existing suburbs, provide water quality benefits and retention requirements for new adjacent residential development, and recharge groundwater. Stormwater is directed into a series of varied depth basins where it is filtered and injected into the aquifer for storage and recovery (ASR). This forms part of a wider pressurized recycled water network in the municipality, distributed to parks, reserves, sports fields and schools. An indigenous plant palette replicating pre-European vegetation systems increases habitat for remnant local wildlife, while a network of paths offer recreational amenities. Since establishment, adjoining areas have benefitted from the increased water, with Cliff's Waterhole being refilled for the first time in recent years.

2.3a

2.3b

2.3a
2.3b
Hong Kong Wetland Park, Urbis Limited & Architectural Services Department of HKSAR Government, Tin Shui Wai, Yuen Long, Hong Kong, China, 2006

Hong Kong Wetland Park is the result of an ecological mitigation area (EMA) for wetlands lost from Tin Shui Wai New Town development. The 150 acre (61ha) conservation, education and tourism facility attracts around 1.5 million vi sitors annually.

2.4a

2.4b

"As a primary goal, we would recommend that the biotic associations within each park be maintained, or where necessary recreated, as nearly as possible in the condition that prevailed when the area was first visited by the white man. A national park should represent a vignette of primitive America."
ALDO LEOPOLD, THE LEOPOLD REPORT (1963)

"These days the historical disinclination of American ecologists to study human-altered systems has been mixed up with an ideological dislike of such systems. Most ecologists are also committed conservationists who, in the correct manner, dislike 'invasive species' and climate change and anything else that reeks of mankind."
EMMA MARRIS, RAMBUNCTIOUS GARDEN: SAVING NATURE IN A POST-WILD WORLD (2011)

2.4a
2.4b
Lady Bird Johnson Wildflower Center, J. Robert Anderson Landscape Architecture and others, 4801 La Crosse Ave, Austin, Texas, 78739, USA, 1982–
The Lady Bird Johnson Wildflower Center (Austin, Texas) was founded in 1982 by former first lady and actress Helen Hays to conserve, restore and create healthy landscapes. It is committed to increasing the sustainable use of native plants to mitigate and address dwindling water supplies, climate change, pollution and invasive species. Over 130,000 annual visitors experience the 279 acre centre (113ha), including 9 acres (3.6ha) of 'maintained' gardens, a 16 acre (6.5ha) Texas Arboretum; savannah meadows and research plots.

Shortcomings

Singular, fixed, and purely scientifically based visions for ecological restoration can miss multidimensional opportunities to synthesize diverse stakeholder requirements, cultural factors and future wider environmental needs. Every site context needs to be analyzed to optimize the best response (high conservation status sites will differ from urban sites with no remnant ecology). 'Nativist' approaches prescribe *endemic* (only locally occurring), *indigenous* (native to a region) and *native* (native to a country) plant species (usually in that order of preference), seeking to restore a site to an 'untouched' state, in isolation from past history (such as indigenous/first nation communities, previously active land management) and site context (biodiversity plantings encouraging wildlife on dangerous road median strips, for example). Although motivated by environmental good, some of the movement's roots in 17th-century conservation, preservation and wilderness movements reflect an outdated, even colonial imperialist notion of an 'untouched native environment' (see Leopold Report quote, below), which cannot be recreated (if indeed it ever existed independently of indigenous and first-nation cultures) and often fails to meet current needs (food, resources, energy).

Key restoration questions

It is important to be broad-minded when considering ecological restoration and the design of new landscapes. What is realistic, effective and will generate the most positive outcomes, and for whom (non-human life forms, endangered species, humanity's sustainability—see Interview, Chapter 2)? What are 'baselines' predicated on (past inaccurate colonial notions of 'natural' landscapes)? What are the legacies of land-use change and industrialization (industrial-scale pollution and toxic accumulations)? How will they accommodate high urban densities and population growth? Do they consider contemporary issues such as finite resource depletion and climate change (scenarios not previously faced)?

"It is in vain to dream of a wildness distant from ourselves. There is none such. It is the bog in our brain and bowels, the primitive vigor of Nature in us, that inspires that dream."
HENRY DAVID THOREAU, JOURNAL (1856)

"Having erected an impossible vision of purity as their ideal, such thinkers are doomed to perpetual disappointment. There can never be any more of this kind of nature, because once touched by humans, it is ruined for eternity."
EMMA MARRIS, RAMBUNCTIOUS GARDEN: SAVING NATURE IN A POST-WILD WORLD (2011)

2.5
Connecticut Water Treatment Facility, Michael Van Valkenburgh Associates, New Haven, Connecticut, USA, 2001–2005
This rich, human-scaled terrain invites a spatial experience of the landscape. Located on the suburban outskirts of New Haven and featuring economical techniques adapted from restoration ecology and bioengineering, the facility is a reserve water source for the South Central Connecticut Regional Water Authority, drawing water from Lake Whitney at the base of the Mill River watershed. On a limited budget of around $5 per square foot ($54m^2), the designed landscape creates a microcosm of the surrounding regional watershed from mountain source to reservoir, assisted by concealing the majority of the built structures below ground. New topography is stabilized using bioengineering methods, with swales guiding site run off through a series landscapes including farmland, meadow, and valley stream, before collecting in a water body recharging groundwater aquifers. Features of the landscape and green roof planting include: native species (not requiring fertilizers or pesticides), seasonal colors and textures, and the anticipation of plant communities' evolution.

Key to diagram:
1 Pre-existing wetlands
2 Lake
3 Island
4 Peninsula
5 Beach
6 Gorge
7 Valley and stream
8 Agricultural garden
9 Mountain and intermittent stream

Progressive scope

Emerging areas include 'novel' ecosystems; post-industrial ecologies (Chapter 3); human-dominated environments and urban ecology; reconfiguring infrastructures (Chapter 4); sustainable and urban agriculture, agroecology and agrobiodiversity (Chapter 5); productive landscapes and ecologies (Chapter 5); outcomes from social, humanitarian and behavioral sustainability dimensions (Chapters 6 and 7); climate change adaptation (Chapter 4); uncertain future scenarios and heightened pressures through landscape-based geopolitical resource issues (fresh water, agricultural land)—all offering opportunities for new areas of practice and mediation to mitigate ecological and social impacts (see Chapters 4, 6 and 10).

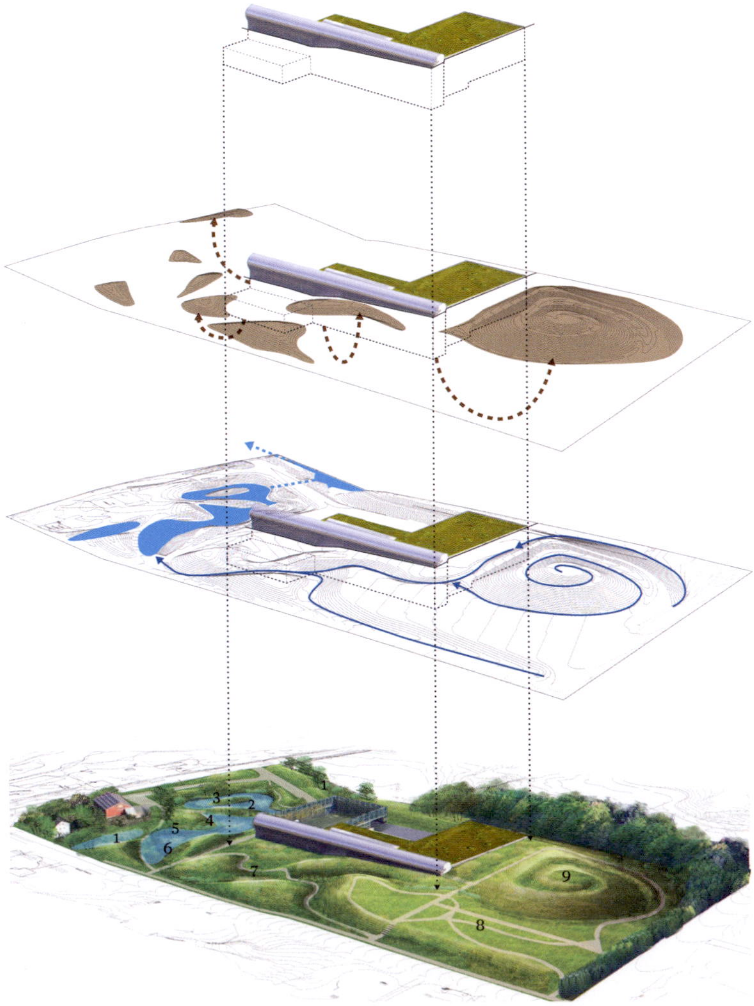

2.5

"And when we [Americans] do make gardens, we tend to favor gardens that are 'wild' or 'natural'—[which] strike me as oxymorons [being] designed to look as though it were not designed. Whether a wildflower meadow, a bog, or a forest, such gardens are typically planted exclusively with native species and designed to banish any mark of human artifice ... There's a strong whiff of moralism behind this movement ... Obviously, the natural gardeners have not rethought the historic American opposition between culture and nature ... They assume we must choose between 'making it pretty' and 'serving the planet'."
MICHAEL POLLAN, BEYOND WILDERNESS AND LAWN (1998)

2.6a

2.6b

2.6c

DECONSTRUCTION AND WASTE MANAGEMENTS PROCESS
EXOTIC INVASIVE FLORA (EIF) EXTRACTION
BUILDING DECONSTRUCTION
BASEMENT REMOVAL (local stone)
ROCK CLEANING
90 ha
25 ha 100% coverage
+/- tons
4.5 ha Urbanisation
1.5 ha Edifications
430 Buildings
1.5 ha Edifications
430 Buildings
4.5 ha Urbanisation
Selective deconstruction (recycling)
beams
wood
glass
ceramic
4/6 months after
70% weight reduction
in situ drying
30-40% volumen reduction
Crasher
Screen
4 axes truck
30% trips vs 2 axes truck
0.5 local soil
1.5 crushed local stone
0.5-1 m dry EIF
asphalt
bedding layer
Landfills
Crushed local stone +
50 cm local soil
Parking pavement
Crushed sifted local stone
walls
2.6d

2.6a (Before)
2.6b
2.6c
2.6d

Restauració del Paratge de Tudela-Culip (Club Med Restoration), EMF Estudi Martí Franch, Parc Natural de Cap de Creus, Gerona, Spain, 2005–2010

This large restoration project in the Mediterranean involved the selective deconstruction of 450 buildings, roads and infrastructure from a former Club Med resort. EMF implemented four key stages (as illustrated in 2.6c): recycling almost all of 42,000m^3 of residue; eliminating invasive exotic species over 222 acres (90ha); restoring orography and drainage to re-establish natural erosion and sediment dynamics; and establishing a network of public circulation to a site that expresses regional *genius loci* through geological and natural elements.

2.7a

2.7b

2.7f

2.7c

2.7g

2.7d

2.7e

2.7a (Before–After)
2.7b
2.7c
2.7d
2.7e
2.7f
2.7g

Mill River Park and Greenway, OLIN, Stamford, Connecticut, USA, 2005–2013

The area's first Puritan settlers renamed the then meandering Rippowam River (inhabited by the Algonquin people) Mill River in 1642, damming it to create the town's original gristmill. Intense industry led to severe degradation—concrete walls inhibited access, compromising ecological systems, while excessive siltation, trash, and debris collected behind the dam, resulting in invasive aquatic plants and blooming algae choking the river.

In 2005, OLIN led a team of ecologists and civil engineers to restore the river and habitats and establish an economically viable, maintainable park. The resulting 14 acre (5.6ha) community greenspace showcases local flora and fauna, restores natural ecological systems, invigorates urban redevelopment, and celebrates community through diverse programming.

2.7a shows the transition before, during and after restoration.

2.7b-g show seasonal variations in water level and vegetation.

"As to how we take action on the ground; we could learn a lot from the way in which the global conservation community has gone from a bunch of hippies in the 1960s to a major corporate and political force today."
RICHARD WELLER (INTERVIEW, CHAPTER 7)

2.8a
2.8b
Scioto Audubon Metro Park, MKSK, Columbus, Ohio, USA, 2009
Scioto Audubon Metro Park is an 80 acre (32ha) reclaimed urban brownfield along the Whittier Peninsula of the Scioto River Dam Area (a nationally recognized unique riverine ecosystem and Important Bird Area) and adjacent to the Columbus downtown business district. During masterplanning, the core planning and design team engaged government agencies and special interest groups to create a strategy to remediate, reclaim, redevelop and revitalize the post-industrial site. The park includes native plantings; prairie; wetland habitat; walking trails, boardwalks and bike paths connecting to adjacent neighborhoods; visitor amenities (including an aviary habitat; athletic fields; park-wide wayfinding; an observation deck and tower) and the region's first nature education center.

2.8a

2.8b

"Ecological design is simply the effective adaptation to and integration with nature's processes."
SIM VAN DER RYN & STUART COWAN, ECOLOGICAL DESIGN (1996)

ECOLOGICAL AND ENVIRONMENTAL PLANNING

Ecological planning is the process of understanding, evaluating and providing landscape use options to both improve the balance between and address the separation of ecological systems and human habitation. Although challenging to separate, *ecological* planning can focus on ecocentric and non-human dimensions (see German & European Green Belts, Wildlands Network, Nature Bridge Crailoo), whereas *environmental* planning can take a more humanist perspective on our place within the wider, interconnected global environment (see Green Belts England, Urban Growth Boundaries). Some approaches combine both (see Baytown Nature Center, Overlay Method—Weller). Ecological planning considers social, political, economic and governance factors that exist within a wider environmental sustainability framework. Environmental legislation and policy provide crucial mechanisms to administer environmental planning and hence its process can be highly politicized.

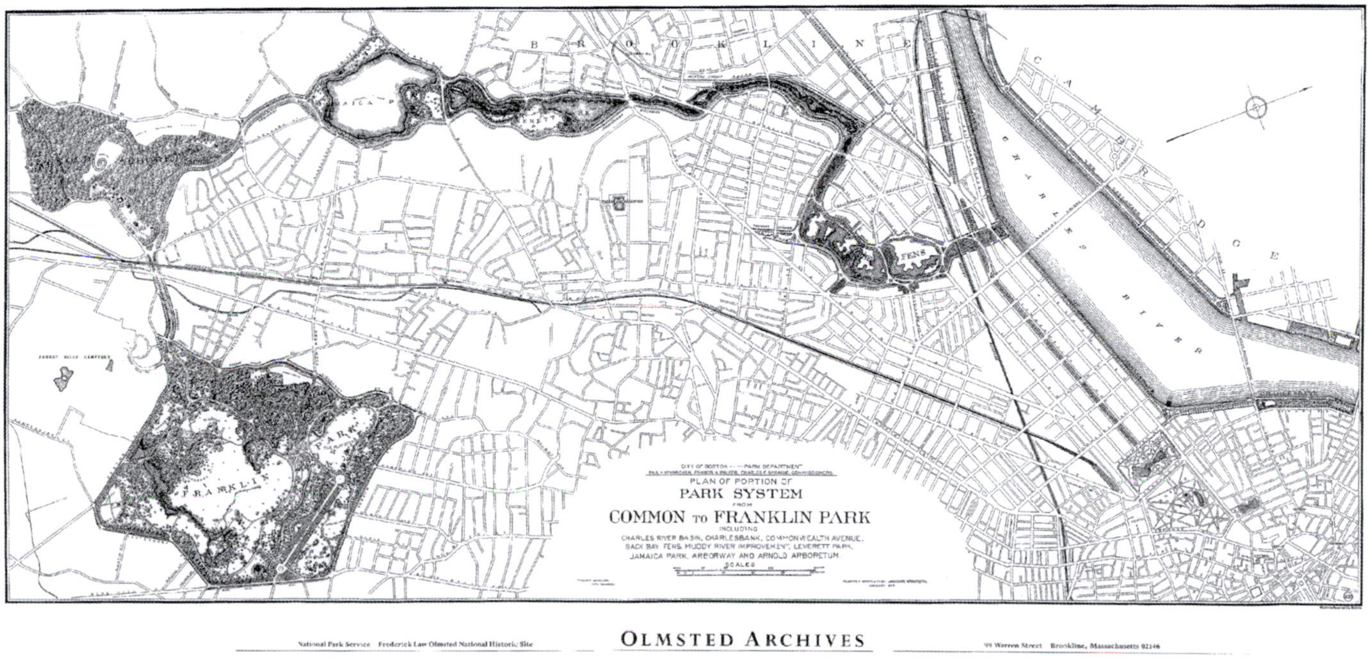
CITY OF BOSTON — PARK DEPARTMENT
PLAN OF PORTION OF
PARK SYSTEM
FROM
COMMON TO FRANKLIN PARK
INCLUDING
CHARLES RIVER BASIN, CHARLESBANK, COMMONWEALTH AVENUE,
BACK BAY FENS, MUDDY RIVER IMPROVEMENT, LEVERETT PARK,
JAMAICA PARK, ARBORWAY AND ARNOLD ARBORETUM.
SCALES
OLMSTED ARCHIVES

2.9

2.9
Emerald Necklace, Frederick Law Olmsted, from 1875, plan drawing 1894, Boston and Brookline, Massachusetts, USA
Most cities have isolated 'islands' of green space. Olmsted's plan for interconnected green space networks coincides with a central concept of ecology that emerged over half a century later. His 1,100 acre (445ha) chain of parks linked by parkways and waterways it is partially constructed.

Newcastle upon Tyne
Sunderland
Bradford
Leeds
York
Liverpool
Sheffield
Manchester
Derby
Nottingham
Stoke-on-Trent
Wolverhampton
Birmingham
Dudley
Coventry
Kidderminster
Redditch
Cambridge
Cheltenham
Oxford
Gloucester
LONDON
Bristol
Keynsham
Bournemouth

2.10

2.10
Map showing the spatial extent of green belts in England, 1935–
Metropolitan green belts act as valuable urban containment devices and significant green buffers, networks and corridors. Constantly under pressure from development, the integrity of green belts is relatively intact in the UK (including that of London, proposed in 1935). While perhaps not the ring of 'countryside' that they were intended to be (and heavily dissected by roads fragmenting green corridor continuity), these peri-urban green spaces act as softscape buffer zones, providing substantial barriers to urban and suburban sprawl and urban mergers. Importantly, green belts help the cleansing process of urban brownfield land by restricting availability of greenfield land for development. Beyond their existing and passive benefits, they possess immense potential for increased ecosystem service provision, multifunctional and productive landscapes (Chapters 2, 3, 4 and 5).

2.11
Urban Growth Boundaries, USA
In the USA, the first urban growth boundary was established in 1958 around the city of Lexington, Kentucky and the first state-wide policy in 1973 when the Oregon legislature passed its landmark law requiring each state municipality to draw a boundary which urbanization could not pass. The US states of Oregon, Washington and Tennessee require cities to establish urban growth boundaries. Each of Oregon's 241 cities has an urban growth boundary (with Portland being a well-known example, first established in 1979). Although not as substantial as green belts, urban growth boundaries—the circumscribing of an entire urbanized area—can help to reduce or stop continuous low density sprawl of cities and suburbia. This land use planning technique assists brownfield cleansing, increased urban density and protects agricultural, rural and conservation land on the peri-urban fringe. Urban growth boundaries can be moved or removed by governments to facilitate the release of land and hence are prone to development lobbying.

2.11

DÄNEMARK
Ostsee
Nordsee
Kiel
SCHLESWIG-
HOLSTEIN
MECKLENBURG-
VORPOMMERN
Hamburg
Schwerin
Müritz
Bremen
NIEDER-
LANDE
NIEDERSACHSEN
POLEN
Oder
BERLIN
Potsdam
Weser
Hannover
Magdeburg
BRANDENBURG
Elbe
NORDRHEIN-
WESTFALEN
SACHSEN-
ANHALT
Neiße
Düsseldorf
Dresden
Erfurt
SACHSEN
THÜRINGEN
BEL-
GIEN
HESSEN
Rhein
Wiesbaden
Mainz
RHEINLAND-
PFALZ
TSCHECHIEN
LUXEM-
BURG
Main
SAAR-
LAND
Saarbrücken
BAYERN
BADEN-
Stuttgart
FRANK-
REICH
WÜRTTEMBERG
Donau
München
ÖSTER-
REICH
Bodensee
SCHWEIZ
LIECHTENSTEIN
0 50 100 km

2.12

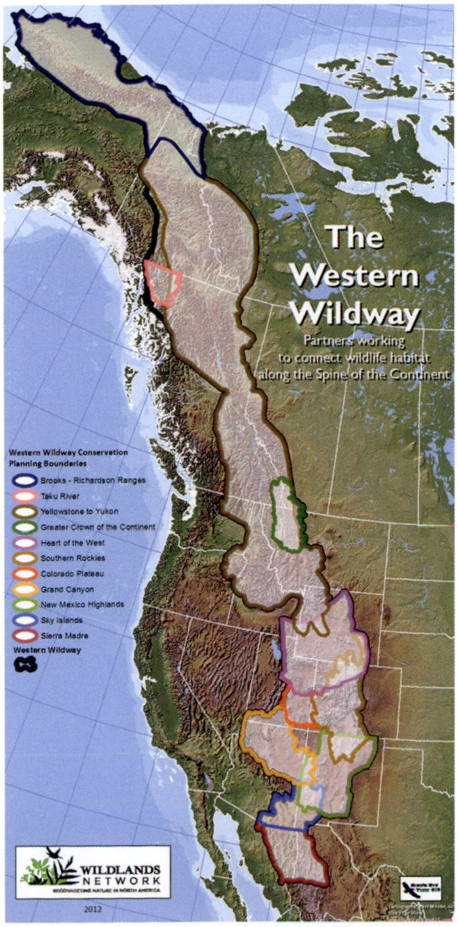
The Western Wildway
Partners working to connect wildlife habitat along the Spine of the Continent
Western Wildway Conservation Planning Boundaries
Brooks - Richardson Ranges
Taku River
Yellowstone to Yukon
Greater Crown of the Continent
Heart of the West
Southern Rockies
Colorado Plateau
Grand Canyon
New Mexico Highlands
Sky Islands
Sierra Madre
Western Wildway
WILDLANDS NETWORK
2012

2.13a

2.13b

2.12

German Green Belt (Grünes Band Deutschland), 1989–

The German Green belt is an 870 mile (1,400km) ecological corridor along Germany's former east–west border sector (part of the USSR's former 'Iron Curtain' boundary dividing Europe and the USSR from the end of World War II in 1945 until the end of the Cold War in 1991). This past network of fences and guard towers enabled several decades of undisturbed natural development largely free from human intervention and is now one of the world's most unique nature reserves.

In addition to the 'no man's land' of the border strip, extensive tracts of inaccessible adjacent land host 600 rare and endangered species of birds, mammals, plants and insects in a system of interlinked biotopes. An initiative of one of Germany's largest environmental groups, Bund Naturschutz (BUND), it informally began in 1975 and more formally in 1989 after the 'Pan-European Picnic', the fall of the Berlin Wall and lifting of the Iron Curtain. Former Soviet leader Mikhail Gorbachev's 2002 endorsement, German Chancellor Angela Merkel's 2005 National Natural Heritage designation, and various other strategies and federal processes have secured the land for nature conservation activities.

2.13a
2.13b

Wildlands Network, 1991–

Wildlands Network (formerly Wildlands Project) restores, protects, and connects wild places in North America, and aims to protect and sustain natural diversity. This science-driven organization began working with partner groups to protect core areas of habitat and create wildlife corridors at scales large enough to facilitate wolves, cougars, and other native predators—populations vital to maintaining healthy landscapes. The Network also engages policymakers to ensure that laws and public policies are helping to protect wild places and animals.

european
greenbelt
Barents Sea
Norway
Finland
Russian
Federation
Estonia
Baltic
Sea
Latvia
Lithuania
Poland
Czech Republic
Germany
Slovakia
Austria
Hungary
Romania
Italy
Slovenia
Croatia
Serbia
Montenegro
Macedonia
Albania
Bulgaria
Black Sea
Turkey
Greece

2.14

2.14

European Green Belt, 2003–

The European Green Belt is an ecological corridor aiming to connect high-value natural and cultural landscapes across 24 countries along the former Iron Curtain. The 2003 initiative merged existing regional schemes into one European initiative divided in three regional sections: Fennoscandian (Norway, Finland, Russia, Estonia, Lithuania, Latvia); Central European (Poland, Germany, Czech Republic, Slovakia, Austria, Hungary, Slovenia, Croatia, Italy); and the Balkan/South eastern European (Serbia, Montenegro, Kosovo, Bulgaria, Romania, Republic of Macedonia, Albania, Greece and Turkey). The 7,770 mile (12,500km) border zone granted nature an almost four decade pause, unwittingly encouraging habitat conservation. Crossing nearly all European bioregions, over 40 national parks are directly situated along it, with more than 3,200 protected nature areas within 31 miles (50km) either side of its corridor. It is a symbol for transboundary cooperation, shared and European natural and cultural heritage, and a restored ecological network consistent with the vision of the European Landscape Convention (see Chapter 4).

2.15a
2.15b
2.15c
Wildlife Bridge Zanderij Crailoo, the Netherlands

The Netherlands began building its network of wildlife bridges in the mid 1980s and has over 600 crossing structures (mainly underpasses) in the national road network, including over 40 bridges (ecoducts) with around 10 more planned. Wildlife bridges can be a solution for habitat and species fragmentation, reconnecting wildlife habitats and facilitating movement across transport infrastructure. Some species require very wide corridors of connecting habitat to reduce opportunistic predators. Zanderij Crailoo, claimed to be the largest in the world at 875 yards long (800m) and 55 yards (50m) wide, makes inroads into the scale required to more meaningfully overcome the devastating impact of the world's vast road network on wild species. Spanning a railway line, industrial zone, roadway, and sports complex, it cost €14.7 million (around $16 million) and took from 2002–2006 to complete. While sometimes perceived to be an expensive measure, neighboring Germany has pledged to build over 100 in the next decade.

Motion sensor cameras (2.15c) capture migration of fauna.

2.15a

2.15b

2.15c

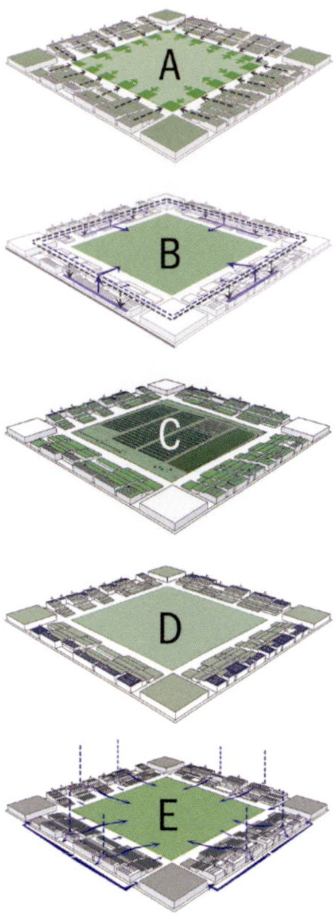
A
B
C
D
E

2.16b

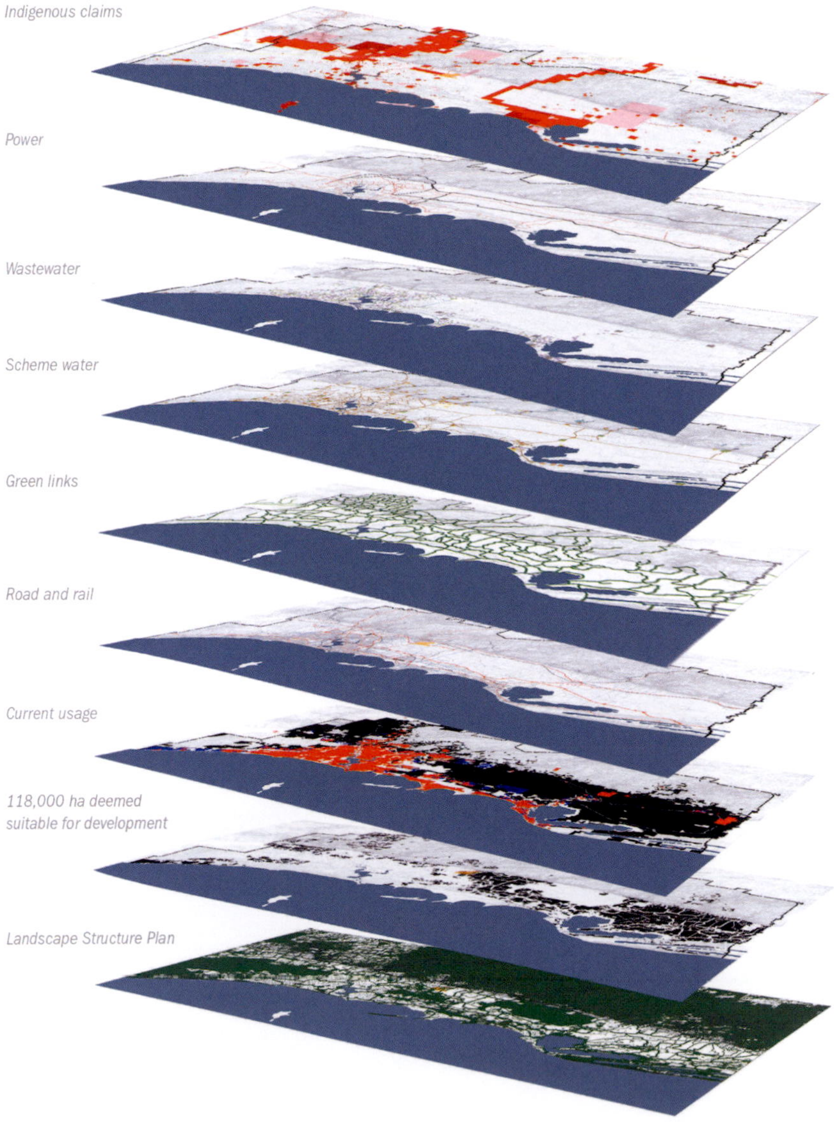
Indigenous claims
Power
Wastewater
Scheme water
Green links
Road and rail
Current usage
118,000 ha deemed suitable for development
Landscape Structure Plan

2.16a

2.16a
2.16b
Ian McHarg overlay method utilized by Richard Weller
Landscape architect Ian McHarg's overlay method provides a clear presentation method for elements of analysis, strategies and designs. It is employed here in Richard Weller's 'Boomtown' for both the analysis of metropolitan Perth, Australia (2.16a) and for the layers of the 'Food City' scenario (2.16b: Compost (A), Greywater (B), Food (C), Energy (solar and wind) (D), and Stormwater (E)) for population growth.

McHarg's seminal book 'Design with Nature' (1969) is still utilized by landscape architecture and planning schools, and his clear methodology of isolating and combining landscape components as layers continues to be used by landscape architects as well as Geographic Information Systems (GIS) (to compile layers of data for maps and spatial outputs).

Contemporary practitioners have included social, cultural and historic elements beyond McHarg's primarily natural science focus, resulting in a well-rounded approach to site analysis and landscape assessment.

"Landscape should be seen as the primary infrastructure which creates value directly and indirectly."
FARRELL REVIEW (2014)

"Nature cannot be managed, not because we lack management intelligence, but because managed things are artifactual, that is, precisely not natural (they are cultural); and any and every attempt to pass off the cultural as the natural necessarily mobilizes the grand Edenic illusion with all its feints."
DENNIS WOOD, UNNATURAL ILLUSIONS (1988)

2.17a
2.17b
Baytown Nature Center, SWA, Baytown, Texas, USA, 1997
The Baytown Nature Center, Brownwood Marsh (20 miles east of Houston), is a 400 acre (162ha) wetland restoration, resulting from a US District Court order to replace damaged and destroyed ecosystems from legal dumping activities of a 200-company consortium in Crosby, Texas. SWA assisted master plan preparation and provided land planning and landscape architectural services for the wetlands parcel. Objectives included protection of valuable existing habitat, enhancement of marginal and degraded habitat, and construction of new habitat niches to create a more resilient bayside ecosystem. The project features an interpretive center with classrooms; auditorium; museum; parking; network of trails; and recreational activities. Plants and animals including deer, fish, crustaceans and 275 bird species have since thrived.

2.17a

2.17b

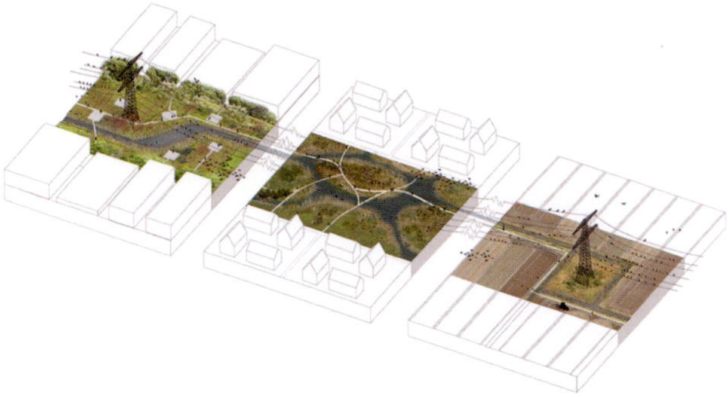

2.18a

Anthropocene = new scope and challenges

Ecological planning's roots can be traced back over 150 years (see, for example, Emerald Necklace and Warren Manning's 1923 national scale plan for the USA). The *Anthropocene epoch* (Chapter 1) recognizes that human activity has and will increasingly reshape and inevitably degrade nature's ongoing processes—'nature' is now a cultural landscape. There is therefore an increasing need for adaptive ecological and environmental planning and design to anticipate anthropogenic effects based on scientifically forecasted future scenarios (see Houston Arboretum).

2.18a
2.18b
2.18c

Ecological Energy Network, LOLA, Fabric & Studio 1:1, the Netherlands, 2012

This first-prize competition winner proposes a green space, recreation and sustainable transport network on land easements used by the power grid. Effectively forming a coherent national ecological network, the transmission area could become the Netherlands' largest national park (planting of non-flammable vegetation types would be crucial if the same concept were applied in drier world regions!).

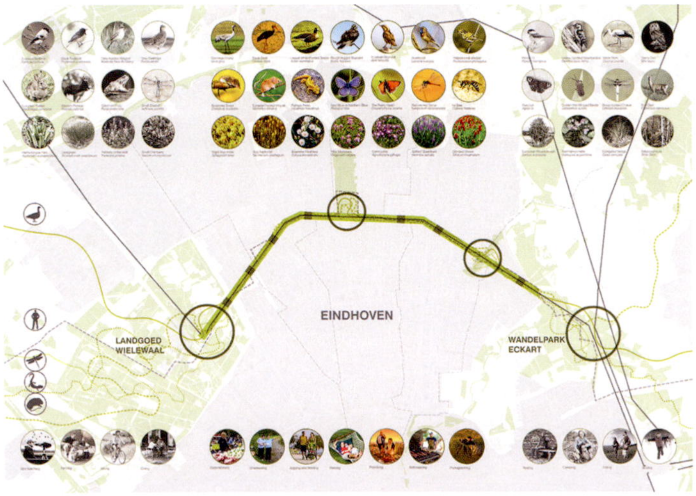
EINDHOVEN
LANDGOED WIELEWAAL
WANDELPARK ECKART

2.18b

2.18c

2.19a
2.19b
2.19c
2.19d

Houston Arboretum and Nature Center, Reed Hilderbrand, Houston, Texas, USA, 2012–

2.19a Impacted by the natural disaster of Hurricane Ike and a recent historical drought, the arboretum represents a landscape in crisis.

2.19b Using baseline inventory data, ecological suitability was determined for each potential landscape type. The result is a diverse and resilient mosaic that is an authentic representation of the arboretum's regional ecological context.

2.19c Restoration will begin with selective clearing of the disturbed landscape, which over the next 40 years, will be regenerated to become a more sustainable ecosystem.

2.19d The proposed design is a more ecologically diverse and resilient landscape, designed to better handle future disturbance.

The 155 acre (63ha) Houston Arboretum and Nature Center is located within one of the largest parks in the USA, the 1,500 acre (607ha) Memorial Park. The arboretum—a critical refuge for native plants and animals and hub for urban environmental education—was a landscape in crisis, with invasive species and sudden, significant tree death (48% tree canopy mortality) due to hurricanes and drought.

The design responds to exhaustive assessment of the site's natural and cultural heritage; diagnosis of the impacts of climate change; extensive stakeholder engagement; and interpretation of regional ecological context. Stakeholder workshops identified two primary goals of achieving landscape diversity and balancing programmed and 'wild' spaces.

Forensic investigation of existing soils, topography, hydrology and remnant vegetation fed into a series of environmental overlays used to determine where optimum conditions existed for varied landscape typologies. For example, 'prairie' consisted of only 2% of the site, yet 49% had characteristics conducive to prairie. This approach helped decision makers embrace the radical changes proposed in the plan.

The design strategy proposes site-contextual ecologies—meadow, savannah, wetland, bayou, prairie, bog, hardwood forests and riparian woods—to develop a more ecologically diverse landscape mosaic, increasing resilience to climate change and future disturbance. Various visitor initiatives maximize experience of distinct landscape characters while preserving sensitive ecological areas. The new plan sets forth a 40-year evolutionary implementation strategy involving nutrient recycling and volunteer employment to restore the site and educate the community of the dynamism of interrelated ecological systems in flux.

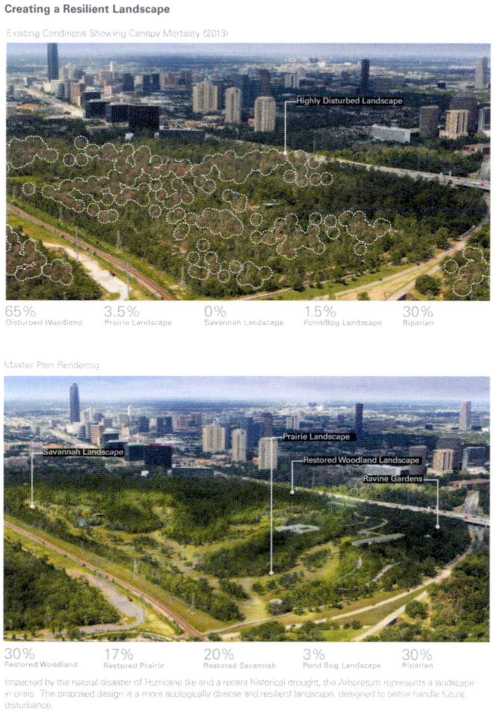
Creating a Resilient Landscape
Highly Disturbed Landscape
65% Disturbed Woodland
3.5% Prairie Landscape
0% Savannah Landscape
1.5% Pond/Bog Landscape
30% Riparian
Master Plan Rendering
Savannah Landscape
Prairie Landscape
Restored Woodland Landscape
Ravine Gardens
30% Restored Woodland
17% Restored Prairie
20% Restored Savannah
3% Pond Bog Landscape
30% Riparian
Impacted by the natural disaster of Hurricane Ike and a recent historical drought, the Arboretum represents a landscape in crisis. The proposed design is a more ecologically diverse and resilient landscape, designed to better handle future disturbance.

2.19a

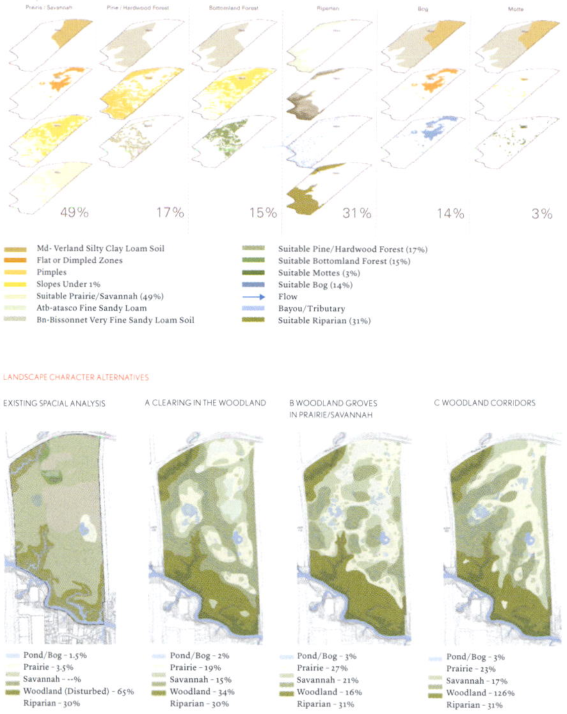
Prairie / Savannah
Pine / Hardwood Forest
Bottomland Forest
Riparian
Bog
Motte
49%
17%
15%
31%
14%
3%
Md- Verland Silty Clay Loam Soil
Flat or Dimpled Zones
Pimples
Slopes Under 1%
Suitable Prairie/Savannah (49%)
Atb-atasco Fine Sandy Loam
Bn-Bissonnet Very Fine Sandy Loam Soil
Suitable Pine/Hardwood Forest (17%)
Suitable Bottomland Forest (15%)
Suitable Mottes (3%)
Suitable Bog (14%)
Flow
Bayou/Tributary
Suitable Riparian (31%)
LANDSCAPE CHARACTER ALTERNATIVES
EXISTING SPACIAL ANALYSIS
A CLEARING IN THE WOODLAND
B WOODLAND GROVES IN PRAIRIE/SAVANNAH
C WOODLAND CORRIDORS
Pond/Bog - 1.5%
Prairie - 3.5%
Savannah - --%
Woodland (Disturbed) - 65%
Riparian - 30%
Pond/Bog - 2%
Prairie - 19%
Savannah - 15%
Woodland - 34%
Riparian - 30%
Pond/Bog - 3%
Prairie - 27%
Savannah - 21%
Woodland - 16%
Riparian - 31%
Pond/Bog - 3%
Prairie - 23%
Savannah - 17%
Woodland - 126%
Riparian - 31%

2.19b

Enjoying the Seasonality of the Prairie and Savannah

2.19c

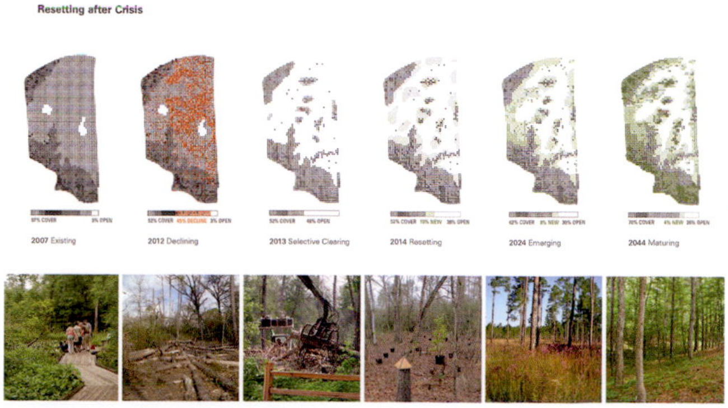
Resetting after Crisis
2007 Existing
2012 Declining
2013 Selective Clearing
2014 Resetting
2024 Emerging
2044 Maturing

2.19d

LAND MANAGEMENT AND MULTIFUNCTIONAL LANDSCAPES

'Land management' is a broad-scale stewardship approach. It identifies diverse qualities of landscape regions, developing synergistic strategic guidance, masterplans and management practices. Mediating economic, social and environmental dimensions (usually on large-scale private and public sites) land management can provide nuanced, symbiotic approaches to land-based activities and processes (such as farming, forestry and conservation). Similarly, multifunctional landscapes seek to maximize benefits through stacking landscape (as well as social) dimensions (see Salisbury Wetlands).

Balancing needs

Large rural areas often contain a mix of seemingly paradoxical activities, such as forestry, farming and conservation. Land management seeks to determine the balance of a given site so that all can survive, co-exist and ideally, thrive (see Orongo Station). Successful land management optimizes possible scenarios such as interventions' scale (private versus industrialized), specific practices (mixed species plantations/monocultures), and conservation versus production requirements to create multifunctional landscape practices (agroforestry, windfarms on grazing land—see Chapter 4) and multidimensional landscapes (combining functional and social elements).

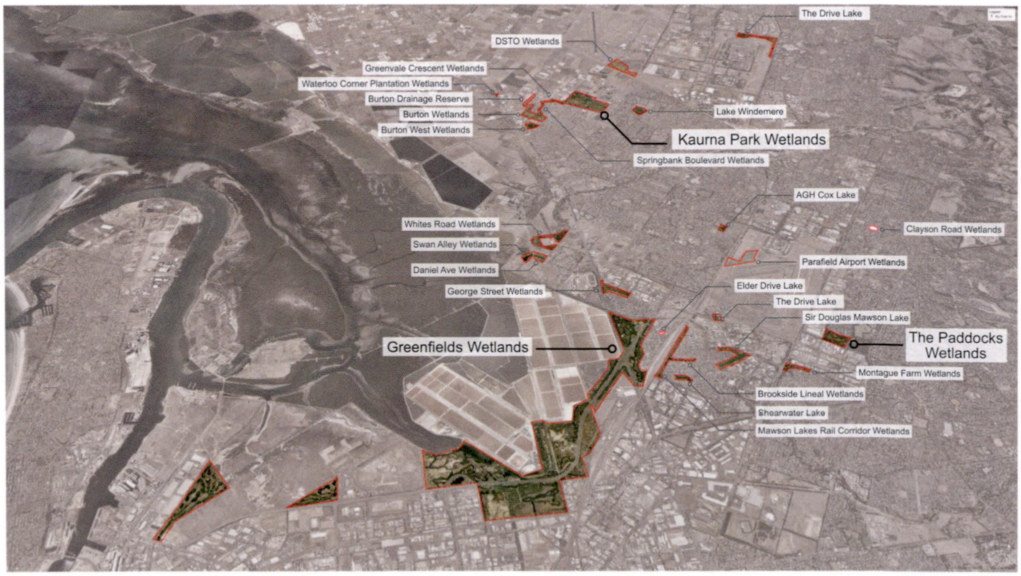
The Drive Lake
DSTO Wetlands
Greenvale Crescent Wetlands
Waterloo Corner Plantation Wetlands
Burton Drainage Reserve
Burton Wetlands
Burton West Wetlands
Lake Windemere
Kaurna Park Wetlands
Springbank Boulevard Wetlands
AGH Cox Lake
Clayson Road Wetlands
Whites Road Wetlands
Swan Alley Wetlands
Daniel Ave Wetlands
Parafield Airport Wetlands
George Street Wetlands
Elder Drive Lake
The Drive Lake
Sir Douglas Mawson Lake
Greenfields Wetlands
The Paddocks Wetlands
Montague Farm Wetlands
Brookside Lineal Wetlands
Shearwater Lake
Mawson Lakes Rail Corridor Wetlands

2.20a

2.20b

2.20c

2.20a
2.20b
2.20c
2.20d
2.20e
2.20f

Salisbury Wetlands, City of Salisbury, Adelaide, Australia, 1970s–

An exemplar of sustainable water cycle management and multidimensional landscapes, the Salisbury Wetlands are a network of over 50 constructed wetlands covering 14,825 acres (6,000ha) of its 62 square mile (161km^2) council area. The wetlands, whose visionary process began in the 1970s, utilize a range of WSUD techniques including trash racks; gross pollutant traps; sedimentation/detention ponds; reedbeds; weirs; and flow/diversion structures, designed to slow and hold the flow of stormwater runoff, allowing sediments to settle and reduce pollutant outfall.

The municipality began monitoring water quality in the 1990s and discovered several key findings: heavy metals were adsorbed into fine clay particles and settled out after a few hours; macrophyte reed beds were facilitating removal of most of the nutrient load; and sunlight was killing harmful pathogens and some of the biotic contaminants in the water.

Aquifer storage and recovery (ASR) (deep bores sunk and water pumped in/out of suitable aquifers) commenced in 1994 and enables winter rainfall to be filtered, stored and extracted for use during the dry summer. The municipality now has over 22 ASR bores, significantly reducing dependence on precious local water supplies in its semi-arid environment and generating economic activity through supplying local industries with recycled water (see Parafield Facility, Chapter 7).

Some of the wetlands dry out, while others offer permanent water bodies, providing a range of habitats and refuge for breeding birds and animals from prolific domestic and wild predators. With over 180 species of nesting birds (including rare species) in one large wetland alone, the wetlands also house a wide range of aquatic plant and animal species including mammals, fish, frogs, insects, macro-invertebrates, tortoises, snakes and lizards.

The wetlands restore habitat, increase biodiversity and ecosystem services; provide flood protection and natural cleansing; facilitate economic activity; help to protect delicate catchments, estuaries and mangroves; provide for recreation and environmental education; enable research and development; and re-establish local distinctiveness.

2.20d

2.20e

2.20f

2.21a
2.21b (During construction)
2.21c
2.21d

Orongo Station Conservation Masterplan, Poverty Bay, New Zealand, Nelson Bird Woltz, 2002–2012

2.21a The hybrid landscape of Orongo Station Masterplan integrates farming operations and restoration efforts and mediates cultural, agricultural and ecological landscapes.
2.21b The wetland during construction.
2.21c and 2.21d The 1,890 foot long earthen dam separates the freshwater from the saltwater wetland and provides a walking path through the environment.

The Orongo Station Conservation Masterplan for a 3,000 acre (1,215ha) sheep farm in New Zealand established extensive ecological restoration while expanding agricultural production and revealing a cultural landscape rich in history. The Station is a site of national significance, being the landing point for the Great Migration of Maori people in 1100, and again for Captain Cook's crew in 1769. British farming methods, particularly sheep grazing, had since subjected it to ongoing resource depletion.

Collaborating with multiple public and private stakeholders, the client and Maori leaders, the masterplan creates multiple, productive farming operations; a restoration regime to repair ecological damage; a series of gardens; and the protection of historic Maori earthwork, defense structures, and a still in use cemetery. Over 500,000 trees were planted to reforest sheep-grazed land and 75 acres (30ha) of fresh and saltwater wetlands have been restored and constructed. By integrating cultural and ecological landscape restoration with active, profitable agricultural operations, Orongo Station serves as a model for sustainable land management.

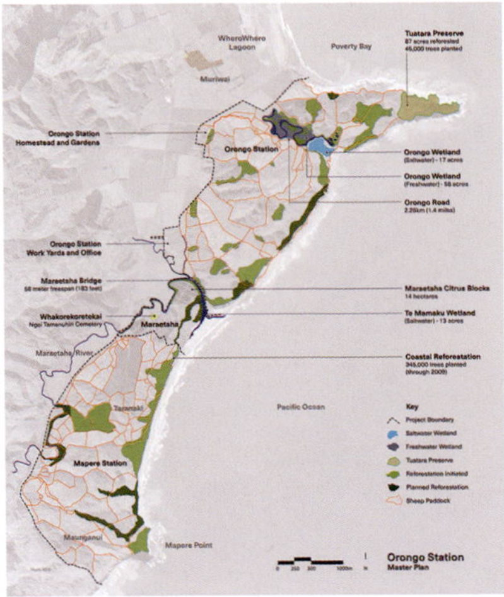

WheroWhero Lagoon
Poverty Bay
Muriwai
Tuatara Preserve
87 acres reforested
46,000 trees planted
Orongo Station
Homestead and Gardens
Orongo Station
Orongo Wetland
(Saltwater) - 17 acres
Orongo Wetland
(Freshwater) - 58 acres
Orongo Road
2.25km (1.4 miles)
Orongo Station
Work Yards and Office
Maraetaha Bridge
56 meter freespan (183 feet)
Maraetaha Citrus Blocks
14 hectares
Whakorekoretekai
Ngai Tamanuhiri Cemetery
Maraetaha
Te Mamaku Wetland
(Saltwater) - 13 acres
Maraetaha River
Coastal Reforestation
345,000 trees planted
(through 2009)
Taranaki
Pacific Ocean
Key
Project Boundary
Saltwater Wetland
Freshwater Wetland
Tuatara Preserve
Reforestation Initiated
Planned Reforestation
Sheep Paddock
Mapere Station
Maunganui
Mapere Point
Orongo Station
Master Plan

2.21a

Multidimensional practice

Land planning and design become increasingly effective when stacking dimensions, functions and elements (rather than having only singular or narrow foci). Environmental restoration, design and land management have the capacity to provide ecosystem services, increase existing and future novel ecosystems' resilience, incorporate effective stewardship, and respond to our dependency on the environment. Urban and built environments must not simply be seen as part of nature, but be understood for their substantial effects on wider ecosystems; their *ecological footprints* (see Chapter 6). Accordingly, symptoms and more importantly, causes, can be determined and concurrently targeted to manage humanity's vast impacts (Chapters 4, 5, 6 and 9), accommodating future needs (Chapter 7).

2.21b

2.21c

2.21d

STUDY/DISCUSSION QUESTIONS

What is a natural landscape? Do these exist? Give an example and explain.

What benefits do natural landscapes provide?

What is a cultural landscape? Is all of the Earth a cultural landscape? Why/why not?

Is there a separation between humans and the environment? Why does this exist?

Do certain landscapes have less value than others? What are the underlying values in assessing the worth of a landscape? Does a landscape have intrinsic value?

What are the values of a) a developer b) ecologist c) landscape architect d) landscape planner e) politician f) you?

Is ecological restoration successful at reinstating natural landscapes?

What is ecological restoration attempting to recreate? i.e. what is its baseline?

Are historic baselines/states/ecosystems best for current and future generations? Why/why not?

Is there an ethical obligation to inform people that a restored (from a cleared site) landscape is not naturally occurring?

Can a restored landscape be a natural landscape? Is 'wildscaping' and 'rewilding' paradoxical or possible?

Is nature 'in-balance'? Can 'balance' be (re)constructed or created by humans?

Would you be willing to stand in front of a bulldozer to stop destruction of 'nature'?

What is "degraded" land? Do degraded landscapes have value?

Some projects involve destroying sites of natural importance and substituting these for protecting or restoring other sites, called 'biodiversity offsetting'. Discuss the issues that result from this approach.

FURTHER READING

Beatley, T. and Manning, K. (1997) *Ecology of Place: Planning for environment, economy, and community*, Washington DC: Island Press.

Douglas, I. and James, P. (2015) *Urban ecology: an introduction*, New York: Routledge.

Fainstein, S. and Campbell, S. (2016) *Readings in planning theory*, Chichester, UK: John Wiley & Sons.

Leopold, A. (1949) *A Sand County Almanac*, New York: Oxford University Press.

Low, T. (2003) *The New Nature*, Victoria: Penguin.

Marris, E. (2011) *Rambunctious garden: saving nature in a post-wild world*, New York: Bloomsbury.

Marsh, W. (2010) *Landscape planning: environmental applications*, Hoboken, NJ: Wiley.

Monbiot, G. (2014) *Feral: rewilding the land, the sea, and human life*, Chicago: The University of Chicago Press.

Mostafavi, M. and Doherty, G. (2010) *Ecological Urbanism*, Germany: Lars Muller.

Ndubisi, F. (2014) *The Ecological Design and Planning Reader*, Washington DC: Island Press.

Randolph, J. (2012) *Environmental land use planning and management*, (2nd ed.) Washington: Island Press.

Reed, C. and Lister, N-M. (2014) *Projective ecologies*, New York: Actar Publishers.

Van der Ryn, S. and Cowan, S. (2007) *Ecological Design*, Washington DC: Island Press.

Weller, R. (2009) *Boom Town*, Western Australia: UWA Press.

ADDITIONAL PROJECTS

You might also like to look for further information on the following projects:

Great Green Wall, Sahara and Sahel, Africa, 2007–

Resuscitating the Fez River, Bureau E.A.S.T., Fez, Morocco, 2008

Bloedel Reserve, Richard Haag Associates, Bainbridge Islands, Washington USA

Magnuson Park, berger partnership, Sand Point Way, Seattle, Washington, USA

Core Area of Lotus Lake National Wetland Park, Tieling City, Liaoning Province, China

Nungatta Station Land Management Masterplan, Material Landscape Architecture, south eastern New South Wales, Australia, 2004–2008

East London Green Grid & All London Green Grid, London, UK

Oostvaardersplassen, the Netherlands, 1968 & 1989–

INTERVIEW Nina-Marie Lister

Professor Nina-Marie Lister is Associate Professor of Urban Planning at Ryerson University and Associate Director of Urban and Regional Planning. She is also Visiting Professor of Landscape Architecture at the University of Toronto as well as Harvard University (2009–2013). As the founding principal of *Plandform*, a studio exploring the relationship between landscape, ecology, and urbanism, Professor Lister's research, teaching and practice focus on the confluence of landscape infrastructure and ecological processes within contemporary metropolitan regions.

*Please note this is an interview excerpt – the full interview is available at www.bloomsbury.com/zeunert-landscape-architecture

Should we be focused on cultivating a more adaptive and opportunistic approach to ecological design rather than one based in theories that don't necessarily equate to human conditions and practices?

Yes! For a number of reasons we could say that normatively, this might be useful. There's so much that has been written on hierarchical dualisms that relate to our destruction of nature and wilderness and that relate to our epistemologies of how we know and understand and make sense of the natural world. Of course, a lot of it relates to our histories of colonization (depending on which cultural perspective you're talking about), so I think there's a huge part of our cultural history at work in the way we have structured our understanding of the natural world. In my own work, I've tended to refer to those as the child or children of a Newtonian deterministic way of knowing about the world. This has served us very well in terms of the modern amenities that have given rise to our civilization, industrialization and our economic system and also the pathologies associated with that. So yes, we should be focused on thinking about renewing and engaging our relationship with the natural world and our understanding of its ecologies, insofar as how they relate to a very diverse and complex set of cultural and social conditions. We are no longer a world of colony and colonies, the Empire and the colonies, we are many of those. We move now around the world at faster speed, we interbreed, we intermarry, we immigrate, we emigrate and there isn't really the kind of insulation, isolation and for lack of a better word—homogeneity—among individuals or groups that we used to see or could rely on. In fact, globalization is from many perspectives, disturbing in its homogenization of everything, but on the other hand, we see a tremendous amount of diversity within the population and in the way that we relate to the natural world. There are huge opportunities for making sense of and interpreting what is left of what we understand to be wild or wilderness. Arguably more important is the landscape that most of us recognize as home—the urban and urbanizing—and these may be the only landscapes that we really understand. I think there's an enormous incentive to have a different, more flexible, nuanced and adaptive approach to engagement with those landscapes.

What are hybridized ecologies and how can we shift our understanding to work with novel ecosystems and hybrid ecologies? What benefits might this provide?

The way in which I have been using that term comes from both agricultural and resource context—the hybridization is the crossing of different species which result in something different and perhaps more adapted to a changing context. Sometimes it is more useful and I tend to think of hybridization as an opportunity to adapt and in many cases particularly in the urbanized environment when landscapes have in many cases been made and remade and often done so after a period of abandonment in a derelict state. There are necessarily emerged combinations of species that are more tolerant of difficult conditions that are associated with contamination or previous abuse, misuse or disuse. Once established, the species can help to complement and build soil in the same way that a native species can. There are benefits to fast-growing hybrid species that can take advantage of harsh conditions that may in the short term improve soil quality, reduce erosion, anchor soil, ameliorate flooding and provide a range of services that we see from a human perspective as valuable and necessary. They may not be aesthetically beautiful in the tradition to which we are accustomed, but they may provide a set of services in their hybridity and contribution to the emergence of a novel set of conditions. They may exist on the edges or help to move an ecosystem towards a more complex succession. These of course aren't ever-permanent states, they are always transitions in time. During that transition, particularly on urban sites that have been challenged, contaminated or left fallow, they can provide a range of benefits, whether it's shading, cooling, or also an aesthetic quality that hasn't been present before. In rapidly changing urban environments that are shifting demographically and culturally, the recognition that these kinds of hybrid environments and the landscapes that result from them add value becomes important, particularly at a time when, for example, we don't have the same kind of municipal budgets that we used to have for ornamental landscapes. We need to look to longer lasting, hardier shrubs and in some cases plants that produce food products, that give color over four seasons and don't have to be annually planted. There are of course changing attitudes toward gardening and landscaping on a larger scale that reflect hybridity. We might see this as an example of people who are environmentally inclined or interested in the processes of ecology who suddenly appreciate these benefits, reflecting a paradigm shift in the last 15 years. Benefits, for example, of pollination, seed dispersal, four season color. They appreciate urban wildlife like butterflies and bees and a variety of songbirds in the garden and are therefore less inclined to put their pesky lawn to the required centermetage and effectively challenge the municipal by-laws about what is acceptable in the garden. So the lawn no longer needs to be a strict species and we may select native species from our area, prairie plants that would occur in our region if left untended. While these might have been perceived as unkempt or messy at one time, we are now re-writing our by-laws to realize that not only do homeowners have choice, but it is a useful thing to do from the perspective of biodiversity and all the aforementioned ecosystem services.

Are productive ecologies a helpful model to break the dualist separation of humanity from nature to transition from this established, anthropocentric worldview?

I still wrestle with terminologies. Hybridization is different but related to the notion of productive. A productive landscape from an ecological perspective is one that I generally understand to be flourishing and has integrity, is resilient in the face of routine or a punctuated period of disruption. It bears fruit metaphorically and sometimes literally, plants repopulate, animals colonize, the flora and the fauna exhibit and feature diversity, it has complexity in the structure, and this of course varies from one ecosystem to another. Productive can mean many things, but in a cultural sensibility that as humans we recognize value from those types of ecology, in that landscapes are not singular in their purposefulness, they're not merely to be viewed from a distance (although beauty I would argue also offers productive and aesthetic landscape values). We can recognize a whole suite of values. I think productive for me means a layered set of values and benefits, so we have a park for purposes of recreation, pleasure-taking, relaxation, leisure, spiritual respite, aesthetic value, but also, perhaps it produces material for human consumption—fruits or vegetables—rather than color alone. It may also provide storm-water management, erosion protection, soil anchoring, in addition to all of the other things, so we suddenly recognize the ecosystem service value of pollination as something to be actively engaged in the design plan. Planting pollinating plants has become almost de rigueur over the past ten years of municipal park design whereas ten years ago I would never have seen someone arguing that the presence of bees or honey bees or butterflies add value. By productive ecologies, I think I'm pursuing the notion that there can be multiple values added through the recognition and of legibility of ecological services and functions. We make these legible to bring understanding, as this gives the opportunity of stewardship and caretaking.

Is it more about the understanding and education to perceive these benefits from novel, hybrid and productive ecologies rather than what is simply visually apparent?

I'm struck by the tension between the pursuit of the spectrum of different ecosystems from urban to wild; there is a continua in places that are more or less inhabited by people. In Canada there is a very large land base of over 10,000,000km^2 and a very low population density relative to that number, we have a different understanding of wildness is. When we say 'park', we could mean a national park that has very few people per square kilometer—or even per seasonal cycle—than a more urban place, where the continuum of that spectrum is much broader. When we talk about productivity, we could equally talk about the productive wild places as we might talk about hybrid, novel, or highly human-dominated ecosystems in the city. In the urban context, I think it is incredibly important to recognize—and again, I'm speaking from a British Commonwealth tradition—that we are a relatively new country with a high degree of immigration with a high degree of ethnic and cultural diversity. In Toronto, for example, more so than most places on the planet, people bring to the city very different sets of cultural values as they relate to the natural world, the outdoor, the garden and the landscape. I think we are challenged to find ways to communicate "what does 'productive' mean in the urban landscape? to our people and our public." One thing we can do is to create a common set of understanding; we can't hope to have stewardship and care for the landscape in any context, without a common sense of understanding and meaning-making. That doesn't mean that we all have to agree on it, it means that we needs some common ways of interpreting and understanding a language that we share. Without that language, whether it's Anne Whiston Spirn's notion of the language of landscape, or Jane Wolf's excellent concepts of legibility and meaning-making, we need a shared understanding, without which there can be no possibility of stewardship with care. The work of designers can make legible these functions, so it becomes really important. There is enormous untapped potential for landscape design in the 21st century urbanizing world to understand the relationship of what different types of ecologies offer different cultural perspectives and how can we make these legible, understood and of value. Once we can give a name to them, and an understanding to the different types of productive values that they offer us, then we can begin a conversation about stewardship and care.

With humanity seemingly out of control, is it helpful to see the earth as a landscape that we inextricably need to manage?

That's a loaded question! Humanity being 'out of control'; are we out of control with our population, do we have an obsessive compulsive desire to manage the world to oblivion? I think we can assert that there are aspects of the Western industrial way of being that take more than their fair share, we might say, that there are aspects of greed and a need for immediate gratification at the expense of others. These are problematic and have long-term implications for the earth's ability to provide for our resources. At the same time, I think it's hugely important to understand that as humans, we are inextricably tied to the biota of the planet. We depend on it for our very ability to breathe, to excrete and to drink and to survive for longer than 24 hours. We need those fundamental services, we need that intimate relationship with the natural world. We are born of it and we are not separate from it. So it does us good to see ourselves as profoundly tied and dependent on the landscapes that we feel we need to manage but the question then becomes not whether or not we manage, or design, or curate or garden, but how we do it. Do we do it respectfully, do we honor the landscape that sustains us, or do we deplete it, to the point where our very survival is at risk? There is a benefit in the conversation, I think, to being somewhat selfish in that we recognize our own need in order to honor the world on which we depend. We are not separate from it and yet nor is it really in our ability to manage in any Newtonian deterministic way. I tend to ask the question not whether or not we can manage the ecosystem but how rather do we manage ourselves. The challenge is how do we manage ourselves and our interactions with the ecologies that sustain us, not to maintain the hubris that we can actually manage that complex a system, but frankly, if we do a bad enough job of it, it will simply eliminate us. Then we will simply be variables. We may find that all (or the few) species remaining around us breathe air that is different, or excrete toxins that will kill us. Will we be the ones that are selected out of the picture? I have no doubt about the continuation and pervasiveness of the ecology around us, I just think that it will look very different and it won't be very hospitable, so it would be good if we paid attention to how we manage ourselves.

3.1

Qian'an Sanlihe Greenway, Turenscape

A section of the 13.4km Qian'an Sanlihe Greenway by Turenscape that has transformed a degraded river system in China.

3
LANDSCAPE AS CLEANSER

We are faced with continuing contamination and relics from industrial production and consumer culture fallout—mines, refineries, factories, landfills and polluted storm and wastewater. The landscape can reverse many of these toxic terrestrial, aquatic and atmospheric systems, acting as healer, cleanser, and even storyteller. Strategic remediation processes contain, process and cleanse pollutants. This chapter's projects demonstrate the success of processes such as (phyto)remediation and water-sensitive urban design (WSUD) to successfully address polluted environments. By guiding inherently abundant 'natural' landscape processes and designing ecosystem services, landscape architecture can transform degraded sites into safe and habitable places with authentic cultural and historic narratives.

POST-INDUSTRIAL TRANSFORMATION AND ADAPTIVE REUSE

Opportunities

Cities and their hinterlands contain many degraded and abandoned industrial sites (such as landfills, quarries, mines, factories, car parks, and ex-military sites). Reconceiving, remediating, repurposing and retrofitting existing ecologically sterile, hardscape-dominated spaces and infrastructures can occur through green infrastructures and ecosystem service generation techniques (wetlands, WSUD biofiltration, permeable paving, water storage) and new social programming. These extend beyond repurposing buildings and include: adaptive reuse of storm and wastewater infrastructures (e.g. concrete culverts, see Emscher Landschaftspark and Duisburg Nord); transport infrastructures (High Line) and streets (Green Streets, Chapter 4); parking lots (Arizona Campus); decorative water features (Perth Wetland); green roofs (Munich, Chapter 4); and installing additional planting in existing barren spaces (legally or through covert, community techniques like 'guerrilla gardening').

"We abuse land because we regard it as a commodity belonging to us. When we see land as a community to which we belong, we may begin to use it with love and respect .... That land is a community is the basic concept of ecology, but that land is to be loved and respected is an extension of ethics."
ALDO LEOPOLD, A SAND COUNTY ALMANAC (1949)

"There are no wastelands in our landscape quite like those we've created ourselves."
TIM WINTON, ISLAND HOME (2015)

3.2a

3.2a (Before)
3.2b
Gasworks Park, Richard Haag Associates, Seattle, Washington, USA, 1970–1975
The 19.1 acre (7.7ha) Seattle Gasworks Park is an oft-cited early exemplar of post-industrial landscape architecture. The lakefront design fought hard to retain structures from the abandoned coal gasification plant. Indigenous soil bacteria consuming hydrocarbons bioremediated the site's surface.

3.2b

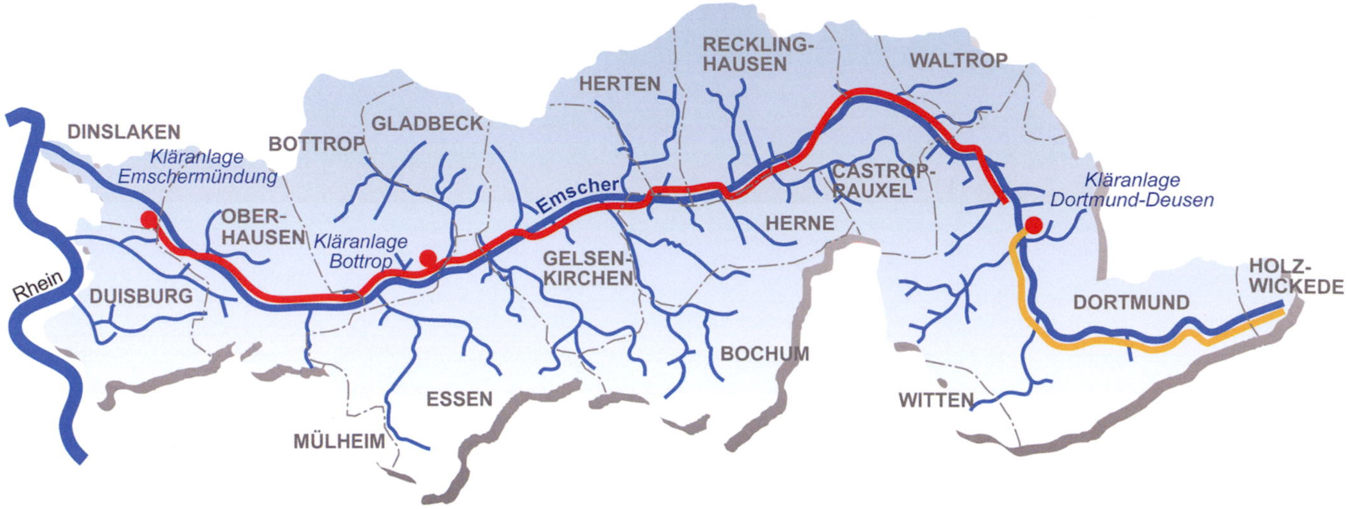
DINSLAKEN
Kläranlage Emschermündung
BOTTROP
GLADBECK
HERTEN
RECKLING-HAUSEN
WALTROP
Rhein
OBER-HAUSEN
Kläranlage Bottrop
Emscher
CASTROP-RAUXEL
Kläranlage Dortmund-Deusen
DUISBURG
GELSEN-KIRCHEN
HERNE
DORTMUND
HOLZ-WICKEDE
BOCHUM
ESSEN
WITTEN
MÜLHEIM

3.3a

3.3b

3.3c

3.3d

3.3e

3.3a
3.3b
3.3c
3.3d
3.3e
Emscher Landschaftspark, Ruhr district, Germany, 1989–
3.3a Yellow=completed, Red=to be completed.
3.3b The Emscher River in Dortmund in 1900.
3.3c Typical before condition.
3.3d Typical after condition.
3.3e View from Duisburg-Nord across part of Emscher Landschaftspark.

The Emscher valley was the heartland of Europe's steel and coal industries, epicenter of German industrialization and one of the most polluted and environmentally devastated regions in the world. By the late 1980s, the area had deindustrialized, with social deprivation accompanied by toxic fallout: slag heaps; tailings; runoff and leachate; decaying structures and an 80km river with heavy metals, untreated sewage and wastewater in its concrete banks.

Its transformation into the huge Emscher Landschaftspark (111,200 acres/45,000ha) used the medium of landscape to create an interconnected 'landscape park', rehabilitating the river and environmentally, socially and economically reinvigorating the region. The state government took a progressive, regional approach, establishing the International Building Exhibition (IBA) Emscher Park in 1989 (coordinating multiple municipalities, private industry, environmental groups and citizens). Themes included: 'Industrial monuments' (retaining and creatively reusing industrial heritage), 'The new Emscher' (regenerating the river system by water association Emschergenossenschaft), 'Working in the park' (employment spaces, social initiatives, education and training) and 'Living in the park' (new types of housing).

The park is composed of cleansed brownfields, reclaimed forests, and recreation providing a cohesive set of green infrastructure for the entire region. Since 1989, over 400 projects have been delivered, ranging from large fallow land areas, small-scale construction schemes, to restoration and reinstatement of biotopes and simple tree plantings. Perhaps the best-known project is Duisburg-Nord Landscape Park (in this chapter).

By mid 1993, €2.5 billion (around $2.7 billion) had been invested in the redevelopment (approximately two-thirds from public funds and one-third from private investments). The process of river regeneration by Emschergenossenschaft requires an investment of €4.5 billion (around $5 billion) for the 218 mile (350km) length.

Authenticity

Many post-industrial and brownfield projects (usually at the client or general public's insistence) attempt to hide or disguise their previous industrial heritage. Shame of a 'dirty' past, or concerns for toxicity and contamination can negatively affect new proposals' value (such as condominiums). Engineers and developers typically consider it easier and more efficient to work on a 'clean slate', while municipal authorities and clients can be fearful of litigation if retaining structures in varying states of decay. Landscape architects can at times take a subtle, more subversive approach to communicate site history as opposed to using obvious images and information on signage. Occasionally, a brave client and/or a persuasive designer manages to integrate old and new, retaining and revealing historical essence, raw forms and site memories in a new vision that gains value from industrial heritage (see Duisburg-Nord, Zhongshan, BP and Ballast Point Parks).

3.4a
3.4b
3.4c
3.4d
3.4e
3.4f
3.4g

Duisburg-Nord Landscape Park, Latz & Partner, Duisburg, Germany, 1990–2002

Duisburg-Nord Landscape Park (DNLP) is part of the extensive Emscher Landschaftspark.

A competition-winning team led by Peter Latz transformed the remnants of a former ironworks and blast furnace plant into a dramatic 568 acre (230ha) landscape park. A long-term masterplan consisted of several sub-projects, including the Blast Furnace Park, the Railway Park, Sinter Park, Waterpark, Adventure Playground, and the Ore Bunker Gallery.

Creatively weaving a powerful social and environmental masterpiece amongst the decaying yet resilient industrial skeleton, the project has helped shift the aesthetic perception of industrial heritage. Yet the project faced challenges and controversy in creating public spaces in a once heavily contaminated blast furnace plant. Fear of pollution has now subsided and the park is a tourist attraction and local asset.

The post-industrial spatial patterns and fragments have been reimagined, reconfigured and interwoven with new elements. A new landscape (with strategically selected materials and hardscape surfaces) has emerged through the harmonious merger with the old. During festivities up to 50,000 people gather in the repurposed spaces, with programming including cultural and corporate functions; a youth hostel; a diving center in an old gasometer; climbing gardens in ore storage bunkers; a high ropes course in a former casting house; a viewing tower in an extinguished blast furnace; light installations and play spaces. Integrated with land art are circulation and hydrology; a range of elevated walkways; careful vegetation management; lawns; meadows; groves and gardens. Entry is free and there are no time limitations.

Ein Geflecht industrieller Strukturen wird Landschaft

3.4a

3.4b

3.4c

3.4d

3.4e

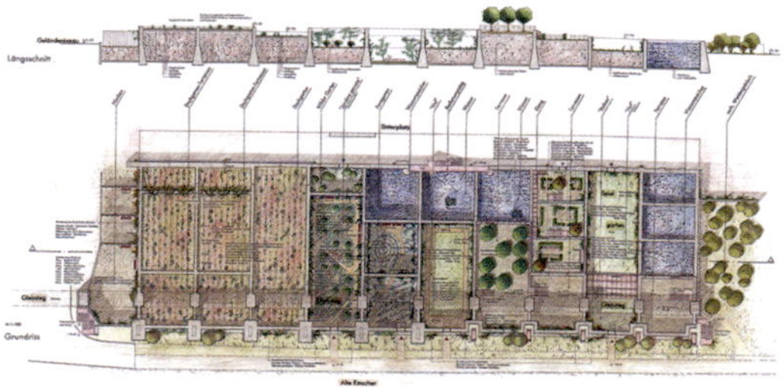

3.4f

3.4g

3.5a (Before)
3.5b
3.5c
Zhongshan Shipyard Park, Turenscape, Zhongshan, Guangdong Province, China, 2001–2002
Zhongshan Shipyard Park is an innovative 1950s shipyard and brownfield site and the first protected industrial heritage site in China. The park demonstrates how landscape architecture can transform a derelict site into a beautiful, meaningful and functional place, as well as stimulate urban renovation.

Despite opposition, Turenscape persistently advocated for the recognition of culture and history not yet designated as formal or 'traditional'. Site inventory uncovered a challenging setting, including daily tidal fluctuations of up to 3.6 feet (1.1m), an existing lake, trees and vegetation, and remnants of industrial machinery. Despite flood regulation recommendations, existing trees were left intact in an island, with bridge networks constructed to address water fluctuations, and integrated terraced planting beds facilitating native salt marsh 'weeds' and a sense of the ocean.

The site reveals stories of socialist China and the Cultural Revolution, artistically and ecologically retaining industrial heritage by preserving, modifying and creating elements dramatizing site character. It merges into the urban fabric through a network of paths, water elements and urban facilities, including reuse of railway lines and machinery, a water tower repurposed as a light tower, docks for tea and club houses, and accessible terraces planted with native plants and beneficial 'weeds'. Kongjian Yu's paper about the project, 'The Culture Being Ignored and the Beauty of Weeds: The Regenerative Design of an Industrial Site', is part of the required middle-school curriculum in Jiangsu Province.

Greenfield overkill

The prevalence of exemplary, realized post-industrial and remediation projects (combined with the number of brownfield and contaminated sites in most cities) helps explain why many built environment sustainability experts look unfavorably on greenfield projects as unnecessary misuse of land. These advocates posit that we should clean up existing and abandoned brownfield areas for built development rather than build on greenfield sites that may have high agricultural land value, remnant ecosystems, or are uncontaminated. Green belts and urban boundaries (Chapter 2) can help facilitate this process as they restrict the freely available supply of greenfield development land within a city.

3.5a

3.5c

3.5b

"Weeds, like valued plants, are complex chemical factories containing chlorophyll and deriving energy from light in photosynthesis.

Weeds, like valued plants, draw insects necessary for pollination of crops.

Weeds are pioneers of degraded landscapes where the soil is worn out and valued plants are missing.

Weeds, in the form of wildflowers, are environmentally and aesthetically essential in shoring up eroding sand dunes.

Weeds are necessary to the healing process of the landscape and help set the stage for future quality growth.

Weeds can quickly cover eroded soil and prevent further erosion.

Weeds play important roles in ecological and economic systems by producing practical benefits that further the interest and wellbeing of society."

JULIA HUGHES JONES, THE SECRET HISTORY OF WEEDS (2009)

3.6a

3.6a (Before)
3.6b
William G. Milliken State Park, Phase 2 Lowland Park, SmithGroupJJR, Atwater Street, Detroit, Michigan, USA, 2010
Previously a contaminated brownfield site with abandoned infrastructure, Lowland Park is the 6.1acre (2.5ha) second phase of 31 acre (12.5ha) Milliken Park and Michigan's first urban state park. It provides riverfront access for the downtown's 39,000 employees, with recreational space for fishing, biking and wildlife viewing, interpretive displays, restored native habitat, and a wetland treating runoff and removing sediments and pollutants from 12.5 acres (5ha) of adjacent parcels 4.5 million gallons annually, over 47 million litres.

3.6b

3.7a

3.7a (Before)
3.7b
3.7c
Arizona State University Polytechnic Campus, Ten Eyck Landscape Architects, Mesa, Arizona, USA, 2009
This LEED-Gold certified project transformed an 18 acre (7ha) concrete and asphalt former military airforce base into a social and academic indoor/outdoor hub sustaining desert life.

Regionally-inspired water features harvest stormwater and mitigate flooding, while native Sonoran Desert plants promote biodiversity and contribute to a sense of place.

3.7b

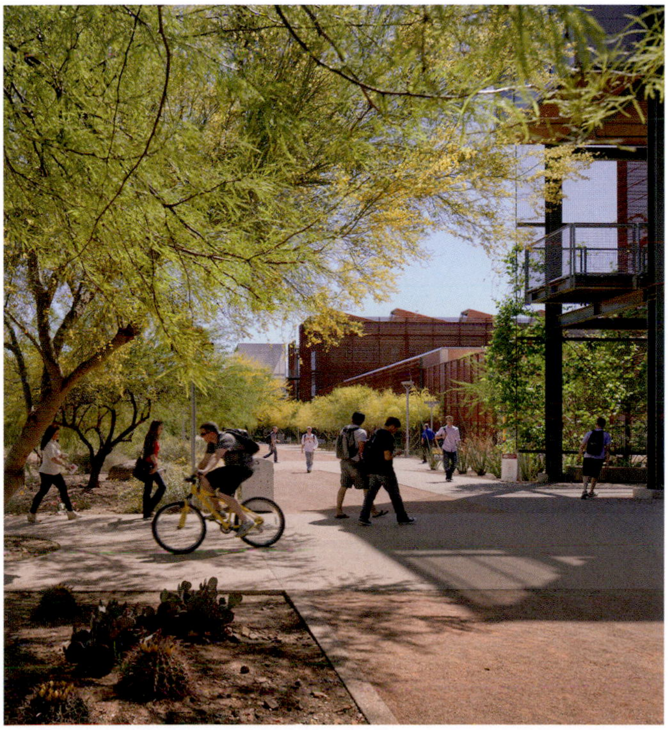

3.7c

OERLIKON
24224

3.8a

3.8a (Before)
3.8b
3.8c
MFO Park, Raderschall Landschaftsarchitekten AG, Neu-Oerlikon, Zurich, Switzerland, 2002
This innovative urban park has created a series of garden rooms, corridors and spaces at various levels under a structure reminiscent of the former engine factory. A range of social programs and events take place amongst the climbing vegetation that displays spectacular colors during fall.

3.8b

3.8c

3.9a (Before)
3.9b
3.9c
3.9d
3.9e

Evergreen Brick Works, Claude Cormier + associés, Toronto, Ontario, Canada, 2006–2010

The 1889 Evergreen Brick Works brownfield site is incised with industrial quarries and heritage, serving as a catalyst for new ideas on relationships between nature, individuals, and cities.

The multidisciplinary team transformed ten of the 40 acre (4 of 16ha) post-industrial ruin into an active, environmentally-based community center and park to reconnect city communities with local natural systems.

Movement of water, cars, electricity, trains, and wildlife are encouraged through increasing site porosity, creating a free-flowing system of sustainability-oriented components. These include the continued development of wetlands and meadows; urban agriculture; a 110,000 square foot (1.22ha) garden and nursery; children's discovery area; conference and event facilities; skating surfaces, and organic farmers' market.

3.9a

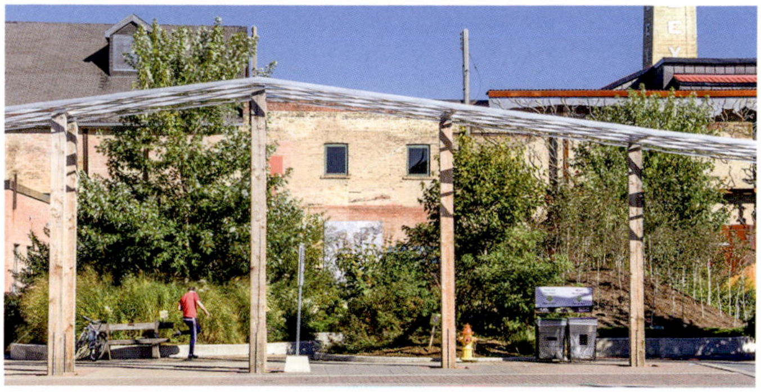

3.9d

3.9b

3.9c

3.9e

ART GALLERY

3.10a

3.10b

3.10c

3.10a (Before)
3.10b
3.10c

Perth Cultural Centre Urban Wetland, Josh Byrne & Associates, Western Australian State Government, Perth, Australia, 2011

Derelict, modernist concrete water features with decayed complex infrastructures exist worldwide. As part of the Perth Cultural Centre Revitalization, an existing water feature has been retrofitted with an urban wetland that treats and filters water through natural processes. The project also includes a carpark, rooftop orchard (see Chapter 5) and play space.

3.11a
3.11b

The High Line, James Corner Field Operations, Diller Scofidio + Renfro, Piet Oudolf, Manhattan, New York, USA, 2009

An extraordinary 6 acre (2.4ha) linear public park across 23 city blocks in Manhattan's West Side was created through adaptive reuse of a disused, elevated post-industrial railway line. The project has transformed the district, demonstrating the power of the urban landscape and public space to catalyze social activation and financial investment.

Widely copied due to its success, most replications fail to acknowledge its unique characteristics (such as the existing railway infrastructure and Manhattan context), authentic response to place, and the highly skilled, contextual design response expressed through materials, furniture, lighting, details and planting.

183

3.11a

3.11b

REMEDIATION

Remediation is the process of making polluted or contaminated sites safe for human access and habitation. It routinely occurs when previously industrial and brownfield land is proposed for residential and commercial redevelopment. There are numerous scenarios in which site cleansing may be required:

- mine sites can leach toxic concentrations of heavy metals into soil, surface and groundwater hydrological systems and air through evaporation from tailings dams;
- oil fields and refineries leave behind heavily polluted soils and structures;
- coal-seam gas extraction (also known as fracking and increasingly used in peri-urban and urban locations) pollutes soil, groundwater and surface water systems;
- nuclear testing, accident and waste sites are beyond remediation capacity and can be toxic for hundreds of thousands of years—the antithesis of a future sustainable legacy;
- agricultural chemical fertilizers and pesticides (both synthetic and organic) pollute soils and agricultural drainage systems, flowing into precious freshwater, groundwater and aquatic and marine environments (together with vast sewerage volumes);
- landfills can seep toxic leachates into groundwater and release dangerous greenhouse gases (particularly methane) into the atmosphere (see Fresh Kills and Vall d'en Joan);
- ex-military land can be polluted and converted into other uses when decommissioned.

Many of these activities can lead to unstable ground surface conditions prone to subsidence. Most large cities have hundreds if not thousands of polluted and contaminated areas with varying levels of toxicity, which may be listed in local, central, state or federal registers. Many of these toxic legacies can be reversed though landscape-based remediation, facilitating natural soil and plant processes. Given time, harmful components can be broken down to safe levels, enabling access and habitation.

"You may delay but time will not."
BENJAMIN FRANKLIN , 'POOR RICHARD'S' ALMANACK (1758)

"Considering that the mercury in thermometers sold to hospitals and consumers in the United States each year is estimated to total 4.3 tons, and it takes only one gram to contaminate the fish in a twenty acre lake, designing a mercury free thermometer is a good thing ... [Mercury in thermometers] account for only about 1% of the mercury used in the United States."
MICHAEL BRAUNGART & WILLIAM MCDONOUGH, CRADLE TO CRADLE (2002)

Scenarios

The extent of remediation required varies on a case-by-case basis depending on the type (arsenic, lead, mercury, cadmium and many others), concentration and stages (solid, gaseous, liquid) of present toxins. Disciplines involved usually include geochemistry, biotechnology, engineering and landscape architecture. In landscape architecture projects, remediation commonly presents several scenarios:

- off-site remediation: removal of polluted soils, structures and fluids to treatment/processing locations or to landfill (many landfills now include measures to contain pollutants and process leachates) if such measures are determined to have reduced risk through relocation;
- on-site remediation: contaminated soils and materials are immobilized on site, and soils may be graded, sorted, washed and treated (see Gasworks Park, Queen Elizabeth Olympic Park). Contaminated materials can be contained in landforms (Renaissance Park), 'sealed' (such as by membranes) and/or 'capped' (such as clay), containing leachate processing and treatment (see Millennium Parklands and Vall d'en Joan);
- phytoremediation: specific plants used to target removal of present toxins in polluted soils and water bodies, which may take considerable time (months, years, decades);
- groundwater remediation: usually involves a combination of biological, chemical, and physical treatment techniques (see Thames Barrier Park).

After remediation, soil deficit may require additional sourcing (see Tejo Park) and a clean surface planting layer may use imported clean fill, cleansed site topsoil or substitute sub-soil as a planting medium (see Queen Elizabeth Olympic Park). Accordingly, the design team will likely inherit a site with different levels, gradients and soil conditions from what previously existed, due to minor or major earthworks. Design may have commenced before remediation and then require re-design (particularly for detailed design and construction documentation) after obtaining a new site survey (and possibly causing delay).

3.12a

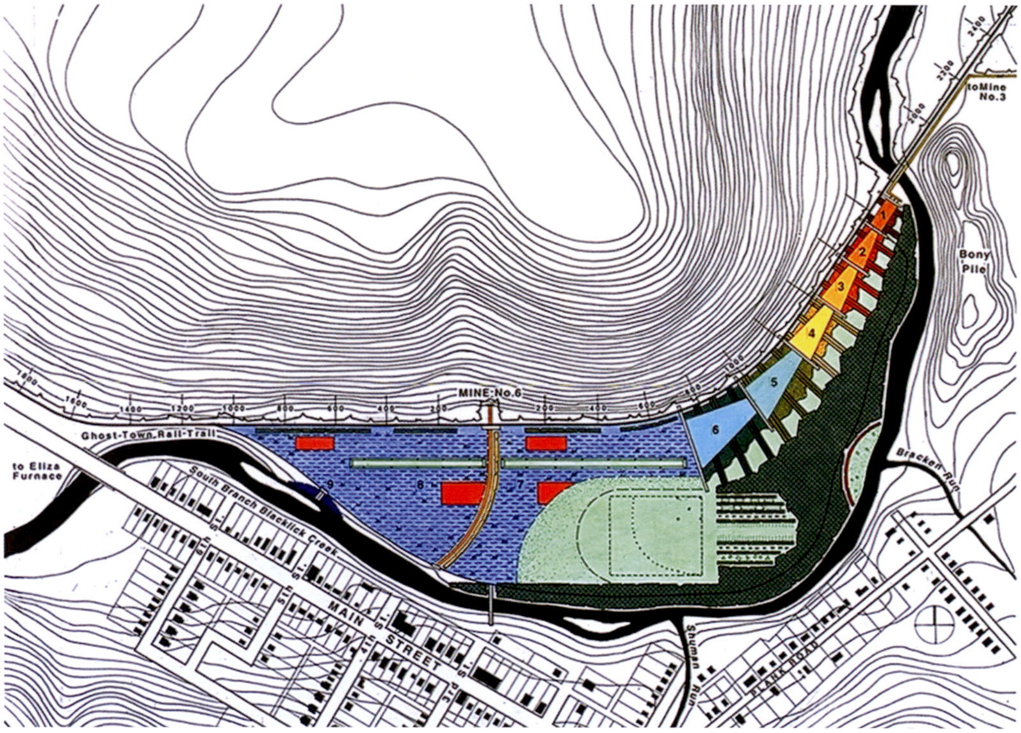

MINE No.6
Ghost-Town Rail-Trail
to Eliza Furnace
South Branch Blacklick Creek
MAIN STREET
toMine No.3
Bony Pile
Bracken Run
Shuman Run

3.12b

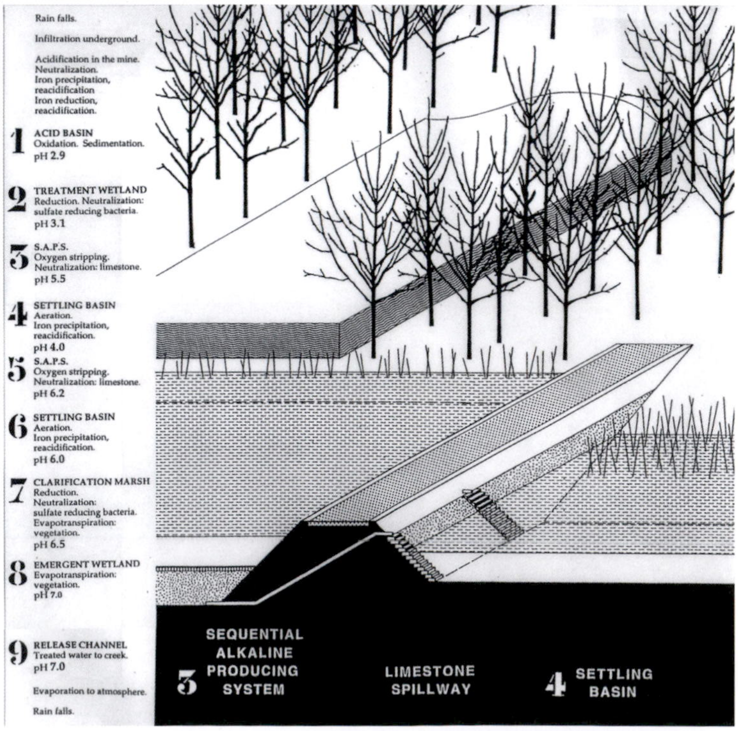

Rain falls.
Infiltration underground.
Acidification in the mine.
Neutralization.
Iron precipitation, reacidification
Iron reduction, reacidification.
1 ACID BASIN
Oxidation. Sedimentation.
pH 2.9
2 TREATMENT WETLAND
Reduction. Neutralization: sulfate reducing bacteria.
pH 3.1
3 S.A.P.S.
Oxygen stripping.
Neutralization: limestone.
pH 5.5
4 SETTLING BASIN
Aeration.
Iron precipitation, reacidification.
pH 4.0
5 S.A.P.S.
Oxygen stripping.
Neutralization: limestone.
pH 6.2
6 SETTLING BASIN
Aeration.
Iron precipitation, reacidification.
pH 6.0
7 CLARIFICATION MARSH
Reduction.
Neutralization:
sulfate reducing bacteria.
Evapotranspiration:
vegetation.
pH 6.5
8 EMERGENT WETLAND
Evapotranspiration:
vegetation.
pH 7.0
9 RELEASE CHANNEL
Treated water to creek.
pH 7.0
Evaporation to atmosphere.
Rain falls.
3 SEQUENTIAL ALKALINE PRODUCING SYSTEM
LIMESTONE SPILLWAY
4 SETTLING BASIN

3.12c

3.12a (Before)
3.12b
3.12c
3.12d
3.12e
3.12f

Vintondale Reclamation Park, DIRT Studio, Vintondale, Pennsylvania, USA, 1994–2004

Vintondale Reclamation Park stands on 35 acres (14ha) of environmentally devastated floodplain wrought by acid mine drainage (AMD) from its previous use as Vinton Colliery. The Environmental Protection Agency (EPA) labelled AMD the biggest environmental problem in the eastern mountains region. Heavy metal-laden water suffocated streambeds with orange sediment, destroying the bottom of the food chain and entire watersheds.

The project connected a team of designers, artists, scientists and historians with government agencies and local communities to combat this environmental destruction and social abandonment common to so many post-mining sites. The strategy focused on making remediation processes visible though a passive water treatment system and 7 acre (3ha) habitat wetland. Horticulture was designed in tandem with hydrology and aesthetics to balance science with art, with a 4 acre (1.6ha) multi-purpose recreation area, gardens, art installations and thirteen native tree species (chosen for their fall colors) to represent the cleansing process of seven keystone-shaped water treatment ponds. Once cleaned and 'legal', the water is released into a wetland with 10,000 native plants, with surrounding habitat provided for deer, wood ducks, geese, beavers and foxes.

3.12d

3.12e

3.12f

3.13a
3.13b (During construction)
3.13c
3.13d
3.13e
3.13f
3.13g

Millennium Parklands, PWP Landscape Architecture, HASSELL, Bruce Mackenzie Design, Sydney Olympic Park, Australia, 1999–2000

Millennium Parklands (now Sydney Olympic Park and the wider setting for the 2000 Sydney Olympic Games) is a 1,112 acre (450ha) park with 15 miles (24km) of waterfront on what was a significantly contaminated 19th century slaughterhouse and 20th century manufacturing and naval munitions storage site. Restoring and enhancing the site's cultural and natural heritage was critical to the design intent, which emphasized recycled materials, indigenous species and new technologies such as facsimile soils, solar energy generation and stormwater recycling.

The park features 124 acres (50ha) of remnant forest, woodlands, mangroves, green corridors and fauna and bird sanctuaries, with Homebush Bay's lowlands restored to waterways and wetlands for more than 180 native bird species.

Bioremediation ponds cleanse aquatic pollution and provide recycled water for irrigation and reuse. Remediation was required for 65% of site soils, which were excavated and contained on-site for decontamination, spatially expressed in landforms and communicated through education programs.

The park reconnects western Sydney's suburbs to its major waterway. Infrastructure, such as roads, was designed to be subservient to the park, with a large network of pedestrian and bicycle paths allowing the 2.5 million annual visitors to experience native ecologies and open rolling topography via a waterfront boardwalk promenade and the preserved historic naval base and Brick Pit.

3.13a

3.13b

3.13c

3.13d

3.13e

3.13f

3.13g

"The great problem to solve is to bring everything, even the smallest details, into the harmony of the whole."
CAMILLE PISSARRO, LE HAVRE (1904)

3.14a

3.14b

3.14a (Before)
3.14b (During construction)
3.14c
3.14d
3.14e
3.14f
3.14g
3.14h

Queen Elizabeth Olympic Park, LDA Design + Hargreaves Associates, Atkins, Arup, Olympic Delivery Authority, Stratford, London, UK, 2005–2008

The 252acre (102ha) Queen Elizabeth Olympic Park is the largest new urban park in London since the Victorian era. Olympic venues can lack purpose and fall into decay following their initial use. Planned as a catalyst for regeneration for east London's Stratford, the Park demonstrates landscape architects' effectiveness as masterplanners, delivering green infrastructure and ecosystem services for ongoing social, environmental and economic viability. Previously a highly contaminated post-industrial brownfield, it contained a post-war munitions dump, battery and match factories, 52 electricity pylons, weed-choked waterways and a 'Fridge Mountain'. Now, over 3.1 miles (5km) of habitat rich parkland, woodland, swales and meadow run along the previously canalized River Lea, which has been transformed into a wetland mosaic (with 300,000 plants), forming an absorbent flood-control measure (approximately 247 acres (100ha) of open space was designed to reduce flood risk, resulting in removal of 5,500 homes from the 'at risk' register). The improved riverbanks divide the 'wilder' north from the more 'urban' south, with the 'South Park Plaza', designed by James Corner Field Operations, were used for part of the post-games downsizing. Many of the lawn areas in the north park, which were by audiences to watch the games and performances from big screens, were converted to species-rich meadows after the games (3.14a–e show the perennial meadows). An onsite soil 'hospital' cleaned nearly two million tons of soil (the largest ever soil-washing operation in the UK), effectively saving 90,000 offsite truck movements, and 95–98% of site material was recycled within the park. Over 650 bird and bat boxes were installed, species relocated and four thousand semi-mature trees planted to fulfil the Biodiversity Action Plan's 111 acre (45ha) new habitat for key species (including otters, kingfishers, water voles, bats, swifts, sand martins, amphibians, reptiles and a range of invertebrates). Other sustainability initiatives include the use of recycled construction materials (recycled concrete in gabions); creation of habitats on brownfield post-industrial substrate; sustainable drainage (SuDS); and species-rich rather than monoculture lawn. A 'Legacy Masterplan' establishes 8,000 new homes in five adjacent neighborhoods; 12 schools; three health centers; a library; commercial districts and ongoing jobs. Extensive new pedestrian, cycleway and road networks were introduced to connect existing communities in proximity to the park, which is being developed separately from the park by the London Legacy Development Corporation.

3.14c

3.14d

3.14e

3.14f

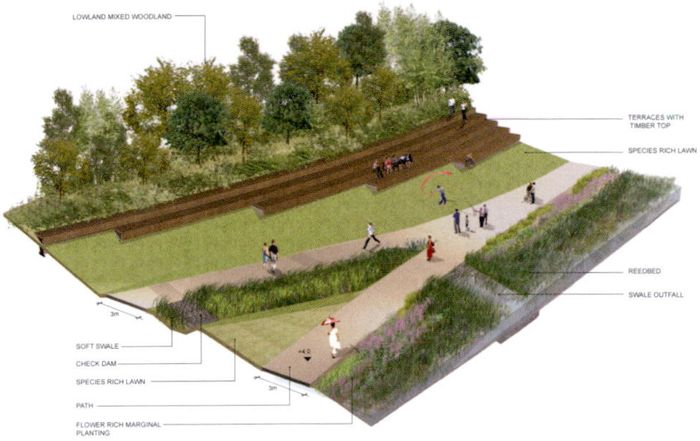
LOWLAND MIXED WOODLAND
TERRACES WITH TIMBER TOP
SPECIES RICH LAWN
REEDBED
SWALE OUTFALL
3m
SOFT SWALE
CHECK DAM
SPECIES RICH LAWN
PATH
FLOWER RICH MARGINAL PLANTING
3m
+4.0

3.14g

3.14h

3.15

3.15

Parque do Tejo e Trancão (Tejo and Trancão Park), Hargreaves Associates & PROAP, Lisbon, Portugal, 1994–2004

Local firm PROAP implemented this 1998 Expo competition-winning design by Hargreaves Associates. Urban and environmental restoration has been partially realized for 160 acres (64ha) of the 222 acre (90ha) degraded, post-industrial area (containing structures, landfill and high indexes of contamination). The design intent was to create a place for recreation and respite featuring the waterfront, and a meaningful environmental education program. Twenty million cubic feet (575,000m^3) of soil dredged from the Tejo riverbed, combined with crushed stone, forms a 10-foot (3m) thick barrier layer between contaminated ground and the new park surface, while a lagoon restocks the water table and irrigates the park.

3.16a

3.16a
3.16b

Thames Barrier Park, Groupes Signes, Patel Taylor, Arup, London Docklands, UK, 1998–2000

Previously a derelict and contaminated 35 acre (14ha) site, this was the first riverside park built in London for over 50 years. Beginning in 1998, remediation dewatered the contaminated water table, removed tars and oils (off-site), and capped contamination through a capillary break layer. A second phase constructed landscapes; a pavilion; water feature; hard surfacing; and planting. The sunken green dock is a reference to the former Prince Regent Dock and provides a sheltered microclimate for a more manicured garden.

3.16b

3.17a

3.17a
3.17b
3.17c (During construction)

Renaissance Park, Hargreaves Associates, 100 Manufacturers Road, Chattanooga, Tennessee 37405, USA, 2006

The post-industrial site of this 22 acre (9ha) $8 million park previously leached contaminants into surface and groundwater, contributing to the pollution of the Tennessee River. Rather than exporting to landfill, waste was extracted on site and stabilized chemically and geotechnically, with 34,000 cubic yards (26,00m^3) of contaminated soil safely sealed within distinctive landforms and 18,000 cubic yards (13,750m^3) of concrete salvaged for on-site fill (saving $1,080,000 in construction cost).

Ecosystem services have been further leveraged through a designed wetland system that collects and cleans the 175 acre (70ha) urban watershed, increasing floodplain storage capacity by 9.32 cubic feet (11,500m^3). A unique vegetative revetment system stabilized the formerly eroding stream through fascines and live-staking, a series of gabion structures and rip-rap armature. The wetland and meadow plantings and preserved remnant floodplain forest quantifiably improve habitat value (with the USEPA Rapid Bioassessment score rising from 60 in 2002 to 122 in 2014).

The park attracts 145,000 visitors annually, has reinvigorated local business and provides a canvas for social engagement, healthy lifestyles, and environmental education through exhibitions and public art (including site-based historic events such as the encampment of liberated slaves).

3.17b

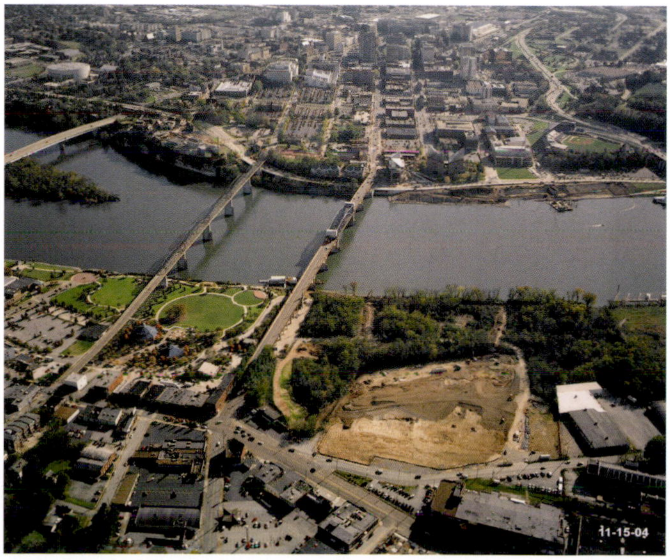
11-15-04

3.17c

Hazard Quad
Munger Valley
Davis Museum
Parking Relocated in New Parking Facility
15
Lulu Wang Campus Center
Physical Plant
Toxic Soil Capped
14
13
Severance Green
12
Alumnae Hall
Toxic Soil Capped
Toxic Soil Removed
Toxic Soil Capped
Toxic Soil Removed
Tower Court
Hay Amphitheater
1
9
10
Toxic Soil Capped
Toxic Soil Capped
8
Cattail Marsh
Toxic Soil Removed
7
2
Events Lawn
Toxic Soil Capped
4
Toxic Soil Removed
Lake House
5
6
Boat House
3
Lake Waban

3.18a

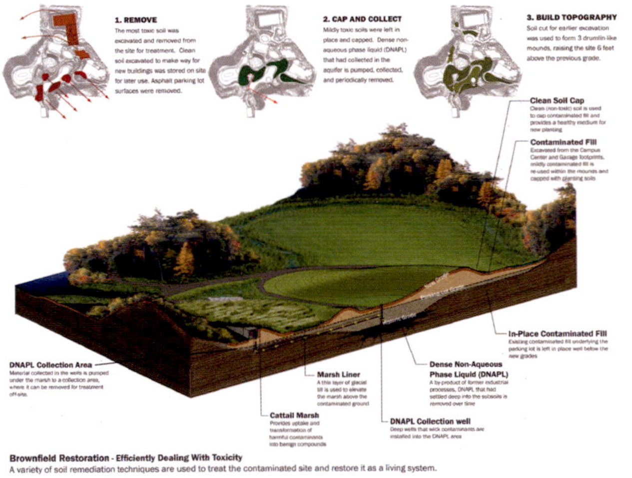

1. REMOVE
The most toxic soil was excavated and removed from the site for treatment. Clean soil excavated to make way for new buildings was stored on site for later use. Asphalt parking lot surfaces were removed.
2. CAP AND COLLECT
Mildly toxic soils were left in place and capped. Dense non-aqueous phase liquid (DNAPL) that had collected in the aquifer is pumped, collected, and periodically removed.
3. BUILD TOPOGRAPHY
Soil cut for earlier excavation was used to form 3 drumlin-like mounds, raising the site 6 feet above the previous grade.
Clean Soil Cap
Clean (non-toxic) soil is used to cap contaminated fill and provides a healthy medium for new planting
Contaminated Fill
Excavated from the Campus Center and Garage footprints, mildly contaminated fill is re-used within the mounds and capped with planting soils
In-Place Contaminated Fill
Existing contaminated fill underlying the parking lot is left in place well below the new grades
DNAPL Collection Area
Material collected in the wells is pumped under the marsh to a collection area, where it can be removed for treatment off-site.
Marsh Liner
A thin layer of glacial till is used to elevate the marsh above the contaminated ground
Dense Non-Aqueous Phase Liquid (DNAPL)
A by-product of former industrial processes, DNAPL that had settled deep into the subsoils is removed over time
Cattail Marsh
Provides uptake and transformation of harmful contaminants into benign compounds
DNAPL Collection well
Deep wells that wick contaminants are installed into the DNAPL area

Brownfield Restoration - Efficiently Dealing With Toxicity
A variety of soil remediation techniques are used to treat the contaminated site and restore it as a living system.

3.18b

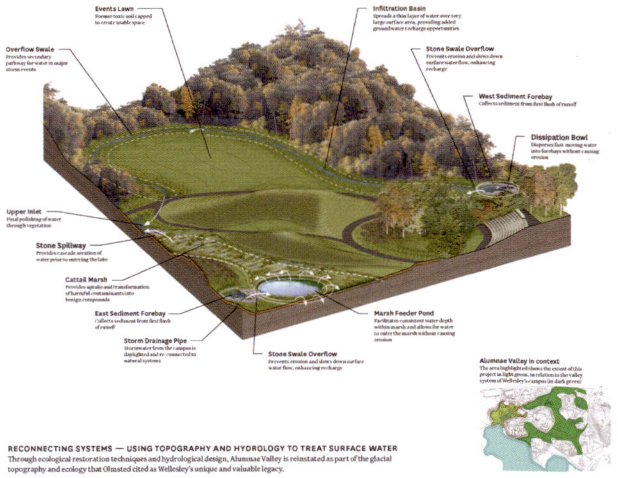

Events Lawn
Former toxic soil capped to create usable space
Infiltration Basin
Spreads a thin layer of water over very large surface area, providing added groundwater recharge opportunities
Overflow Swale
Provides secondary pathway for water in major storm events
Stone Swale Overflow
Prevents erosion and slows down surface water flow, enhancing recharge
West Sediment Forebay
Collects sediment from first flush of runoff
Dissipation Bowl
Disperses fast-moving water into forebays without causing erosion
Upper Inlet
Final polishing of water through vegetation
Stone Spillway
Provides cascade aeration of water prior to entering the lake
Cattail Marsh
Provides uptake and transformation of harmful contaminants into benign compounds
East Sediment Forebay
Collects sediment from first flush of runoff
Marsh Feeder Pond
Facilitates consistent water depth within marsh and allows for water to enter the marsh without causing erosion
Storm Drainage Pipe
Stormwater from the campus is daylighted and re-connected to natural systems
Stone Swale Overflow
Prevents erosion and slows down surface water flow, enhancing recharge
Alumnae Valley in context
The area highlighted shows the extent of this project in light green, in relation to the valley system of Wellesley's campus (in dark green)

RECONNECTING SYSTEMS — USING TOPOGRAPHY AND HYDROLOGY TO TREAT SURFACE WATER
Through ecological restoration techniques and hydrological design, Alumnae Valley is reinstated as part of the glacial topography and ecology that Olmsted cited as Wellesley's unique and valuable legacy.

3.18c

"Trees are responsible for half the photosynthesis on land ... feed oxygen and minerals into the ocean; create rain; render mercury, nitrates, and other toxic wastes in the soil harmless; gather and neutralize sulphur dioxide, ozone, carbon dioxide, and other harmful pollutants in their tissue; create homes and building materials; offer shade; provide medicine; and produce a wide variety of nuts and fruits. They ... are vital to myriad aspects of the earth's ecosystems."
JIM ROBBINS, THE MAN WHO PLANTED TREES (2012)

Phytoremediation

Phytoremediation is an emerging practice of particular interest to landscape architects due to its use of plants (and associated microbiota, soil amendments and agronomic techniques) to remove low to moderate levels of toxicity from soil and water (phytofiltration). Through phytoextraction and rhizofiltration, certain species of trees and plants (over 400 from over 45 families known to be 'hyperaccumulators') are able to absorb contaminants (phytoaccumulation) into their biomass, where they can be broken down by microbial processes to safe levels.

Time planning

Phytoremediation's success is dependent on allocated time, pollutant levels and horticultural skill, with some plants becoming contaminated then consigned to landfill, incineration or recontamination. Site clean up to legally safe levels can take years or even decades, hence may be unsuitable for commercially-focused clients with short time frames, and is currently uncommon on valuable urban sites. With increased understanding of time required and longer-term project planning, phytoremediation can feature more dominantly in planning, design and construction projects and post-industrial cleansing.

3.18a
3.18b
3.18c
Alumnae Valley Landscape Restoration, Michael Van Valkenburgh Associates, Wellesley College, Wellesley, MA, USA, 2001–2005
When Frederick Law Olmsted Jr surveyed Wellesley College in 1902, he emphatically recommended that the natural topography of glacial landforms, valley meadows, and native plant communities be preserved. At the time of its construction, the landscape-based campus structure challenged the more homogenous quadrangle schemes favored by schools like Harvard and Princeton. As the college developed, the valley became the site for its physical plant, industrialized natural gas pumping and, finally, parking lot over a toxic brownfield. The site's reconceptualization includes an appreciation for its history, with topography fulfilling a dual role of ecological design solution and experiential enhancement. The restored Alumnae Valley now reclaims its place in the natural hydrological system that structures the campus, continuing its tradition of challenging landscape orthodoxy not by returning to Olmsted's master plan but by advancing its principles to become a living part of the contemporary campus.

3.19a
3.19b
3.19c
3.19d
3.19e
3.19f
3.19g
3.19h

Freshkills Park, James Corner Field Operations, Staten Island, New York, USA, 2001–

Freshkills is the largest park developed in New York City in over 100 years. James Corner Field Operations' (JCFO") vision for the remediation of 1,000 acres (405ha) of closed landfill and 450 acres (182ha) of intact ecosystems will create a 2,200 acre (890ha) $650 million parkland. The construction of such a large urban park presents multiple logistical, administrative and political challenges during its 30 year phasing.

The park has been designed in five major sections, supporting 750 acres (304ha) of active and passive recreation, event spaces and miles of trails providing spectacular views of downtown Manhattan. A network of meadows, plantings, habitats and programs will reflect different slope and soil-water gradients, solar aspects and adjacent contexts.

Sustainability initiatives include: landfill gas energy generation ($12 million in annual revenue and enough heat for approximately 22,000 homes); emerging energy technologies; reforestation; habitat restoration including new meadows, salt marsh, coastal habitat and shoreline stabilization; resilience planning for climate change and sea level rise; improvement of water quality; soil production; urban agriculture; seed harvesting and tree nurseries; scientific research and research plots; and goats to graze weeds facilitating ecological recovery.

JCFO generated evocative and progressive graphic techniques in the initial 2001 competition-winning scheme and subsequent masterplan, articulating strategic ecological restoration strategies while expressing landscape's temporal flux. The resultant merging of natural and engineered beauty with performance advances the emerging field of landscape urbanism beyond theoretical discourse.

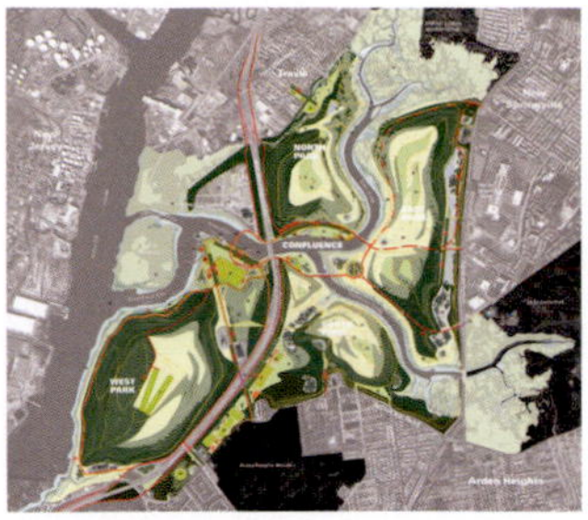
3.19a

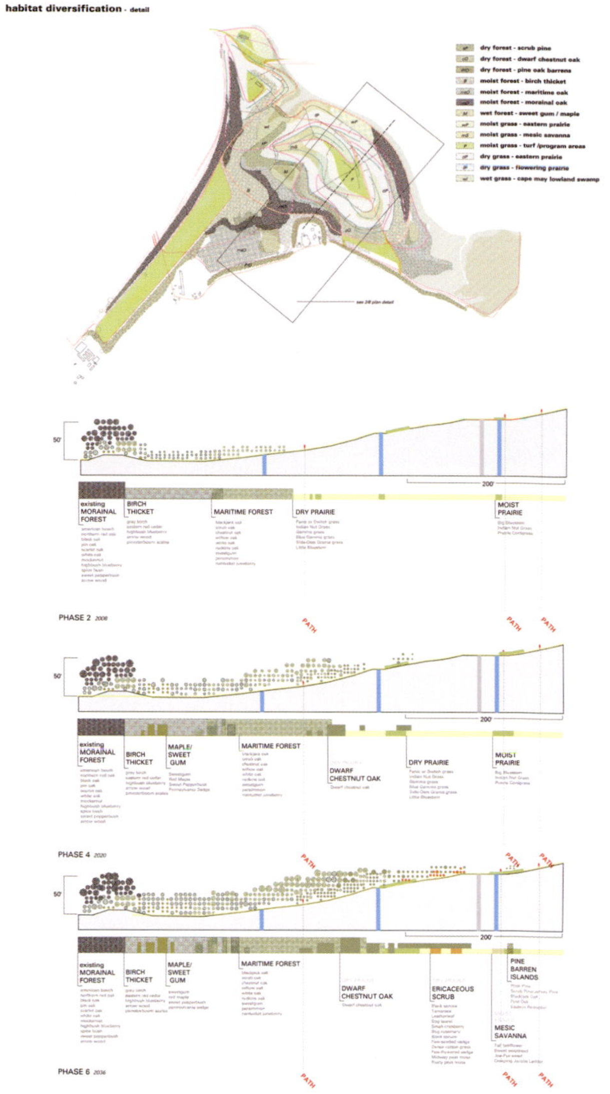
habitat diversification - detail
PHASE 2 2006
PHASE 4 2020
PHASE 6 2036
existing MORAINAL FOREST
BIRCH THICKET
MAPLE/ SWEET GUM
MARITIME FOREST
DWARF CHESTNUT OAK
DRY PRAIRIE
MOIST PRAIRIE
ERICACEOUS SCRUB
PINE BARREN ISLANDS
MESIC SAVANNA
PATH
3.19b

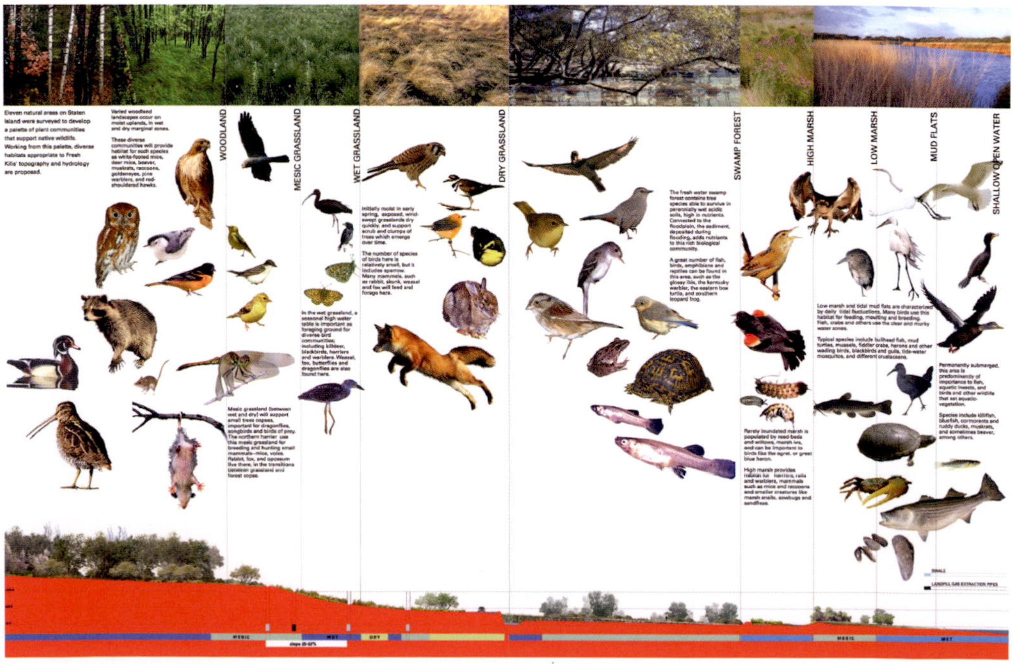
WOODLAND
MESIC GRASSLAND
WET GRASSLAND
DRY GRASSLAND
SWAMP FOREST
HIGH MARSH
LOW MARSH
MUD FLATS
SHALLOW OPEN WATER
3.19c

3.19d

3.19e

3.19f

3.19g

3.19h

3.20a (Before)
3.20b
3.20c
3.20d

Former BP Park, McGregor Coxall, Waverton, Sydney, Australia, 2005

Sydney Harbour is a nexus of post-industrial sites searching to find new use. The Former BP Park is emblematic of moves to reclaim the harbor foreshore for the people of Sydney, placing important site heritage within an ethic of environmental responsibility. The 6.2 acre (2.5ha) Former BP Park on Sydney Harbour had a 60-year oil storage history, where contamination from the 31 tanks and facilities had seeped too deeply into the porous sandstone geology for remediation to remove all traces. McGregor Coxall's design incorporates phytoremediation planting and an integrated WSUD stormwater collection and filtration system that continues to cleanse the site, directing water into detention ponds and filtered by aquatic plants before discharge into Sydney Harbour. This has created new ephemeral wetland habitats for a variety of frogs, ducks and bird species, indicating successful cleansing. During remediation, existing soil was mixed with imported organic matter and reused across the site rather than consigned to landfill. Provenance plant seed was collected from nearby Balls Head and propagated to reinstate the site's original flora.

The skillfully detailed design reconnects demolished industrial structures that left behind dislocated historic fragments during the remediation process, contrasting them with contemporary structures within the regenerating bushland. Low cost, durable galvanized steel and *in situ* concrete walking platforms, viewing decks and stairs wrap around the dramatic sandstone cliff, projecting over the water-sensitive, wildlife-attracting ecosystem below.

3.20a

3.20b

3.20c

TANK # BB5
M3 - 11.010
LIGHT
DIESEL OIL
1922–1997

3.20d

3.21a

3.21b

3.21c

3.21d

3.21a (Before)
3.21b
3.21c
3.21d
3.21e

Ballast Point Park, McGregor Coxall, Sydney, Australia, 2006–2009

This 6.2 acre (2.5ha) waterfront park is located on a formerly contaminated Sydney Harbour site. The park has a richly layered history of indigenous occupation, a 1860s marine villa ('Menevia'), sandstone quarrying for shipping ballast, and Caltex petroleum distillation from the 1920s until 2002. Retention and interpretive initiatives reveal this cultural heritage (see Chapter 7). Environmental initiatives include recycled materials (see Chapter 9), eight vertical wind turbines, WSUD, and ecological rehabilitation with over 55,000 provenance-sourced indigenous plants.

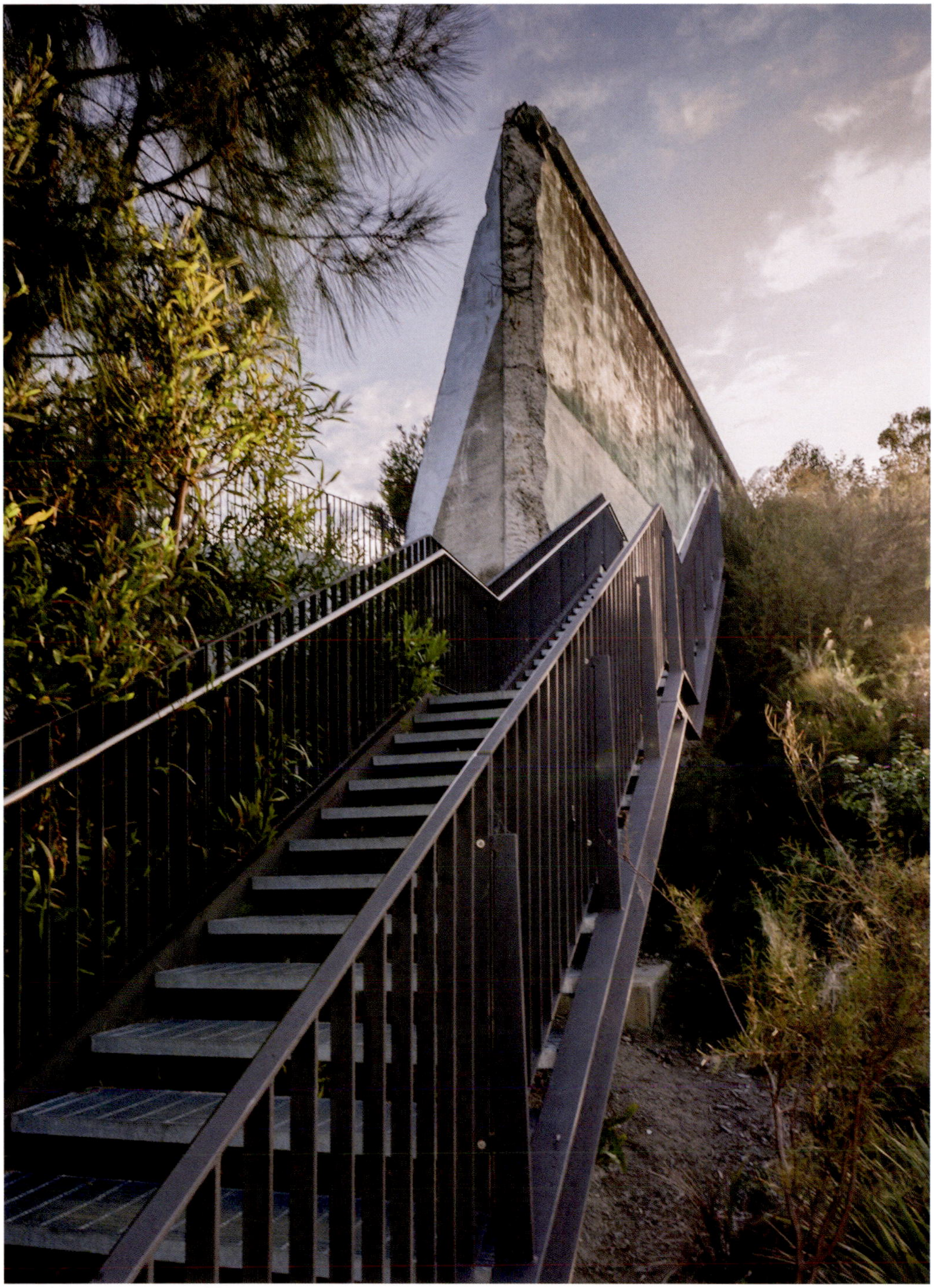

3.21e

Land value

Land value often drives the costly remediation process. Subsequently, planning authorities and local municipalities are pressured by governments (lobbied by developers) to release cheaper greenfield land for development. Valuable sites (such as inner urban growth areas like Berlin's Kreuzberg) may financially justify remediation, still allowing for development profit. If a site is of public interest for reuse as green open space (see BP and Ballast Point Parks), then a local municipality may seek funding or cover costs. Site clean up may or may not be paid for by the company responsible for contamination.

3.22a (Before)
3.22b
3.22c
3.22d
3.22e

Qian'an Sanlihe Greenway, Turenscape, Qian'an City, Hebei Province, China, 2006–2011

3.22a The 2006 site condition, significantly degraded by sewage and a former garbage dump.
3.22b The project created water-centered public spaces integrating stormwater management, habitat restoration, recreation and art to catalyze urban development.
3.22c The lushly revegetated upper Greenway's newly created stream with pedestrian and cycling paths on both river edges.
3.22d The Folding Paper installation integrates shelters, seats, boardwalk and lighting, while being woven around existing trees. Planted wild chrysanthemum can be harvested as Chinese medicine and requires little maintenance.
3.22e Existing trees retained through 'islands'.

The 8.3 miles (13.4km) long, 330–985 feet (100–300m) wide Greenway is a diversion of the Luan River through Qian'an City. Water mills were constructed in 1917, and by the 1970s the river had become badly polluted by sewage and waste from continuous industrial development and population growth. The municipal government commissioned Turenscape through the Sanlihe River Ecological Corridor Project for ecological restoration, urban design and sewage and waste management.

Design strategies across the upstream water source, city, and downstream wetland park include preservation of existing trees on boardwalk connected islands, pedestrian and cycling paths, art integration and a green river strategy. The existing concrete channel was removed and replaced with a multiple water course, riparian wetland and ecological purification system to regulate floods, remediate urban stormwater runoff and create wildlife habitat. The Greenway has assisted significant urban development and demonstrates how neglected ecologies can be regenerated as green infrastructure and multidimensional landscapes with ecosystem services in short timeframes.

3.22a

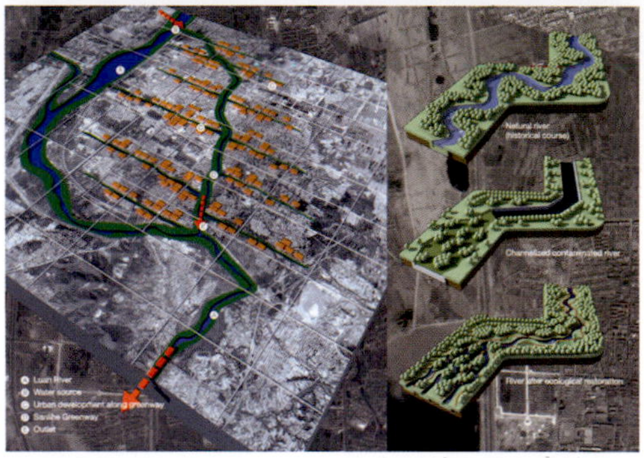
Natural river
(historical course)
Channelized contaminated river
River after ecological restoration

3.22b

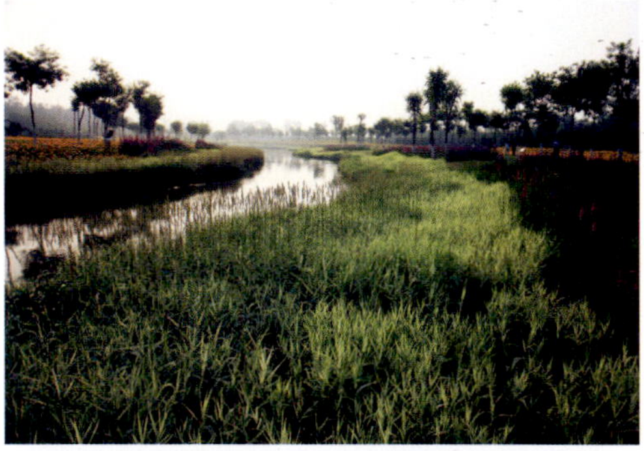

3.22c

3.22d

3.22e

3.23a
3.23b
3.23c
3.23d

Vall d'en Joan Landfill, Batlle i Roig Arquitectes & Teresa Galí-Izard, Garraf, Begues, Barcelona, Spain, 2001–

3.23a Plan view aerial photographs showing the transformation between 1956, 1994, 2000 and 2014.
3.23b Site panoramas showing transformation between 2004, 2005, 2007 and 2009.

For 30 years, 148 acres (60ha) of Barcelona's landfill filled the site to a depth of 263 feet (80m). Leachate contaminated the Castelldefels aquifer through porous limestone geology, and landfill greenhouse gases (especially methane) contributed to around 20% of Barcelona's total greenhouse gas (GHG) emissions.

The design approach sought to address the technical complexities of landfill decommission while recovering lost natural landscape values. Surface water systems (terrace and plot system, perimeter channels and irrigation networks) are separated from landfill water collection to prevent contamination, slow runoff and erosion and assist revegetation. Leachate treatment reduces seepage and simplifies landfill-capping barriers, while underground storage pools and a water treatment plant cleanse water before discharging. The landfill is sealed with a waterproofing sheet, a metre thick layer of draining gravel and a geotextile filter, on which topsoil was placed.

Low water requirement native vegetation (pine, evergreen oak, shrubs and grasses) have been planted to establish communities and agricultural crops of local legumes to regenerate soil.

A biogas system of over 150 wells capture landfill gas and pipe it to a plant to generate an average of 12,500kW of electricity.

The design team added public visitation space not originally envisaged by the client, including an information center (retrofitted into a remnant building), carpark and connecting terraces with the adjacent Garraf Natural Park. Gabion walls filled with waste materials serve as ongoing reminders of the site history that will visibly dissipate as the vegetation matures.

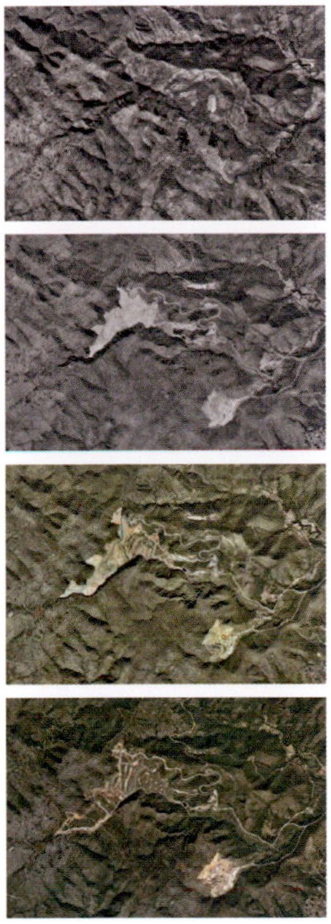

1956
1994
2000
2014

3.23a

2004
2005
2009
2014

3.23b

3.23c

3.23d

"Do unto those downstream as you would have those upstream do unto you."
WENDELL BERRY

ENVIRONMENTAL WATER CYCLE MANAGEMENT

Landscape architects are frequently involved in environmental water cycle management despite it being a specialized subset of environmental and hydrological engineering. Three main terms differ across regions to describe very similar practices:

1. *Water sensitive urban design* (WSUD), used in Australia and the Middle East (among others regions);
2. *Sustainable drainage systems* (SuDS), more commonly used in the UK (sometimes referred to as 'sustainable urban drainage systems');
3. *Low impact development* (LID) a North American term for improved stormwater management practices.

Though both WSUD and SuDS reference the term 'urban', they also include rural and complete water system management. WSUD arguably encompasses the broadest scope and is therefore used henceforth to represent all approaches. Extensive benefits include:

- hydrological filtration systems cleansing storm and wastewater using natural filter mediums (rocks, soil mediums with mixes of gravel, aggregates, sand, charcoal) and suitable plant species (aquatic and ephemeral) (see Wetlands and Biofilter Projects);
- mechanical filtration systems (UV filtration, filter membranes) can be coupled with natural systems, such as in urban sites with reduced areas (see Adelaide Botanic Wetland);
- flood mitigation through slowing stormwater runoff/outfall;
- increasing groundwater recharge; through infiltration, permeable surfaces and aquifer storage and recovery (ASR);
- wastewater reduction through reducing stormwater inflow into wastewater systems and thus reducing volumes of intensive treatment;
- pollutant cleansing through wetlands, biofiltration, grey and black water treatment/recycling;
- visual amenity including landscape features, street trees and vegetation;
- biodiversity value providing habitat plantings and water sources for wildlife;
- potable water supply from filtered rainwater storage;
- non-potable water supply through ASR, water bodies and storage cisterns; and
- recreational amenity and education opportunities.

"The 30–40 additives commonly introduced into water supplies are often pollutants in themselves to that increasingly sensitive sector of society developing allergies to any type of modern pollutant. The additives represent the end point of the technological fix: pollution is 'fixed' by further pollution."
BILL MOLLISON, PERMACULTURE: A DESIGNERS' MANUAL (1988)

"Unfortunately, it has taken a series of water-related disasters to make people see that status quo engineering standards—the pipes, walls and levees—may not be the only or best way for handling water… Cities are looking toward green infrastructure as a means to not only better deal with stormwater, but to also mitigate flooding, increase biological diversity, and provide cleaner water and air."
MARK HOUGH, URBANISM AND THE LANDSCAPE ARCHITECT (2013)

Naturally engineered?

Contemporary water systems combine both natural and highly engineered techniques. Dams, reservoirs and river systems of protected watersheds provide high quality supplies (see Catskill, Chapter 7); pipelines and diversion channels supply water from often far away catchments; electricity enables filtration, sterilization, pumping and distribution; and industrial chemicals (some of which are considered pollutants/carcinogens depending on concentration) can be added to kill pathogens and improve appearance. Desalination (Chapter 1) is an intensive, industrial, unsustainable method that bypasses freshwater resources to use energy to convert seawater into potable water.

Flood management legacy

20th-century hydrological and civil engineering flood management ('grey' hydrological systems) typically involved draining flood-prone lands through excavating drainage lines and installing concrete-lined channels in creek and river beds. This has effectively reduced flood events and removed large volumes of water to facilitate urban development. Yet this environmentally damaging process (with its often brutal visual impact) excludes living systems and biodiversity, lacks groundwater recharge, results in poor water quality (due to not having any natural filtration) and is highly insensitive to aquatic systems. Since the 1970s, far more attuned WSUD approaches have improved hydrological and design outcomes (see Salisbury Wetlands, Chapter 2, Turenscape projects).

WSUD opportunities

Urban locations provide many opportunities to implement WSUD measures, such as daylighting and removing culverts and underground pipes; removing waterways' hard edges; installing biofiltration and wetlands near stormwater pipes to filter large urban hardscape catchments; using WSUD street tree pits and biofilters to clean road and parking lot surface runoff and promote tree growth; utilizing underground tanks for cleansed water storage for reuse; creating wetlands for habitat and amenity; utilizing ASR to provide seasonally-optimized recycled water supply; and supplying water-intensive urban industries (see Parafield Wetland, Chapter 7; aquaculture and urban agriculture, Chapter 5). WSUD benefits larger infrastructures (such as potable water filtration and wastewater plants) by diversifying and decentralizing hydrological systems (see Chapter 4).

Maintenance

WSUD systems almost always require higher maintenance than grey hydrological systems in order to operate effectively. This can prove to be a barrier where clients desire minimal maintenance (although arguably provides 'green' job creation). Improved water legislation, standards and regulations (such as increased minimum retention times and site water quality discharge requirements) can promote inclusion of WSUD and normalize maintenance regimes.

Alternative sources

Numerous cities worldwide have initiated water saving programs (although as these can be unpopular, governments often focus on supply over usage). Some regions (such as parts of Australia) mandate or install recycled water systems (*dual reticulation*) to provide two water supplies (potable and recycled water), reducing unnecessary potable use for toilet flushing and irrigation. Very few, however, effectively utilize rainwater and its storage collected from rooftops. Rainwater can supply significant urban water demands when correctly configured, for example, through avoiding mosquito infestation, bypassing primary contamination with a 'first flush' system, optimizing cistern size, and providing suitable filtration (if for potable use).

Treatment intensity

Storm and wastewater require a less intensive treatment process than desalination for reuse as potable supply. Various regions and cities worldwide utilize treated wastewater to partially supplement potable supply, either planned (Texas and Orange County, USA; Singapore; Hampton, London, UK; Southeast Queensland and Canberra, Australia) or unplanned (where downstream supplies are drawn after upstream wastewater discharge: London, UK; Mississippi River, USA; Adelaide, Australia). Decision makers minimally or covertly deploy these approaches due to poor public perception, yet they are more sustainable than desalination.

Nutrient recovery

Positively, water systems are increasingly being reconceived as 'resource loops'. Many cities process wastewater for agricultural use as sewage sludge (over 30% in the European community) or as biosolids (notable volumes in Australia) and capture modes can be employed at various stages. This reuse of nutrients and/or nutrient water reduces nutrient loss, soil exhaustion and problematic wastewater discharge into aquatic ecosystems. Near Amsterdam, for example, the authority has coupled its water treatment with a waste to energy plant (see Energy Landscapes, Chapter 4) in order to increase multifunctional benefits and synergies (see Waternet, Chapter 9).

Wetlands projects

Since wetlands' value was realized in the latter decades of the 20th century, they have been created in countless locations across the globe. The intent for wetland creation varies, as benefits include: flood mitigation; wildlife habitat; water cleansing through phytoremediation, sediment and pollutant capture; water storage and reuse; amenity and recreation benefits; as well as expressing pre-existing landscape characters and the *genius loci* of place regions. More recently, wetlands have been established in increasingly urban contexts with corresponding aesthetics, requiring careful engineering and technical detailing to ensure their optimization. Wetlands require considerably more surface area to provide water filtration services than biofiltration, however, their amenity, habitat and urban cooling benefits can offset this fact.

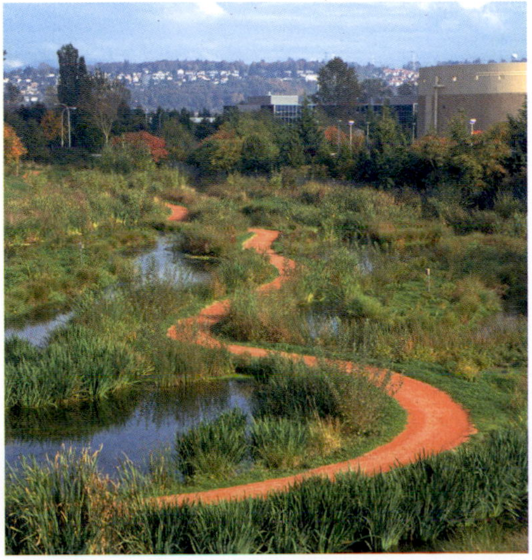

3.24b

3.24a (Before)
3.24b
Waterworks Gardens, Lorna Jordan, Renton, Washington, USA, 1996–1997
An environmental art park filtering and holding stormwater, with water purification symbols throughout its designed forms.

3.24a

3.25

3.26

3.25
Potsdamer Platz, Atelier Dreiseitl, Berlin, Germany, 1997–1998
This 3.2 acre (1.3ha) site is an early example of an 'urban' wetland (with an architectural and metropolitan design aesthetic, as opposed to non-contextual 'naturalistic' design).

3.26

Parc Diagonal Mar, AECOM (then EDAW) + EMBT + Robert A. M. Stern Architects, Barcelona, Spain, 1997–2002

Resulting from Spain's first public/private sustainability agreement, Parc Diagonal Mar is located on a former railyard. A sculpted wetland cleanses water and provides for irrigation, porous pavements minimize stormwater runoff and native plants give habitat for indigenous bird species. Extensive commercial development accompanied the park with adjoining tower buildings and shopping complex.

3.27

Haute Deûle River Banks – New Sustainable District, Atelier des paysages Bruel-Delmar, Quai Hegel, Lille, France, 2008–2015

The project traces the memory lines of the Haute Deûle canal, cleansing stormwater runoff and offering a convivial space in the inland water shipping site that forged the identity of the Bois Blanc district. The water garden (shown here) acts as cleanser and storage, evolving with rainfall rhythms to become an emblematic place for the new district.

3.27

3.28a
3.28b

Wusong Riverfront, SWA, Kunshan, Suzhou, China, 2009–

Unprecedented population and commercial growth in Kunshan, China (near Shanghai) has resulted in environmental degradation and riverfront loss of identity. SWA's masterplan for the 236 acre (96ha) pilot site aims to restore and create a new waterfront district, providing wildlife habitat, education and ecosystem services downstream. Existing stormwater pipe outlets, previously discharging sludge and industrial effluents directly into the inner bay, are redirected to a 'kidney' water treatment system, bio-swales, channels and ponds that settle, filter, aerate, and bio-process pollutants in alternating oxic and anoxic environments.

3.28a

3.28b

3.29a
3.29b

St Jacques Ecological Park, Atelier des Paysages Bruel-Delmar, 35136 Saint Jacques de la Lande, Ille-et-Vilaine (35), France, 2007–2013

A 99 acre (40ha) urban park with large areas of wetlands creates a hybrid ecology based on geography, history, economics and land use.

3.29a

3.29b

"Nobody knows what a sustainable human settlement looks like or how it functions. Some people say that small European towns in the Middle Ages, or prehistoric hamlets for instance, were 'sustainable'; both models, however, were based on the same non-sustainable paradigm: resources were extracted from the environment, while waste was thrown back. The fact that they were small is what made such settlements 'apparently sustainable', since disruption to the natural environment was minor. "

MIGUEL RUANO, ECO URBANISM (1998)

3.30a

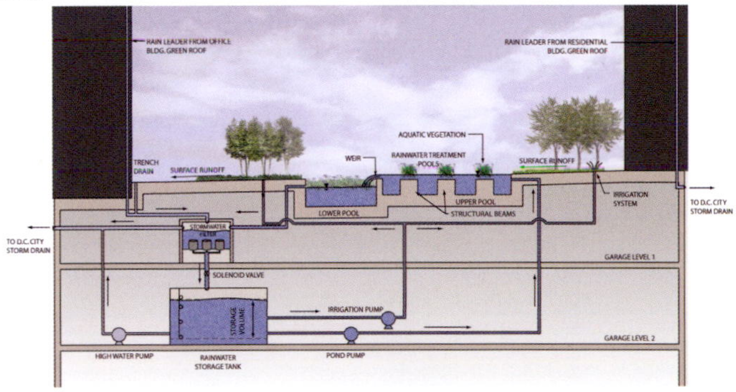
RAIN LEADER FROM OFFICE BLDG. GREEN ROOF
RAIN LEADER FROM RESIDENTIAL BLDG. GREEN ROOF
AQUATIC VEGETATION
RAINWATER TREATMENT POOLS
WEIR
TRENCH DRAIN
SURFACE RUNOFF
SURFACE RUNOFF
IRRIGATION SYSTEM
LOWER POOL
UPPER POOL
STRUCTURAL BEAMS
TO D.C. CITY STORM DRAIN
TO D.C. CITY STORM DRAIN
STORMWATER FILTER
GARAGE LEVEL 1
SOLENOID VALVE
IRRIGATION PUMP
STORAGE VOLUME
GARAGE LEVEL 2
HIGH WATER PUMP
RAINWATER STORAGE TANK
POND PUMP

3.30b

3.30a (Before)
3.30b
3.30c
3.30d

The Avenue, Sasaki Associates, Houston, Texas, USA, 2011

The Avenue is a 3.5 acre (1.4ha) mixed-use transit oriented development (TOD), six blocks northwest of the White House. It features a 58 foot wide (17.6m) active streetscape (34 street trees with 900 cubic feet (25.5m^3) of structural soil each), terraces, 4,000 cubic foot (372m^2) green roof, and courtyards. Much of the landscape comprises of at grade green roof, capping five levels of underground parking, where 76,000 gallons (288kl) of annual stormwater from a 40,000 square foot (3,700m^2) area are harvested, filtered, stored underground and pumped back for irrigation and to replenish the water feature. The wider complex includes high-efficiency irrigation systems and drought-tolerant plants throughout public and private green spaces.

3.30c

3.30d

3.31a

3.31b

3.31a
3.31b
Adelaide Botanic Gardens Wetland, Paul Thompson, David Lancashire Design, Adelaide, Australia, 2010–2014
The multidimensional design of the A$10 million 6.4 acre (2.6ha) wetland combines physical, biological, mechanical and hydrological processes, serving as a model for urban ecosystem service provision. It remediates a formerly polluted site, ameliorates flooding, purifies stormwater and provides habitat, while fusing landscape architecture with engineering and art. Stormwater is diverted into a sedimentation pond where fine clays settle before water passes into a macrophyte basin. An Aquifer Storage and Recovery system then injects filtered water into the aquifer, where it can be drawn into the storage basin for irrigation when required. The ASR system supplies the 25 acre (51ha) botanic garden's irrigation network (in time, anticipated to meet 100 megalitres and equivalent to 40 Olympic swimming pools).

Biofilter, bioretention and raingarden projects

Infiltration basins, *bioretention*, *biofiltration/biofilters* and *rain gardens* refer to terrestrial (as opposed to aquatic/wetland) stormwater treatment devices. They are usually planted depressions with a dedicated soil medium that are graded to capture diverted stormwater runoff from impervious urban areas. They provide a spatially efficient means of filtering urban stormwater runoff (less area than wetlands) and thus have become popular in urban locations worldwide. Biofilters require optimization of their drainage/soil medium porosity to ensure that they are neither too free-draining nor 'boggy'. Depending on intent, rain runoff is diverted into biofilters which can hold water *in situ* for several hours to several days to allow for sediment and pollutant capture, and reduction of flood risk within their stormwater system and watershed. Biofiltration can feed filtered water into storage tanks (usually underground) and surface bodies to be utilized for reuse in non-potable demands such as irrigation and toilet flushing. If another form of treatment is added, such as UV and/or chemical treatment, recycled water can be used for water features and situations where 'primary' public contact occurs, but this is determined by local water authority regulations and/or regular on-site monitoring.

Additional biofilter projects are also located in the 'Green Street Projects' in Chapter 4.

3.32

3.32
University of Sydney, TCL & DesignFlow, Sydney, Australia, 2010
This biofilter/bioretention/raingarden is coupled with an urban wetland and part of a wider campus redevelopment project. While the biofiltration provides significantly more filtration (based on comparative area), the wetland offers the amenity of a permanent water body. Both are situated within a graded depression, draining filtered water into underground storage tanks, then used for irrigation across the campus.

3.33a
3.33b
Federal Way Schools Support Services Center, Site Workshop & Bassetti Architects, Federal Way, Washington, USA, 2012
Located within the Hylebos watershed, a series of cisterns, detention ponds and rain gardens collect and treat stormwater runoff across the site, complemented by indigenous trees and plantings providing habitat. Materials, energy and waste reduction, and water and air quality were carefully integrated into the design, which included a variety of indoor and outdoor spaces.

3.33a

3.33b

Turenscape projects

Turenscape's work in river and hydrological systems in China is impressive, demonstrating testing and realization of theory and concepts at scales mostly unrealized in Western countries. Their numerous projects span a breadth of scale from large river systems through to human-scale elements.

3.34a

3.34a (Before)
3.34b

Yongning River Park (The Floating Gardens), Taizhou City, Zhejiang Province, China, 2002–2005

Turenscape convinced the local authority to cease concrete channelizing of the river and utilize ecological flood control and stormwater management solutions. The result is a 52.6 acre (21.3ha) park composed of two layers, where a natural matrix (wetland and local vegetation suitable for ecosystem processes and flooding) overlaps a human matrix (tree, path and story box matrixes). The design response needed to ensure river accessibility to tourists and locals and includes native plants and common trees typically neglected in the region.

3.34b

3.35a

3.35b

3.35c

3.35d

3.35a (Before)
3.35b
3.35c
3.35d

Tianjin Qiaoyuan Park, Qiaoyuan, China, 2005–2008

The park converted a 54 acre (22ha) garbage dump into low-maintenance green space for 20,000 nearby residents. Features include: 21 pond 'bubbles' (wet and dry cavities ranging from 33–130 feet (10–40m) in diameter and 3.3–5 foot (1.1–5m) in depth) to treat stormwater; observation platforms (built from around 3,000 cubic feet (85m^3) of salvaged railroad ties); regionally sourced soil, plants, and limestone; and interpretive signage describing natural species and processes. Rich, seasonal vegetation creates an intentionally 'messy' aesthetic, with 99% native species (40% perennials in 58 varieties and 34% woody plants in 50 varieties). The five species of herbaceous plants increased to 58 following park construction and 96 two years after opening, and hedgehogs, foxes, ducks, geese, and weasels have been observed on the site.

3.36a

3.36a (Before)
3.36b

Houtan Park, Shanghai, China, 2007–2015

The Huangpu riverfront park is a regenerative landscape of ecological infrastructures providing multiple social and ecosystem services to treat polluted river water and recover the degraded waterfront from the former brownfield site. The restorative design constructed wetlands; ecological water treatment and flood control; reclaimed industrial structures and materials; urban agriculture; and productive landscapes. The design is executed to evoke past memories, while demonstrating a new landscape aesthetic based low maintenance and high performance.

3.36b

3.37a

3.37b

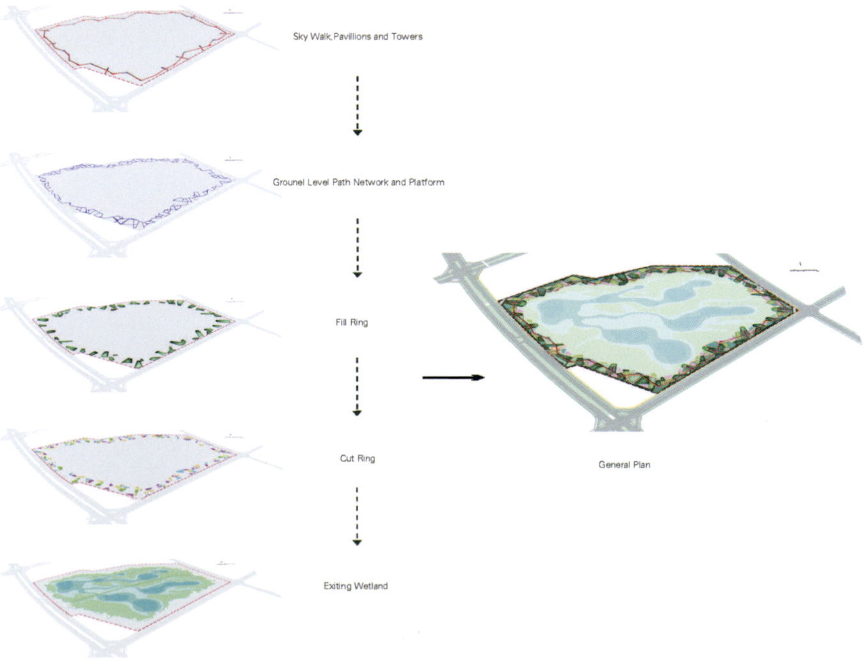
Sky Walk, Pavilions and Towers
Grounel Level Path Network and Platform
Fill Ring
Cut Ring
Exiting Wetland
General Plan

3.37c

3.37a
3.37b
3.37c
3.37d
3.37e

Qunli Stormwater Park, Haerbin, Heilongjiang, China, 2009–2010

Commencing in 2006, the 6,753 acre (2,733ha) Qunli New Town involves construction of 12.4 square miles (32 million m^2) of building space in 13–15 years, with only 16% zoned as green space. In the center lay a dying 84.5 acre (34.2ha) wetland, which Turenscape have transformed into a 'green sponge' urban stormwater park with multiple ecosystems services. Annual rainfall is 567mm and primarily falls from June to August, when flooding and waterlogging can occur. The wetland site is surrounded on four sides by roads and dense development.

An encircling cut and fill, pond-and-mound ring surrounds the existing wetland to provide a cleansing buffer zone, evenly distributing and filtering urban stormwater runoff before it flows into the wetland.

Path networks, platforms and viewing towers, native wetland grasses, meadows and groves of native *Betula* trees create a variety spatial experiences and habitats and the park is now listed as a national urban wetland park.

3.37d

3.37e

3.38a

3.38b

3.38c

3.38d

3.38e

3.38f

3.38g

3.38h

3.38a, b, c, d (Before)
3.38e
3.38f
3.38g
3.38h

Minghu Wetland Park, Liupanshui, Guizhou, China, 2009–

Developed as part of a municipal campaign to improve the urban environment, design of the 222 acre (90ha) park seeks to recover the channelized River Shuicheng, provide ecological infrastructure, improve water quality, and create resilient public green space. Through a three-year design and construction process (phase one—77 acres/31.2ha), a large section of the river has been regained as the lifeline of the city. The concrete embankment (installed in 1975–1980) was removed to restore the natural riverbank and waterways, which were integrated into a stormwater management and ecological purification system revitalizing riparian ecologies and maximizing self-purification capacity. A series of ribbon-like terraces create wetland pockets slowing water flow, settling pollutants, regulating seasonal variations, and facilitating vegetation growth. Low maintenance native plants and wildflowers, pedestrian pathways and bicycle routes sweep through a 50–65 foot (15–20m) wide greenway, while interpretative signage educates visitors about the landscape's regenerative and cultural significance.

Is it dishonest to design in a manner that makes no reference to the historic past of a site? Is this different in a residential area to a commercial or industrial site?

Why would a developer or local authority not want to reveal the past uses of a site? Is this ethical?

Is there a difference between preserving historic residential/civic buildings and historic industrial buildings/structures? Why/why not?

What is your favorite post-industrial or adaptive reuse project and why?

What opportunities exist for adaptive reuse in your city/region?

Is it better to leave pollutants in place on site or to move them elsewhere? What circumstances and factors might affect this?

Should the party responsible for a polluting a site be responsible for its clean-up? Why does this regularly fail to occur in practice? Why are companies not held accountable?

What types of scenarios are examples of where phytoremediation could occur?

What factors effect how long phytoremediation will take?

What are some examples of plants suited/adapted to your locality that are effective at removing pollutants from soil and water?

Is a desalination plant that is powered by wind energy a sustainable project (e.g. in Sydney, Australia)? Discuss.

Which is more effective in treating stormwater—wetlands or biofiltation? Why? What considerations might there be other than effectiveness?

Is rainwater readily drinkable? What conditions affect this? Why is rainwater not more commonly utilized?

Can wastewater be made drinkable? What cities currently do this?

What common problems are encountered with WSUD? How can these be factored into the design process?

FURTHER READING

Barbaux, S. (2010) *Jardins Ecologiques: Ecology, source of creation*, France: ICI Interface.

Berger, A. (2006) *Drosscape: Wasting Land in Urban America*, New York: Princeton Architectural Press.

Dreiseitl, H. and Grau, D. (2010) *Recent waterscapes: planning, building and designing with water*, Basel: Birkhäuser.

Dunnett, N. and Clayden, A. (2007) *Rain gardens: managing water sustainably in the garden and designed landscape*, Portland, Oregon: Timber Press.

France, R. (2008) *Handbook of regenerative landscape design*, Boca Raton: CRC Press.

Howe, C. and Mitchell, C. (2012) *Water sensitive cities*, London: IWA.

Hoyer, J. (2011) *Water sensitive urban design: principles and inspiration for sustainable stormwater management in the city of the future*, Berlin: Jovis.

Jorgensen, A. and Keenan, R. (2012) *Urban wildscapes*, Oxon, UK: Routledge.

Kennen, K. and Kirkwood, N. (2015) *Phyto: principles and resources for site remediation and landscape design*, Oxon, UK: Routledge.

Margolis, L. and Robinson, A. (2007) *Living Systems: Innovative Materials and Technologies for Landscape Architecture*, Switzerland: Birkhäuser.

Robbins, J. (2012) *The man who planted trees: lost groves, the future of our forests, and a radical plan to save our planet*, New York: Spiegel & Grau.

ADDITIONAL PROJECTS

You might also like to look for further information on the following projects:

Candlestick Point State Recreation Area, Hargreaves Associates, San Francisco, USA

Seattle Art Museum's Olympic Sculpture Park, Weiss/Manfredi & Charles Anderson Landscape Architecture, Seattle, Washington, USA, 2007

Henry Palmisano Park, site design group, Chicago, Illinois, USA, 2004

Cultuurpark Westergasfabriek, Gustafson Porter, Amsterdam, the Netherlands, 2004

Schöneberger Südgelände Park, Group Odious, Berlin, Germany, 2008–2009

Hunter's Point South Waterfront Park, Thomas Balsley Associates & Weiss/Manfredi & ARUP, Queens, New York, USA, 2013

Tanner Springs Park, Atelier Dreiseitl, Portland, Oregon, USA, 2005

Water Park, Alday Jover & Christine Dalnoky, Ranillas Meander, Zaragoza, Spain, 2005–2008

Kitsap County Administration Building, SvR, Site Workshop & Miller Hull Architects, Port Orchard, Washington, USA, 2002–2006

Thornton Creek Water Quality Channel, SvR Design Company, NE Thornton Place, Seattle, Washington, USA, 2003–2009

Edinburgh Gardens Rain Garden, GHD & DesignFlow, Melbourne, Australia, 2010–2012

Menomonee Valley Redevelopment Plan and Community Park, Wenk Associates, Milwaukee, Wisconsin, USA

Taylor 28, Mithun, Seattle, Washington, USA, 2004–2009

Kroon Hall Quad, OLIN, New Haven, Connecticut, USA, 2009

Waitangi Park, Wraight Athfield Landscape + Architecture, Wellington, New Zealand, 2002–2005

INTERVIEW Tony Wong

Professor Tony Wong is Professor of Civil Engineering at Monash University and Chief Executive of the Cooperative Research Centre for Water Sensitive Cities (Australia and Singapore). Professor Wong is internationally recognized for his award-winning urban design projects, research and strategic advice in sustainable urban water management and water sensitive urban design. He has previously served on the Australian Prime Minister's Science Engineering and Innovation Council's '*Water for Cities*', and has been cited as having defined "a new paradigm for design of urban environments that blends creativity with technical and scientific rigor".

When and why did sustainable urban water management/WSUD/LID/SuDS come about?

Sustainable urban water management started from a perspective of environmental protection whether it be WSUD, LID or SUDS. There are subtle differences between these three terms—WSUD focuses on integrative urban design in delivering sustainable urban water management for improved sustainability (and resilience) outcomes. In doing this, WSUD is less focused on the simple application of technology. In Australia, WSUD was first conceived as a new planning framework in the mid 1980s but didn't get much traction (mainly, I believe, due to an inability of those who first developed the idea to articulate tangible outcomes that would meet the needs of the community and industry at that time). In the early 1990s, water quality protection of major rivers and bays that receive stormwater became an important focus. In Melbourne, where WSUD really took off in the early 1990s, the protection of Port Phillip Bay was a key concern of the state government (following the significant initiatives in the USA to protect Chesapeake Bay from stormwater pollution). It was around the same time that research activities undertaken by the CRC (Cooperative Research Centre) for Catchment Hydrology at Monash University started to address the role of constructed wetlands, and then in late 1990s, of biofilters in stormwater cleansing with these features being incorporated into urban landscapes. Concurrently, such stormwater Best Management Practices (BMPs) were also being investigated in the USA. They were subsequently integrated into urban development and coined LID where the focus on water infiltration and filtration were espoused. In the UK, infiltration was also extensively investigated and coined Sustainable Urban Drainage (SuDS).

What are WSUD's key aims?

The key aims of WSUD are to manage urban water (whether stormwater or wastewater) in a manner that best recognises the resource potential of these different water streams, the potential for their impact in reducing the incidences and severity of floods, their potential to reduce the vulnerability of cities to drought and more recently the potential to recover resources from our sewerage, beyond water, e.g. energy and nutrients. The harnessing of these potentials is through good urban design and architecture (both building and landscape). We often use the notion that WSUD is the practice and Water Sensitive City (or precinct) is the outcome. WSUD is expressed in many different forms, from the green walls of buildings that also cleanse greywater while utilizing it as a water source for irrigating the green wall itself; to stormwater treatment along ecological landscapes that form part of the blue and green corridors of a city; the blue/green corridors being corridors for flood detention and safe passage; to the recycling of treated wastewater for non-drinking water uses such as toilet flushing; and to maintain green landscapes in cities while preserving higher quality water for drinking purposes. Ecological landscapes can promote multiple ecological and ecosystems benefits, create a sense of place and provide important amenity in cities. My key argument here is that spaces in the public domain are essential features of public amenities. However, these urban landscapes must be functional beyond providing spatial amenities. Our knowledge of the traditional 'values' of open spaces and landscape features needs to be bolstered with an understanding of the 'ecological functioning' of the urban landscapes that capture the essences of sustainable water management, microclimate influences, facilitation of carbon sinks and use for food production.

WSUD seems to facilitate the blending of vision and creative problem solving, technical and scientific rigor, and practical application and realization. What are the keys to this?

The city is a melting pot of many of the challenges we face today and there are many lenses through which different disciplines of practice can interpret resilience. In the contemporary urban water management perspective, resilience as a principle needs to encompass biophysical (anthropogenic and natural) and social/institutional resilience. Adaptability of infrastructure and institutions is fundamental. From an urban water management perspective, urban water systems need to have a level of robustness in their (combined biophysical and social) capacity to accommodate major system 'disturbances' (such as floods, droughts, heat waves and waterway health degradation) and the adaptive capacity to create opportunities from these disturbances for innovation and development or even the pursuit of new trajectories. Recent occurrences in the last decade of record breaking climatic events—whether it be floods or droughts or heat—have focused on the political language of resilience. The need for ensuring resilience has a higher level of urgency to communities and governments than what 'sustainability' was ever able to achieve in the last 20+ years since the Rio Summit. The reality of course is that we have reached this level of urgency as a result of not having been effective in mainstreaming sustainability in fostering economic development.

The key to success in blending vision and creative solutions is in fact in the practice of urban design—the practice of blending innovative solutions across multiple disciplines into the urban form. I have always been fascinated with the practice of urban design often led by architects and more recently landscape architects. I see engineers can play an important influencing role in this process, and the successful projects are usually those where the urban designers are inclusive and understand the interplay between technology, terrestrial and aquatic ecology, and the built form.

In our need to transition to a post-carbon era, why do governments utilize desalination plants over alternatives such as rainwater, stormwater and wastewater systems to provide a more sustainable water supply?

Many of the decisions to build desalination plants have been made in the midst of crisis. Desalinated water is a reliable source of water but the most expensive amongst all the possible sources of water—but it provides certainty and in a crisis, governments need the certainty of their decisions. Many of the more sustainable solutions require longer incubation in society because of the diffuse nature of their implementation. The fact that many of the desalination plants in Australia (with the exception of Perth) have come online at a period when dams are filling have certainly taken some of the shine off these projects. Nevertheless these facilities are of strategic importance to the water supply security of many of these cities—they provide an era of stability in terms of water supply security over the next 20 years or so in enabling a greater and more holistic development of water management strategy to secure the sustainability and resilience of these cities. It would be a grave mistake if cities chose not to invest in incubating more sustainable solutions just because they now have a desalination plant. Population growth, increasing water consumption and more severe droughts would mean that there will come a time when we will be faced with the need for building another desalination plant if we do not use the time we have now to develop and implement more sustainable solutions.

Is WSUD largely dependent on legislation mandating its implementation?

The adoption of a water sensitive approach to urban development and redevelopment needs to be supported by enabling legislation and regulation. This should include clear articulation of outcomes—but not prescription of the means towards achieving the outcomes. Outcomes stipulated could include (i) the quality of stormwater to be attained before its discharge to the receiving waters; (ii) the level of substitution of the traditional sources of drinking water with alternative water sources (stormwater and recycled wastewater for example) which may in some cases be treated to drinking water standards; (iii) the reduction in peak discharges for a range of flood scenarios; (iv) ecological values of urban streams; (v) the reduction in local temperature attributed to WSUD urban heat management just to name a few.

How reliant is WSUD on maintenance? Is this something that clients need to be willing to accept?

WSUD features in the public realm are green infrastructure—the operative word being infrastructure. These assets must be managed as community assets with clearly defined maintenance and operation provisions. We have to look beyond the public realm as simply a place that provides amenity and recreation for local communities. In fact, if we are to get really serious about green infrastructure, we need to clearly articulate from the outset what range of functions we expect from this infrastructure. The detention and safe passage of floodwaters, the cleansing and harvesting of stormwater, support for mitigating urban heat, productive landscapes and maintaining urban biodiversity are just a few of the functions that should be identified and clearly articulated from the beginning. And of equal—if not greater—importance, a whole of government approach combined with a more robust economic valuation framework is essential. With this in place, we can fully recognize all the economic and community benefits that can be achieved from green infrastructure. Then maybe we can say we're really getting serious about green infrastructure.

Australia is increasingly implementing its 'purple-pipe' system for supply of recycled water. Are other regions following or leading the implementation of these types of systems?

Yes, the delivery of recycled water for non-drinking purpose is an important step in reducing our dependency exclusively on drinking water from the mains (eg. the traditional source of water) for all of our water usage. Many cities around the world are experiencing severe droughts at the moment—Sao Paulo, Bangkok just to name two current hot spots. However, many of these cities are still not looking at the total water cycle and therefore are missing out on realising the full potential that a water sensitive approach to urban water management can deliver. Furthermore, bringing in a 'purple-pipe' is a large scale operation taking many years to implement—and not necessarily one that offers a solution to an immediate drought crisis.

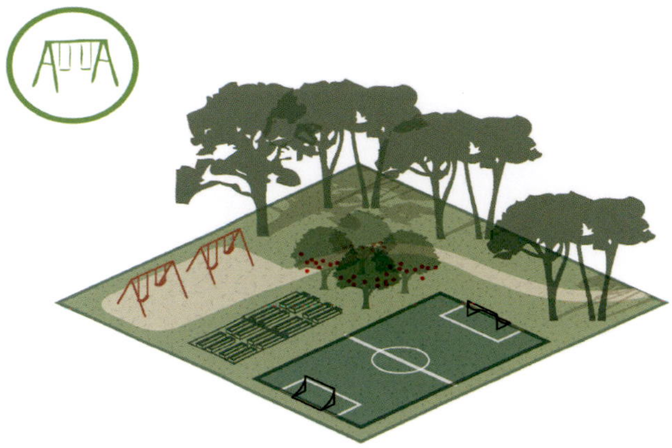

COMMUNITY OPEN SPACES

LANDSCAPES FOR RECREATION, SOCIAL LIFE, AND SMALL-SCALE FOOD CULTIVATION

PLAYGROUNDS

NEIGHBORHOOD PARKS

SPORTS FIELDS

REGIONAL PARKS

PLAZAS

RECREATION CENTERS

TRAILS / GREENWAYS

URBAN GARDENS

FARMERS MARKETS

CEMETERIES (EXISTING)

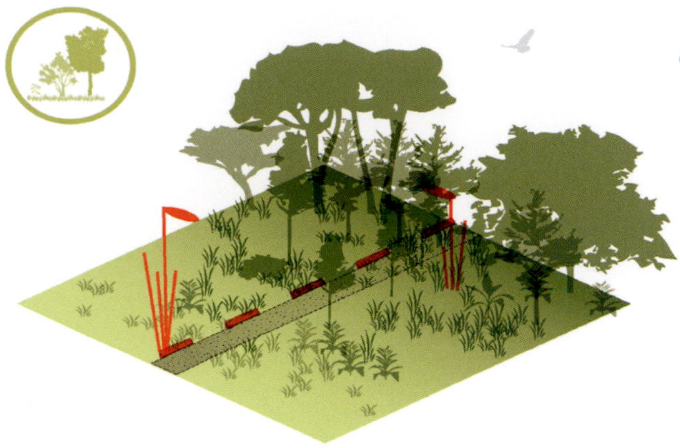

ECOLOGICAL LANDSCAPES

MEADOWS AND FORESTS THAT PROVIDE HABITAT AND OTHER ENVIRONMENTAL BENEFITS

NATURE PARKS

INDUSTRIAL NATURE PARKS

RAPID REFORESTATION

SUCCESSIONAL ROAD

ROADS TO RIVERS

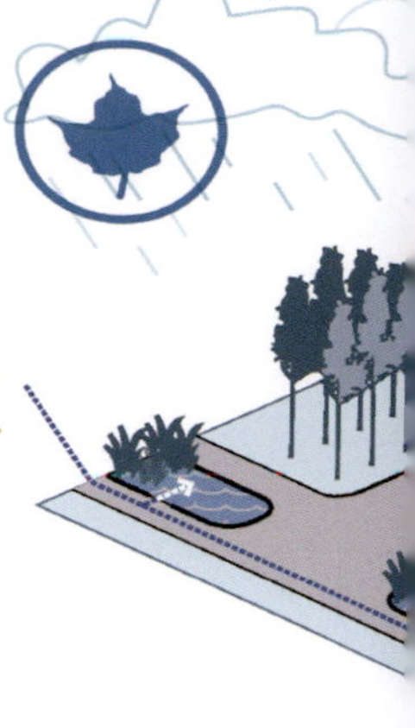

BLUE+GR INFRAST

LANDSCAP CAPTURE S AND CLEAN

LARGE LAKE

SMALLER RET

INFILTRATION

SWALES + INF MEDIANS

ROAD-SIDE P WIDE ROADS

GREEN INDUS

CARBON FOR

4.1
Detroit Future City
A shrinking Detroit population requires adapting over-subscribed 'grey' infrastructure systems to more ecologically and cost-effective effective green infrastructure networks suited to reduced demand.

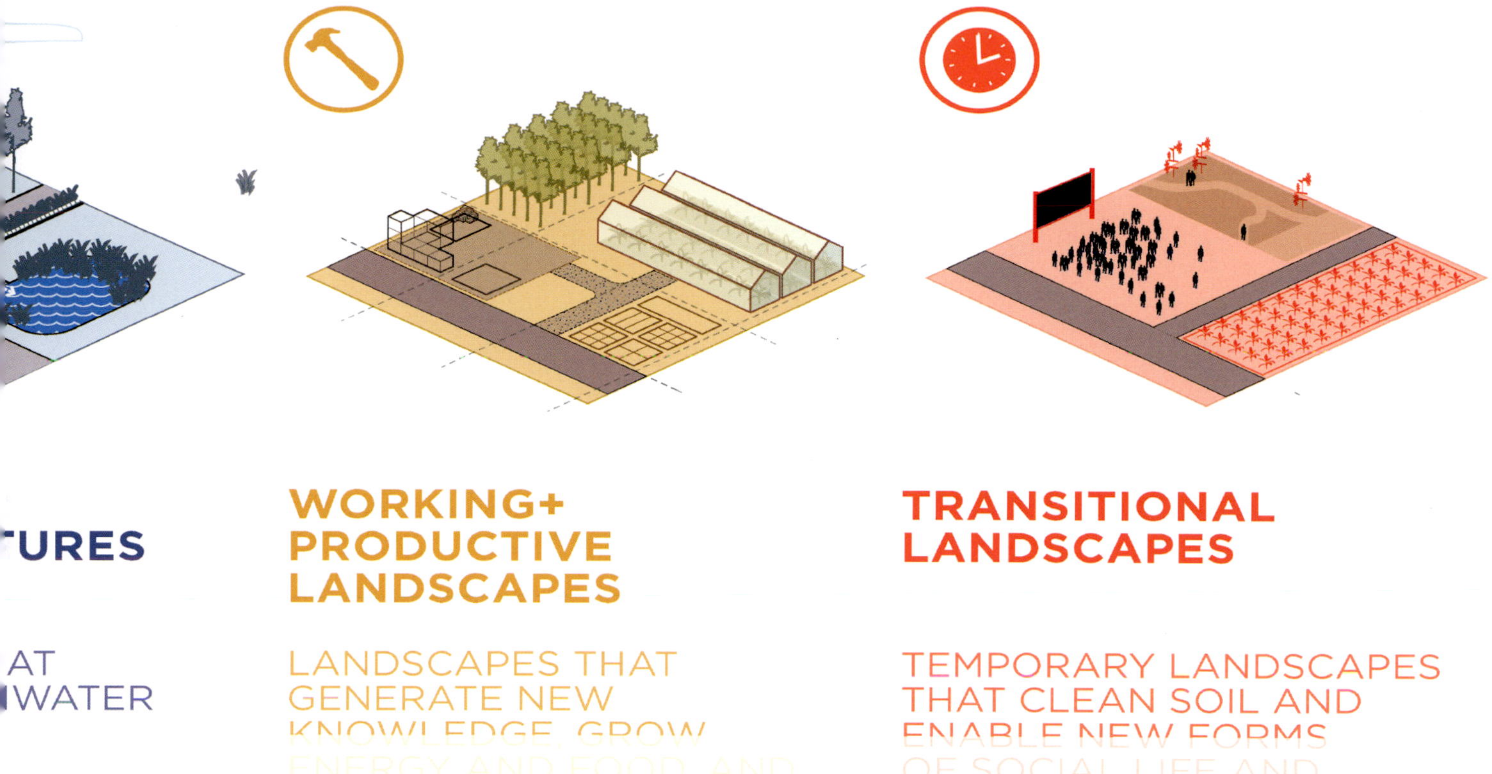
WORKING+ PRODUCTIVE LANDSCAPES
LANDSCAPES THAT GENERATE NEW
TRANSITIONAL LANDSCAPES
TEMPORARY LANDSCAPES THAT CLEAN SOIL AND

4
ENVIRONMENTAL INFRASTRUCTURE

Can planning and landscape architecture more significantly implement environmental infrastructure (EI) to mitigate non-renewable, grey infrastructure networks' environmental harm? How can EI generate solutions for new pressures such as climate change, while incorporating multifarious social benefits? To answer such questions, new forms of landscape architectural practice must extend beyond current, limited 'green infrastructure' endeavors (crossing ecological planning (Chapter 2) and blue-green networks (Chapters 2 and 3)) and even counter-productive visual, character and environmental impact assessments. Landscape architects can harness spatial, communicative and interdisciplinary skills to manifest performative, renewable outcomes beyond the merely visual. These assist environmental sustainability by offsetting and mitigating fossil fuel consumption in energy, waste and transportation infrastructures (and water—Chapter 3). While small projects are incrementally important, substantial environmental inroads require major network reconfiguration.

GREY INFRASTRUCTURE'S LEGACY

Importance and pressures

Infrastructures are support systems of civilization. These often invisible or unnoticed networks provide historically unprecedented levels of comfort, efficiency, and health to those who can afford to access them. It is easy to take such everyday services for granted (for example, sanitation/sewage/wastewater; potable water supply; flood protection; transport systems; electricity; natural gas; and telephone/data/digital/satellite technologies) until they falter or fail. Yet their stability faces heightened pressures and is regularly tested to breaking point.

Slow pressures include gradual population growth, ageing components, lack of maintenance/replacement, and increasing climate change impacts (like sea level rise).

Rapid pressures are usually the result of natural disasters and extreme climate events, such as flooding, storm surge, hurricane/typhoons/cyclones, extreme heat/cold, wild/bushfires and landslides—all of which are projected to increase in intensity and frequency from climate change.

Limitations of centralized grey infrastructure

Infrastructures and their centralized networks (distributing large outputs of electricity, potable water and natural gas, and processing garbage and sewerage wastes) have traditionally been the domain of engineers (for example, civil, hydrological, mechanical, structural, electrical and environmental).

Environmental sustainability concerns

These large-scale, fossil-fuel reliant infrastructures reflect a segregated working approach of separate (or closely aligned) disciplines rather than collaborative teams from wide-ranging professions:

- their design almost always excludes ecological and social dimensions (for example, lacking ecosystem service provision, excluding biodiversity through hardscape treatments to aquatic systems (Chapter 3) and excluding public access and social opportunities;
- they follow a linear resource path of energy input to waste output rather than circular arrangements (e.g. generating electricity without utilizing heat, using fossil fuels instead of renewable resources);
- they possess singular, rather than multiple functions and dimensions.

Social sustainability concerns:

Under democratic government, state-owned centralized infrastructure systems worked effectively. Although low numbers of these large installations make them potentially more vulnerable to network failure, terrorism and extreme climate events (such as fresh water supply systems, pipelines (oil, gas), and electricity infrastructure like nuclear plants) they have proved reliable to date. Increased economic deregulation and privatization from the 1980s has resulted in corporate owned essential public services, infrastructure assets and/or their ongoing operation contracts. This threatens affordability due to commercially oriented profiteering (Chapter 7) and can reduce maintenance and long-term investment.

"The American Society of Civil Engineers said in 2007 that the US had fallen so far behind in maintaining its public infrastructure … that it would take more than a trillion and half dollars over five years to bring it back up to standard … It's easy to imagine a future in which growing numbers of cities have their frail and long-neglected infrastructures knocked out by disasters and then are left to rot, their core services never repaired or rehabilitated. The well-off, meanwhile, will withdraw into gated communities, their needs met by privatized providers."
NAOMI KLEIN, THE SHOCK DOCTRINE: THE RISE OF DISASTER CAPITALISM (2014)

"Designers must acknowledge the hierarchy associated with the design of urban systems, where the numbers alone provide an indication of the food chain of the disciplines … professional membership in 2010 included 26,700 landscape architects, 38,400 urban and regional planners, 141,000 architects, 551,000 construction managers, and 971,000 engineers (combining civil, mechanical, industrial, electrical, environmental)."
PIERRE BÉLANGER, LANDSCAPE INFRASTRUCTURE: URBANISM BEYOND ENGINEERING (2012)

"The public sector has its public works departments: roads here, parks and rivers over there, water and supply and sanitary over here … without an integrated strategy. We need tighter, more hard-core systems of integration between the landscape of infrastructure and urbanism, where site systems interface with spatial experiences and connect with ecological processes."
JOSEPH E. BROWN, INTERVIEW: PEERING INTO THE FUTURE (2009)

"The United States Department of Defense is the largest contractor and land developer in the world. Despite its budget of over 500 billion dollars and a portfolio of nearly 30 million acres of lands and facilities, neither does there exist a clear cartographic inventory of this military-industrial infrastructure, nor has any recent scholarly enterprise been undertaken to visualize and analyze the presence of US military-bases and related industries worldwide."
PIERRE BÉLANGER & ALEXANDER S. ARROYO, LANDSCAPE OF DEFENSE: MILITARY GEOGRAPHIES AND ALTITUDES OF URBANIZATION (2016)

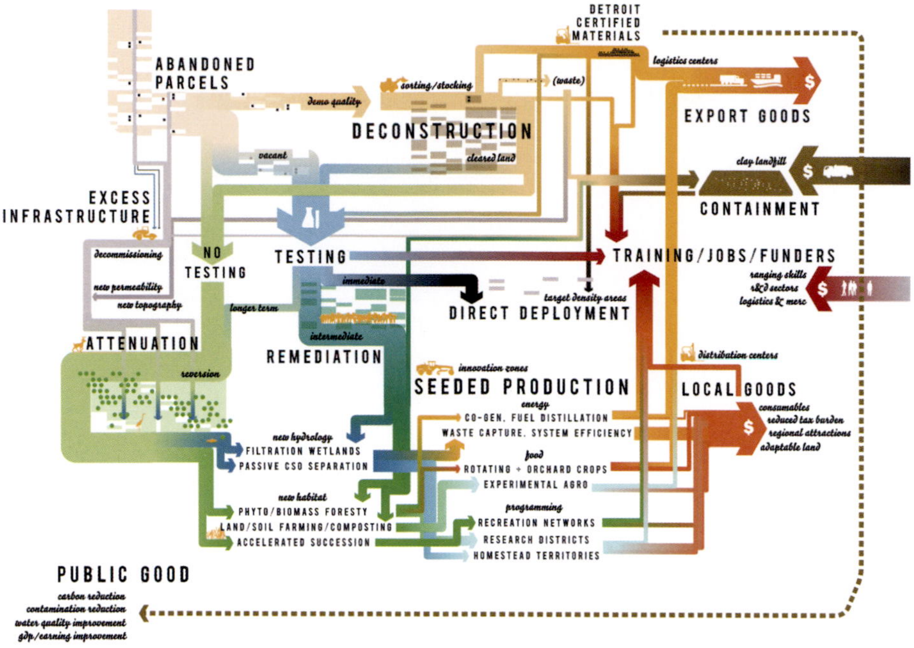
DETROIT
CERTIFIED
MATERIALS
ABANDONED
PARCELS
demo quality
sorting/stocking
(waste)
logistics centers
EXPORT GOODS
DECONSTRUCTION
vacant
cleared land
clay landfill
CONTAINMENT
EXCESS
INFRASTRUCTURE
decommissioning
new permeability
new topography
NO
TESTING
TESTING
TRAINING/JOBS/FUNDERS
ranging skills
R&D sectors
logistics & merc
immediate
longer term
target density areas
DIRECT DEPLOYMENT
intermediate
ATTENUATION
REMEDIATION
reversion
innovation zones
SEEDED PRODUCTION
distribution centers
LOCAL GOODS
consumables
reduced tax burden
regional attractions
adaptable land
energy
CO-GEN. FUEL DISTILLATION
WASTE CAPTURE. SYSTEM EFFICIENCY
new hydrology
FILTRATION WETLANDS
PASSIVE CSO SEPARATION
food
ROTATING + ORCHARD CROPS
EXPERIMENTAL AGRO
new habitat
PHYTO/BIOMASS FORESTY
LAND/SOIL FARMING/COMPOSTING
ACCELERATED SUCCESSION
programming
RECREATION NETWORKS
RESEARCH DISTRICTS
HOMESTEAD TERRITORIES
PUBLIC GOOD
carbon reduction
contamination reduction
water quality improvement
gdp/earning improvement

4.2a

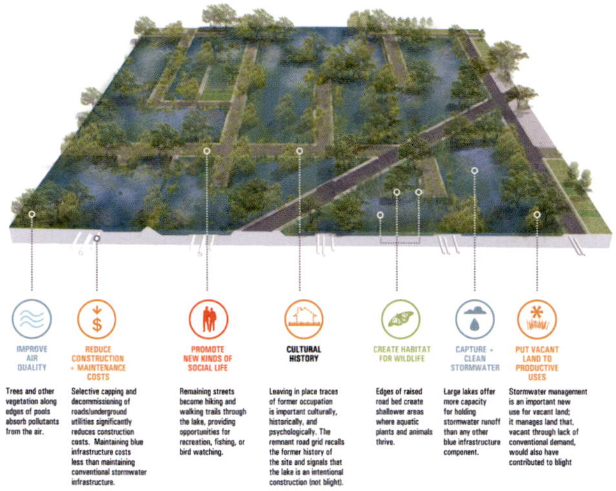
IMPROVE AIR QUALITY
Trees and other vegetation along edges of pools absorb pollutants from the air.
REDUCE CONSTRUCTION + MAINTENANCE COSTS
Selective capping and decommissioning of roads/underground utilities significantly reduces construction costs. Maintaining blue infrastructure costs less than maintaining conventional stormwater infrastructure.
PROMOTE NEW KINDS OF SOCIAL LIFE
Remaining streets become hiking and walking trails through the lake, providing opportunities for recreation, fishing, or bird watching.
CULTURAL HISTORY
Leaving in place traces of former occupation is important culturally, historically, and psychologically. The remnant road grid recalls the former history of the site and signals that the lake is an intentional construction (not blight).
CREATE HABITAT FOR WILDLIFE
Edges of raised road bed create shallower areas where aquatic plants and animals thrive.
CAPTURE + CLEAN STORMWATER
Large lakes offer more capacity for holding stormwater runoff than any other blue infrastructure component.
PUT VACANT LAND TO PRODUCTIVE USES
Stormwater management is an important new use for vacant land; it manages land that, vacant through lack of conventional demand, would also have contributed to blight

4.2b

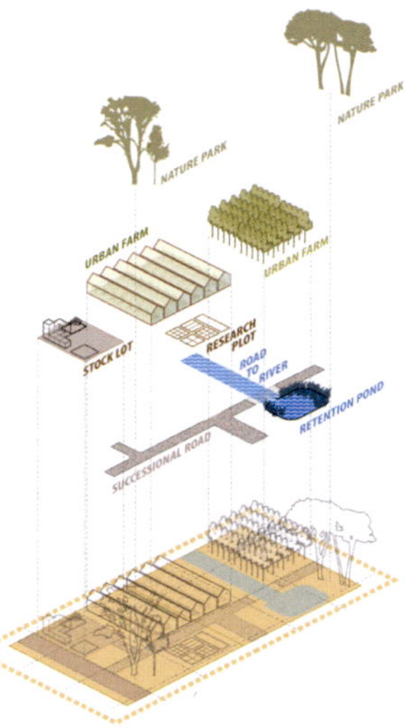
NATURE PARK
NATURE PARK
URBAN FARM
URBAN FARM
STOCK LOT
RESEARCH PLOT
ROAD TO RIVER
RETENTION POND
SUCCESSIONAL ROAD

4.2c

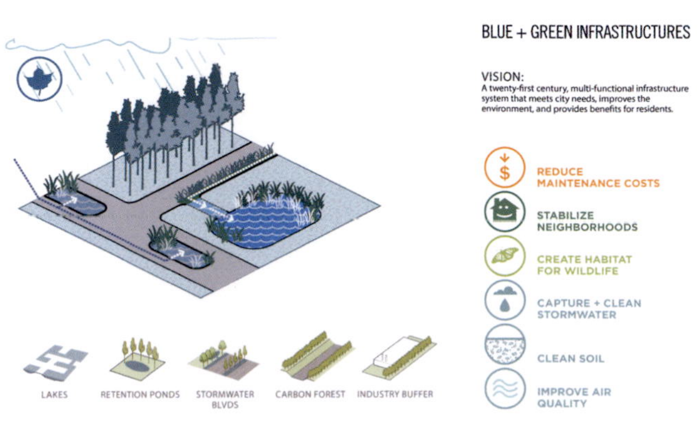
LAKES
RETENTION PONDS
STORMWATER BLVDS
CARBON FOREST
INDUSTRY BUFFER
BLUE + GREEN INFRASTRUCTURES
VISION:
A twenty-first century, multi-functional infrastructure system that meets city needs, improves the environment, and provides benefits for residents.
REDUCE MAINTENANCE COSTS
STABILIZE NEIGHBORHOODS
CREATE HABITAT FOR WILDLIFE
CAPTURE + CLEAN STORMWATER
CLEAN SOIL
IMPROVE AIR QUALITY

4.2d

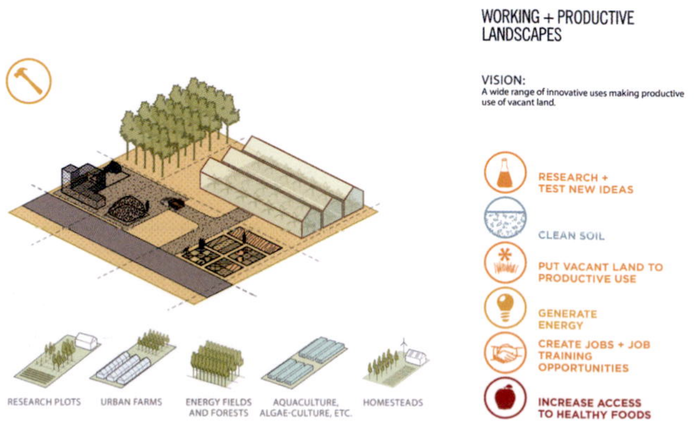
RESEARCH PLOTS
URBAN FARMS
ENERGY FIELDS AND FORESTS
AQUACULTURE, ALGAE-CULTURE, ETC.
HOMESTEADS
WORKING + PRODUCTIVE LANDSCAPES
VISION:
A wide range of innovative uses making productive use of vacant land.
RESEARCH + TEST NEW IDEAS
CLEAN SOIL
PUT VACANT LAND TO PRODUCTIVE USE
GENERATE ENERGY
CREATE JOBS + JOB TRAINING OPPORTUNITIES
INCREASE ACCESS TO HEALTHY FOODS

4.2e

EXISTING: CURRENT LAND USE

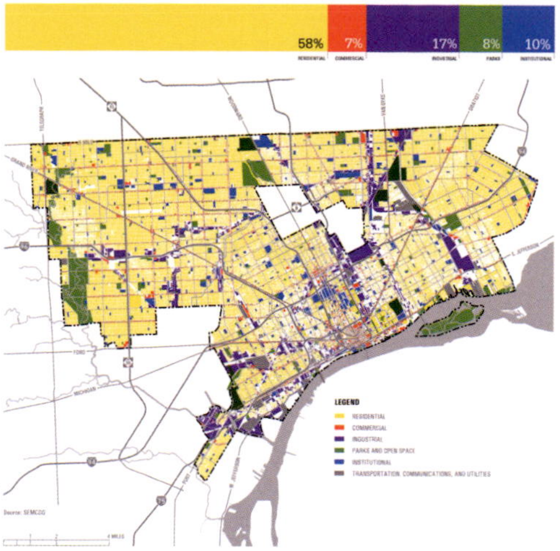
58%
7%
17%
8%
10%
LEGEND

4.2f

PROPOSED: 50-YEAR LAND USE SCENARIO

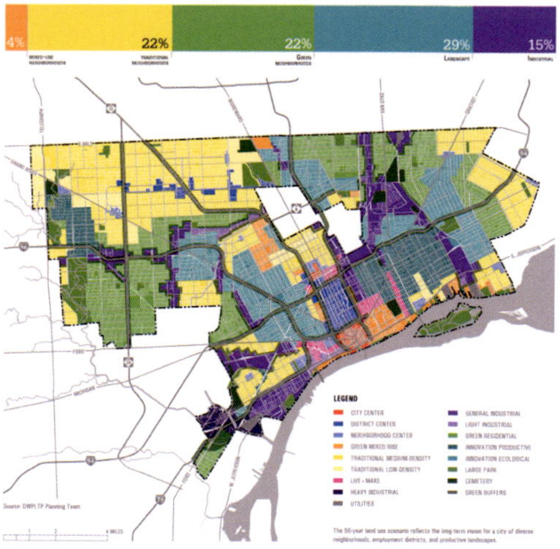
4%
22%
22%
29%
15%
LEGEND

4.2g

4.2a
4.2b
4.2c
4.2d
4.2e
4.2f
4.2g
Detroit Future City, STOSS, Detroit, Michigan, USA, 2011–2012
The Detroit Strategic Framework is the first to accept that the city that may not regain its peak population of nearly 2 million and address its future in the context of systems with a need for civic capacity and engagement, beyond land use and economic growth. STOSS' collaborative process (responding to 24 month long public engagement), formulated a 50 year, city-wide vision to improve and create synergies between Detroit's social, economic and environmental systems. Focusing on landscape, ecology, open space, blue/green infrastructure and agricultural urbanism, it harnesses the productive and generative capacity of landscape to improve ecologies, economies and health.

LANDSCAPE'S ROLE

Scope

Traditionally, landscape architecture's role with respect to grey infrastructure has been restricted to the following:

- integrating and disguising visual impact of large scale grey infrastructures (power, water and waste plants, roads and railways, industry and landfills often in peri-urban and non-urban locations (see Energy Landscapes and Connecticut Facility, Chapter 2);
- micro scale visual management (placement and screening of site services such as stormwater pits and transformers);
- adding 'parsley to the pig': decorative and surface treatments intended to beautify grey infrastructure projects;
- Transforming decommissioned infrastructure sites (Chapter 3).

Environmental infrastructure

Landscape architecture can facilitate renewable and decentralized infrastructures. This is distinct from what the landscape architectural profession calls 'green infrastructure' (Chapters 2 and 3), which refers to creating interconnected 'blue-green' corridors and landscape surface treatments, passive recreational networks and WSUD systems, often for large, unsustainable grey infrastructures such as expansion of roadways and sprawling subdivisions (see Interviews, Chapters 4 and 7). Although 'green infrastructures' demonstrate biophilia, biodiversity, air pollution and other benefits, these are somewhat insignificant when measured against the scale of grey infrastructure resource consumption. Environmental Infrastructures (EI) are potentially much more substantial, reimagining and structurally reconfiguring grey infrastructure systems as renewable, environmentally sustainable, multidimensional support systems that are socially integrated, increasingly visible and aesthetically incorporated at macro and micro scales.

"An object seen in isolation from the whole is not a real thing."
MASANOBU FUKUOKA, THE ONE STRAW REVOLUTION: AN INTRODUCTION TO NATURAL FARMING (1978)

Challenges

Challenges to successfully implementing EI primarily include visual objections (see Energy Landscapes), status-quo grey infrastructure preferences (and powerful corporations' persuasive lobbying and political donations for their continuance), and limiting land and jurisdictional boundaries. Such artificially imposed cartesian land parcels are usually at odds with broad-scale ecological and regional interconnectedness, being arbitrary in relation to bioregions, natural features and infrastructure zones such as watersheds, public transport networks, road systems, coastlines and waterways. Projects crossing multiple municipalities can be difficult to coordinate and integrate, causing piecemeal, ineffective or contextually disconnected plans, strategies and design outcomes (see European Landscape Convention). Boundaries also reinforce private land ownership and enclosure ideologies and can contradict indigenous/aboriginal/first nation/native title (where relevant), amongst many other social issues (Chapter 7).

4.3
European Landscape Convention, Council of Europe member states, 2000/04
Val d'Orcia in Tuscany, Italy
The European Landscape Convention organizes European co-operation on landscape issues, transcending individual countries, raising awareness of living landscape value and promoting protection, management and planning. Adopted October 20, 2000 in Florence, Italy, it came into effect March 1, 2004 (Council of Europe Treaty Series no. 176). It is open for signature by member states of the Council of Europe and for accession by the European Community and European non-member states. It is the first international treaty to be exclusively concerned with all dimensions of European landscape (including everyday and degraded landscapes) and covers natural, rural, urban and peri-urban areas. This image shows the UNESCO World Heritage Val d'Orcia region in Tuscany, Italy, which was listed in 2004 and cited for its cultural significance on landscape thinking since Renaissance times.

4.3

Multidimensional infrastructure

EI reflects a shift away from single discipline engineering towards multifunctional infrastructure systems. Beyond functionality, however, EI requires multidimensional operation at multiple scales with diverse benefits. How can we, for instance, optimize large infrastructures such as airports, ports and road systems to operate at both city and human scales? Until the last few decades, many ports were centers of human activities for both work and socialization, but are now highly mechanized and over-scaled and have lost social dimensions (see Amager Plant). Social opportunities are missed if infrastructure is measured only in tonnage and economic values of outputs. Similarly, grey approaches have poorly accommodated non-human life forms, in many cases seeking to exclude, suppress and control ecological systems. Can environmental infrastructures realize increased resilience and sophistication through combining multiple dimensions such as economic, social, ecological and productive?

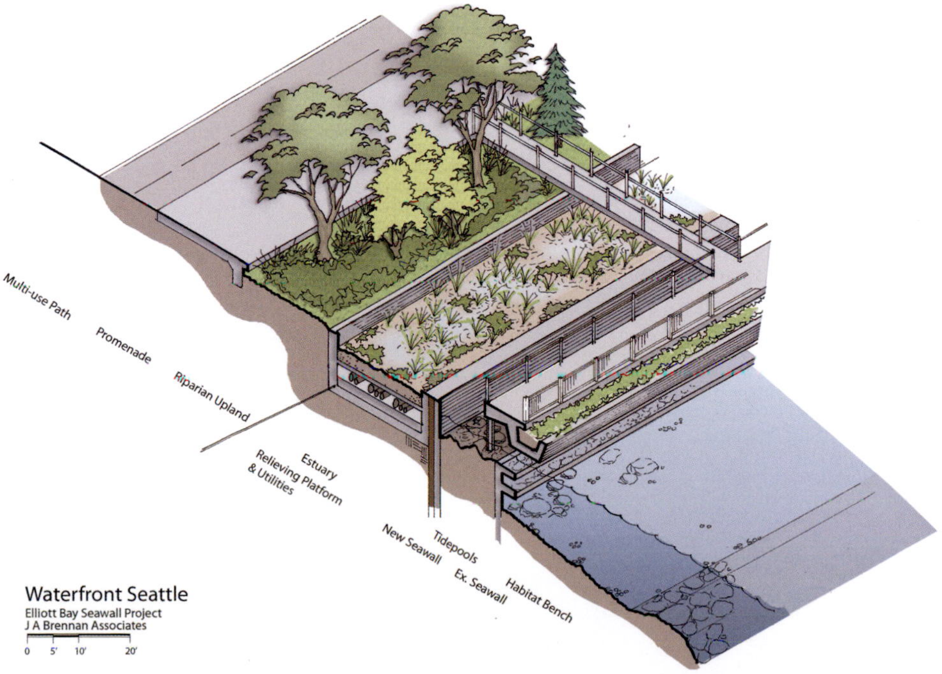

Multi-use Path
Promenade
Riparian Upland
Estuary
Relieving Platform & Utilities
Tidepools
New Seawall
Ex. Seawall
Habitat Bench
Waterfront Seattle
Elliott Bay Seawall Project
J A Brennan Associates
0 5' 10' 20'

4.4

4.4
Elliott Bay Seawall Replacement, J. A. Brennan Associates, Seattle, Washington
The vision for the 1.5 miles (2.4km) of Seattle's dense, urban waterfront is an ecologically friendly environment with pebble beaches, off-shore reefs and aquatic day lighting to simulate natural habitat, increasing aquatic plant and animal populations, and enhancing salmon migration.

Decentralized, small-scale infrastructure

At the individual site and project scale, decentralized infrastructures have been steadily gaining momentum. Although currently small in output when compared with monolithic grey infrastructures, decentralized initiatives collectively contribute to greater resilience and if carefully planned and executed, improve sustainability and environmental performance. Renewable and environmental systems include (micro) wind turbines; solar photovoltaic panels; solar thermal electricity, hot water and heating; greywater and/or blackwater recycling systems; rain and recycled water cisterns; geothermal heat pumps; waste and nutrient recycling and composting. Some of these are better suited to detached structures/buildings (harvesting water from a roof) and some are expensive to retrofit rather than build into new developments (geothermal wells and underground tanks). These renewable technologies are increasingly mass-produced and thus less expensive, or can be assisted by government incentives (purchase subsidies; 'green loans'; renewable energy feed-in tariffs). Connecting renewable infrastructures to centralized networks is usually mutually beneficial (for example, grid connected PV panels to generate income and avoid storage batteries) to improve efficiencies through balancing supply and demand.

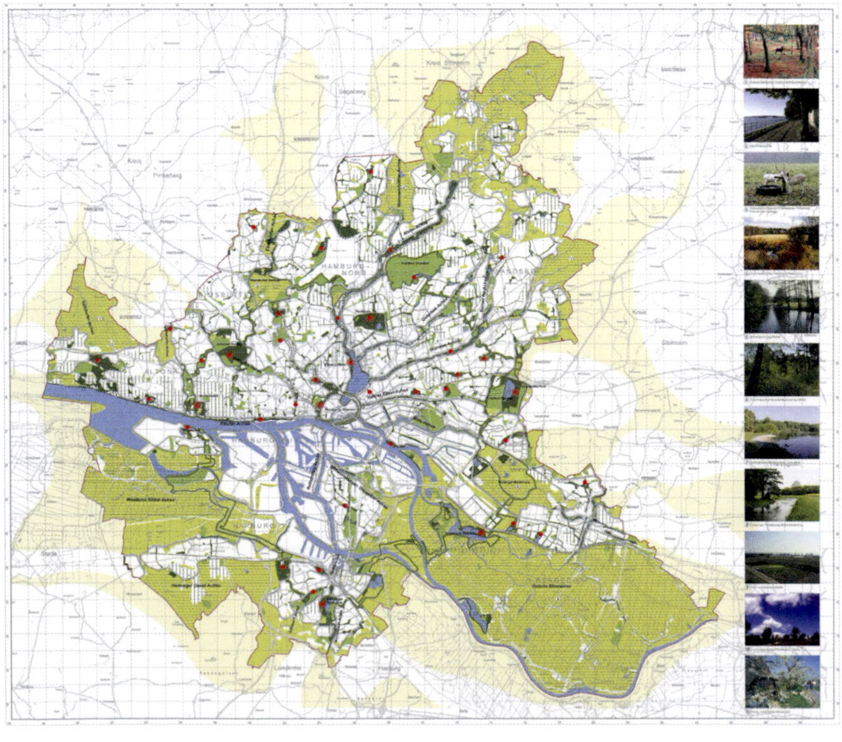

4.5

4.5
Hamburg Green Network, Hamburg, Germany, 2010–
Although central Hamburg isn't planning to ban cars (as has been misreported elsewhere), the city is improving alternative transport means. A new 'green network' covering 40% of the city will be completed in the next 10–15 years, making biking/walking possible from any point. This will partially involve undergrounding sections of the crowded A7 autobahn with green space to facilitate at grade connections (see also Madrid Rio, Chapter 4).

Audiences

To achieve environmental infrastructure, practitioners need to continue to expand into large project leadership roles with greater effective advocacy. Notable results are more likely where landscape architects and environmental system-thinkers are well positioned in government (see Chapter 7), or can effectively communicate visions and strategies to clients, municipalities, mayors, stakeholders and public audiences (see Interviews, Chapters 4, 7 and 10).

Environmental planning mechanisms' shortcomings

Environmental Impact Assessments/Statements (EIA/EIS) are planning tools used to identify and assess environmental impacts of proposed projects. They are routinely initiated by developers seeking approval for large infrastructure schemes. EIA/EIS usually focus only on site-specific, direct immediate environmental impact from the construction of the project itself and not subsequent impacts from site activity (continuing impacts from airports, for example, greatly exceed construction impact). Depending on their context and the integrity of the democratic and governmental processes, EIAs can become diluted (for example, consulting firms preparing EIAs are also frequently part of the developers/clients' team who are proposing the project). Accordingly, the impartiality of their assessment may be adversely influenced as they can lack independent appraisal. EIA/EIS are reactive rather than proactive, providing minimal scope for encouraging new and innovative environmental infrastructures. Although public submissions are usually possible, EIA/EIS do not consider alternatives (for example, a wind, solar or tidal farm(s) to substitute a nuclear or coal power station). Subsequently, EIA/EIS influence on decisions can be minimal.

4.6

4.6
Munich Green Roof
Local, state and national governments can mandate green roofs on new buildings, increasing energy efficiency and boosting production, reducing urban heat islands, slowing stormwater runoff, and increasing biodiversity—benefits which become significant at city and network scales. In 1997, the City of Munich in Germany mandated inclusion of vegetation on all flat roofs larger than 100 square meters. Similar regulations have been instituted in: Basel, Switzerland (2002, leading the world in per capita green roof use), Toronto, Canada (2009) and Copenhagen, Denmark (2010). A French law (2015) requires new building rooftops in commercial zones to be partially covered in either plants or solar panels.

RESILIENCE TO CLIMATE CHANGE

Environmental infrastructures (EI) need to be resilient and adaptive to future pressures. Some landscape architects have recently begun contributing to climate change adaptation strategies for settlements and their infrastructures. This is a challenging process that lacks easy solutions. Development that has occurred in problematic locations is placed under additional vulnerability and strain, such as settlements in flood prone areas, low-lying coastal sites and estuaries (see Ouse Valley) and on unsuitable soil/ground conditions with notable examples including New Orleans, USA, where 2005 Hurricane Katrina caused US$81 billion of damage (See Dutch Dialogues); much of the Netherlands, where nearly half of the country's surface area is both below and less than 3.3 feet (1 m) above sea level (see Room for River); and other susceptible settlements (such as Canvey Island near London).

"Regrettably, cities seem to underestimate the urgency of adaptation strategies—no known legally binding climate related urban design guidelines have been adapted yet."
JANA MILOSOVICOVA, URBAN DESIGN FOR THE CLIMATE CHANGE (2012)

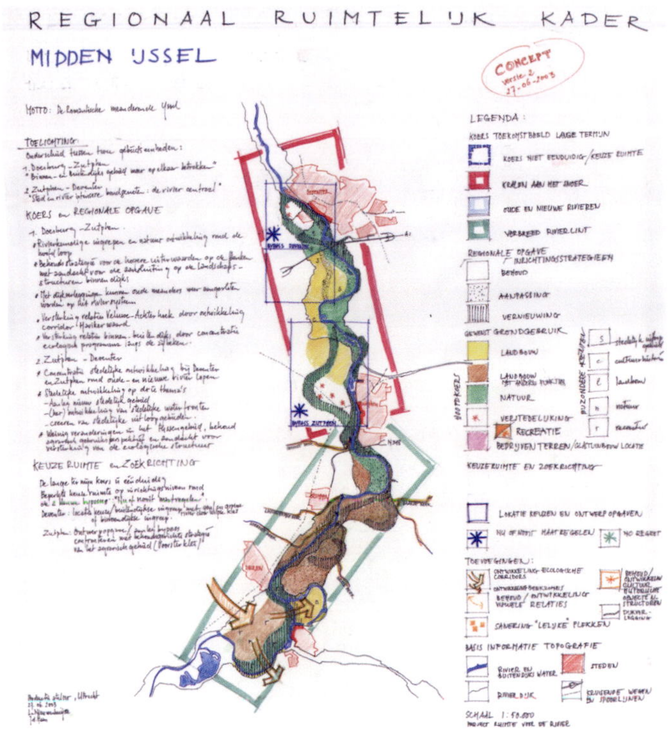
REGIONAAL RUIMTELIJK KADER
MIDDEN IJSSEL
CONCEPT
LEGENDA

4.7a

4.7b

4.7c

4.7a
4.7b
4.7c
Room for the River, H+N+S Landschapsarchitecten, the Netherlands, 2002–2003
Government initiated, Room for the River addresses flood protection, environmental improvement and landscape character in the Netherlands' river areas. The 12-year strategy seeks safety and coherence between individual river measures and dyke relocation, new retention areas and lowered floodplains, coupled with a long-term plan for 2050 accommodating climate change and higher peak drainage flows. Conceptually expressed strategic measures give rise to distinctive new hydrological regions. 'Beads on the string; concentration and dynamics' concentrates and links the river in dynamic areas, while morphological processes inspire floodplain extension in 'Old and new rivers, robust and natural'. 'The widened river ribbon: linear and balanced' equitably spreads the difficulties of large-scale change through substantial excavation of floodplains and dyke relocation.

4.8
Dutch Dialogues, H+N+S Landschapsarchitecten, the Netherlands, 2007–2011
Regional and catchment scale planning is required to understand the forces that can impact an entire region. Following Hurricane Katrina's devastating impacts, H+N+S worked with a multidisciplinary team (including water management experts, engineers and urban planners, government bodies and New Orleans' residents) to strategize more resilient solutions.

A series of workshops and ongoing projects identified integrated urban design and engineering approaches to reducing flood risk and alleviating tropical storm impact with focus given to how water can assist economic redevelopment.

Orleans Canal
Lake Pontchartrain
Levee
New Pump Station
New Pump Station
Purification
Bayou
London Avenue Canal
Pump Station
Pump Station

4.8

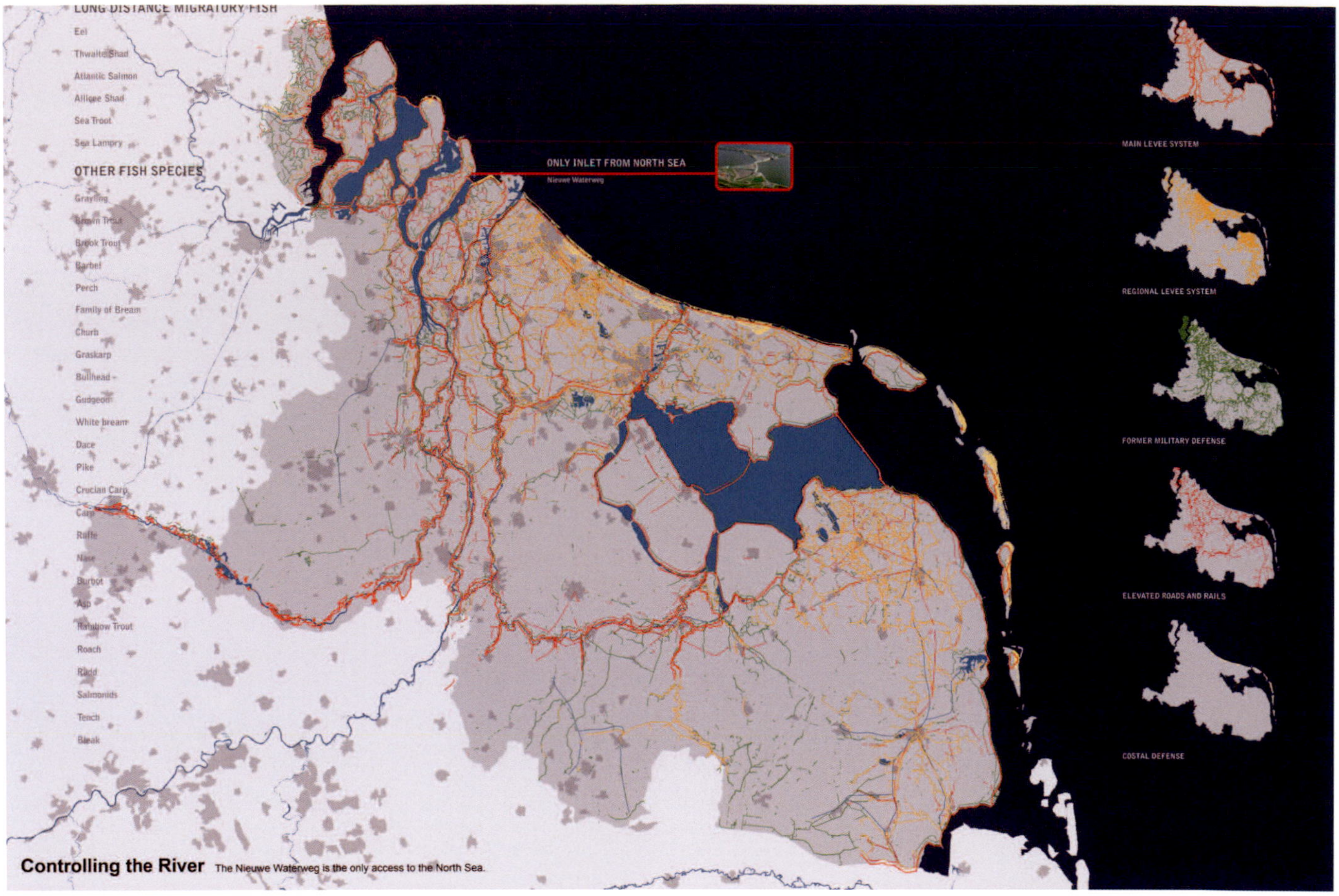
LONG DISTANCE MIGRATORY FISH
Eel
Thwaite Shad
Atlantic Salmon
Allice Shad
Sea Trout
Sea Lamprey
OTHER FISH SPECIES
Grayling
Brown Trout
Brook Trout
Barbel
Perch
Family of Bream
Chub
Graskarp
Bullhead
Gudgeon
White bream
Dace
Pike
Crucian Carp
Carp
Ruffe
Nase
Burbot
Asp
Rainbow Trout
Roach
Rudd
Salmonids
Tench
Bleak
ONLY INLET FROM NORTH SEA
Nieuwe Waterweg
MAIN LEVEE SYSTEM
REGIONAL LEVEE SYSTEM
FORMER MILITARY DEFENSE
ELEVATED ROADS AND RAILS
COSTAL DEFENSE
Controlling the River The Nieuwe Waterweg is the only access to the North Sea.

4.9a

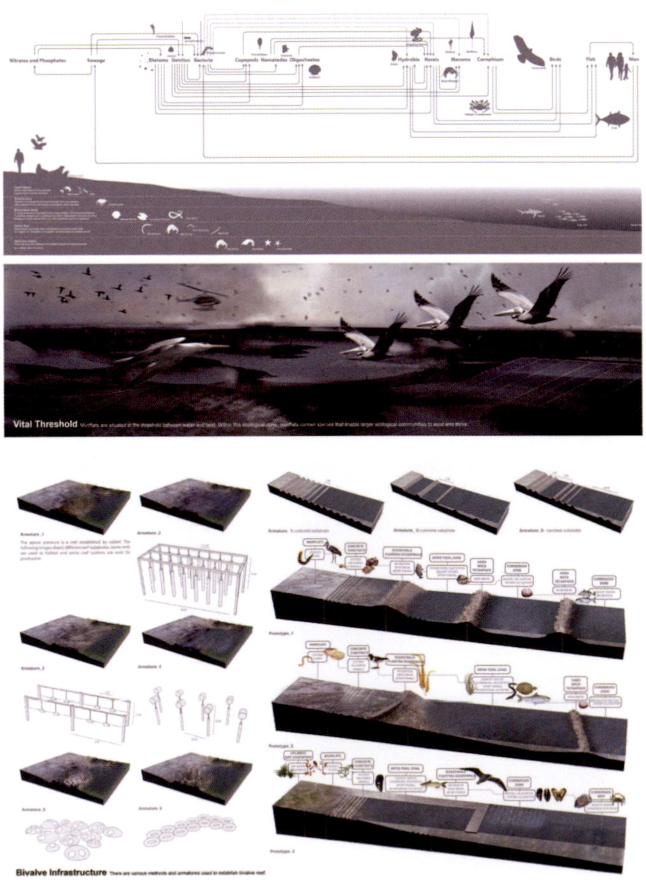
Vital Threshold
Bivalve Infrastructure There are various methods and armatures used to establish bivalve reef.

4.9b

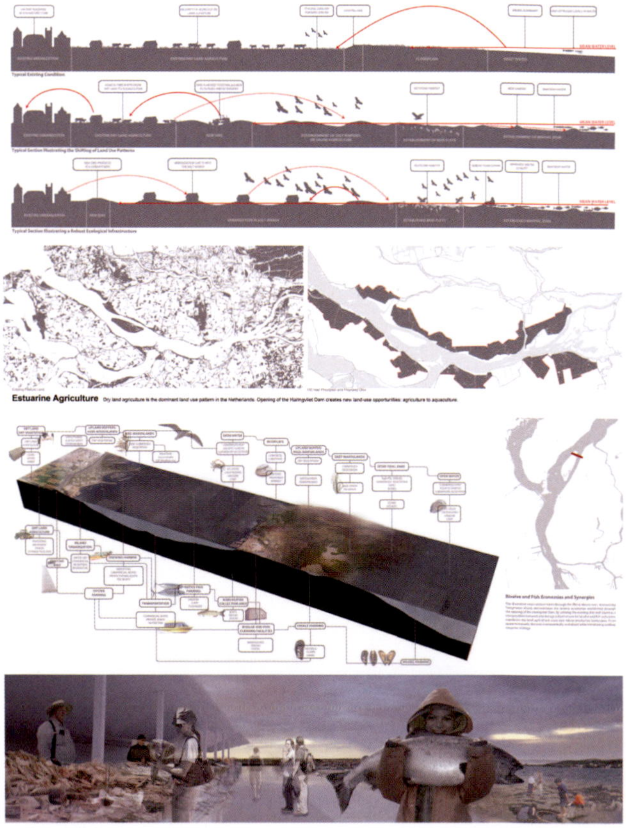
Estuarine Agriculture Dry land agriculture is the dominant land use pattern in the Netherlands. Opening of the Haringvliet Dam creates new land use opportunities: agriculture to aquaculture.

4.9c

4.9a
4.9b
4.9c
DeDamming the Dutch Delta, Harvard GSD studio by Nina-Marie Lister and Pierre Bélanger, student work by Kimberly Garza and Sarah Thomas, Dordrecht, the Netherlands, 2009–2010
This Harvard student project examines the productive capacity of an ecologically healthier landscape region of the Rhine-Meuse Delta in Dordrecht. By deconstructing landscape infrastructures of dykes and dams from hard and fixed to adaptive and flexible systems dependent on biological infrastructures, it incorporates natural ebb and flow, acknowledging floods as anticipated, recurring landscape conditions with economic and ecological potential from the fluctuating gradient and biological productivity of mixed salt and fresh waters.

Climate challenges

The economic and cultural value of vulnerable settlements (and the political pressure this creates) can determine the approach taken, usually either 'retreat', 'accommodate', or 'protect'. Climate change scenarios for settlements can rarely be solved by conventional approaches to engineering (or might be prohibitively expensive). At present (and depending on the wealth of the locality or country) resources are usually allocated into attempting their perpetuity (higher seawalls or dykes, larger flood mitigation basins and deeper channels). Processes involving 'retreat' have already been occurring in low-lying nations in the Pacific, creating 'climate refugees'. This will become more commonplace as climate change impacts increase. If such planned and staged measures are not coordinated and undertaken in a timely manner, emergency scenarios (such as storm surge or major flooding) may prove disastrous. Occasionally, a local municipality (and vocal taxpayers) may not be willing to divert funds into expensive and possibly futile measures of continued protection (as was the case for a series of previously expensive houses built on fragile sand dunes prone to storm surge erosion in Byron Bay, Australia). The resilience of both engineered and natural systems in vulnerable locations can often benefit from big-picture, lateral approaches to green infrastructure strategy that are readily accommodated through lateral landscape architectural design thinking (see DeDamming Delta).

4.10
Adapting to Climate Change: Launching the Debate in the Lower Ouse Valley, LDA Design, Ouse Valley, Sussex, UK, 2014
Artist's impression of how the coastline could look with offshore breakwaters to preserve the Seaford beach and salt marsh.

Climate change is complex, with uncertain impacts and ranging adaptation options. Led by LDA (and working with the Coastal Futures Group, communities and climate/flood/coastal specialists), this consultation and planning project looked beyond traditional flood defenses and planning for a 11,850 acre (48km^2) area. It aimed to identify long-term climate change and sea-level rise risks and opportunities over the next 150 years, planning for the future through alternative adaption processes and practical actions by community members with limited resources. Engagement and communications ranged from landscape visualizations, historic case studies, illustrated scenarios to public exhibitions, workshops, and online consultation.

4.10

TRANSPORT

Suburbia

Prior to 20th-century infrastructure advancements, many urban areas were cramped, disease-prone and impoverished. Understandably, the countryside was seen as the desirable and healthy place to be. Models such as Ebenezer Howard's Garden Cities concept aimed to combine the best aspects of both the city and the countryside through a detached home on a piece of land accessible to urban amenities. The subsequent rise of detached and low-density housing has led to one of the world's most spatially dominant outcomes—suburbia. This model became inextricably co-dependent with private motorized transport and fossil fuel industries, serviced by extensive road networks and surfaced by crude oil by-products. As population growth continues and oil reserves decrease, sprawling suburbs and their congested trunk roads have lost some favor to urban areas now serviced by high quality infrastructures, abundant social amenities and effective public transportation systems. As yet, there are no absolute answers in the low/medium/high density sustainability debate, however, sub-optimal conditions are generated through very low (isolation, obesity) or high (overshadowing, high wind) densities and their reliance on energy intensive infrastructures (such as lift and mechanical systems for high density and long-distance transport required by low density).

"The way a city grows, the direction in which it spreads, is a factor not so much of zoning or real estate activity or land values but of highways."
J. B. JACKSON (1909–1996)

"Be wary of the automobile; on no account let it dominate this land."
CHRISTOPHER ALEXANDER, SARA ISHIKAWA AND MURRAY SILVERSTEIN, A PATTERN LANGUAGE (1977)

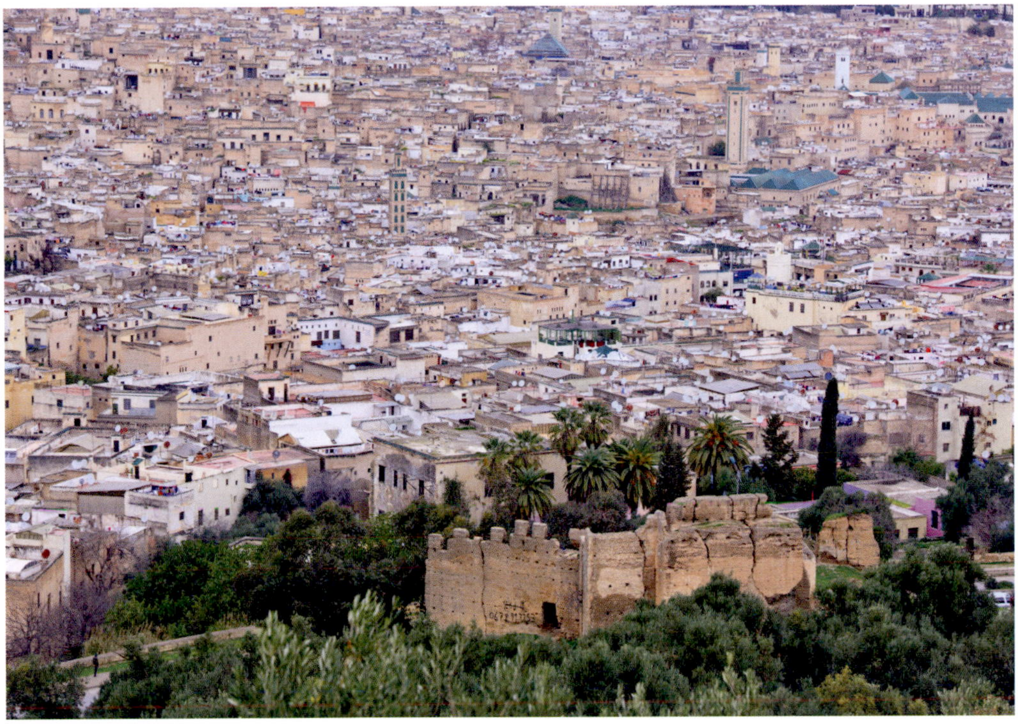

4.11

4.12

4.11
Fes-al-Bali, Fes, Morocco
There are over 10,000 retail businesses, over 13,000 historic buildings and 222 inhabitants per acre (550/ha) in the 741 acre (300ha), car-free Fes medina. Both Fes and Venice, Italy (constructed on mudflats with over 20 million annual visitors) are UNESCO World Heritage sites and believed to be the largest contiguous car free areas in the world by population/area.

4.12
Low-density sprawl from the air, Arizona
Low-density housing typologies, such as in Phoenix, Arizona, USA, typify the adage 'a pint of gas (petrol) to buy a pint of milk'.

Motorized domination

There are over 1 billion motorized vehicles in use in the world. In under a century, motorized transportation infrastructure has become the public urban landscape's most dominant feature, with vast road systems filling up significant percentages of total urban areas in addition to carparks, over/underpasses and buildings catering for vehicles (as well as the resultant pollution, noise, danger, impacts on the environment and animals). The explosion of private motor vehicle use led to removal or diminishment of public transport infrastructure and services in many locations. Increased homogenization (furthered by generic roadside 'big-box' retail chain stores worldwide) has further affected regional identity, place attachment and loss of more socially oriented spaces and transport modes like main/high-street precincts and tramways (although in some areas, these are making a resurgence, such as in new urbanism, TODs and smart cities).

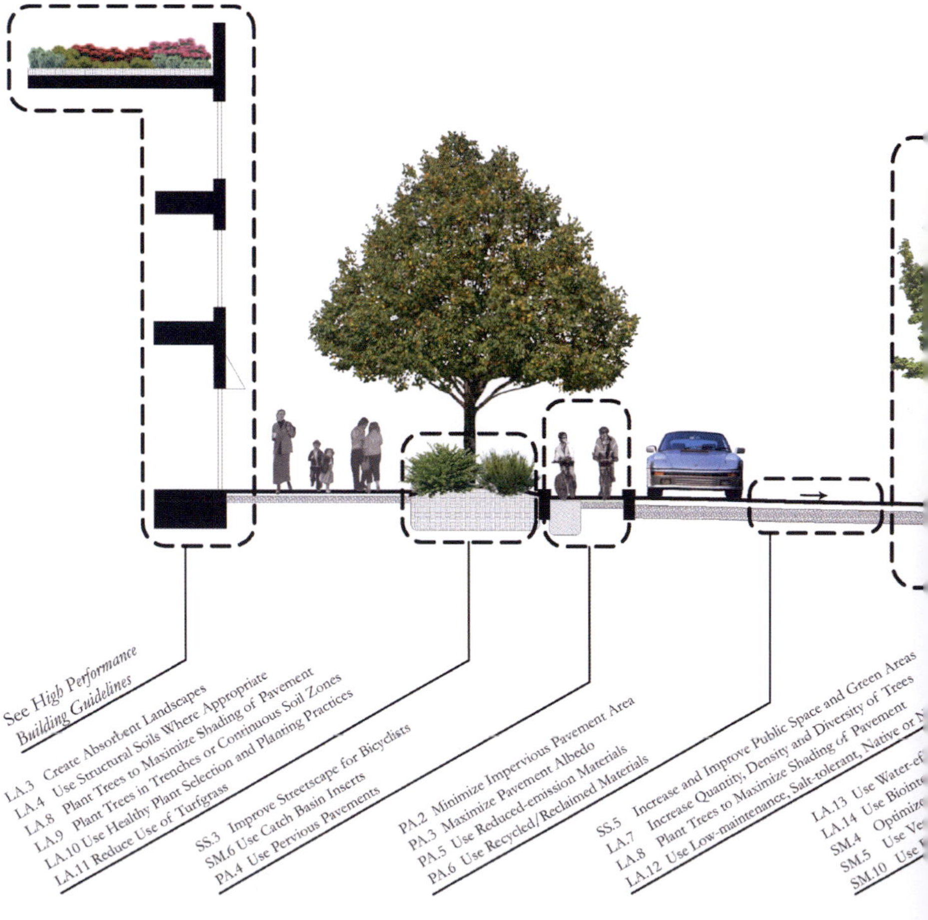
See High Performance Building Guidelines
LA.3 Create Absorbent Landscapes
LA.4 Use Structural Soils Where Appropriate
LA.8 Plant Trees to Maximize Shading of Pavement
LA.9 Plant Trees in Trenches or Continuous Soil Zones
LA.10 Use Healthy Plant Selection and Planting Practices
LA.11 Reduce Use of Turfgrass
SS.3 Improve Streetscape for Bicyclists
SM.6 Use Catch Basin Inserts
PA.4 Use Pervious Pavements
PA.2 Minimize Impervious Pavement Area
PA.3 Maximize Pavement Albedo
PA.5 Use Reduced-emission Materials
PA.6 Use Recycled/Reclaimed Materials
SS.5 Increase and Improve Public Space and Green Areas
LA.7 Increase Quantity, Density and Diversity of Trees
LA.8 Plant Trees to Maximize Shading of Pavement
LA.12 Use Low-maintenance, Salt-tolerant, Native or
LA.13 Use
LA.14 Use
SM.4
SM.5 Use
SM.10 Use

4.13b

"The suburban rings of our [US] cities have poor prospects in the future. They therefore represent a massive tragic misinvestment, perhaps the greatest misallocation of resources in the history of the world. It is hard to say how this stuff might be reused or retrofitted, if at all, but some of it, perhaps a lot, may end up as a combined salvage yard and sheer ruin."
JAMES KUNSTLER, A REFLECTION ON CITIES OF THE FUTURE (2006)

"If you plan cities for cars and traffic, you get cars and traffic. If you plan for people and places, you get people and places."
FRED KENT, PROJECT FOR PUBLIC SPACES

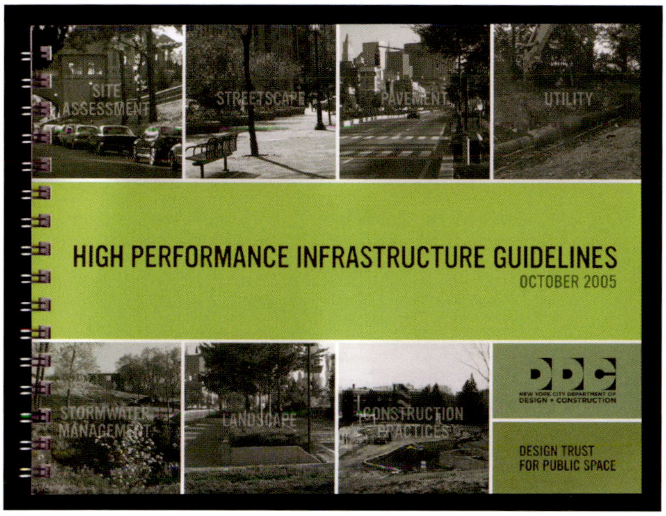

SITE ASSESSMENT
STREETSCAPE
PAVEMENT
UTILITY
HIGH PERFORMANCE INFRASTRUCTURE GUIDELINES
OCTOBER 2005
DDC
STORMWATER MANAGEMENT
LANDSCAPE
CONSTRUCTION PRACTICES
DESIGN TRUST FOR PUBLIC SPACE

4.13a

4.13a
4.13b
High Performance Infrastructure Guidelines: Best Practices for the Public Right-of-Way, Design Trust & New York City Department of Design and Construction, New York City, New York, USA, 2005
This handbook details sustainability practices for city streets, sidewalks, utilities, and urban landscaping and is a useful resource for planners, designers, engineers and public officials involved in constructing, operating and maintaining the right-of-way.

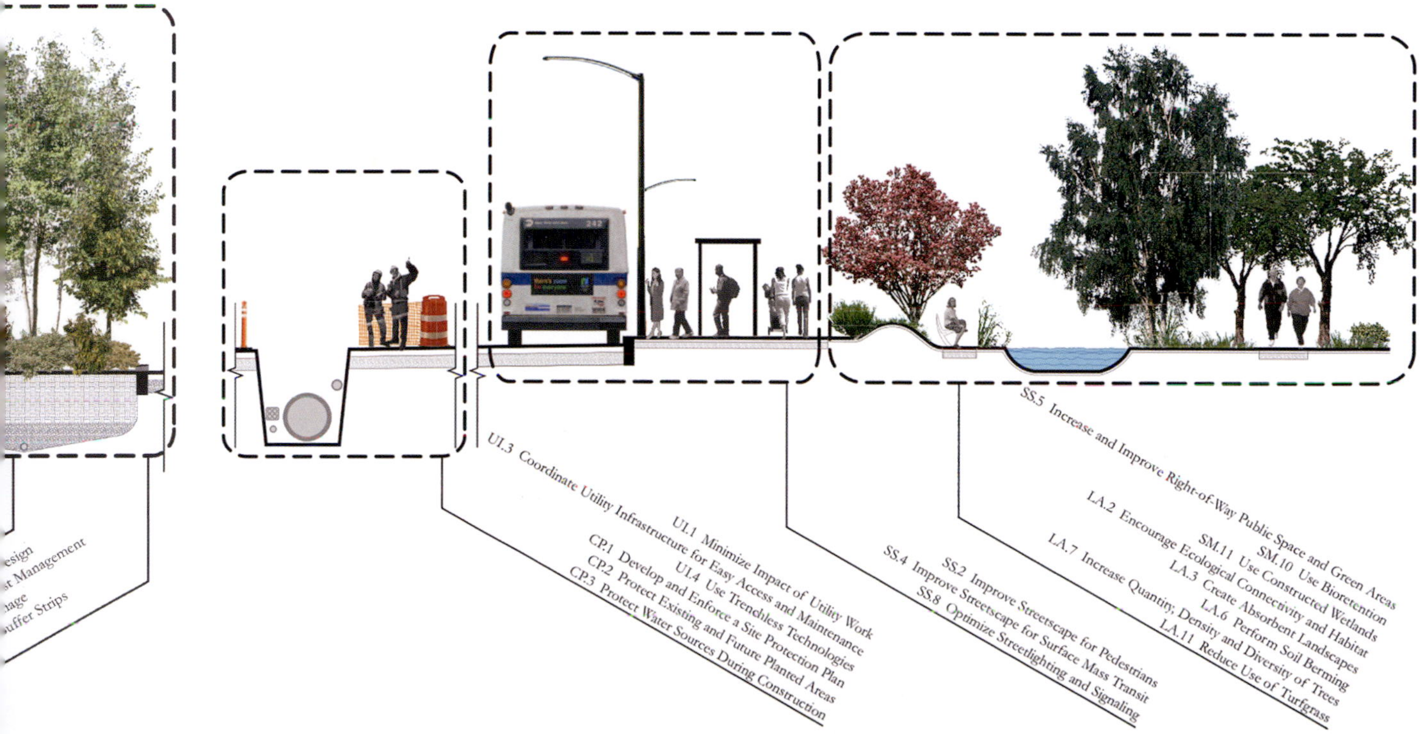

UI.3 Coordinate Utility Infrastructure for Easy Access and Maintenance
UI.1 Minimize Impact of Utility Work
UI.4 Use Trenchless Technologies
CP.1 Develop and Enforce a Site Protection Plan
CP.2 Protect Existing and Future Planted Areas
CP.3 Protect Water Sources During Construction
SS.4 Improve Streetscape for Surface Mass Transit
SS.2 Improve Streetscape for Pedestrians
SS.8 Optimize Streetlighting and Signaling
SS.5 Increase and Improve Right-of-Way Public Space and Green Areas
LA.2 Encourage Ecological Connectivity and Habitat
SM.10 Use Bioretention
SM.11 Use Constructed Wetlands
LA.3 Create Absorbent Landscapes
LA.7 Increase Quantity, Density and Diversity of Trees
LA.6 Perform Soil Berming
LA.11 Reduce Use of Turfgrass

Where are we headed?

Just as infrastructure systems for fossil fuel powered vehicles have rapidly risen to dominate the last century of urban planning and design, they may also dissipate and change form over the next century. Such a scenario requires repurposing in light of post-carbon agendas, resource scarcity and desire for safer, more sociable spaces. Reducing our dependence on cars and creating affordable, integrated and effective public transport systems will be a major component of 21st-century planning and design, requiring progressive and multidimensional transport solutions.

4.14
Curitiba, Brazil
Curitiba's bus rapid transit (BRT) system is considered an exemplar of public transport. The BRT includes 37 miles (60km) of median busways, carrying 70% of Curitiba's commuters per day (around 2 million people). Beginning in the 1970s and part of a master plan for radial transport corridors and integrated land use and density, the innovative BRT system enables efficient, affordable and pragmatic service (see Chapters 7 and 9).

Monte Moriá

4.14

"The continued expansion of new road and air infrastructure no longer makes any sense. The current forecasts of a massive increase in air and road travel over the next thirty years are based entirely on historical data, and may soon be rendered meaningless by peak oil. New airport terminals and major road developments run the risk of turning into expensive white elephants. Instead, we must start preparing for a probable contraction in all travel modes that depend on crude oil."
OIL DEPLETION ANALYSIS CENTER, PREPARING FOR PEAK OIL (2007)

"The whole systems approach looks at a broad range of problems ... The engineering mentality is always to take one issue at a time [hence] we lose the possibility of being really good designers ... If you ... only focus on how you move the most number of cars most efficiently, you get one type of street. If you think of the street as having many agendas, like walking, biking, cars, lingering, meeting, the ecology of street trees ... you design for all of them [and] get a much richer environment."
PETER CALTHORPE, INTERVIEW: ASLA (2011)

4.15
Tramway, Nantes, Pays de la Loire, France
Like many European cities, Nantes has an effective light rail network. Reintroduced from 1985 after removal in the 1950s, the 27 mile (43km), three line, 83 station tram network is part of a larger network spatially and hierarchically prioritizing sustainable initiatives. Features include: bus rapid transit; 1,000 share bicycles at over 100 stations; hundreds of kilometers of bicycle paths; minimized car parking; narrow private vehicle lanes; pedestrian priority; and expansion of sidewalks and public space.

BUS

4.15

4.16a
4.16b
4.16c
4.16d

River Torrens Linear Park, Land Systems & HASSELL, Adelaide Australia, 1978–1997

Totalling 11.6 square miles (30km^2), the 31 mile (50km) park was Australia's first linear park or greenway and a prime example of green infrastructure. Since colonization in 1836, dams have altered the once seasonal flows of the River Torrens (*Karra wirra-parri* in Kaurna language). Following mid-20th century suburbanization, landscape architecture prevailed over engineering to save the river from being converted into a concrete-lined, underground storm water pipe to mitigate flood risks below a major roadway.

Proposed in 1970s, the design divided the length into 26 sectors and was implemented from 1982–1997, costing $20 million (excluding the bespoke public transport corridor (the 'O-Bahn' express busway). State and local governments divided responsibility between land acquisition, environmental reinstatement and the transport corridor (state) and path system and ongoing maintence (local).

Multidimensional components include: flood mitigation; stormwater filtration: wetlands; revegetation and restoration; recreation and sport; and a vehicle-free pedestrian/cycle system. Revegetation has since strengthened remnant trees across a generous easement creating a meaningful green corridor linking the extensively vegetated Adelaide Hills across the plains to the coast. More recently, some local governments along the park have implemented planting strategies of indigenous shrubs and groundcovers to reduce the expanse the original design's often irrigated and mown lawn.

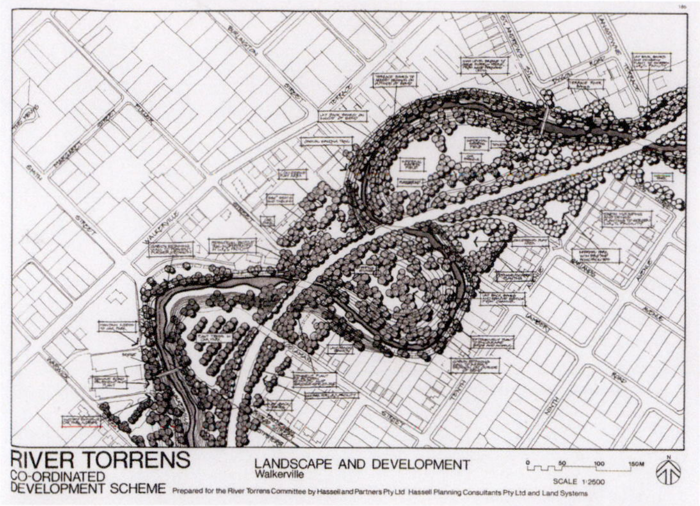
RIVER TORRENS
CO-ORDINATED
DEVELOPMENT SCHEME
LANDSCAPE AND DEVELOPMENT
Walkerville
SCALE 1:2500
Prepared for the River Torrens Committee by Hassell and Partners Pty Ltd Hassell Planning Consultants Pty Ltd and Land Systems

4.16a

4.16b

4.16c

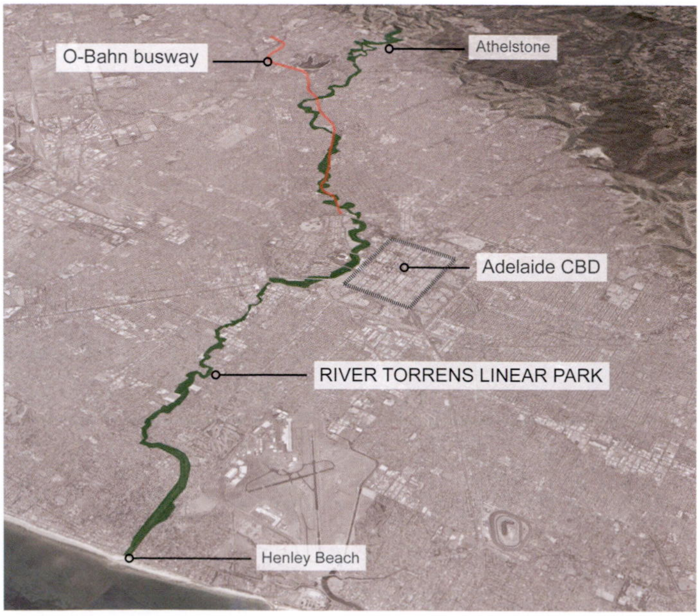
O-Bahn busway
Athelstone
Adelaide CBD
RIVER TORRENS LINEAR PARK
Henley Beach

4.16d

00766
한화증권

4.17a

은퇴설계의

4.17b

4.17a
4.17b

Cheonggyecheon Stream, Seoul, South Korea

This rare example of significant roadway reclamation (16 lanes) in a highly urbanized area prioritizes amenity and respite, significantly reducing urban heat island effect and offering urban corridor habitat to more than 40 bird and 20 fish species. The few pillars retained from the former highway stand as reminders of one of the city's most polluted areas, where traffic was further reduced by improving bus networks. Though on the site of a former stream, water from the Hangang River is pumped and treated, achieving permanent, significant flow but missing WSUD opportunities to cleanse the linear waterway's urban runoff and stormwater.

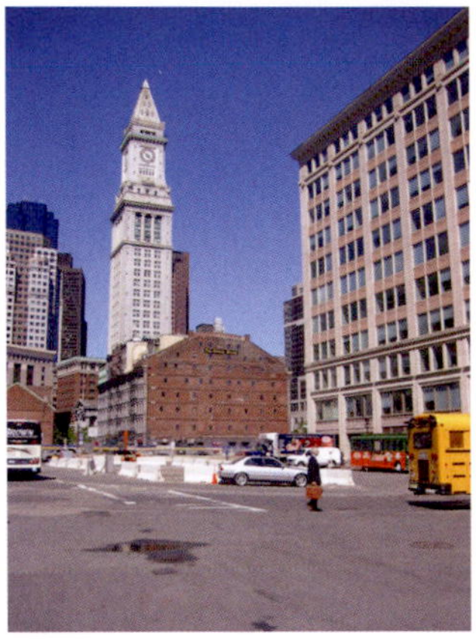

4.18a

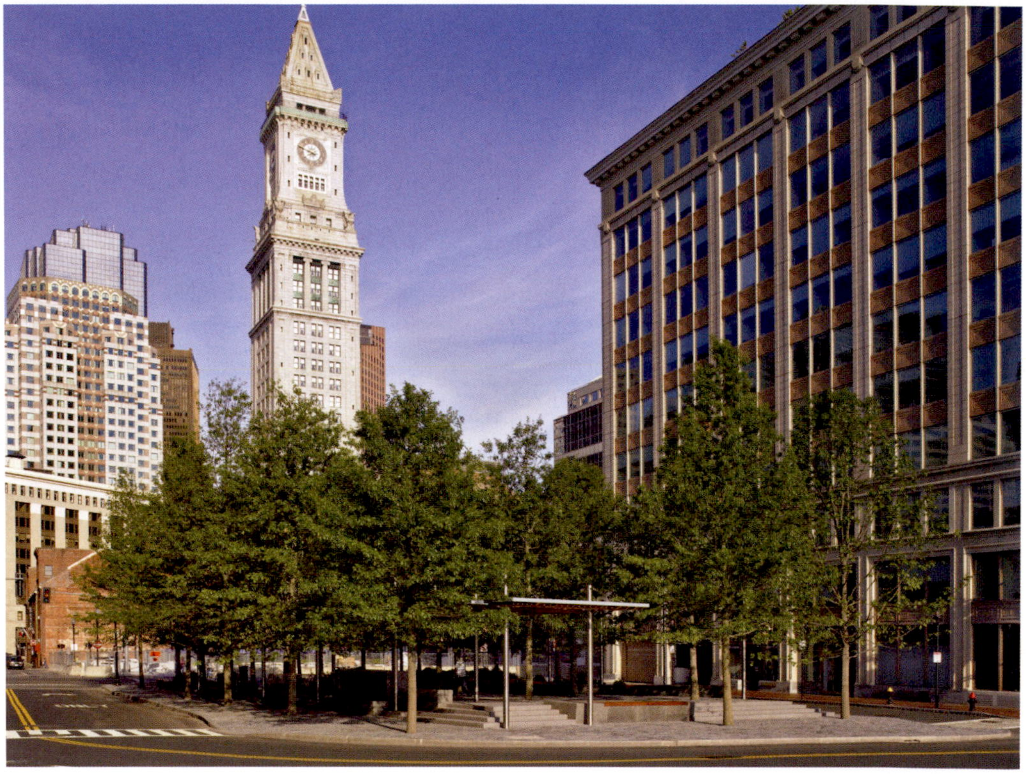

4.18b

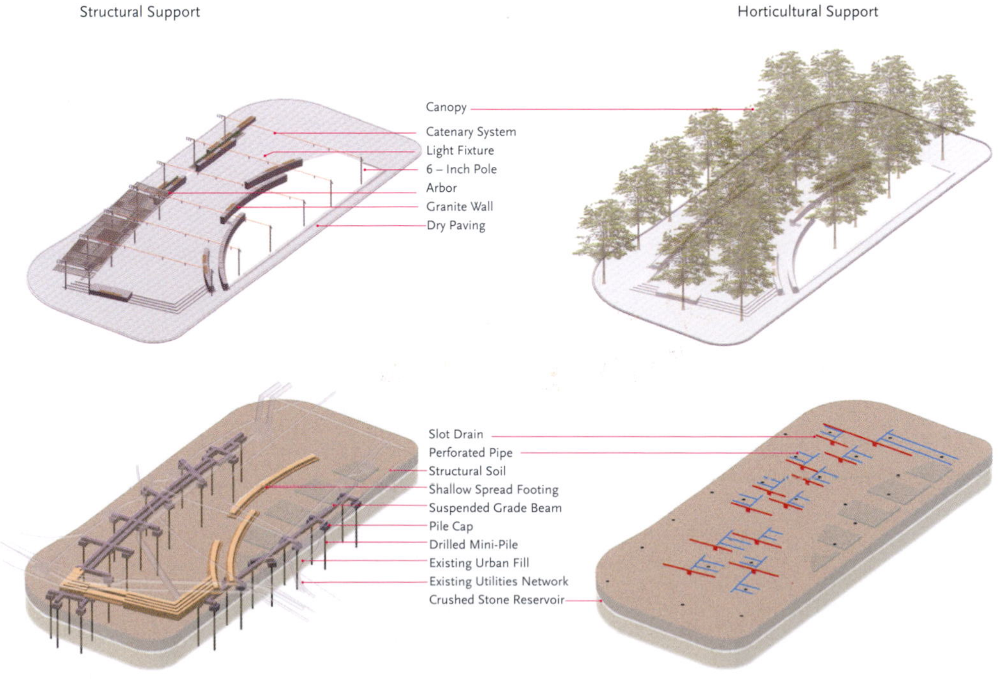
Structural Support
Horticultural Support
Canopy
Catenary System
Light Fixture
6 – Inch Pole
Arbor
Granite Wall
Dry Paving
Slot Drain
Perforated Pipe
Structural Soil
Shallow Spread Footing
Suspended Grade Beam
Pile Cap
Drilled Mini-Pile
Existing Urban Fill
Existing Utilities Network
Crushed Stone Reservoir

4.18c

4.18d

4.18a (Before)
4.18b
4.18c
4.18d

Central Wharf Plaza, Reed Hilderbrand, Boston, Massachusetts, USA, 2004–2008

Great cities possess great trees. A 4,000 square foot traffic island became a 13,000 square foot ($370m^2$/$1,200m^2$) plaza in part of what was once the busiest commercial port in North America, and mid 20th-century CE parking lot. Made possible through the Big Dig and the creation of the Kennedy Greenway, the densely planted island of 25 mixed-species oaks contrasts with nearly treeless adjacent areas, demonstrating the value of a high quality, below-grade infrastructure network and urban tree canopy stewardship.

Key benefits include: urban heat island mitigation (10.4°F average reduction at ground level); infiltrating all stormwater runoff for up to a 25-year, 24-hour storm event (369,000 annual gallons/1.4 million liters); annual carbon sequestration of over 3,600 pounds (over 1,600kg); 57% increased tree growth rate (compared to a typical urban oak by providing over 1,500 cubic feet of soil per tree); and high pedestrian usage (over 1,550 pedestrians observed in 5.5 hours (approximately 280 pedestrians per hour).

Backward dominance

At present, traditional traffic planning and engineering almost always takes precedence over 'cities for people', even with involvement from advocates for 'complete streets'. It is often difficult for landscape architects to influence transport planning and streetscape design, which can be dominated by traffic engineers, powerful and well-financed motoring lobbies who are solely concerned with vehicular volumes and rapidity of flow. Local businesses may believe that vehicles and parking are needed for their viability, yet complete streets regularly demonstrate economic (and social) vibrancy.

"Not everything that can be counted counts, and not everything that counts can be counted."
WILLIAM BRUCE CAMERON, INFORMAL SOCIOLOGY: A CASUAL INTRODUCTION TO SOCIOLOGICAL THINKING (1963)

"No city seems to have a department of people, pedestrians and public life, but I have seen lots of traffic departments with lots of statistics on cars in our cities."
JAN GEHL, LECTURE: CITIES FOR PEOPLE (2012)

"Good street design contributes both economic benefits and public value … investment in design quality brings quantifiable financial returns and people value improvements to their streets. Simply improving street design can make a major difference to market values. For the first time we can see that the best streets really are paved with gold."
CABE, PAVED WITH GOLD: THE REAL VALUE OF GOOD STREET DESIGN (2007)

"All around the world, highways are being torn down and waterfronts reclaimed; decades of thinking about cars and cities reversed; new public spaces created."
MICHAEL KIMMELMAN, IN MADRID'S HEART, PARK BLOOMS WHERE A FREEWAY ONCE BLIGHTED (2011)

"Portland, Oregon, has put in almost 200 miles of bike trails for the cost of one mile of urban freeway. This isn't an issue of retrofitting; it is often just a matter of changing the way we think about our most valuable public space: our street network. For too long, we have assumed that streets, paid for by all taxpayers, belong only to cars, and that the rest of us—bicyclists, pedestrians, sidewalk cafes, merchants, etc.—should have to compete for a small slice of sidewalk space."
EARL BLUMENAUER, THE DIRT, ASLA (2009)

Macro-micro

A clear vision directed on improving transport planning and design is required to span the breadth of scale from regional networks through to the detailed design of individual streetscapes. Otherwise, transport becomes a piecemeal jumble rather than a holistic and integrated system. The very nature of making cities less vehicular oriented often necessitates a gradual, incremental approach to retrofitting vehicular dominated environments and thus a clear, long-term strategy is crucial in realizing a coordinated network (see Copenhagen).

4.19

Copenhagen's Bicycle and Pedestrian Network, Denmark

Forty years ago, Copenhagen traffic was typical of any other city. Since the 1960s, the city instigated the slow and deliberate process of reducing parking and increasing car restrictions, pedestrian zones, (and later) car-free zones, raised streetside bicycle tracks, and off-road trails and bridges. This led to what is now one of the lowest European rates of car ownership, 200 miles (360km) of bicycle lanes, with new planned cycle superhighways. Over half the population cycles to work every day (around nine times more than Portland, Oregon, with the most cycle commuters in the US) and half of all inner-city trips are by bicycle—all in a city with a seasonally challenging climate for cycling. In 2014, Copenhagen was recognized as the 'European Green Capital' for its wider achievements such as clear harbor and drinking water and accessible green networks (96% of residents can reach a large green or blue area in less than 15 minutes).

4.19

4.20
Groningen's Bicycle Network, the Netherlands
Though Amsterdam is well known for its cycling presence (its canals, buildings and restrictive road dimensions having somewhat necessitated a cycle-friendly approach), Groningen (population 190,000) is regularly voted the Netherlands' most cycle friendly city. Since the 1970s, Groningen enacted policies to prioritize walking and cycling and discourage cars. Now, bicycle is often the fastest form of transport through the city center's pedestrianized streets and cycle lanes, with the central train station's 10,000 bicycle parks filling to capacity on weekends.

4.20

Where does it work well?

There are several examples of progressive transport networks (e.g. central Copenhagen, Denmark and Madrid, Spain). Various small cities and towns such as Ghent in Belgium, Oxford in the UK, the fledgling Masdar in the UAE and many historic city centers like Venice, Italy and Fez, Morocco (which were built long before motorized vehicles) maintain car-free areas. Some cities undertake temporary car-free measures on specific streets, on weekends or for special events (see Ecomobility). This is a strategy that can facilitate more permanent pedestrian-centric spaces and behavior over time. Alternative transport solutions such as light rail/trams (notable networks include Vienna, Austria; Prague, Czech Republic; Berlin, Germany; Budapest, Hungary; Bucharest, Romania; Toronto, Canada; and Melbourne, Australia), are being widely expanded, reinstated, installed and utilized, although this can prove slow, expensive and difficult. Very few examples of commendable transport systems exist in low density suburban environments, which through their dispersed patterning, almost preclude effective public transportation. Yet despite challenges, both the reclamation of vehicular lanes for light rail, buses, bicycles and taxi/car sharing/electric vehicles and the widening sidewalks for pedestrian safety, amenity and pedestrian-only zones are nonetheless gaining momentum.

4.21a

4.21b

4.21c

4.21d

4.21e

4.21f

4.21g

4.21h

4.21i

4.21j

Salón de Pinos

4.21k

4.21a (Before)
4.21b
4.21c (Before)
4.21d
4.21e (Before)
4.21f
4.21g (Before)
4.21h
4.21i
4.21j
4.21k

Madrid Rio, West 8, MRIO arquitectos (Burgos & Garrido, Porras La Casta, Rubio & A-Sala), Gines Garrido Colomero, Madrid, Spain, 2006–2011

This ambitious project, instigated by then mayor Alberto Ruiz-Gallardón, targeted Madrid's M-30 ring road motorway and undergrounded 26.7 miles (43km) of road within a single term of office (accruing significant infrastructure debt in the process). West 8's team were the only submission in the 2005 invited international competition to design the reclaimed area above the tunnel exclusively through landscape architecture. The '3 + 30' design divided the 198 acre (80ha) urban development into a trilogy of initial strategic projects for 47 subprojects initiated by the municipality, private investors and residents.

With a combined total budget of €410 million (around $450 million), the first subprojects were realised in 2007 and in April 2011 the entire project was complete and opened to the public. In addition to the various squares, boulevards and parks, a series of bridges improves connections between urban districts along the river.

Although tunnels add amenity at ground level, sustainable transport planning is required to reduce vehicular use (and negative effects of tunnel chimneys) and Madrid is implementing measures to reduce private vehicles, expand its car-free zone, increase affordable public transport networks, and redesign 24 of its busiest streets for pedestrians.

"Any bicycle lane that is unsafe for an 8 year old is not a bicycle lane."
ENRIQUE PEÑALOSA, INTERVIEW: THE PLAN (2012)

4.25a

CANBERRA100

4.25b

4.25a
4.25b
Canberra Centenary Trail, Harris Hobbs Landscapes & Fresh Landscape Design, Canberra, Australia, 2012–2013
Created to celebrate Canberra's centenary in 2013, this 90 mile (145km) walking/touring cycling loop through urban and rural areas provides spectacular views of native grasslands, woodlands and river environments. The project concentrated on approximately 18.6 miles (30km) of new trail sections needed to complete the loop and was carefully designed and constructed to navigate ecological constraints. It includes a non-vehicular access campground, bridges, photo points, interpretative signage and brings health and economic benefits to local communities.

Green street projects

While streetscape reconfigurations may represent small gains in increasing the sustainability of larger transport networks, they are nonetheless important signifiers of welcome change in repurposing vehicle-dominated transport environments. Streetscape design involves high attention to detail due to spatially constrained sites and complex concentrations of infrastructures. Competition for space amongst stakeholders and disciplines with competing interests frequently utilizes mediation skills of the landscape architect in realizing complete streets.

4.26

Vancouver Greenways and Streets, Canada

These linear public pedestrian/cycling corridors connecting parks, nature reserves, neighborhoods and retail areas are distinct from dedicated cycle lanes and resident-maintained neighborhood greenways. The Vancouver Greenways Plan (1991) by the Mayor's Urban Landscape Task Force and chaired by Landscape Architect Moura Quayle, designed this system of border-to-border streets, including: sidewalks, ramps, intersection controls, infiltration bulges, wayfinding, public plantings, benches, water fountains, and public art.

4.26

4.27a

4.27b

4.27c

4.27d

4.27a
4.27b
4.27c
4.27d

SEA Streets (Street Edge Alternatives) & Seattle Natural Drainage System, Seattle, USA, 1999–

Completed in 2001, Seattle's Street Edge Alternatives pilot project (SEA Streets) is designed to closely mimic the natural landscape prior to piped infrastructure systems. Two years of monitoring demonstrated that SEA Street reduced total stormwater runoff by 99%, through swales, 11% fewer impervious surfaces and over 100 evergreen trees and 1,100 shrubs. Seattle Public Utilities' subsequent project, Seattle Natural Drainage System, is part of ongoing stormwater and WSUD initiatives in collaboration with local residents.

4.28

4.28

Victoria Park Public Domain, NSW Government Architect's Office + HASSELL + Dr Tony Wong & Dr Peter Breen, Sydney, Australia, 2002

Originally a lagoon and swamp prior to European settlement and then brownfield, the 62 acre (25ha) public domain site fuses constructed ecologies with contemporary urbanism. The integrated design took advantage of inherent site constraints—Botany Basin sand formations, impermeable ancient swamp peat beds, the high water table, and the slight fall of the flat terrain—to overcome problems of ponding, flooding and a generally marshy land surface.

Street drainage is inverted, with dual carriageways draining inwards from the footpath edge to a saw tooth, permeable kerb and central bio-remediation swale. Water is filtered by sand beds, grasses and groundcovers, removing particulate matter and contaminants. The plantings, selected for drought and flood tolerance, assist nitrogenous waste uptake creating a root mat which keeps the sand filters stable and free draining. The bio-swale system treats first flush stormwater, while a system of weirs and inlets beneath pedestrian bridges across the swales capture excess flows. Subsurface pipes channel peak flows to the central park detention, falling to a sedimentation pond and constructed wetland set within a grove of paperbarks.

4.29a

4.29b

4.29a
4.29b
Haute Deûle Sustainable District, Atelier des paysages Bruel-Delmar, Quai Hegel, Lille, France, 2008–2015
The project's streets express the old Haute Deûle canal lines and irrigation ditches (Chapter 3). Stormwater collection and filtration is used across all surfaces in the district.

4.30

4.30

Cermak Road, Chicago, Illinois, USA 2009–2012

The two mile (3.2km) "greenest Street in America" (Chicago Department of Transport, 2013), cost $14 million to build 21% less than traditional road reconstruction. The project utilizes partially self-cleaning cement developed by the Vatican to keep their new churches clean (titanium dioxide treatment reacts with sunlight, breaking down nitrogen dioxide from exhaust gases). Green features include: 23% recycled asphalt and concrete (and 60% of construction waste recycled in other projects); a permeable surface; wind and solar operated LED street lighting; native plant bioswales; street trees; improved public transport; cycle lanes and a bicycle-sharing system.

4.31

4.32a (Before)
4.32b
4.32c
4.32d

Dutch Kills Green, WRT, Margie Ruddick Landscape, Marpillero Pollak Architects, Michael Singer Studio, 27th Street & Queens Plaza, Long Island City, Queens, New York, USA, 2011

Dutch Kills Green (Queens Plaza Pedestrian and Bicycle Improvement Project) is one of two pilot projects for New York City's High Performance Infrastructure Guidelines (Chapter 4). Formerly a dangerous tangle of elevated trains and bridges across a sea of asphalt roads and parking lots, the design integrates green space, a dedicated bike path, 206 new trees and grasses, stormwater filtration, public art and links Queens and Manhattan bikeways.

4.31

Lonsdale Street, TCL & DesignFlow, Dandenong, Melbourne, Victoria, Australia, 2011

This project forms part of a major street redevelopment prioritizing pedestrians/cyclists and creating garden rooms along the boulevard with lighting artwork. WSUD measures include: road median rain gardens, a treated water harvesting scheme irrigating vegetated road areas, and bioretention street tree pits on the pedestrian pathways.

4.32a

4.32b

4.32c

4.32d

"Landscape should be seen as the primary infrastructure which creates value directly and indirectly."
FARRELL REVIEW (2014)

ENERGY LANDSCAPES

Visual management

Landscape architectural involvement with energy infrastructures has traditionally been restricted to visual and scenic character considerations through 'visual resource management'/'visual management systems' and their contemporary counterparts, 'landscape visual impact assessment' (VIA/(L)VIA) and 'landscape character/scenic assessments' (LCA). A fundamental goal of these processes is to conceal, disguise or obscure large scale infrastructure, such as power plants, mines, quarries, highways, ports, airports, industrial zones, railways and industrial processes like forestry and agribusiness. Removing these 'eyesores' from ground/road level or residential view is seen to create pleasing, harmonious landscape aesthetics and increases economic/property values and tourism. Accordingly, successful visual management creates a deceptive view, hiding much of the industrialized reality of contemporary rural landscapes. This has been partially counteracted in recent decades through widespread public access to aerial photography (such as Google Earth/Maps) that reveals 'hidden' infrastructures.

Misrepresentation

Misrepresenting or intentionally concealing everyday, essential landscape processes hinders rather than assists environmental outcomes by providing misinformation (and hence misunderstanding), a false view of reality and furthering disconnect between our lifestyles and the energy required to sustain them. Greenhouse gas (GHG) reducing renewable energy infrastructures (solar, wind, tidal farms) require large spatial footprints and surface areas to meaningfully contribute to the extensive amount of energy production required through electricity consumption. Yet public preference routinely impinges their acceptance in the landscape, as concealment of small numbers of grey infrastructures has been feasible while camouflaging large renewable energy infrastructures is not. Consequently, (L)VIA favors singular and discrete infrastructures (a coal/gas/nuclear power plant) over a diffuse scattering (wind/solar farm) to minimize visual and character 'impact', and therefore concentrated finite fossil fuels over less energy dense renewable resources.

Visual or environmental baseline?

Because (L)VIA and LCA examine the extent of change by using the existing character as baseline, they can assume that it is desirable or, more pertinently, performing optimally (some regions, such as Scotland, are addressing this shortcoming). They primarily apply to new projects, while ubiquitous existing infrastructures (existing electricity transmission towers, roads, 'unsightly' features) and monocultural, ecologically sterile landscapes (industrialized agriculture, grazing landscapes) can escape interrogation due to unconscious familiarization. While aesthetics and sustainability performance need not be mutually exclusive, shifting the dominant perceptions of landscape beauty to align with the Anthropocene epoch's pressing concerns (climate change mitigation, decreasing finite resource consumption and lessening hazardous waste burdens for future generations) will improve sustainability outcomes (Chapter 6).

"The landscape we see in the built world is a veneer. What we consider solid ground is actually a contrived set of impressions and solutions."
JANE AMIDON, RADICAL LANDSCAPES: REINVENTING OUTDOOR SPACE (2001)

"Energy = Space. Without those handy little packages of gas, oil and coal from below the surface, we can only get energy from sources on the surface. Because of the 'low energy density' above ground, this switch requires radical new ways of thinking in terms of urban planning and the development of the built-up environment."
ANDY VAN DEN DOBBELSTEEN, URBAN METABOLISM (2014)

"For [James] Corner, the narrow agenda of ecological advocacy that many landscape architects profess to is nothing more than a rear-guard defense of a supposedly autonomous 'nature' conceived to exist *a priori*, outside of human agency or cultural construction. In this context, current-day environmentalism and pastoral ideas of landscape appear to Corner, and many others, as naïve or irrelevant in the face of global urbanization."
CHARLES WALDHEIM, THE LANDSCAPE URBANISM READER (2006)

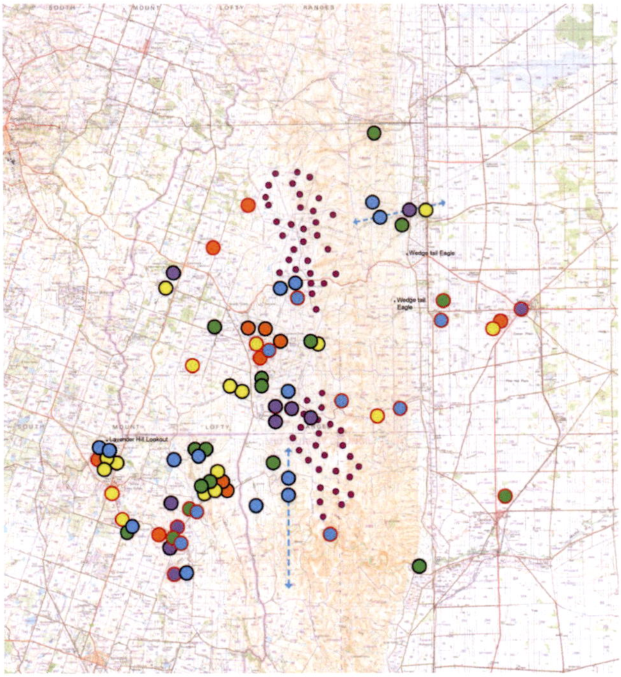

4.33a

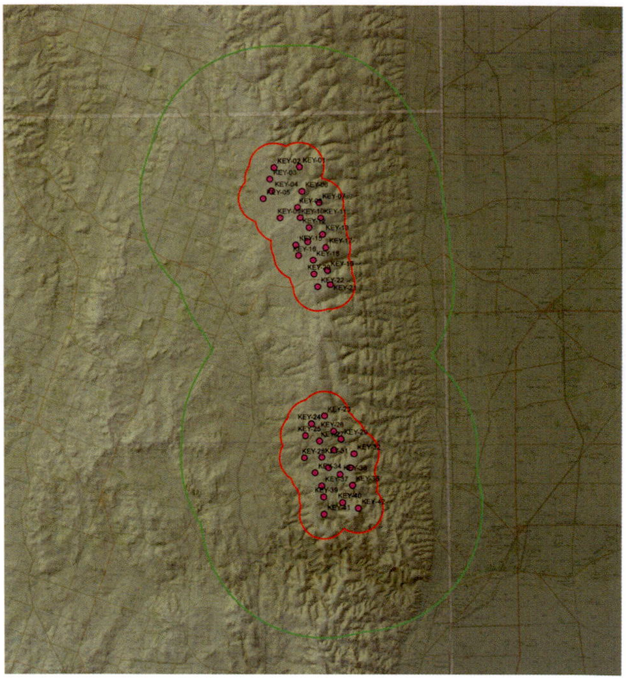

4.33b

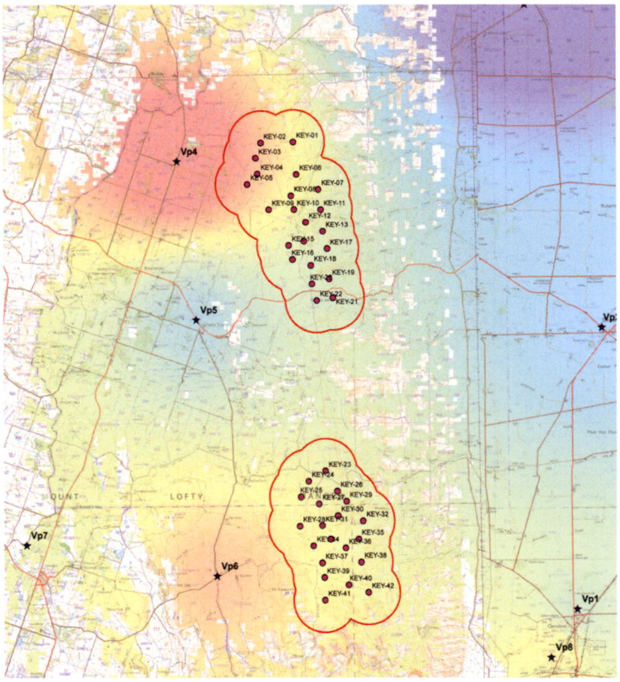
Vp4
Vp5
Vp6
Vp7
Vp1
Vp8

4.33c

4.33d

4.33a
4.33b
4.33c
4.33d

Keyneton Wind Farm, Brett Grimm Landscape Architect & WAX Design, Eden Valley, South Australia, 2011

The visual assessment for a 42 turbine wind farm considered the landscape character and potential visual effect. This comprised of:

a. *Community cognitive mapping*: community engagement mapped the landscape values to provide baseline landscape character interpretation, degree of sensitivity and scenic quality.

b. *Digital terrain model*: GIS topographic profile of ridgelines, promontories, valleys and drainage catchments are correlated to the design of the turbine array.

c. *Visual effect assessment interpolation*: GIS mapping is used to provide a distance weighted relative visual impact layer. The 'GrimKe matrix methodology' is used to evaluate the visual impact from various viewpoints and is cartographically mapped.

d. *Photomontage and wire line*: GPS validated photomontages are developed to represent the proposed development from key public viewing locations.

4.34
German bio-energy villages
Jühnde was the first of several German bio-energy villages (Mauenheim, Bollewick, Feldheim, Strohen and Bad Oldesloe). Renewable biomass (woodchips, silage, animal manure) supplies residents with heat and electricity (co-generation), effectively producing twice as much energy production as consumption.

4.34

Walking the talk

Renewable energy installations can bring landscape architects' spatial skills to the fore and test claims of contributing to a more sustainable society and development. The urgency to break dependence on non-renewable, polluting energy sources (oil, coal, natural gas, uranium) necessitates stewardship, advocacy and leadership to mediate the challenging and politicized process of mass-implementation of renewable energy.

4.35

Stacking functions to mitigate subsidies

Improved rural land management is needed to mitigate urban areas' intensive demands (Chapter 2). A traditionally romantic, pastoral idyll still commonly dominates conceptions of the 'countryside' in many nations, freezing it in an archaic vision. Many rural landscapes are monocultures, missing opportunities to stack functions, such as combining grazing/agriculture, ecology/conservation and wind/solar farms on one site. Income produced through leases to power generators can mitigate government and taxpayer subsidies directed to land-rich landowners for single purpose grazing (as occurs in most of Britain, with many governments worldwide also subsidizing fossil fuel energy generation). To further enhance multidimensional outcomes, agricultural subsidies (such as those in the EU) would be adjusted to incorporate conservation and ecological restoration areas as opposed to current regulations dictating blanket pasture coverage for subsidy eligibility (as in the UK).

4.35
Swansea Tidal Lagoon Power Plant, LDA Design, Swansea Bay, UK, 2012–
View from the western seawall towards the bay. The 6-mile (9.6km) long seawall will house underwater turbines.

The proposed (at the time of writing) tidal power plant is claimed to be the world's first purpose built tidal energy project, covering approximately 2,930 acres (1,185 ha). The Nationally Significant Infrastructure Project (NSIP) will establish itself as a sailing and visitor destination and with a 120 year design life, is expected to generate 500GWh of annual electricity (equivalent to powering 155,000 homes). LDA's major roles within the interdisciplinary team included landside and lagoon masterplanning; objectives and operational framework; project design coordination and Development Consent Order application; design documentation; land negotiation planning support; public consultation; and strategic review of the EIA.

Who leads renewable?

Some countries, such as Denmark, Portugal, Spain and Germany have more substantially embraced solar and wind power as higher proportions of their overall energy generation, where accordingly, offshore and onshore wind and solar farms form part of the contemporary coastal and landscape visual matrix. This is not always based on aesthetic preferences or a progressive environmental outlook; it can be a result of the lack of domestic fossil fuel resources or an unwillingness to reply on imported energy supply.

Waste to energy

'Waste to energy' (W2E) plants are being increasingly implemented in many cities, whereby garbage is incinerated to produce electricity (and sometimes heat and gas). The European Union has over 450 W2E plants in operation (particularly prevalent in countries with limited land area). These plants are an improvement over archaic garbage incineration that lacks electricity/heat/gas production and arguably, sending waste to landfill, which results in groundwater pollution and methane release (methane is exponentially worse as a GHG than CO_2 and even where landfill methane energy production is in place a significant amount escapes to air (see Fresh Kills, Vall d'en Joan, Chapter 3)). Amsterdam's W2E and water filtration plants have been coupled to increase synergies and efficiency (see Waternet, Chapter 9). Though an evolution, W2E is still part of the single facility, engineering/technological approach to infrastructural design and can discourage more sustainable processes such as recycling. Thus, W2E is less preferable to sophisticated garbage, recycling and composting sorting systems (such as in areas of Germany and Europe) and 'zero-waste' initiatives run by some municipal governments (such as in parts of the USA (notably San Francisco) and Australia), which facilitate high resource recovery rates (Austria, Germany, the Netherlands and Belgium), behavioral change and create significant employment.

4.36a
4.36b
4.36c

Amager Bakke Waste to Energy Plant, BIG Architects, TOPOTEK 1, ManMadeLand, Copenhagen, Denmark, 2011–

Copenhagen's existing waste-to-energy plant is Europe's oldest (almost 50), burning up to 400,000 tons of yearly waste. Now under construction, BIG's design for Copenhagen's new plant incorporates public space and access, most notably through a 7.7 acre (31,000m²) ski slope/hill. Day-pass purchase allows access and bus routes and cycle paths are proposed to improve access.

4.36a

4.36b

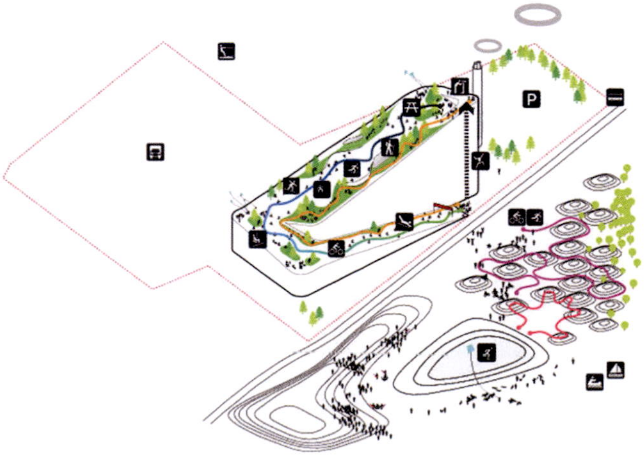

4.36c

STUDY/DISCUSSION QUESTIONS

Outline the pros and cons of both centralized and decentralized infrastructure systems. What approach would form an ideal solution?

Brainstorm opportunities for 'greening' infrastructure. For example:

What opportunities exist in urban, suburban, peri-urban and rural locations?

Should we shift focus from increasing supply of energy/electricity or to strategies to reduce energy demand and consumption?

What strategies can be employed to shift the debate on energy projects beyond merely visual and 'character' impact? How can other factors be prioritized in assessment?

Develop strategies for improving the EIS (Environmental Impact Statement) process that allows for alternative solutions or projects.

What barriers exist to realizing integrated and systematic transport planning? What are possible solutions to these?

Should we seek to reduce the dominance of private motor vehicles in urban centers? Why? Why does this prove challenging?

What strategies could be employed to demonstrate to stakeholders that pedestrian and cyclist friendly streets are also good for commerce?

Is evidence-based, technical knowledge important in streetscape planning and design? Why?

Find best practice examples of:

- the 'complete streets' approach;
- an exemplary public transport network with multiple modes;
- cycle friendly city;
- shared street network;
- widespread WSUD/SuDS streetscape network;
- renewable energy infrastructure incorporated into towns/cities.

What are ways to ensure that rapidly developing cities and economies don't repeat the mistakes that many developed cities are now trying to rectify?

FURTHER READING

Adger, W., Lorenzoni, I. and O'Brien, K. (2010) *Adapting to climate change: thresholds, values, governance*, Cambridge: Cambridge University Press.

Austin, G. (2014) *Green infrastructure for landscape planning: integrating human and natural systems*, Abingdon, Oxon: Routledge.

Benedict, M. and Mcmahon, E. (2006) *Green infrastructure: linking landscapes and communities*, Washington DC: Island Press.

Farr, D. (2008) *Sustainable urbanism: urban design with nature*, Hoboken, NJ: Wiley.

Gehl J. (2010) *Cities for people*, Washington: Island Press.

Landscape Institute (2013) *Guidelines for landscape and visual impact assessment*, Third Edition, Oxon, UK: Routledge.

Maas, W. (1999) *Metacity datatown*, Rotterdam: MVRDV/010 Publishers.

Pollalis, S., Schodek, D., Georgoulias A. and Ramos, S. (eds) (2012) *Infrastructure Sustainability and Design*, Oxon, UK: Routledge.

Rouse, D. (2013) *Green Infrastructure: a landscape approach*, Chicago, IL: American Planning Association.

Sarté, S. (2010) *Sustainable infrastructure: the guide to green engineering and design*, Hoboken, NJ: Wiley.

Sijmons, D., Hugtenburg, J., Hoorn, A. V. and Feddes, F. (2014) *Landscape and energy: designing transition*, Rotterdam: Nai010 Publishers.

Stremke, S. and Dobbelsteen, A. (2013) *Sustainable energy landscapes: designing, planning, and development*, Boca Raton, FL: Taylor & Francis.

Tumlin, J. (2012) *Sustainable transportation planning: tools for creating vibrant, healthy, and resilient communities*, Hoboken, NJ: Wiley.

ADDITIONAL PROJECTS

You might also like to look for further information on the following projects:

100 Resilient Cities, Rockefeller Foundation, 2013–

Bay Area Climate Change Education Needs Assessment Report, Institute at the Golden Gate, 2014

Climate Change Adaptation Toolkit, Net Balance, 2012

Landscape Succession Strategy, Melbourne Gardens, 2016–2036

Street Design Manual, New York City Department of Transportation, New York, USA, 2009 and 2013

Elmer Avenue Neighborhood Retrofit, Stivers & Associates, Los Angeles, California, USA, 2010

Desert Claim Wind Project, Jones & Jones, Kittitas County, Washington, USA.

INTERVIEW Dirk Sijmons

Professor Dirk Sijmons was appointed as the first State Landscape Architect of the Netherlands (2004–2008) and is Chair of Landscape Architecture at TU-Delft University. In 1990, he co-founded H+N+S Landscape Architects, which received the Prince Bernard Culture award in 2001, and in 2002 he received the Rotterdam-Maaskant award. Professor Sijmons has worked for several government ministries and the State Forestry Service and curated IABR-2014 with the theme *Urban-by-Nature*. His book publications in English are *Landscape* (1998) and *Greetings from Europe* (2008), and most recently, *Landscape and Energy* (2014).

What led to the Netherlands appointing a State Advisor on Landscape or a State Landscape Architect, given that this uncommon in most other parts of the world?

A strong, socially democratically-inspired institutional design approach existed following the Second World War until the beginning of the 1990s in all kinds of state institutions, such as the State Forestry Service (where I was Head of Landscape Architecture). This slowly faded away in the wake of global neo-liberalization. To compensate this loss (and the work either becoming privatized or vanishing altogether), a State Landscape Architect position was created to advise the ministers and to let Parliament know that we are still involved and worried about landscape matters and their new ventures.

While privatization and global neo-liberalization might seem like a rather negative approach, a very positive outcome came from it. The Netherlands had and continues to have a strong tradition in architectural policy. We have had a State Architect for over 200 years. Architectural policy, over time, evolved from architecture itself, to policy of architecture and urbanism, to the jump of architecture, urbanism and landscape architecture. Following this broad trajectory, the State Architect needed the help of some 'right hands'. I was invited to be the first State Landscape Architect, while another colleague worked on large infrastructure and another on cultural heritage within the portfolio.

During your time as State Advisor on Landscape, what key themes did you focus on? Did you have the scope to determine these yourself, or were they informed by your boss/the Minister?

My direct political boss (as I was independent) was the Minister of Agriculture, Natural Affairs and Landscape. I was able to offer unsolicited advice but was also asked to advise on issues (for example, the up-scaling of dairy farming following concerns about industrialization of the countryside). I jumped on the wagon with two elements I considered the largest concerns we are facing, both linked to climate change: firstly, the adaptation of our country to rising sea levels (and the resultant character change of our rivers) and secondly, the mitigation of the problem by trying to reduce CO_2 emissions (synonymous with the transition to renewable energy solutions).

Did you encounter any general resistance to change or reactions based on visual impact on the landscape?

There are all kinds of fears and emotions projected onto spatial effects. I was recently very surprised at the enormously emotional response to wind turbines in parts of the world such as in Australia, which I think has to do with people feeling that we are at the end of what Peter Sloterdijk calls the "era of fossil expressionism" and are very uncertain about what the future will bring (even to the extent of the diagnosis of new bodily diseases resulting from wind-farms—a phenomenon similar to mid-nineteenth century recordings to the response to train travel—which soon disappeared). My intuition though, is that when you dig a bit deeper, we all need to get used to the change from energy being a plume on the horizon from an enormous coal or gas power-plant whereby we only had to flick a switch in our homes to access it, to energy becoming decentralized and closer to our direct living environment. It's a very new phenomenon.

Do you think that we should be focusing on more decentralization and self-sufficiency?

Decentralization is an option and a real asset for people to take power into their own hands: it is therefore not only *electrical* power that is to be decentralized, but *real* power. Ultimately, we need to establish equilibrium between top down and bottom up elements, because we can't do much without the grid that has to be completely retrofitted. We also need to be able to mitigate or store energy when above 25% renewables are deployed due to production fluctuation. Some of the infrastructure will be big, some small. Tesla are already producing hydrogen cells for domestic use, but that won't solve the problem completely, as we also need economies of scale. In our part of the world, wind energy will be the main player, in Southern Europe, solar energy. What is required is an exploration of very large scale, centralized, wind turbines parks on the North Sea which is a fantastic possibility and investment opportunity.

Traditionally, this process would have been led by engineering. Are landscape architects and planners taking an increased interest due to the scale of harnessing renewable above ground energies as opposed to in-ground fossil fuels?

I think we as landscape architects must take an increased interest, as all the discussions are about space and horizon and spatial quality. We have a large role to play but we must take it and we must conquer it because the energy world—whether it be centralized or very decentralized—does not automatically have the phone number of their friendly neighborhood landscape architect in their address books so we have to show that our discipline can bring extra value to the field. I am absolutely dedicated to help conquer these new types of commissions for landscape architects.

How do you think we can improve the collaboration between technical experts such as engineers and spatial experts like landscape architects to focus on sustainability initiatives?

First and foremost, the energy world is a very technical world. Space is not on the critical path in a quantitative way, perhaps with the exception of biomass production, which is a very different topic. In its more symbolic guise as landscape, suddenly space *is* on the critical path because of broad public reactions and resistance (in Amsterdam, for example, we have an action group trying to save traditional roofs from being conquered by blue photovoltaic cells). Landscape architects can mediate to show that by designing the receiving landscape, for instance, wind turbines have to be placed and thus show that there is a difference between good and bad design. We must not, however, be overly ambitious in believing we can solve the problem or bring the discussion to a halt through mere good design. I do believe that bridging being in the field and bringing together discussions between the people affected and the technicians is an important place for us to be and role to play.

When you were acting as State Advisor, was it challenging to integrate this broad, interconnected thinking into more short term political and planning cycles?

In the energy field, yes, I think we are only at the very start of discussions. Beyond the spatial, I believe that landscape architects can also play a cultural and emotional role in 'national therapy' following the changes to our energy system. That aside, I believe we have been especially successful working at the frontier of adaptation. A key instance is that of linking hydrological effectiveness, robustness and aesthetic fullness through our large national river program (encompassing 34 projects that are part of the 'Room for the River' project). As a State Advisor when this project was being devised, I had the opportunity to broaden the discussion by saying that we not only have to improve our water safety but also have the ambition to increase the beauty of the river area and increase land-use functions such as leisure, nature reserves and urban planning. The success of the project was assisted by a long-term vision of the effects of climate change on our low-lying country and narrow watercourses and a long history of debates about spatial quality, together with collaboration between hydrological engineers and landscape architects.

In the Anthropocene and as landscape architects, what other key issues should we be focusing on?

One of the reasons that Paul Crutzen introduced and coined the term 'the Anthropocene', was the change of land-use all over the globe, not only through urbanization but also the reclamation of wild-lands. While I was curating International Architecture Biennale Rotterdam in 2014, I therefore tried to focus on divining urban conditions as containing not only the built-up areas, but also those of food-production, leisure, nature, strip-mining, airfields (and so on) and to view them as one large artifact, perhaps our biggest. This is a new way of working for landscape architects, because urban densities are decreasing the world over and we urgently need to find sustainable solutions. Vitally, for planners perhaps even more than for landscape architects, we need to review the 'automatic pilot' of urban land-use, whereby due to the high market value of urban land, agriculture shifts to reclaim wild areas. Instead, we need to find peaceful configurations of urban landscapes where water production, nature and leisure can have their relatively stable position. Future commissions are likely mirror those such as in Europe and parts of the United States where ecoducts are being built to address disconnections such as those between fresh and salt water.

You suggested that planning perhaps needs to take more control of some of these economic issues which have more recently have been left to the market. Do you think we need to try to help the process of reclaiming control of how the city evolves?

We can no longer go back to the heyday of what in Holland we call 'the era of makeability'—that is, that we can make everything and solve all our problems through spatial means. You could in a way, think along the lines (and I'm not sure whether this is in the scope of landscape architects or planners), that as capitalism is unlikely to radically change we must refine the market within the capitalist system. One such example is the change of a value-added tax to a carbon tax as a sound way of making CO_2 emissions fiscal. These are the kind of measures—like decentralizing the CO_2 market—that we need in order to create tail-wind for the sustainability movement to make positive changes in time.

Is this part of an increasing urgency around these key issues?

We are moving very slowly in the Netherlands in combatting climate change. Holland is, I believe, in 34th place in-between Latvia and Bulgaria (perhaps partly due to our very strong fossil-fuels lobby). In my book *Landscape and energy: designing transition*, I outline what would need to be done in order to reach our goals. We are not moving anywhere near fast enough to combat the urgency of staying under 450 million ppm—in fact, we have already passed the 400 million ppm. The movement simply doesn't have enough momentum yet.

You've have had a very successful career—what insight or advice would you give to young, emerging landscape architects and planners?

I would advise them to not only look at spatial form but to look 'under the hood' to see what processes are steering these forms and how these can be influenced, by singling them out and looking at the landscape expression that they could give. I observe that there are a lot of formative forces that only need the landscape architect's magic wand in order to make their contribution to landscape formation. Ultimately, landscape is a living entity and it is the role of the landscape architect or planner to work, upkeep and constantly garden.

Do you think that landscape architects or other professional organisations should be more active in counter-lobbying?

There is a line of where the responsibility of a discipline lays and I'm not entirely sure if it is right to overstep it, despite having pushed that boundary often during my working career. Do landscape architects just accept a client's commission and execute it well? It is certainly also a legitimate professional view. My opinion has always been that the landscape architect's job is to mediate between humankind and nature. Not only does this have a symbolic meaning and expression but also one at the core of our discipline and on this basis, we might have a legitimate right of entry into the discussion.

5.1
Sheep Grazing in Central Park, circa 1935
Food and productive systems existed in urban areas until relatively recently. Although small interventions are returning in many developed cities, medium and large-scale agriculture is largely absent or diminishing.

5
LANDSCAPE AND FOOD

Landscape architects, planners and architects have become increasingly engaged in key issues, policies, legislative mechanisms and projects regarding the planning, security, sovereignty, integrity, locality and design of food systems and urban agriculture. Reversing a trend of over half a century of exclusion and discouragement in the global north, these activities are expanding existing token areas of community gardens, allotments and small foodscapes. These bolster the resilience of the problematic global food system to increase food security, agrobiodiversity, and food sovereignty. Planning is essential in improving how and where we produce food, while landscape architects need to develop their ability to instigate and execute successful urban and peri-urban food interventions and expand from the limiting ornamental plant legacy.

FOOD SYSTEMS

Since the Neolithic Revolution around 12,000 years ago, food production and settlements retained strong proximity until the onset of the agricultural Green Revolution in the mid 20th century. Unprecedented changes in agricultural systems in the past century have led to dramatic change in the way we live and inhabit the Earth. In 1960, the world's population stood at 3 billion people and now passes 7 billion. Feeding 4 billion extra people is an extraordinary agricultural feat, but one with highly questionable long-term sustainability and extensive negative impacts on the Earth's living systems. During this time, planning and policy in most developed cities discouraged or excluded urban agriculture through non-sympathetic legislation and zoning, failing to protect valuable metropolitan agricultural land from development and other land uses that have, in many cases, rendered soils toxic and infertile.

"The first supermarket supposedly appeared on the American landscape in 1946. That is not very long ago. Until then, where was all the food? Dear folks, the food was in homes, gardens, local fields, and forests. It was near kitchens, near tables, near bedsides. It was in the pantry, the cellar, the backyard."
JOEL SALATIN, FOLKS, THIS AIN'T NORMAL: A FARMER'S ADVICE FOR HAPPIER HENS, HEALTHIER PEOPLE, AND A BETTER WORLD (2011)

"Fine fruit is the flower of commodities. It is the most perfect union of the useful and the beautiful that the earth knows. Trees full of soft foliage; blossoms fresh with spring bounty; and, finally, fruit, rich, bloom-dusted, melting, and luscious."
ANDREW JACKSON DOWNING, THE FRUIT AND FRUIT TREES OF AMERICA (1845)

"Food is energy. And it takes energy to get food. These two facts, taken together, have always established the biological limits to the human population and always will."
RICHARD HEINBERG, WHAT WILL WE EAT AS THE OIL RUNS OUT (2005)

"Edible, adj.: Good to eat, and wholesome to digest, as a worm to a toad, a toad to a snake, a snake to a pig, a pig to a man, and a man to a worm."
AMBROSE BIERCE, THE DEVIL'S DICTIONARY (1911)

"Sometimes a population grows so rapidly that it overshoots carrying capacity before negative feedback can stop the increase. If a population overshoots, it usually depletes its food so severely that negative feedback in the form of more deaths and fewer births quickly reduces it below carrying capacity."
GERRY MARTEN, HUMAN ECOLOGY: BASIC CONCEPTS FOR SUSTAINABLE DEVELOPMENT (2001)

"Globalisation, which attempts to amalgamate every local, regional, and national economy into a single world system, requires homogenising locally adapted forms of agriculture, replacing them with an industrial system—centrally managed, pesticide-intensive, one-crop production for export—designed to deliver a narrow range of transportable foods to the world market."
HELENA NORBERG-HODGE, FROM THE GROUND UP: RETHINKING INDUSTRIAL AGRICULTURE (2001)

"How could intelligent beings seek to control a few unwanted species by a method that contaminated the entire environment and brought the threat of disease and death even to their own kind?"
RACHEL CARSON, SILENT SPRING (1962)

5.2
Leberecht Migge
German landscape architect, regional planner, writer and self-titled 'architect for horticulture' Leberecht Migge championed self-sufficiency through small family gardens and social gardening principles. This 1932 diagram portrays how settlement food gardens could expand as families grew.

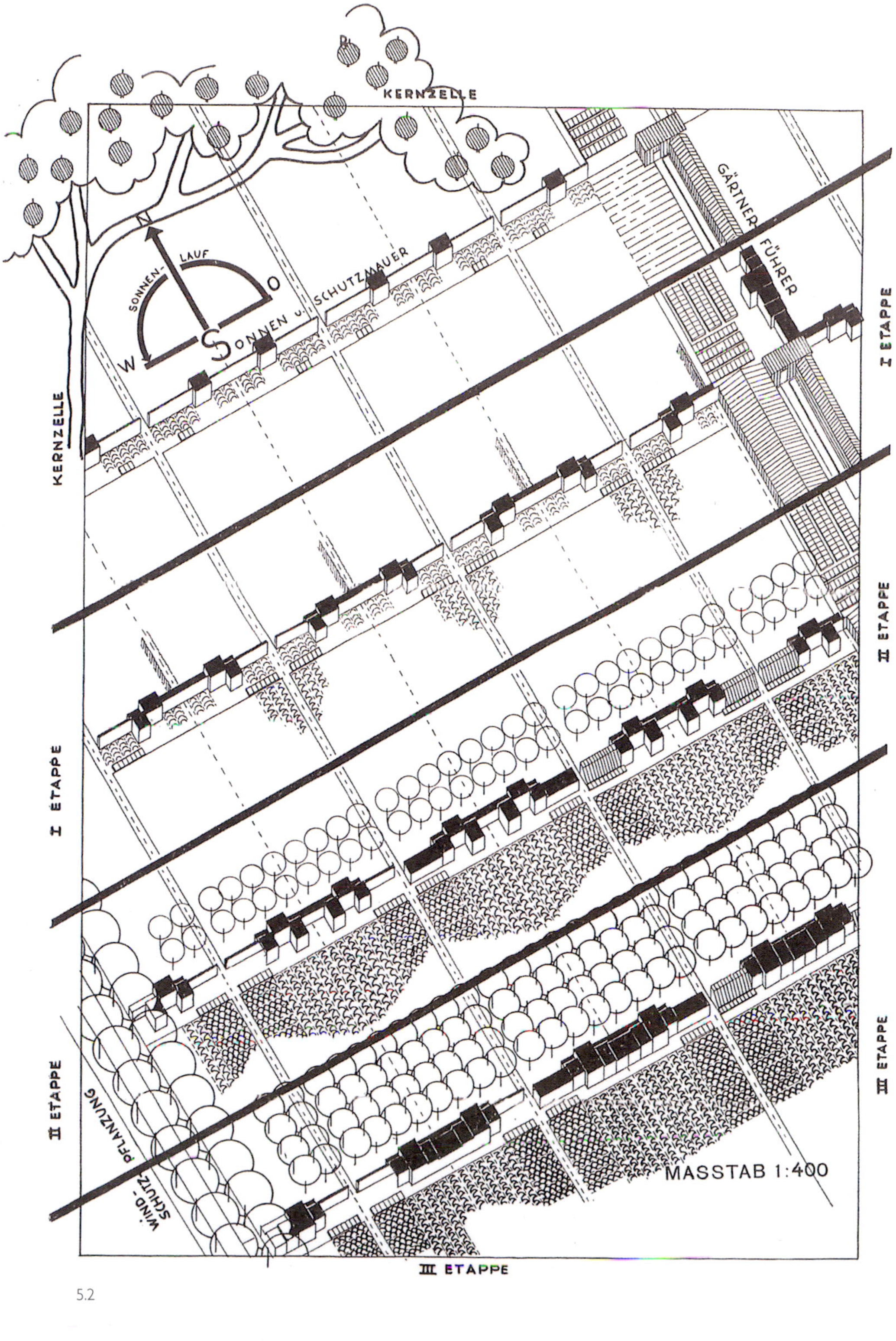
KERNZELLE
KERNZELLE
SONNEN-LAUF
W
S
O
SONNEN u. SCHUTZMAUER
GÄRTNER FÜHRER
I ETAPPE
I ETAPPE
II ETAPPE
II ETAPPE
III ETAPPE
III ETAPPE
WIND-SCHUTZ-PFLANZUNG
MASSTAB 1:400

5.2

"The modern food system consumes roughly ten calories of fossil fuel energy for every calorie of food energy produced."
RICHARD HEINBERG, WHAT WILL WE EAT AS THE OIL RUNS OUT (2005)

"We are slaves in the sense that we depend for our daily survival upon an expand-or-expire agro-industrial empire – a crackpot machine – that the specialists cannot comprehend and the managers cannot manage. Which is, furthermore, devouring world resources at an exponential rate."
EDWARD ABBEY, EARTHLY WORDS: ESSAYS ON CONTEMPORARY AMERICAN NATURE AND ENVIRONMENTAL WRITERS (1994)

"The total distance for all transportation [of Australia's 29 most common food items] is 70,803km, equivalent to travelling nearly twice around the circumference of the Earth (40,072km), or travelling around Australia's coastline three times."
SOPHIE GABALLA & ASHA BEE ABRAHAM, FOOD MILES IN AUSTRALIA: A PRELIMINARY STUDY OF MELBOURNE, VICTORIA (2008)

"The American Prairie as it was, with all of its diversity and grasses, actually produced more carbohydrates and protein per hectare than modern agriculture. But conventional agriculture has not engaged this rich ecosystem on its own terms."
WILLIAM MCDONOUGH & MICHAEL BRAUNGART, CRADLE TO CRADLE (2002)

Green revolution

The 1940s to 1960s witnessed a shift in farming practices to increase crop production through large-scale mechanization, high-yield crop varieties, artificial fertilizers and pesticides, with the global food system vastly transforming to become both extraordinarily productive and ecologically destructive. This agricultural 'Green Revolution' is in no way 'environmental' as its name suggests. While mechanized efficiency requires little human input, the amount of invested fossil fuel energy for the corresponding return of food energy is remarkably inefficient. The correspondingly massive, worldwide spatial expansion of agricultural land is dramatically transforming and destroying natural systems. *Agribusiness* is a more fitting term than *agriculture* for the great majority of food grown, processed, transported and consumed in developed countries. In most cases, the 'culture' of agriculture has been lost and food has become an economic commodity to be processed, marketed and traded for maximum profit.

"A whole generation of citizens thought that the carrying capacity of the earth was proportional to the amount of land under cultivation and that higher efficiencies in using the energy of the sun had arrived. This is a sad hoax, for industrial man no longer eats potatoes made from solar energy, now he eats potatoes partly made of oil."
HOWARD ODUM, ECOLOGICAL ECONOMICS (1971)

"To put it simply, [we] have been eating oil and natural gas for the past century, at an ever-accelerating pace. Without the massive 'inputs' of cheap gasoline and diesel fuel for machines, irrigation, and trucking, or petroleum-based herbicides and pesticides, or fertilizers made out of natural gas, [we] will be compelled to radically reorganize the way food is produced, or starve."
JAMES KUNSTLER, THE LONG EMERGENCY (2006)

Agro impacts

The impact of agriculture on the environment is immense: it is the largest global consumer of freshwater resources, it occupies around 40% of the Earth's surface; it is responsible for extensive land clearance for fields and plantations; it uses and releases enormous amounts of pollutants and chemicals into the environment; inconceivable distances are covered by regular food items to reach consumers (food miles); and 20–50% of food is wasted in developed countries. In the meantime, populations continue to become further urbanized (at over 50%), pushing agriculture from metropolitan regions. This results in a spatial and visual disconnection between people and agriculture, in which food production becomes increasingly imperceptible. The availability of food is taken for granted, while knowledge and skill bases diminish relative to population size.

"The amount of grains fed to US livestock is sufficient to feed about 840 million people who follow a plant-based diet."
DAVID PIMENTEL & MARCIA PIMENTEL, SUSTAINABILITY OF MEAT-BASED AND PLANT-BASED DIETS AND THE ENVIRONMENT (2003)

"Becoming vegan is the most important and direct change we can immediately make to save the planet and its species."
CHRIS HEDGES, SAVING THE PLANET, ONE MEAL AT A TIME (2014)

"Globally, in the last 100 years, much of the genetic biodiversity and cultural knowledge of our food plants has disappeared as a result of the industrialization of our food production."
KOANGA INSTITUTE, OUR VISION (2015)

Food security

The United Nations (UN) definition of food security is focused on daily calorific consumption and nutrition. A broader meaning encompasses the security of our food supply through measuring natural systems' carrying capacity, input longevity, and resilience to provide the volume of food required relative to the needs and/or demand of the global population; a collective rather than individual definition. Concerning issues of food security are manifold and include that at present, around half of the world's population survive on food that is the direct result of using synthetic nitrogen in agriculture (fertilizer), produced by large amounts natural gas. Not only is natural gas a finite resource and a significant contributor to climate change, but nitrogen fertilizers destroy microorganisms and soil carbon, cause acidification in soils (significantly reducing soils' ability to support high yielding crops) and eutrophication in water systems.

Dietary footprint

More detailed examination of food security reveals that dietary choices have significant impacts on landscapes and resource consumption. Certain products such as beef, seafood and dairy require immense productive areas and embody resources and practices such as freshwater consumption, grain crops (fed to animals) and ocean dredging (fed to farmed fish). Such consumer products and choices accordingly shape and degrade vast landscape and seascape areas. A large urban park, for example, may only supply adequate pasture for a small herd of cows or cattle, yet could provide significantly more food as a public market garden (and social value, employment, training).

"Since the 1900s, some 75% of plant genetic diversity has been lost as farmers worldwide have left their multiple local varieties and landraces for genetically uniform, high-yielding varieties … Today, 75% of the world's food is generated from only 12 plants and five animal species."
FOOD AND AGRICULTURE ORGANIZATION OF THE UNITED NATIONS (FAO), WHAT IS HAPPENING TO AGROBIODIVERSITY? (1999)

"Institutions do not save seeds. Humans with hearts do."
GARY PAUL NABHAN, SEED SAVERS EXCHANGE ANNUAL CONFERENCE (2013)

Agrobiodiversity

Biodiversity does not simply entail indigenous or native biodiversity; by definition, it encompasses all life forms. *Agrobiodiversity* (agricultural biodiversity) is a lesser-known issue than the loss of native plant and animal species commonly associated with biodiversity loss. As a result of agricultural industrialization, the world has lost the majority of the global genetic biodiversity of food plants and thus, greatly reduced its diversity and resilience. Signatory nations to the Convention of Biological Diversity (signed by 150 government leaders at the 1992 Rio Earth Summit) possess a legal obligation to preserve agrobiodiversity. Yet this important issue is largely unknown, overlooked or misunderstood (and greatly overshadowed by the prominence and awareness of the loss of indigenous and native biodiversity). Many nations are failing to meet or even address agrobiodiversity issues, which are facilitated through perpetuity of diversified farming practices, which can also provide multiple ecosystem services, reduce environmental externalities and the need for off-farm inputs. It is also crucial to ensure that seed collection, seed use and seed swaps maintain freedom from corporate control and patents (see Modes of Production, Chapter 7). These factors indicate a broader need to address sociocultural, power and economic factors within the global, industrial food system (Chapter 7).

5.3
Svalbard Global Seed Vault, Norway
The world's largest seedbank is carved into the arctic permafrost of a Norweigan hill slope. Other significant seedbanks include London's Millennium Seed Bank in Kew and the USA's federal facility in Fort Collins, Colorado. The Seed Savers Exchange in Iowa, USA run a participatory preservation program focused on endangered garden and food crop heritage heirloom seeds.

A
B
C
D
E
F
G

5.3

"We need the World Bank, we need the IMF, we need all the big foundations, we need all the governments to admit that for 30 years we all blew it, including me, when I was president. We blew it. We were wrong to believe that food is like some other product in international trade. And we all have to go back to a more environmentally responsible, sustainable form of agriculture. We should go back to a policy of maximum food self-sufficiency."
BILL CLINTON, UNITED NATIONS WORLD FOOD DAY SPEECH (OCTOBER 16, 2008)

Food sovereignty

'Food sovereignty' concerns people's rights to define, control and partake in their own food and agricultural systems. It encompasses how food is produced, distributed, traded and consumed and includes concerns regarding healthy and culturally appropriate food generated through ecologically sound and socially sustainable methods. The importance of policy and legislative mechanisms in enabling food security and sovereignty are crucial and thus, planning is an essential discipline in improving how and where we produce food. Within food sovereignty movements are a range of sub-pursuits and concerns such as: local food; community supported agriculture (CSA); food justice; cooperatives; slow food; civic agriculture; food deserts; healthy food; and 'peasant', family and artisanal agriculture. Yet despite the burgeoning activity in urban agriculture in many developed countries, at present, there are few opportunities to gain employment in agricultural production and food systems—especially at a living wage—thereby missing opportunities to strengthen local food security and diversify career prospects.

Self-reliance

Movements such as *permaculture* (permanent agriculture, permanent culture), *transition towns and networks*, *homesteading*, *grow your own*, allotment and community gardens highlight a growing awareness of and demand for food sovereignty and a desire to avoid consumer vulnerability from sole reliance on the resilience of food systems that are largely out of individual control. While still marginal with minimal effect upon the vast global food system, such practices offer a pragmatic and important response to escalating challenges heightened by global geopolitical issues of peak oil, increasing resource scarcity, climate change, and ineffective governmental recognition of the importance of local and national food self-sufficiency.

Each pin on this map represents a current or possible food growing space. Map your own site or watch an existing site to get involved.
Get Started
Add a Site
Selwyn Park Community Garden
61A Selwyn Street, Albion
The Selwyn Park Community Garden was established in 2010 and is solely run by the local community as a demonst...
4 people watching
Melbourne
Leaflet | Map data © OpenStreetMap contributors under ODbL | Map imagery © Mapbox
Active: There is an active food garden at this site. Get involved!
Proposed: People are working to start a food garden at this site. You can keep an eye on its progress by "watching" it.
Potential: This site could become a food garden! Sign in to start watching it and organizing your new community garden.
Unsuitable: Someone identified this as a potential food garden site, but unfortunately it's not suitable. Click the marker to find out why.

5.4

5.4

3000 Acres, 3000 Acres & Planisphere, Melbourne, Australia, 2013–

3000 Acres is a Melbourne initiative to bridge traditional grassroots food production and city planning policies. An online platform with detailed toolkit connects people, land and resources, targeting vacant land, establishing community, business, and government relationships and enabling project self-organization.

5.5

Garden Enfield, Enfield London Borough Council, London, UK, 2013–

This vision to re-establish a vibrant and sustainable market gardening industry builds on Enfield and the Lee Valley's food growing heritage, aiming to create around 1,200 jobs. Based on the 2020 Sustainability Programme and Enfield Food Strategy and Action Plan, the project was awarded £600,000 by the Greater London Authority (GLA) for a cooperative growing model, progressively increasing land area while exploring sales avenues. Some of the extensive initiatives include: food growing and technology centre; apprenticeships, work experience placements and volunteering opportunities; organic food box scheme; public pop up stalls; and the establishment of school food growing projects. This photograph shows harvesting of black grapes in an Enfield glasshouse in 1937.

5.5

5.6a

5.6a
5.6b
5.6c
5.6d

Shenyang Architectural University Campus, Turenscape, Shenyang City, Liaoning Province, China, 2003–2004

Turenscape considers food production and sustainable land use as survival issues in a country where continued urbanization of 1.37 billion people consume precious agricultural and arable land. A 7.5 acre (3ha) foodscape in their 52 acre (21ha) university campus design demonstrates that agricultural landscapes can become part of the urban environment and cultural identity. With pressing time and budget limitations (one year design and implementation with landscaping at \$US0.10 per square foot (\$1m^2), the design utilized the original site's good soils and viable irrigation system from its past use as a regionally distinctive 'northeast rice' field. Rice, native plants (as borders) and crops (such as buckwheat) grow in rotation, demonstrating productive landscape feasibility and including student participation. The rice produced is harvested and distributed, serving both as a keepsake for visitors and a source of identity for the newly established, suburban campus.

5.6b

稻香飘校园
育米如育人
袁隆平
赠品
Paddy-rice scenery area of Shenyang Architectural and Civil Engineering University.

5.6c

5.6d

"Planners, urban designers, and even developers, are recognizing 'farming as another mixed use that adds vitality to the community'. After a half-century hiatus, agriculture is finding a place next to public spaces, entertainment and cultural venues, employment opportunities, recreational amenities, educational institutions, and shops and markets as principal constituents of great communities."
DARRIN NORDAHL, PUBLIC PRODUCE (2009)

"The issue of food is the premier topic to return circular thinking to the city ... For the city revolves around people, and people need to eat. Good food grows on good soil, requiring good water and nutrients. Also because of the ongoing urbanisation, these ingredients will become ever scarcer. Unless the city will start to think in terms of closed, organic cycles to replace the industrial-age notion of linear production chains."
JAN WILLEM VAN DER SCHANS, URBAN METABOLISM (2014)

"Seasoned landscape architects ... [are] lopsidedly focused on ornamentals. Currently, edible landscapes are a niche market ... Landscape architects will need to be versed in ornamental and edible plants, and how to plant them in combinations that not only create beautiful compositions that realize the principles of integrated pest management and companion planting, while providing utility, joy, comfort, and relief to people in public space."
DARRIN NORDAHL, PUBLIC PRODUCE (2009)

"I believe the city should own tracts of land for the growing of vegetables and fruits, where the citizens can see and understand that their real existence comes out of Mother Earth, and that the merchant or the peddler is only a means of delivery."
JENS JENSEN, A GREATER WEST SIDE PARK SYSTEM (1920)

FOOD PLANNING, POLICY AND DESIGN

The ability for land planning and design to influence food systems is considerable and ranges from the macro to the micro.

Landscape Planning is beginning to realize that the exclusion of food from modernity's 20th-century urban agenda was a poor oversight. Both strategic and statutory planning can facilitate urban and peri-urban agriculture at a range of scales. The America Planning Association (APA), since around 2005, has attempted to redress this through a range of initiatives including numerous policies, guides and events.

Landscape Architecture as the profession that "dominates the design and delivery of the public realm in urban environments" (see Interview, Chapter 7), can significantly facilitate the design and delivery of civic urban agriculture. The skills of landscape architects are ideally matched to navigate the technical and social challenges presented through inclusion of productive and edible species in the public realm. Yet very few landscape architects have experience in public foodscape design and execution and fail to possess extensive knowledge of productive plant species.

5.7

5.7
Broadacre City
Frank Lloyd Wright's Broadacre City is an early example of agrarian urbanism that implicitly grasps and spatially articulates the need for communities to grow their own food. At his Taliesin Fellowship, student architect apprentices labored in on-site food production.

> "When a civilisation is in decline, there is a clear point when the food source occurs too far away from the city."
> AUSTRALIAN SCHOOL OF HUMAN ECOLOGY, CIVILISATIONAL DECLINE (2007)

> "There needs to be a fundamental paradigm shift that recognizes the total dependence of human beings on natural systems. Man-made landscapes must become 'productive' as opposed to 'consumptive'."
> JOSE ALMINANA, ASLA INTERVIEW (2009)

Facilitatory mechanisms

Urban food production cannot usually financially compete with the economic return generated by other uses of land (see Interview). Most contemporary cities' policy and planning mechanisms have failed to protect productive agricultural land from more immediately financially lucrative uses such as (low-density) residential housing. In transition to a post-carbon era, it is vital to ensure that planning policy protects such land and facilitates agriculture as a legitimate urban land use to reduce food miles (for food transportation) and to increase the resilience and self-sufficiency of urban and peri-urban food systems (see Garden Enfield). Policy, legislative and financial mechanisms can assist through concessions/subsidies for small-scale urban and peri-urban growers (as provided in most rural, developed agricultural systems). Such initiatives can increase employment and agrobiodiversity, food security, sovereignty, local and national self-sufficiency. Providing 'agricultural parks' in a similar system to national parks and conservation areas (but with more participatory involvement) deserves increased exploration to facilitate the protection of valuable urban and peri-urban agricultural land and its ongoing sustainable management. This could additionally create opportunities for non-landowners seeking agricultural careers and employment beyond the realm of rural and conventional, mega-scale monoculture farming.

Inclusion of food

Through working on large-scale planning and public green space projects, landscape architects can expand 'the commons' and urban/peri-urban food production, deploying significant areas for food-based activities (see Life on the Edge). Historically, agriculture and edible plants have been largely excluded from landscape architectural design, with species used wholly for ornamental value or 'native' relationship to place (see Chapter 8). Thankfully, this is expanding to include productive landscapes, aesthetic foodscape design, continuous productive urban landscapes, agrarian urbanism (and various other related practices) to create effective and efficient local food systems that generate multiple environmental, social and economic benefits.

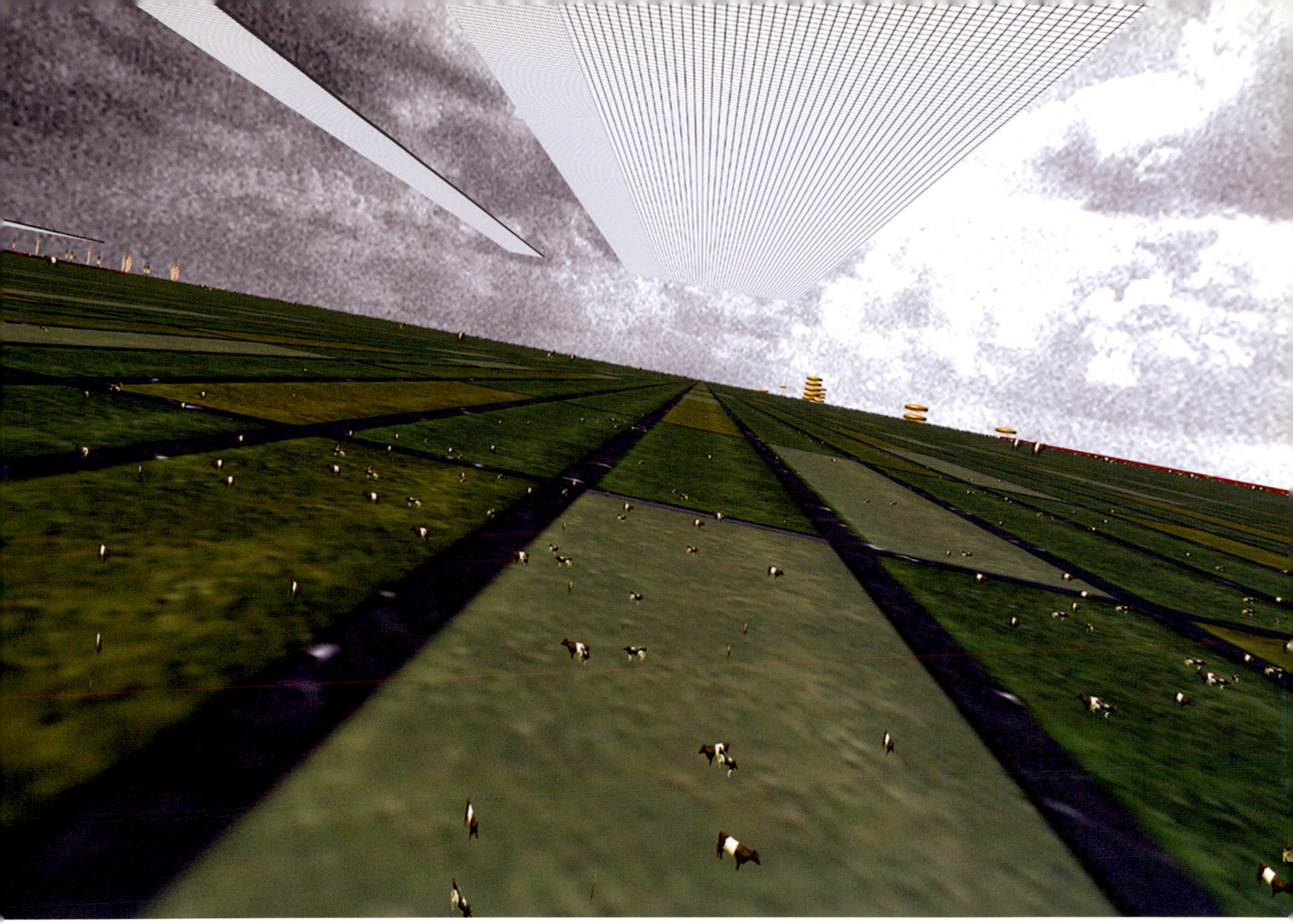

5.8

5.8
MVRDV Meta City Data Town—Agricultural Sector
MVRDV's 'big data' installation (and subsequent book METACITY/DATATOWN (The Hague, the Netherlands, 1998)) conveys the spatial extent of cities' components, posing if globalization has exploded beyond our grasp. Their hypothetical 400 by 400km city datascape, four times denser than the Netherlands, reveals the agricultural sector to be the largest land consumer, with vastly different spatial and corresponding energy impacts of vegetarian versus meat-eating societies.

"In the same way that when we came to recognize the supreme ecological value of wetlands we erected high bars to their development, we need to recognize the value of farmland to our national security and require real-estate developers to do 'food-system impact statements' before development begins. We should also create tax and zoning incentives for developers to incorporate farmland (as they do now for 'open space') in their subdivision plans; all these subdivisions now ringing golf courses could someday have diversified farms at their centre."
MICHAEL POLLAN, FARMER IN CHIEF (2008)

"But as China has become more urbanized and 'civilized,' this vernacular landscape has gradually been deprived of its productivity, its support to and of life, and its natural beauty. Like the peasant girls whose footbinding crippled them, it has gradually been adapted by the minority urban upper class and transformed into artificial decorative gardens. The aesthetic of uselessness, leisure, and adornment has taken over as part of a larger overwhelming urge to appear 'modern' and sophisticated."
KONGJIAN YU, BEAUTIFUL BIG FEET: TOWARD A NEW LANDSCAPE AESTHETIC (2010)

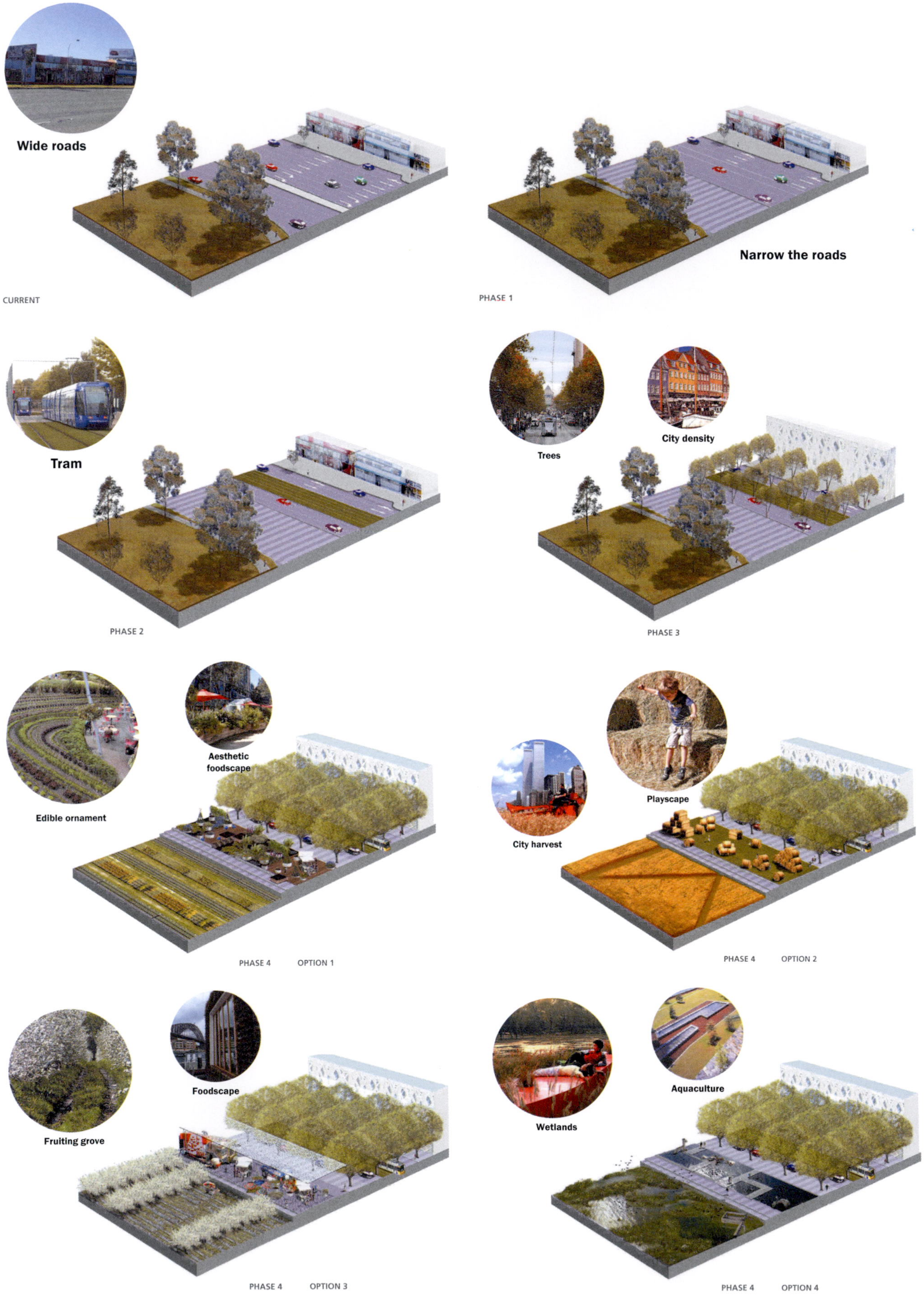
Wide roads
CURRENT
Narrow the roads
PHASE 1
Tram
PHASE 2
Trees
City density
PHASE 3
Edible ornament
Aesthetic foodscape
PHASE 4 OPTION 1
City harvest
Playscape
PHASE 4 OPTION 2
Fruiting grove
Foodscape
PHASE 4 OPTION 3
Wetlands
Aquaculture
PHASE 4 OPTION 4

5.9

5.9
Life on the Edge, TCL, Adelaide, Australia, 2011
This government design exercise explored possibilities of reconfiguring a major road corridor on the western edge of Adelaide and its encircling parklands. As one of three teams commissioned by the Integrated Design Commission, TCL's 'the edible ornament' addressed public transport and density to propose aesthetic urban agriculture through a civic, participative, productive and activated vision of the city. The drawings show the current road corridor, phases 1, 2 and 3 of the proposed redevelopment, and four options for phase 4 of the redevelopment. These four options included aesthetic foodscapes and community market gardens; farmers markets and orchards; crops and playspaces; and water filtration wetlands and aquaculture.

Opportunities

Planning and policy initiatives can increase the frequency and incidence and, in turn, the resilience of urban food systems. This can involve prioritizing local agriculture over food-mile intensive global agriculture; protecting historical and cultural agricultural landscapes, practices and traditions; attempting to provide a food supply system that reduces reliance on finite resources; increasing resilience to climate change and its threats to food supply; engaging local people through paying a living wage and fulfilling employment; and utilizing *agroecology* to protect ecosystems and biodiversity.

5.10a
5.10b
5.10c
Nanhu: Farm Town in the Big City, SWA Group, Jiaxing, China, 2011
The design challenges typical rural-to-urban land transformation whereby agricultural landscapes are wiped clear of historic and cultural significance. Agriculture and urbanization are married the creation of a dense urban village. An extensive canal network, abundance of water, flat land, and fertile soil give potential for a model agricultural center of food production for the surrounding mega cities. Three major hurdles were identified: low efficiency in agricultural land organization, a stagnant and polluted canal system, and an uneconomic rural population density. The design proposes an infrastructural overhaul to treat heavily polluted water and a village that maintains an agricultural character and is compact, walkable, tightly-knit and with proximity to open space.

FARM REFORM STRATEGY
STEP 1: physical site components
STEP 2: service components
STEP 3: integration
labor + technology
niche markets
community/tourism
organic agriculture
5.10a

AGRICULTURAL VARIETY
ORGANIC FARM
FAMILY FARMS
ECO-TOURIST FARMS
GARDEN PARKLAND
5.10b

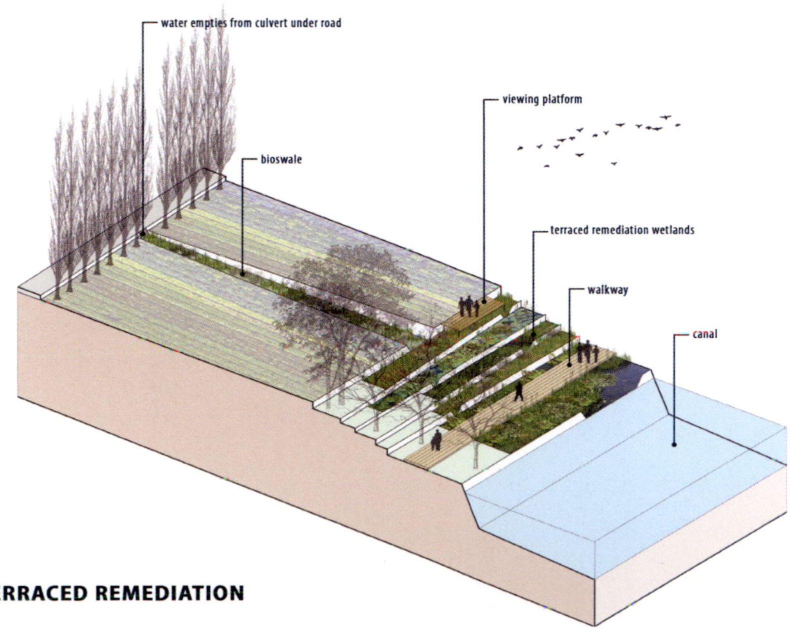
water empties from culvert under road
viewing platform
bioswale
terraced remediation wetlands
walkway
canal

TERRACED REMEDIATION

5.10c

5.11a
5.11b
Agriculture at Garraf Waste Landfill
Agricultural land is a precious resource, especially in close proximity to major cities. Here, a farmer ploughs the remediated land of a former landfill in Barcelona, Spain (see Chapter 3).

5.11a

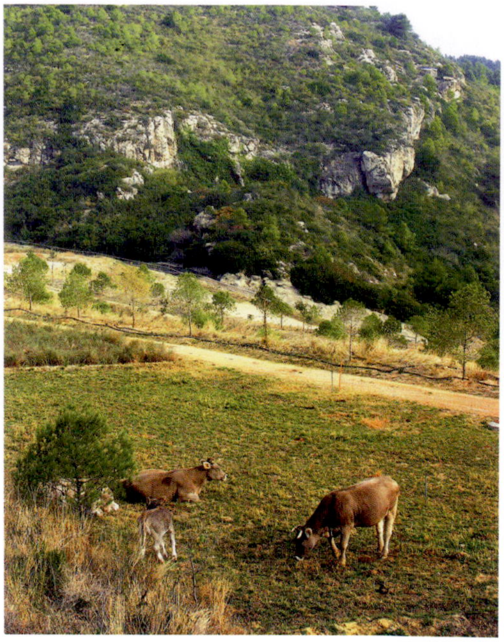

5.11b

Beyond community agriculture

While some municipalities and regions provide allotments, community gardens and other forms of socially oriented urban agriculture, very few offer scope to employ urban residents in food production or actively nurture a local food industry (see Garden Enfield). Some municipalities, though, have adjusted their policies to facilitate food and agriculture by, for instance, changing laws to allow urban beekeeping (New York City), chickens/animals and rooftop agriculture.

5.12
Urban Beekeeping
Urban beekeeping (shown here in Brooklyn) is on the rise to counter an alarming decline in bee and pollinator populations. Urban bees can produce complex honey from the greater variety of plant sources than typical rural monocultures, while avoiding agricultural chemical impacts—a primary source of their decline. The urban heat island effect increases bees' seasonal range, however, drawbacks include vehicles, construction dust and air pollution hazards and potential increased swarms from inexperienced beekeepers.

5.12

"There will always be risks associated with growing and consuming food. Some concerns are valid, though most are based on naïveté. Nevertheless, these perceptions may prove to be formidable obstacles to implementing a public produce program in many communities. The truth is that farms today have few regulations in place to ensure absolute safety of fruits and vegetables, and there is perhaps greater potential for municipal government and citizenry to work together to ensure a healthier- and safer-food system."
DARRIN NORDAHL, PUBLIC PRODUCE (2009)

"So important are insects and other land-dwelling arthropods that if all were to disappear, humanity probably could not last more than a few months."
EDWARD O. WILSON, THE DIVERSITY OF LIFE (1992)

Design execution

Concerns regarding urban agriculture and public health need to be carefully considered, yet planning and policy often remains entrenched in a 20th-century paradigm of 'urban modernity', where aesthetic concerns restrict urban agricultural activities. Urban agriculture can be deployed to complement green space benefits (like aesthetics, recreation, education and health). This can be assisted by guidance and leadership through landscape architects' skills to facilitate masterplanning; community engagement; spatial execution; horticultural expertise; maintenance; and distribution in local economic, community and social networks. Perhaps more importantly, looming challenges of food security (Chapter 1) vastly overshadow shallower concepts of visual preferences, styles and trends.

Urban synergies

Urban contexts offer synergies and conditions well suited to urban agriculture, including complementary practices such as WSUD, productive landscapes, and green infrastructure. These further include:

- excess nutrient utilization in agriculture such as phosphorus and nitrogen in wastewater and urine;
- ecologically degraded land and under-activated urban and peri-urban land;
- biodiversity through diversified farming practices;
- stormwater runoff treatment with WSUD to facilitate reuse as agricultural irrigation;
- compostable food/green waste and biodegradable materials from urban regions;
- local food production for local consumption,
- social participation and education;
- income and employment.

Although urban agriculture faces hurdles in urban contexts (aesthetics, risk, maintenance and knowledge), the possibilities and benefits deserve significantly increased exploration.

"There are only seven meals between civilization and anarchy."
LULA DA SILVA, CONFRONTING THE CHALLENGE OF THE GLOBAL FOOD CRISIS IN THE AMERICAS (2008)

"It has been estimated that almost half the people on the Earth are currently fed as a result of synthetic nitrogen fertilizer use."
J.W. ERISMAN , HOW A CENTURY OF AMMONIA SYNTHESIS CHANGED THE WORLD (2008)

ALLOTMENT, COMMUNITY GARDENS AND PUBLIC FOODSCAPES

Urban agriculture in developed cities usually exists at a community or local scale and typically includes allotments; community gardens (see P-Patch); school gardens; small urban farms; rooftop agriculture (see Gary Comer); temporary events (see Wheat Festival); exhibitions; and private enterprises (see Eden Garden). These are usually small, ranging between 0.025–7.4 acre (0.01–3ha) and often 'grassroots', community-led (see Incredible Edibles) or small entrepreneurial growing interventions, rather than highly organized or professional operations. Yields may not be the primary focus for individuals or groups who are often involved for social and recreational reasons, and growing costs may even exceed the relative economic return. Thus, the social dimensions of urban agriculture currently dominate discourse as they regularly involve positive and transformative stories regarding community cohesion, engagement, health and intergenerational education (Chapter 7). The physical, psychological and health benefits are well documented and discussed in various media and publications.

5.13

5.14

5.13
Barnängen, Stockholm allotment garden in 1915

5.14
Allotment Gardens, Munich

European allotments are documented in the 18th and early 19th centuries and can be traced to Anglo-Saxon times. Sweden's first allotment garden was inspired by examples in Copenhagen, Denmark, and established in Malmö, 1895, followed by Stockholm in 1904. Laws enabling and restricting access and allotment provision differ between countries.

5.15

5.15

P-Patch, Picardo Farm, Seattle, Washington, USA

P-Patch is a specific term used in Seattle for gardening allotments, named after the city's first community garden, Picardo Farm. Established in 1973, it contains 259 allotments in 98,000 square feet (9,105m^2) and has a waiting time of over two years.

5.16

Wheat Harvest Festival, Champs–Elysees, Paris, France, 1990

A temporary wheat field on the iconic Avenue des Champs–Elysees during a one-day harvest festival held to raise awareness of the importance of farming work. Wheat grown on large pallets was brought into the city and arranged to form a vast wheat field, then harvested by farmers.

5.16

5.17

5.17
The Eden Project Food Garden
The edible garden adjoining the cafe at The Eden Project (Chapter 7) directly links food production and consumption. It is executed with spatial simplicity and a high degree of skill in managing the timing and featuring the aesthetics of the edible plants.

Access to land

Such local food movements are an expression of people (whether consciously or unconsciously) asserting inalienable rights to land, air and water, or perhaps our innate need for these connections. Some countries and regions facilitate this process better than others. Allotment systems in the UK and Europe are one successful example, but can be grossly over-subscribed (such as in London where waiting lists commonly exceed ten years). Community gardens enable access to land for growing food (such as in the USA, Canada and Australia) but are generally more sporadically deployed, less widespread than allotments and without the same level of cultural entrenchment (and also frequently over-subscribed). Both allotments and community gardens usually provide small, marginal, leftover, less lucrative land that can be reclaimed by councils or property owners when they wish, severing place attachment formed by gardeners, removing productive landscapes and building over valuable soils.

"The soil is the great connector of lives, the source and destination of all. It is the healer and restorer and resurrector, by which disease passes into health, age into youth, death into life. Without proper care for it we can have no community, because without proper care for it we can have no life."
WENDELL BERRY, THE UNSETTLING OF AMERICA: CULTURE AND AGRICULTURE (1977)

"Teaching kids how to feed themselves and how to live in a community responsibly is the center of an education."
ALICE WATERS, MOTHER JONES MAGAZINE (JAN–FEB 1995)

Allotments and community gardens

Allotment and community gardens are plots of land made available for individual and non-commercial gardening or growing food plants, sometimes through local municipal governments. These gardens can differ in their structure, though most are governed by zoning laws that stipulate growing for individual and not commercial purposes. Allotments are cultivated individually with plots (usually between 50 and 400m^2 (around 500 and 4,500 square feet)) formed by subdividing land into parcels (sometimes several hundred) assigned to individuals, groups or families and usually managed through an allotment association. Community gardens are more varied: the entire area might be tended collectively by a group of people, or it can be a combination of individual and community areas, or sometimes purely individual plots (as per the European allotment system).

POLLINATION STREET

5.18

5.18
Incredible Edibles, Todmorden, West Yorkshire, England, UK, 2008–
This public urban gardening and local food project plants edible species in neglected public land, sharing harvests with the community. There are now more than 20 'Incredible Edible' towns worldwide.

5.19a

5.19b

5.19c

SOUTH

5.20a

5.20b

5.19a (Before)
5.19b
5.19c

Huerta de la Partida, West 8, Madrid, Spain, 2007–2009

Part of the Madrid Rio project (Chapter 4), this extensive urban orchard was prompted by destruction of the original orchard in Royal Palace during its conversion into a transportation hub in the 1950s. Contrary to the initial tendency to create a historical replication, the Huerta is a modern interpretation of the orchard that makes reference to ancient paradise gardens. A wide variety of fruit trees (such as fig, almond and pomegranate) have been planted in groups and arranged in alternate lines to create an enclosed garden. The restored river, previously channelled underground, now meanders through the landscape.

5.20a
5.20b

Gary Comer Youth Center, John Ronan Architects & Hoerr Schaudt, Grand Crossing, Chicago, Illinois, USA, 2006

This 8,160-square-foot (758m^2) vegetable and flower green roof garden contained within the center forms a highly graphic outdoor classroom supporting youth horticultural programs. The garden collects and recycles rainwater and reduces heat loss and climate control costs. The microclimate allows for near year-round gardening, while 18–24 inches (455–610mm) of soil facilitates diverse growing options contained in recycled plastic 'lumber' raised beds. A full-time gardener creatively maintains the garden for horticultural learning, environmental awareness and organic food production—over 1,000 pounds in 2009 used by students, elderly locals and the center's café.

5.21

Perth Cultural Centre Urban Orchard, Josh Byrne & Associates, Western Australian State Government, Perth, Australia, 2011

This once neglected carpark rooftop is now a publicly accessible community garden, with organic seasonal fruit, vegetables, herbs and companion plants. Constructed with local and recycled materials, the space also accommodates major events such as concerts and festivals. The gardens are managed with involvement by volunteers and involve hands-on training programs. The use of turf slows stormwater flows and provides a cooling surface treatment as opposed to paving in the heart of the city.

5.21

5.22a
5.22b
5.22c

Lafayette Greens: Urban Agriculture, Urban Fabric, Urban Sustainability, Kenneth Weikal Landscape Architecture, Detroit USA, 2010

This 0.425 acre (172m²) downtown Detroit urban foodscape garden is based on productivity, beauty and inspiration. It contains an orchard, rainwater cistern, bioswale, children's garden, and special events area, and uses recycled and salvaged materials such as pallet wood, doors and chalkboard panels. Founder Peter Karmanos rented the land from the City of Detroit to encourage community engagement. Produce is donated to garden volunteers and Detroit's Gleaners Food Bank.

Modernity = marginalization

Much urban agriculture is temporary, informal or unofficial, occurring on vacant land and 'meanwhile' leases (see Union Orchard). This reflects its current marginal status in policy, legislation and also, the lack of public perception and recognition of its place in the city. Urban agriculture interventions can stimulate local economic development and then face displacement. While this can be seen as a measure of success, it is also symptomatic of the commercial focus in urban development and governance, where a lack of protection in policy and planning mechanisms against gentrification is frequently uncommon (Berlin has notable exceptions). In these situations it is important to design for disassembly and the ease of transportation to allow decampment to new, cheap, under-activated areas.

5.22a

5.22b

5.22c

5.23a
5.23b

Union Street Urban Orchard, Wayward Plants, Bankside, London, UK, 2010

From derelict site to thriving community orchard, this 'meanwhile' (temporary) space design was a feature project of London's 2010 Festival of Architecture. Wayward Plants facilitated carpentry and gardening training during a six-week community build, with over 100 volunteers helping construct the site from reclaimed materials. The biodiverse orchard of 85 fruit trees and countless rescued plants hosted workshops, urban agriculture discussions, film screenings, musical performances and community meetings. After one fruit harvest, the dismantled garden and trees were given to local housing estates and community gardens, turning 'meanwhile' temporality into an ongoing legacy.

5.23a

The Union Street
RBAN
CHARD

5.23b

STUDY/DISCUSSION QUESTIONS

Why do human populations overshoot their carrying capacity? What happens? Can you think of actual examples?

Are landscape architects focused on ornamental plant species? Why/why not? Why have some formerly productive plant species been made to produce no fruit?

Should landscape architects and designers, horticulturalists and nurseries shift their focus from ornamental plants to edible, productive and useful plants? Why/why not?

Should landscape architects engage with food and productive projects? Why and if so, in what contexts? What roles can landscape architects play in food-related projects?

What are some of the challenges of using edible and productive plants in public spaces? What are some strategies to overcome these challenges?

Can edible planting look good? Find examples, both historic and contemporary. What are some design strategies to achieve pleasant aesthetics?

What is agribusiness? Does it lack 'culture'?

What are genetically modified (bioengineered) foods? How does this differ from millennia of plant breeding practices? Are there ethical concerns? Why/why not? What impacts can genetically modified plants have on the landscape and for farmers?

What is agroecology?

What is agrobiodiversity?

What is agroforestry?

Is agricultural biodiversity or native biodiversity more important? To whom? Why?

To what extent are fossil fuels employed in our food system? Provide examples.

Is urban agriculture important in the developed world? In the developing world? What are the key differences?

What is permaculture and its principles? Why is permaculture not more widespread in education, the public realm and policy? Who are its key proponents?

To what extent should public green space be utilized for the public growing of food?

What other systems and infrastructures is urban agriculture dependent upon? What synergies and opportunities exist for mutual benefit in urban environments?

FURTHER READING

Ableman, M. (2005) *Fields of plenty: a farmer's journey in search of real food and the people who grow it*, San Francisco: Chronicle Books.

Bohn, K. and Viljoen, A. (2014) *Second nature urban agriculture: designing productive cities*, Oxon, UK: Routledge.

Carpenter, N. and Rosenthal, W. (2011) *The essential urban farmer*, New York: Penguin Books.

de la Salle, J. and Holland, M. (2010) *Agricultural urbanism: handbook for building sustainable food & agriculture systems in 21st century cities*, Manitoba: Green Frigate Books.

Fukuoka, M. (2009) *The one-straw revolution: an introduction to natural farming*, New York: New York Review Books.

Gorgolewski, M., Komisar, J. and Nasr, J. (2011) *Carrot city: creating places for urban agriculture*, New York: Monacelli Press.

Hodgson, K. (2010) *Urban agriculture Growing healthy, sustainable communities*, Chicago: APA Planners Press.

Holmgren, D. (2002) *Permaculture: Principles & Pathways Beyond Sustainability*, Hepburn, VIC: Holmgren Design Services.

Méndez, V., Bacon, C., Cohen, R. and Gliessman, S. (2015) *Agroecology: A transdisciplinary, participatory and action-oriented approach*, Boca Raton: CRC Press.

Miazzo, F. and Minkjan, M. (2013) *Farming the city: food as a tool for today's urbanisation*, Amsterdam: Trancity valiz.

Mollison, B. (1988) *Permaculture: A Designers' Manual*, NSW: Tagari.

Nordahl, D. (2009) *Public Produce: The New Urban Agriculture*, Washington DC: Island Press.

Philips, A. (2013) *Designing urban agriculture: a complete guide to the planning, design, construction, maintenance and management of edible landscapes*, Hoboken: Wiley.

Roberts, P. (2008) *The End of Food*, Boston: Houghton Mifflin.

Viljoen, A., Bohn, K. and Howe, J. (2005) *Continuous productive urban landscapes: designing urban agriculture for sustainable cities*, Amsterdam: Elsevier.

Waterman, T. and Zeunert, J. (2017) *The Routledge Handbook of Landscape and Food*, Oxon, UK: Routledge.

You might also like to look for further information on the following projects:

CERES, Melbourne, Australia, 1982–

Cuccagna Project, Milan, Italy, 2011–

Garden of Amaranths, Emmanuel Louisgrand, Lyon, France, 2002–2008

Food Urbanism Initiative, Verzone Woods Associates, Switzerland, 2010–2013

Prinzessinnengarten, Berlin, 2009–

Zuidpark, Amsterdam, the Netherlands, 2012–

Wanzhuang eco-city, Arup, Wanzhuang, China

Fairmont Hotel Gardens, Vancouver, Canada

Del Aire Fruit Park, Fallen Fruit, Los Angeles, USA, 2012

New York City Rooftop Farms, Brooklyn, USA

Uncommon Ground Restaurant, Chicago, Illinois, USA

MUSC Urban Farm, Urban Edge Studio, Crop Up, Charleston, South Carolina, USA

Productive Neighborhoods, Berger Partnership, Seattle, Washington, USA, 2011

Bee and Bee Hotel, St Ermin's Hotel in London, UK

Back to Front Manual: For Growing Food in Front Gardens, Leeds, UK, 2011

INTERVIEW Tim Waterman

Tim Waterman is Senior Lecturer and Landscape Architecture Theory Coordinator at the University of Greenwich, and teaches at the Bartlett School of Architecture, University College London. He is the author of *Fundamentals of Landscape Architecture* and, with Ed Wall, *Basics Landscape Architecture: Urban Design*. Tim is honorary editor of *Landscape*, the journal of the Landscape Institute and his writing has appeared in multiple publications, including the *Journal of Architecture* and *Landscape Architecture Magazine* (LAM). His research explores the interconnections between food, taste, place, and democratic civil society.

While food and landscape are inextricably linked, foodscapes are largely absent, diminishing and tokenistic in most urban environments. Is food production in urban and peri-urban areas important? Why?

Discussions of urban agriculture, at least in the west, regularly drift almost immediately into technological speculation; from vertical farms to green roofs to aquaculture/pisciculture. The hard truth of the matter is that the most important and productive agriculture of the future is still likely to be involved with growing plants in the soil. Agriculture is largely dependent upon cheap and abundant arable and pasture land and is likely to remain so for the foreseeable future. The high price of much inner-city urban land is the most effective deterrent to the development of urban foodscapes. Only the most outrageously high-value crops, such as Cannabis, are viable. Thus we tend to see many urban foodscapes that are tokenistic simply because they aren't large enough to produce a meaningful amount or high enough value of food. At worst, urban foodscapes are mere greenwash, and at best they establish a positive intention. A lettuce-encrusted living wall, for example, in most cases, is valuable for its symbolic or didactic power or its ability to connect us to nature; and this is often enough to justify the expense and effort.

Peri-urban areas I see quite differently from agriculture in the urban core. These have historically been the areas from which cities have drawn their sustenance, and a virtuous loop of waste as fertilizer (food waste, manure, and so on) and the production of high-value fruit, herb, and vegetable crops combined with low food miles is still a compelling argument for encouraging peri-urban agriculture. It is probably an unfashionable argument, but I would like to see a very different approach to urban jobs, again based in a historic model. No one should work at a desk all year. The planting and harvest months should be spent in the fields. This is part of that other great benefit of urban agriculture, the reconnection of human lives to cycles of nature.

Do you think that there is a perception that food production that isn't part of the mechanized, rural, agribusiness paradigm is tokenistic or fluff? Why?

Big agribusiness has worked hard to convince people that no alternative to the existing food system is either necessary or possible, and this where the perception of alternative methods as unviable has largely arisen. This has gone hand in hand with the development of the high modern state, which is characterized by a drive towards simplification and legibility (which helps with taxation and control, for example). The reality, though, is that our agricultural interactions with planetary processes and forces are never simple. In fact, traditional agricultural methods everywhere are far more complex and fascinating than modernist methods. What we need is to begin to wean ourselves off of the monolithic agribusiness model in favor of agricultural and biological diversity over the next few generations. This will be immensely intellectually, politically, and physically difficult, and will require humility and cooperation. In other words, all those subjective, emotional, earthly 'fluffy' qualities that modernist objectivity has tried to engineer out.

With the strength of heritage movements, why is food heritage a relatively absent issue/discipline?

Food heritage is no longer an absent discipline. The field of food studies has grown massively, particularly in the last decade, and heritage is an important component, particularly in the study of foodways. Foodways are the social, cultural, and economic frameworks, often highly local, that figure in the production and consumption of food. History and tradition are emplaced in the landscape through foodways, or perhaps I could say that the landscape is emplaced in history and tradition. Not only in academia is food heritage being taken seriously. The Slow Food Movement, which originated in Italy, is a good example of a popular revival of food heritage and associated culinary and landscape practices.

Similarly, while there is widespread awareness on the loss of native and indigenous biodiversity, why is the devastating loss of agrobiodiversity so little known?

Again, the awareness of the need for agrobiodiversity has burgeoned in recent years. Heirloom varieties of fruits and vegetables are being rediscovered, and even some supermarkets (often real bad guys in the food and landscape story) are offering unusual produce. They're certainly responding to consumer pressure, which is a good indicator of increasing awareness. Writers and commentators such as Michael Pollan, Eric Schlosser, Alice Waters, and Carolyn Steel have had a tremendous influence in raising awareness.

Western, global food systems, through agribusiness, treat food as an economic commodity. How can we increase the diversity of our food systems and increase our democratic right to access land?

Access to land is one of the biggest and thorniest issues that we will face in the future, and it's a many-sided question. Farmers in much of the developed and developing world are aging and not being replaced by a younger generation, and small farms and mixed farms are still in decline. Food is treated as an economic commodity, and so is land. The work of the enclosures and the clearances, so closely tied to the development of the current market conditions, continues even today. The ideal, presumably, is an empty countryside where no one can see the results of the pillaging of the land and the slave-like conditions of migrant labor. This system, though, is fragile, and I believe that it is coming to an end. New types of markets must emerge that are not based upon exploitation alone. Land ownership patterns must change to allow new generations of young farmers to emerge, to become stewards of the land and advocates for it, and there must also be a focus on creating a good quality of rural life for them. The countryside everywhere, while it may often be beautiful, is also often lonely and boring. This needn't be the case.

How can planners and landscape architects play a role in moving beyond tokenistic gestures of food production in urban areas and realize more substantial interventions supported by policy, legislation and financial incentives?

Planners and landscape architects need to become much more aggressive. They need to work to create new markets and new types of markets. They need to become developers. They need to become activists. They need to work directly with communities and food producers to create new opportunities. They can't just keep on with business as usual, because the current market, agriculture, and the food business is simply not giving us what we need for the long-term survival of our species on this planet!

Why does landscape have a strong tradition that it seems resistant to break from of using horticulturally sterile, ornamental plant species as opposed to productive and fruiting species? i.e. why do we place more emphasis on visual performance than a broader measure of productivity?

I once asked a representative of the Royal Parks in London why there were no fruit trees planted. The representative responded that there were numerous problems that they had been unable to overcome. First, that fruit trees take specialized care, for example pruning and thinning of fruit. Second, that people often damage fruit trees when harvesting from them, which incurs expense, from repairing the damage to replacing dead trees. Third, that they worried that people would injure themselves climbing the trees to harvest the fruit; a proper orchard would be equipped with ladders, for example. These are all powerful deterrents to changing how the service plants its parks. What is needed is consistent pressure for change in many arenas: in behavior and manners; in horticultural training; in park staffing; in health and safety regulations; and so on and on. The fact that a meaningful movement to accomplish such changes is already in place, and that news items regularly appear about householders challenging conventions by replacing suburban front lawns with gardens, for example, should be ample encouragement to those wishing to work for change in these areas. Again, I must stress that humility and cooperation are key to this.

Do you think aesthetics will diminish in importance as we descend into the challenges of climate change and resource scarcity?

If we're not working towards a beautiful, sensuous world, then we are not living. Landscapes have always presented life-and-death challenges as much as they've provided a home and a place of sensual delight. This contrast is part of the wonder of life. If we abandon aesthetics, we abandon the future.

VOTA MEA REDDA

6.1
Hypotopia
A student-built physical protest spatially expressing what could be built with €19 billion (the Austrian government's amount of 'bailout' to a failed bank).

6
LANDSCAPE ACTIVISM, ART AND BEAUTIES

This chapter presents somewhat rare but pertinent artistic and provocative works and discourse rooted in landscape, to inspire critical thought and subsequent action about sustainability issues. These social, environmental and political activist pieces advocate change through less conventional methods, offering social commentary and new practice opportunities. Immersive, beautiful landscapes are offered as additional great works of art for their capacity to engender reflection, deep connections with the environment and concerns for places and their sustainability.

"The aims of art are incommensurate (as the mathematicians say) with social aims. The aim of an artist is not to solve a problem irrefutably, but to make people love life in all its countless, inexhaustible manifestations."
LEO TOLSTOY, TOLSTOY'S LETTERS (1828–1879)

"Art does not reproduce the visible; rather, it makes visible."
PAUL KLEE, CREATIVE CREDO (1920)

ACTIVIST LANDSCAPE ART

Although activism and provocation are rare landscape architecture dimensions, they can provide less constrained techniques to harness and leverage social influence. Artistic and creative mediums can capture the imagination, influencing new ways of seeing, being, feeling, and understanding. When imbued with direct intent, the artistic medium can foster awareness about sustainability issues and care for people, places and the environment.

6.2
Paul Klee, Twittering Machine, 1922
Labelled 'degenerate art' by Adolf Hitler, this work, which shows birds tied to a hand-crank, highlights art's provocative capacity. Interpretations range from the appropriation of art for propaganda to a critique of the machine age.

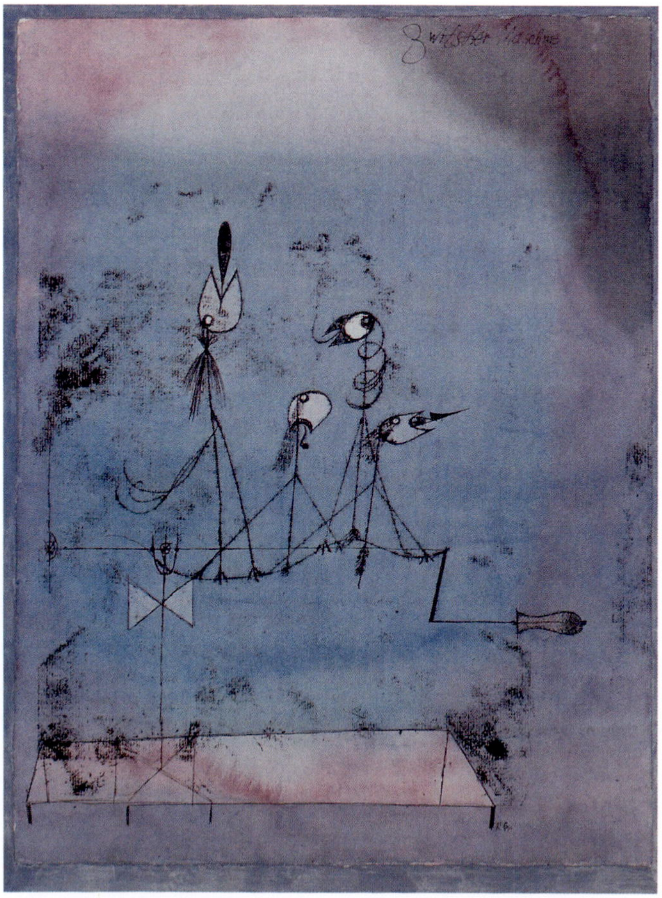

6.2

6.3
PARK(ing) Day, Rebar, San Francisco, USA, November 16, 2005
Over 70% of downtown San Francisco's outdoor space is dedicated to private vehicles. In 2005, local firm Rebar addressed the imbalance of public land through a temporary conversion of a single metered parking space into a park. Following their guidelines, this now annual global event sees artists and activists collaborate to temporarily transform parking spaces into temporary public places and 'parks'.

6.3

Diminishing scope?

Landscape architecture has been traditionally understood as a balance between art and science, combining aesthetic considerations with structural, empirical design solutions. In many societies, economic support for the arts and humanities has waned while the sciences have continued to grow, aided by conservative, commercially focused governments (Chapter 7). This has perhaps contributed to landscape architecture's diminishing artistic scope (as is reflected by the comparatively minimal number of sourced projects featured in this Chapter).

"True, thought lost its scholastic curlicues, ceased to be cyclical and began to run in one direction, forward."
GÜNTER GRASS, ALBRECHT DÜRER AND HIS LEGACY (2002)

"Because of their very nature, science and logical thinking can never decide what is possible or impossible. Their only function is to explain what has been ascertained by experience and observation."
RUDOLF STEINER, LECTURE: EDUCATION AS A FORCE FOR SOCIAL CHANGE (1919)

"What is called 'objectivity', scientific for instance (in which I firmly believe, in a given situation) imposes itself only within a context which is extremely vast, old, firmly established, or rooted in a network of conventions … and yet which still remains a context."
JACQUES DERRIDA, LIMITED INC (1977)

"Many of land art's prominent figures displayed a chilling insensitivity to nature, regarding the great outdoors as nothing more than a colossal sketch pad on which to impose their artistic egos."
DAVID BOURDON, DESIGNING THE EARTH: THE HUMAN IMPULSE TO SHAPE NATURE (1995)

Land art

While the best known artistic practice related to landscape, much 'land art' simply uses the land as artist's canvas. Accordingly, land art frequently lacks environmental motivation. 'Double Negative' by Michael Heizer, for example, excavated 244,000 tons of rock to create a simple spatial gesture in Nevada, USA. In contrast, some land art can embody powerful environmental meanings and social sustainability through harnessed processes (see Wheatfield—A Confrontation; 'leak').

6.4

6.4
Wheatfield—A Confrontation, Agnes Denes, Battery Park Landfill, lower Manhattan, New York, USA, 1982
This four-month land-art project is perhaps Hungarian-American conceptual artist Agnes Denes' best-known work. Denes planted and harvested a field of wheat on 2 acres (8,100m^2) of rubble-strewn landfill near Wall Street and the World Trade Center (now the site of Battery Park City and the World Financial Center), facing the Statue of Liberty.

Its placement on land worth $4.5 billion created a powerful statement of misplaced priorities and issues such as commercial mismanagement, world hunger, waste, and ecological concerns.

Following 200 soil truckloads, 285 cleared, hand dug and sown furrows and four month's maintenance, over 1,000 pounds (454kg) of healthy wheat was harvested, distributed to 28 cities around the world in an exhibition called 'The International Art Show for the End of World Hunger', and subsequently planted.

Landscape and art

Landscape architecture usually involves inter-disciplinary collaboration, working in the public realm and operating within an ethic of social responsibility. Artists may work without a client or on commissions that provide creative freedom, greatly enabling exploration and evocation of ideas. Specific artistic motivation varies, but often has a visual or spatial intent to capture emotionally heightened, transcendent power and beauty. Artistic work can invoke transformative experiences or provoke subversive, intentional and political agendas about environmental and social concerns (Sweet Barrier Reef). The artistic medium can focus on a key issue or singular concern (for example, the plight of the Amazon) bringing it to prominence, whereas the complexity of most landscape projects rarely affords this clarity. Built environment practitioners possess an ability to represent ideas to scale, which can add great value to the expression of a concept (see Hytopia).

6.5a
6.5b
Sweet Barrier Reef, Ken & Julia Yonetani, Venice Biennale, Italy, 2009
This sugar reef representing the Australian sugarcane industry's impact on the Great Barrier Reef was exhibited at the 2009 Venice Biennale. High levels of suspended sediments (nitrogen, phosphorus and herbicides) from sugarcane agriculture are carried through storm and river water, leading to coral bleaching and death. While pondering the work's allusions to sugar as symbol of consumerism, colonization, modernization and environmental impact, spectators were served sugary sweets while models danced to Strauss' 'The Blue Danube'.

6.5a

6.5b

6.6a

6.6b

6.6a
6.6b
'leak' 2010, Rosemary Laing, Cooma-Monaro district, New South Wales, Australia
For her series 'leak', Rosemary Laing built an oversized domestic timber house frame on a sheep paddock, which appears to have fallen upside-down or unceremoniously sprouted from a mound of eucalypts. The resulting visual collision contrasts the pastoral idyll and present-day suburban contagion. Here, the landscape is subjugated and on the verge of a destructive metamorphosis. The confusion of phenomenological relationships questions whether a balancing act between nature and humanity is a possibility or a perpetual predicament.

6.7

6.7
Hytopia, Students from the Technical University of Vienna , Vienna, Austria, 2014
Developed as a protest statement by a group of civil engineering, urban planning and architecture students, the model questions, 'what could you build with €19 billion?' This amount coincides with a government bailout of a failed Bavarian bank, spatially demonstrating its enormous scale over a four-month construction period in Vienna's main Karlsplatz Square. Containing over 1,200 components, €2.15 billion of planned transport infrastructure, power and waste plants, it was built from concrete and timber blocks donated by businesses. The meticulously designed city factors the costs of social and technical infrastructures and could theoretically house 102,574 inhabitants.

6.8a

6.8b

6.8a
6.8b
Carrascoplein, Carrasco Square, West 8, Amsterdam, the Netherlands, 1997–1998
The empty space near Amsterdam's Sloterdijk railway and bus station was a dark, challenging site dominated by elevated railway lines, columns, and car, tram, cyclist and pedestrian transit. West 8 responded through a meld of design and symbolism, creating a restrained and surreal landscape of new grass, asphalt, illuminated iron tree stumps, a clad column simulating a Beech trunk, and white dots when the ground surface is undercover or unfavorably shaded. In 2015, the 'stobben' (tree stump) artworks were relocated to the Amsterdamse Bos (forest) art-route, where they light the atmospheric and dark Dutch forest.

6.9

Festival Garden, West 8, Chaumont-sur-Loire, France, 1999–2000

This 'still life' show garden of terracotta pot-shards, sprawling pumpkins and bones was created at the peak of the French Mad Cow and Foot-and-Mouth Disease outbreak, challenging the 'taboo' of sale of meat and articulating a dialogue between life and death. The enclosed garden of inert mineral fragments juxtaposed with the once-living bone remains is reminiscent of an artificial landscape (much like Holland itself, where West 8 are based) and questions both our impacts on nature and what is 'natural'.

6.9

6.10a
6.10b

Surrogate Trojan, Richard Goodwin, Adrian McGregor, Russell Lowe, Newcastle, New South Wales, Australia, 2007–2008

Three Greenpeace activists were arrested on 6th December 2006 for attempting to prevent an international grains trader bringing 57,000 tons (metric) of Canadian genetically modified (bioengineered) canola seed into a Newcastle plant, to be shifted silently around Australia through margarine, mayonnaise, canola oil and animal feed. Like the Trojan horse, vessels slip in and out of ports, drawing little attention to their hidden cargo and its potential effects. Placed directly opposite the grain silos on the Newcastle Harbor for the 'Back to the City' Festival, the temporary installation 'Trojan' container sat on a bed of canola seed, while an inside projection screened animated footage of environmental concerns.

6.10a

TROJAN

6.10b

"Landscape architecture is a troubled profession, more distinguished by what it lacks … It has no historiography, no formal theory, no definition, direction, or focus. A vast schism currently exists between its academics and professional practitioners [where] designers yoked to the bottom line crank out pedestrian design."
HEIDI HOHMANN & JOERN LANGHORST, LANDSCAPE ARCHITECTURE: A TERMINAL CASE (2004)

Professional limitations?

While design can facilitate ideation, it can be constrained by commercially oriented clients. Commercially restrictive design pressures (Chapter 7) may be compounded within the relatively small landscape profession, where deliberate controversy can affect commercial, professional or institutional reputation. Additionally, accredited/registered practitioners are bound to professional charters (for example of ASLA, LI, AILA) potentially limiting their scope as outspoken activists.

6.11
Splice Garden, Martha Schwartz Partners, Cambridge, Massachusetts, USA
This 875 square foot (61m^2) rooftop garden is part of an art collection for the microbiology research Whitehead Institute and intends to create an unsolvable visual puzzle for the building's scientists. The dark and inhospitable ninth story courtyard site with high surrounding walls, inability to hold additional weight, lack of water source, low budget and no maintenance staff, precluded living plants. By providing enough signals for the site to read as a garden, the design could imply a larger landscape through abstraction, symbolism and reference. Its narrative relates to the institute's work and is a cautionary tale about the inherent dangers of gene splicing. The garden is a 'monstrous hybrid', a forced coupling of French Renaissance and Japanese Zen. Traditional elements are deliberately distorted, projected from vertical surfaces or precariously teetering on a wall's edge. All plants are plastic, while the green colors are composed of colored gravel and paint. Typical Zen rocks are replaced with French topiary pompoms, while rolled steel covered with Astroturf forms clipped hedges (doubling as seating).

6.11

Pastiche or profound?

In conventional landscape practice and public domain design, an artistic outcome is often incorporated into a project through sculpture, murals and patterns in pavements, walls and structures. 'Environmental' art commonly manifests as representational in character and there are countless projects that tangibly evoke a site's location or historical characteristics (such as wave pavement patterns by the beach). There can be a fine line between literal symbolism, pastiche and a significant work of art. Craftspersonship, mastery of the medium, innovation and sophisticated execution is crucial. Many projects (as with tourism) may actually be contributing to the destruction of the elements that they represent, without any ironic or educational intent.

Activism

Some projects involve an artistic curator or consultant who may select an appropriate artist(s). Various landscape practitioners are artists in their own right. Design team members, stakeholders or clients may develop the brief or key themes for the artist. Activist landscape work is rare, due to the public and usually permanent nature of landscape-based artistic interventions. Artists or designers may employ an ironic, 'tongue-in-cheek' approach to bypass political correctness, or subversively imbue hidden meanings (such as the political messages in Stowe Gardens, England). Ambitious artistic briefs are usually the result of private situations free from censorship and the neutrality of most government-controlled public contexts. Opportunities exist in unsolicited, competition, academic, and unofficial (guerrilla, illegal) design and these can expand a predominantly service-based profession into greater realms of expression.

6.12

Ecological Footprint, Richard Weller, Boomtown, Perth, Australia, 2009

This image conveys the ecological footprint of a detached house in Perth—the immense 'estate' area of productive land required to provide the resources demanded by its inhabitants. Weller states, "This then is the true dimension of an average Western Australian suburban property. In this sense suburbia's aristocratic pretensions have now been fully realised." This equates to an ecological footprint of 14.50 hectares per person (35.8 acres), consisting of Food and beverages 6.69ha; Clothing 0.50; Other products 1.56; Housing 0.1; Energy supply 0.41; Trade 2.02; Other services 1.13; Degraded land 0.74; Other 1.25.

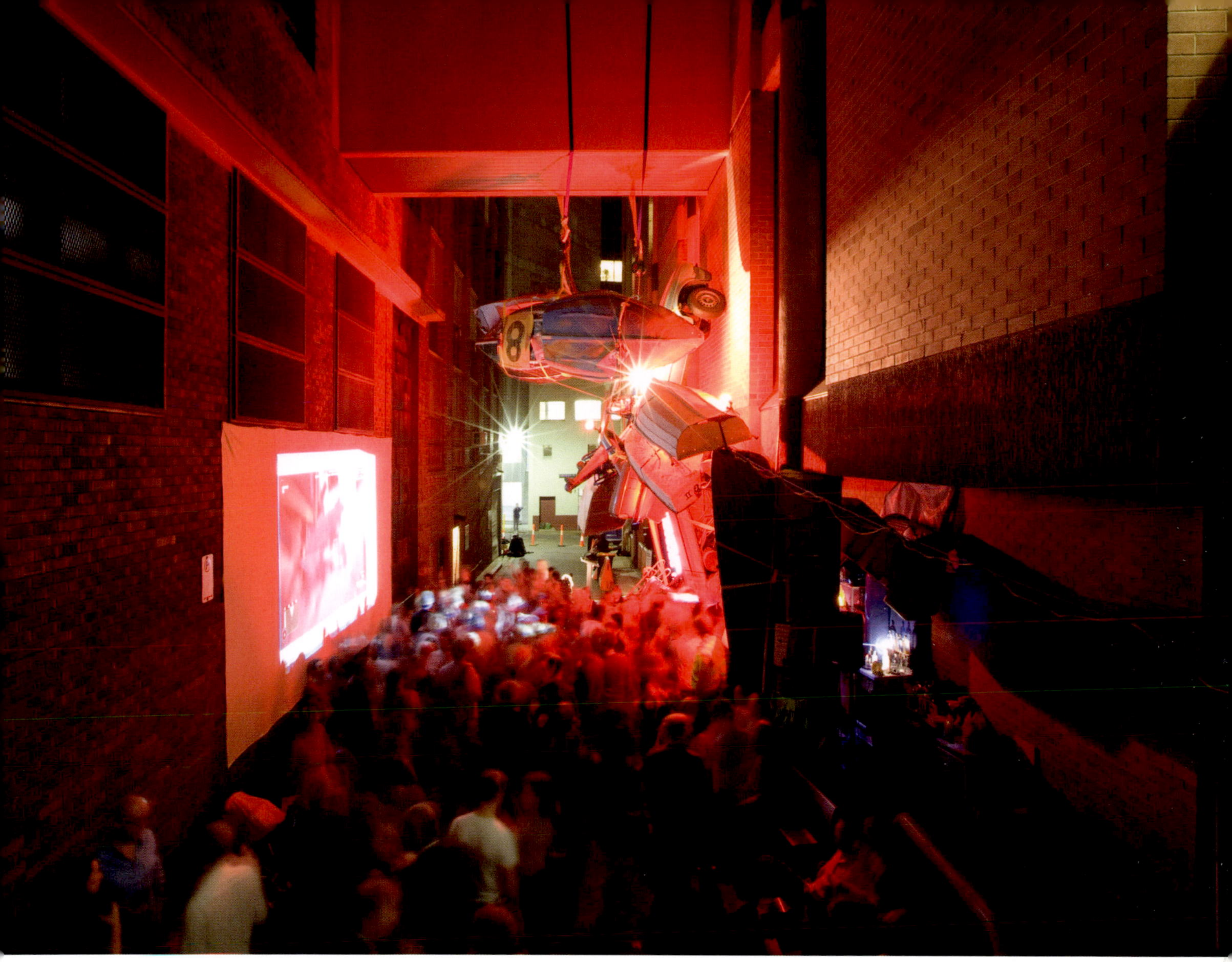

6.13

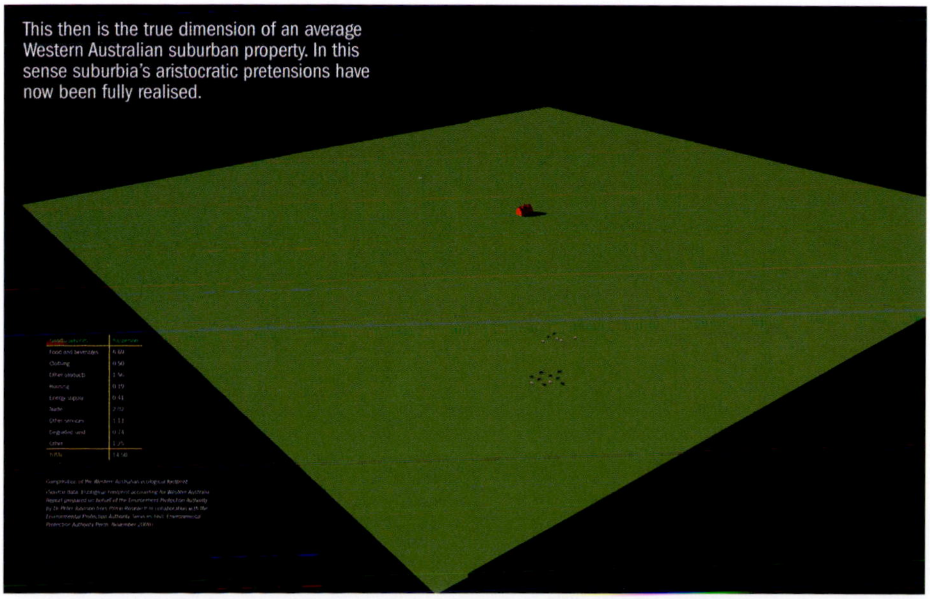
This then is the true dimension of an average
Western Australian suburban property. In this
sense suburbia's aristocratic pretensions have
now been fully realised.

6.12

6.13

Seven Metre Bar, Richard Goodwin, Adrian McGregor, Russell Lowe, Sydney, New South Wales, Australia, 2009

According to NASA scientist James Hansen, sea levels could rise up to 75 meters (246 feet) from polar ice cap melt. The Seven Metre Bar temporary installation (chosen from 500 registrations/68 submissions to activate Sydney's under-utilized laneways) sits at an elevation of 7 meters above sea level and aimed to spark dialogues on climate change and sea level rise. The installation was built primarily from salvaged junk and featured cars, boats and materials tangled within columns like seaweed. Volatile weather scenarios were projected onto the bar, the ferocity of which intensified as the patronage increased.

"Ethics and aesthetics are one."
LUDWIG WITTGENSTEIN, JOURNAL (1916)

"We can be ethical only in relation to something we can see, feel, understand, love, or otherwise have faith in."
ALDO LEOPOLD, A SAND COUNTY ALMANAC (1949)

LANDSCAPE BEAUTIES AND SUSTAINABILITY

Can beauty be measured? Landscapes can powerfully shape experience. Whether 'natural' or designed, beautiful landscapes can ignite connection, passion and concern. Like artists, some landscape architects attempt to create heightened and even transcendental states for those who spatially experience their work. If this enables people to see and feel at 'one' with nature, or connect personally to a particular place (such as a local conservation area or design site or street trees), theme (native plants or animals) or issue (threat of development), it can engender beneficial outcomes for stewardship and ethical action.

6.14
Asher Brown Durand, The Kindred Spirits, 1838
Extensive land clearance for forestry and agriculture greatly diminished the 'hostile wilderness', long considered the 'uncivilized haunt of beasts'. Durand's painting heralds a significant shift in perception from previously negative views of wildness to romanticized. Today, in the Anthropocene, the concept of untouched 'wilderness' has been reframed as a contemporary myth (see Chapter 2), yet its enduring image harnesses immeasurable energy in conservation activism.

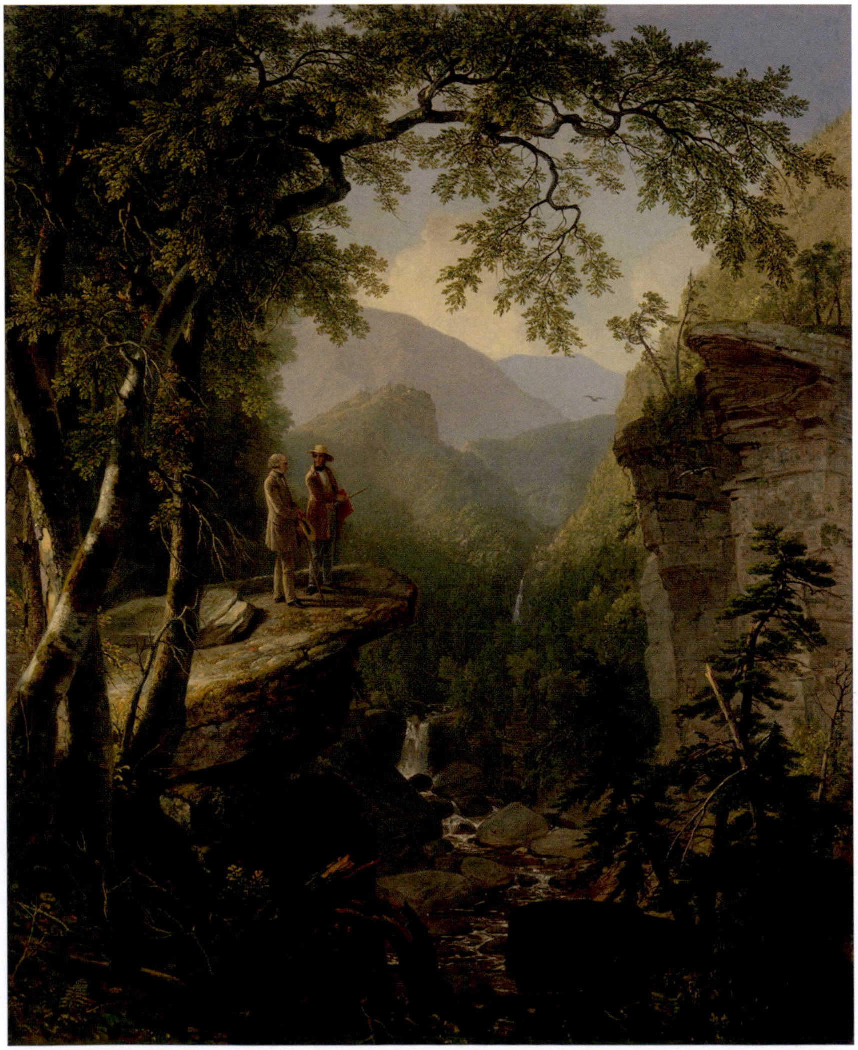

6.14

"The single most effective action that can be accomplished for the future of nature is to motivate and inspire large numbers of people."
ROBERT FRANCE, GREEN WORLD, GRAY HEART?: THE PROMISE AND THE REALITY OF LANDSCAPE ARCHITECTURE IN SUSTAINING NATURE (2003)

"Creating desire is essential to sustainability… But in the rush to embrace quantifiable and demonstrable technological solutions, we have overlooked the important role of human nature. In fact, if you consider design a creative rather than merely an imitative endeavor, desire is the impetus to the process. Thus design too has been under-represented in the discourse on sustainability."
MARTHA SCHWARTZ, SEX AND THE CITY LANDSCAPE: DESIRE AND SUSTAINABILITY (2009)

6.15a (Before)
6.15b
6.15c
6.15d
6.15e

The Australian Garden, TCL & Paul Thompson, Cranbourne, Melbourne, Australia, 1995–

The Australian Garden is a retrofitted 62 acre (25ha) former sand quarry on Melbourne's south eastern outskirts and an exploration and expression of the coexistence of the Australian people and their landscape and flora. The project is a radical departure from established European landscape traditions (unsustainable in a subcontinent with vastly different climate and soil) and the standard botanic garden presentation of scattered global plant collections in broad groupings.

The garden presents artistic interpretations of bio and landscape character regions, assembling plant associations in spatial compositions, drawing visitors to perceive beauty in the native landscape and helping to engender ecological literacy. The design highlights the tension between the natural landscape and our human impulse to alter it, using that tension as a driving creative impulse for exploration, expression and interpretation to celebrate Australia's environments.

6.15a

6.15b

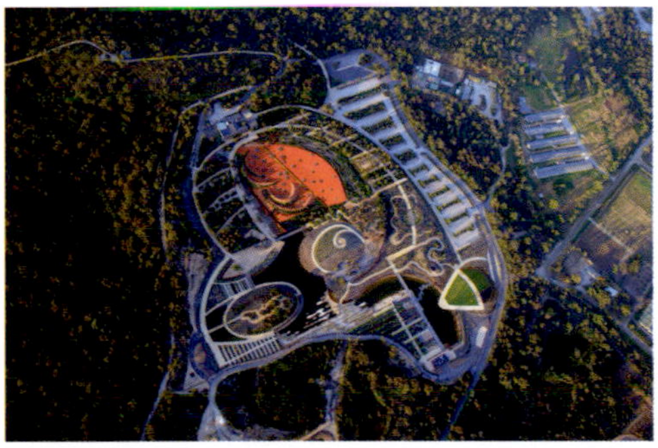
6.15c

6.15d

6.15e

STUDY/DISCUSSION QUESTIONS

Has a particular place/site/design or experience/scenario stimulated a care for nature (or landscape architecture) for you?

Have you ever experienced sublime immersion in nature? Have you ever experienced fear in nature? Are these connected?

Are there any sustainability issues that generate a desire to express your ideas and feelings? What are they? What artistic mediums do you feel inclined to use to represent these?

Are developers neutral? What about artists? What is the baseline of measurement that they/you default to? Who determines and shapes social norms?

What is activism? Does activism exist in design and in landscape architecture? Can you find any examples?

Why do you think that people are drawn to art and activism to express environmental issues and their ideas and views?

Do you have a favorite landscape project that expresses a meaning or message? How has this been executed?

Are there any projects or installations that have changed the way you 'see' and feel? If so, what were the characteristics or conditions that led to this?

Is landscape architecture a troubled profession? Why or why not? If you think it is, what should it address to improve its situation?

Does much land art display a 'chilling insensitivity to nature'? Is this different to development projects displaying a similar insensitivity?

Can beauty be measured? Does it effect your affinity for a place?

Who determines what is considered aesthetic or beautiful? Is this individual or collective?

What are the dominant perceptions of landscape beauty? How have these changed over time? How do these impact sustainability?

What is the difference between 'banal' and 'ugly' in the landscape? Does dissonance have a similar effect?

FURTHER READING

Bell, B. and Wakeford, K. (2008) *Expanding Architecture: Design as Activism*, NY: Metropolis Books.

Bourdon, D. (1995) *Designing the Earth: The Human Impulse to Shape Nature*, New York: Henry N. Abrams, Inc.

Davis, J., Greenhill, J. and Lafountain, J. (2015) *A companion to American art*, Chichester: Wiley Blackwell. (See Braddock, Chapter 26, p. 447–467).

Deming, E. (2015) *Values in landscape architecture and environmental design: finding center in theory and practice*, Baton Rouge: LSU Press. (See Meyer, p. 30–53).

Garrard, G. (2012) *Ecocriticism*, New York: Routledge.

Gregg, M. and Seigworth, G. (2010) *The affect theory reader*, Durham, NC: Duke University Press.

Hohmann, H. and Langhorst, J. (2005) 'Editor's Choice – Landscape Architecture: A Terminal Case', *Landscape Architecture* 95/4 pp. 26–45.

Jacobs, J. (1961) *The Death and Life of Great American Cities*, New York: Random House.

Meyer, E. (2008) Sustaining beauty: The performance of appearance, *Journal of Landscape Architecture* 3(1) pp. 6–23.

Scapegoat journal.

Shepard, B. (2016) *Sustainable urbanism and direct action: case studies in dialectical activism*, London: Rowman & Littlefield.

You might also like to look for further information on the following projects:

Not A Cornfield, Lauren Bon & Metabolic Studio, Los Angeles, USA, 2005–2006

365 Bales, Stephen Grossman, New Haven, Connecticut, USA, 2000

Garden of Australian Dreams, Room 4.1.3, Canberra, Australia

Terra Form Australis, HASSELL & Holopoint & the Environment Institute, Vencie Biennial, 2010

A Line Made By Walking, Brogan Bunt, Mt Keira, Wollongong, Australia, 2013

Parco di Levico, Stefano Marinaz, Trento, Italy, 2010

Waste Landscape, Elise Morin and Clémence Eliard, Paris, Bucharest and The Hague, Europe, 2011–2013

The Black Cloud, Heather and Ivan Morison & Sash Reading, West Yorkshire, UK, 2009

Vacant Lot of Cabbages, Barry Thomas, Wellington, New Zealand, 1978.

INTERVIEW Elizabeth Meyer

Professor Elizabeth Meyer is a landscape architect, theorist and critic at the University of Virginia, where she has served as Landscape Architecture Department Chair, Director of the Graduate Landscape Architecture Program, Dean and Edward E. Elson Professor. Her teaching and scholarship have garnered honors, grants and awards from the Council of Educators in Landscape Architecture, the American Society of Landscape Architects, the Graham Foundation and the National Endowment for the Arts. Professor Meyer is an ASLA Fellow and advises leading firms working on significant historic and cultural landscapes.

In your manifesto, *Sustaining Beauty* and the follow up *Beyond Sustaining Beauty*, you argue that the aesthetic experiences in landscape are essential for sustainability. What is the relationship between aesthetics and sustainability?

The primary point that I wanted to make in the manifesto was that focusing solely on ecological performance was limiting the effectiveness of design and that unless there was a major change in how the larger public perceived and felt connected to the bio-physical world, all of the 'green bandaids' in design (e.g. rain gardens or high-performance landscape infrastructure) weren't going to be enough, because a truly sustainable community requires changes to everyday practices and a larger re-imagination of the relationship between humans and the non-human world.

Through explorations in my earlier work I realized that aesthetic experience was fundamentally relational—it has to do with effects, being in the world, seeing and encountering, and how this affects one's psyche. Aesthetics is the art and science of perception, not just a formal category of how something looks. As I started thinking about the issues of perception and relationships, I realized that many of the people who talk about being environmentalists, mention an encounter they had as a 'free-range kid', such as a relationship to a creek, water body or forest patch. They learnt more later because they came to wonder and care about that place. And that was a relationship—it wasn't data or information or knowledge; it was felt.

I think if you care about the sustainability or resilience of the built environment, you have to change how people feel about the world, not just change the ecological performance of a place. So I would say that there are four components to sustainability— there's environmental and ecological performance; there's a concern for social equity; a need for economic prosperity; but a fourth issue is aesthetic experience of all types and not just beauty.

Why do you think sustainability is so obsessed with technology, quantification and technical considerations?

In the culture that we live in—a neoliberal, capitalistic economy—there's such a desire and need to quantify. Whether it's the push for evidence based design, where all of a sudden, lab scientists have more say than theoretical scientists (you can see that in our fields too), I think part of it is being part of the neo-liberal capitalist economy where the bottom line is how much something is financially worth. That has fuelled the interest in ecosystem services with particular focus on the regulating and providing of services that water, soil, plants and wildlife give to human beings. I have explored ecosystem services in relationship to aesthetics and for example, the UN Millennium Goals/ Assessment helped progress thinking on the importance of quantifying, measuring, exchanging ecosystem services and these include a category called cultural services. Within that category are things like spiritual sites, recreational and aesthetics. There is more work to be done here on qualitative metrics related to the role of aesthetics in ecosystem services. I do think that even scientists recognize that the value of qualitative metrics, but we as designers haven't been good at claiming that category. We've gone down the modernist, functionalist, technologist routes instead of arguing for qualitative metrics that design can offer. I'm intrigued by new research between neuroscience, environmental psychology and design for which qualitative metrics can result from, and frankly, I think a lot of it can also surface from the narratives of oral histories from people in particular communities.

Do you think we can convince policy and decisionmakers that the issues you're talking about—ethical agency, landscape beauty, aesthetics, deserve as much or more devotion than dominant empirical science?

I think part of the answer to that comes from the accounts of scientists, environmentalists and designers who talk about their own childhood and early adult experiences. I have former students (e.g. from anthropology and the liberal arts), as well as ecologists (e.g. Stewart Pickett) and colleagues (Kristina Hill) who all talk about the power of narrative as an art of rhetoric and persuasion. We have a tendency to think that we have to quantify things but stories and narratives neurologically connect with people in very powerful ways. I have a friend who's a psychotherapist and she talks about the fact that the stories we tell about each other actually change the structure of our brain, help us to not only deal with trauma but also to re-imagine new habits. So we have to find the right form for these narratives, they may not all be written, they may be a combination of info-graphics and writing that explain the powerful connections in terms of people's public health and wellbeing that have been made through their everyday experiences in constructed or found landscapes in their communities. There's a lot of potential there, if people are collaborating, particularly with anthropologists, environmental psychologists and public health professionals.

I think to see the role of some landscape architects, not just in making, not just in criticizing, but in communicating and to realize the power of that. I think that professional organisations such as ASLA in America—while they do a lot of things very well—they haven't used their role as a central clearinghouse for our profession in this way yet. I think that that's a logical place for that to be a primary role, as some other professions are probably doing this better.

Culturally, can we shift to appreciating the beauty in productive, working, and abandoned landscapes in the urban context? We seem to value wildness or a wild aesthetic in non-urban locations but in cities the instinct still seems to be to 'scape' everything, with aesthetic tastes still entrenched in formalism and approaches that dominate and subjugate natural systems?

That's a great question, I think about that a lot because my close friend and colleague Julie Bargmann is really interested in the urban wild, spontaneous vegetation and the role that a landscape architect could play in curating that and not destroying it. I think there's a couple of things to keep in mind here. I already think that there's a generational change. There is much more interest in the urban wild from an aesthetics of 'thrift', understanding that things that work have their own intrinsic beauty, that conceptions of beauty and aesthetics change over time and they change over time in relationship to changing social conditions and political conditions, not just design conditions, and I think we have to recognize this. The philosopher Kate Soper, in an essay on cultural hedonism and aesthetic reenvisioning, talks about the fact that there are already existing spatial practices that are connected to new forms of sustainability and new conceptions of beauty. We just need to be aware of those. So I think about, in the United States, the number of young people right out of school who are drawn to live in cities like Detroit or New Orleans, that have radically different urban landscapes because of either neglect or disinvestment or disaster and slow response and neither city, given the scale of the issue, could ever be fixed by design. The communities that live there also see the raw material and the resilience of things that are working and finding a home, productive landscapes, and emerging habitats developing. So I think we need to harness what's already started to happen. In my experience a lot of designers are caught up in what they think the public wants, instead of actually having their ear to the ground about actually changing perceptions.

I read a lot of nature writing outside of design writing. There's a magazine in the States called 'Orion', which is a beautiful collection of essays, poetry and photography about people and places. I'm really struck by the difference of what is discussed and presented there compared to 25 years ago. That's obviously a rarefied group, because these are people who are interested with people's relationship to places and the natural world, but what they perceive to be the natural world is anything but the untouched and pristine. More specifically, I think more projects like Südgelände Nature Park in Berlin can occur in other places, bringing city dwellers and suburban dwellers in close proximity to these disturbed, spontaneous vegetation sites. These need to be done in a way that it's clear there's a design hand that's curated the sequence or the proximity (I say proximity because at times, if it's a tricky, gooey, toxic site, immersion might not be wise yet). So these provisional encounters with sites that are still off limits might be one way to start and frankly the other—and we've been having some of these conversations here in Virginia—is starting to demonstrate to officials in localities who are charged with management and maintenance, how much more resilient some of these tough plants are. It's curious the native plants bias has swung so much that there's often a lack of recognition that with the erratic weather we've been having, the extremes between drought and flood and changes in sea-level rise, their native place has moved. So that there's a practical way that these places can be re-introduced as resilient and capable of less care than some other kinds of landscapes.

Is there an objective, universal standard for sustainable beauty or is it in the eye of the beholder?

If I think about what I should have done differently in that manifesto and that I've commented on more recently in my piece, 'Beyond Sustaining Beauty', was to put the 'beauties' in the plural and to get away from any sense that there's a universal standard. The other general issue is that when I titled that manifesto, I used the term beauty as a shorthand for aesthetics, but because I did that and wasn't explicit about the range of beauties that are possible, I think that caused some misinterpretation of my intentions. In my second piece I talk about changing conceptions of beauty, connected to things like dissonance, and dissonant beauty in surrealist art. Maria Hellström Reimer's fantastic essay, 'Unsettling Ecoscapes' talks about the importance of creating challenging, uncanny and at times discordant everyday landscapes to stretch our sense of aesthetics from a normative conception of beauty to ugliness. There are other authors who also discuss the idea that 'ugly' is not the opposite of beauty; 'banal' is the opposite of both. The beautiful and ugly are related to each other.

What key findings have resulted from your recent research?

I have refined the premise of 'Sustaining Beauty' to think about the essence of the socio-ecological social agency of landscape—what is it about a landscape that has the ability to remake the way we think about ourselves as a socio-ecological community? A few points I'll share:

1. The beautiful or aesthetics may be connected to appearance but they're not exhausted by it. Because they're connected to experience, time would be required to apprehend the beautiful and so that gets to repeat visits to a place, and living in a place as a fundamental part of understanding aesthetics and sustainability. From a one time visit, you don't see sustainable beauty, you experience it over time.

2. Aesthetic experience requires duration and it exists in the exchange between what you see and what you know. The art critic Arthur Danto writes about this, where he says that there's always a gap between what you see and what you feel and it's processed by what you know. This gets back to your question about whether there's one kind of sustainable beauty or not; your own experience is going to affect that, where you grew up, what kind of language you speak, so that's important, to realise that the visual is actually only one part and it's experienced over time and it's in relationship to past experience.

3. I connected this point to Elaine Scarry's writing on beauty but I now realise that positive psychologists are writing about it as well; aesthetic experience draws us near to something and it makes us want to know more and to act. Jonathan Haidt, who's written a book called *The Happiness Hypothesis* talks about aesthetic experience in urging us to create response. That's fascinating because there's the agency of a designer but there's also what would you do as a citizen, your creative act.

4. Aesthetic experience builds emotive intuition that combines feelings and knowledge. It's something you experience, but it's in relation to what you know and calls into question what you know and essentially this back and forth between feelings and knowledge produces its own form of cognition—a new way of knowing that connects feelings and knowledge. This is where this new body of literature on theories of effect—which is pervasive in the humanities now and is starting to make its way into architecture and landscape architecture—is fascinating because it is interested less in sensual experience and more in the relationship between materials, bodies, emotions and action. That was a useful new area for me because it allowed me to pull away from aesthetic theory alone or phenomenology, both of which have limitations and to connect to this new area of what is sometimes called 'social aesthetics' or 'theories of effects'. These are things that I learned about in response to criticisms of my essay that allowed me to develop a more nuanced argument about the potential reason and the effects of adding aesthetics to the sustainability agenda. It's one thing for me to speculate about the action, and another thing for me to realize that a whole range of other disciplines are thinking very deeply right now about the connection between bodies, emotions, networks of bodies, and systems and changing ethical practices.

7.1
Northala Fields
This London project effectively paid for itself through generating income as a 'waste-fill' depositary.

7
SOCIAL SUSTAINABILITY: INFLUENCE BEYOND SITE

Landscape architecture is not simply the process of designing surface treatments, spatial forms and objects, but increasingly, the ethical planning and creative problem solving for systems, processes and strategies. A voracious global market seeking continual growth can lack social accountability. Landscape architecture and design thinking can facilitate socially oriented, lateral solutions and benefits extending beyond a project brief or site, effectively transcending conventional disciplinary boundaries to increase the social sustainability and resilience of settlements and communities at local, national and global scales. This is an inherently politicized process requiring skillful mediation, communication, community engagement, interpretive design, leadership skills and an ability to compromise, helping to facilitate social sustainability outcomes in areas such as education and health.

"The right to the city is … a common rather than an individual right since this transformation inevitably depends upon the exercise of a collective power to reshape the processes of urbanization. The freedom to make and remake our cities and ourselves is … one of the most precious yet most neglected of our human rights."
DAVID HARVEY, NEW LEFT REVIEW (2008)

"Plant spacious parks in your cities, and loose their gates as wide as the morning, to the whole people."
ANDREW JACKSON DOWNING (1815–1852)

"There is a long tradition in critically debating landscape not as something simply 'out there', but as an activity and process."
WERNER KRAUSS, THE ANTHROPOLOGY OF POST-ENVIRONMENTAL LANDSCAPES (2012)

ETHICS

Ethics concern moral principles, standards and codes governing behavior. Environmental and professional ethics are usually touched upon in design education (to significantly varying extents between programs), however, their realization can become constrained within the business and corporate-dominated world of design practice. Personal values may not align with professional ethics, which in turn may contradict business practices. The perpetual-growth, free-trade capitalist economic system places commercial pressures on businesses to accept commissions and clients that might be potentially ethically and environmentally questionable. Design is no exception and commercial practices face a constant threat of securing adequate income. Maintaining ethical environmental standards can reduce commercial viability by restricting client bases and ruling out unsustainable commissions such as new nuclear or coal fired power stations (toxic waste, climate change), mining projects (uranium and subsequent weapons proliferation, coal extraction), and desalination plants (see Chapter 1). Frequent ethical dilemmas encountered in landscape projects include unnecessary removal of existing trees, soil and vegetation, and building poor quality housing, infrastructures, social services and landscapes. A design practice may accept ethically or reputation-compromising commissions but try to disguise their involvement (for example, by not listing it in their completed projects). Other firms may refuse to be involved based on their ethical standards. At an individual level, a designer may face the challenge of working on projects confronting his or her value system while employed by another organization.

7.2
Birkenhead Park, England, Joseph Paxton, Park Drive, Birkenhead, Merseyside, UK, 1847
Britain's first publically funded civic park was intended to act as a 'green-lung' antidote to the heavily industrialized region. The conversion of 226 acres (91ha) of marshy grazing land to 'natural' rather than formal garden was initially funded by Parliament and then private sale and inspired Frederick Law Olmsted in such seminal projects as New York's Central Park.

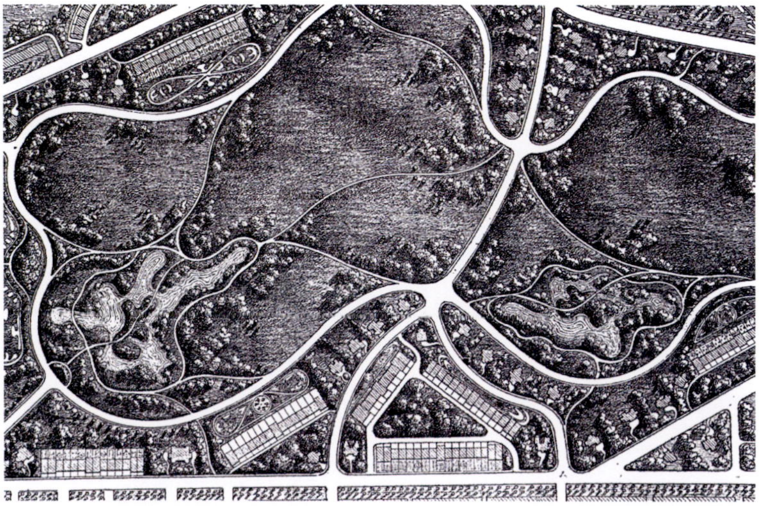

7.2

"How is it possible to gain that ability to act to sustain what needs to be sustained in conditions that devalue and negate that with sustaining capability for the sake of short term gains and immediate gratification?"
TONY FRY, A NEW DESIGN PHILOSOPHY (1999)

"I see landscape as being 'systems of flow' that humans may attempt to guide, spaces being influenced by forces with which people may try to negotiate towards their better inhabitation of the planet."
THIERRY KANDJEE, INTERVIEW: FUNDAMENTALS OF LANDSCAPE ARCHITECTURE (2015)

7.3a
7.3b
7.3c
7.3d
7.3e

Urban Metabolism: Sustainable Development of Rotterdam, James Corner Field Operations + FABRICations, Rotterdam, the Netherlands, 2013–2014

This project examined how 'urban metabolisms' can improve sustainable outcomes in city development. Nine categories of 'material flows' at regional and metropolitan levels were analyzed (cargo; people; waste; biota; energy; food; water; air; and sand and sediments). Drawings and animated videos articulate invisible metabolisms in the dynamic urban landscape, focusing on entropy and waste. Ecological planning initiatives then focused on context-specific strategies—channel heat, connect biotopes, capture nutrients, and catalyze industry. Specific possibilities including a subterranean heat network utilizing industrial waste, ecological matrix from unused port slips and aquaculture, and a micro manufacturing and logistics precinct. Part of the 6th International Architecture Biennale of Rotterdam, the work also provided the municipality with potential pilot strategies and urban locations.

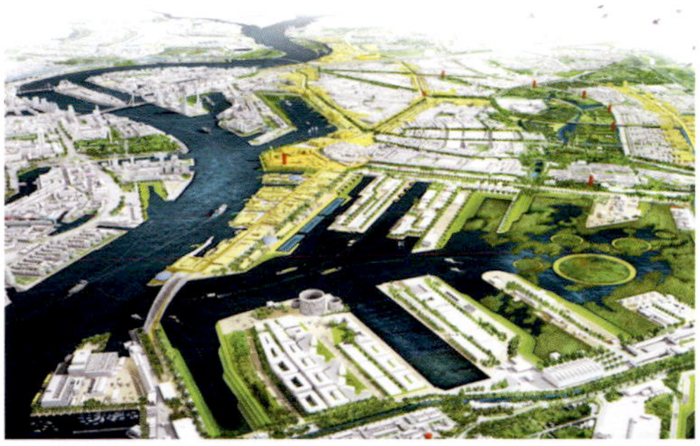
7.3a

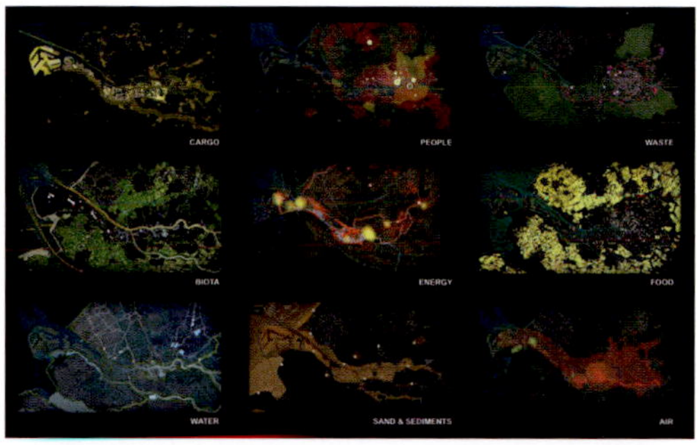
CARGO
PEOPLE
WASTE
BIOTA
ENERGY
FOOD
WATER
SAND & SEDIMENTS
AIR
7.3b

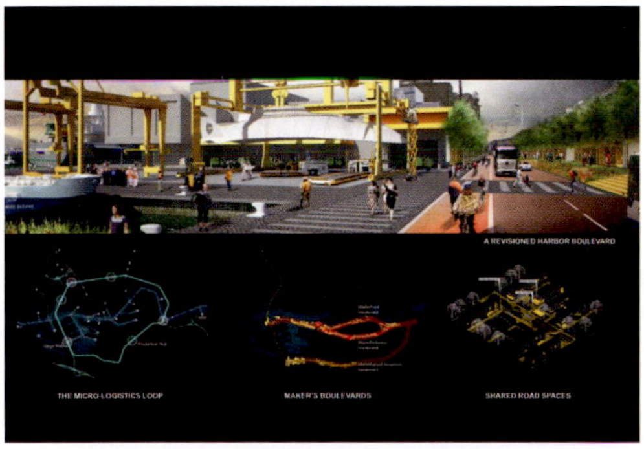
A REVISIONED HARBOR BOULEVARD
THE MICRO LOGISTICS LOOP
MAKER'S BOULEVARDS
SHARED ROAD SPACES
7.33c

SOUTH ROTTERDAM'S NUTRIENT COLLECTIVE
REGIONAL ORGANIC WASTE INFRASTRUCTURE
NEIGHBORHOODS WITH SEPARATE ORGANIC WASTE INFRASTRUCTURE
UNDER-UTILIZED OPEN SPACES & ADJACENT NEIGHBORHOODS
7.3d

WALHAAVEN PORT SPONGE PARK
ELECTRIC UTILITIES CORRIDORS
STACKED ELECTRICAL INFRASTRUCTURE
SEDIMENT ACCRUES AROUND VACANT PIER
7.3e

"What difference does it make how much is laid away in a man's safe or in his barns, how many head of stock he grazes or how much capital he puts out at interest, if he is always after what is another's and only counts what he has yet to get, never what he has already? You ask what is the proper limit to a person's wealth? First, having what is essential, and second, having what is enough."
LUCIUS ANNAEUS SENECA, LETTERS TO LUCILIUS (65 CE)

Civic boundaries

There are numerous examples of ethical dilemmas arising in design practice. Are projects' worth or usefulness diminished if their clients' or sponsors' environmental, social and ethical practices have been found to be detrimental or brought into public scrutiny? Should project sponsors be able to 'advertise' their involvement through naming rights or on-site signage? Are these issues heightened in the context of health or child-focused projects?

Distorted definition

In the built environment context, the term *development* almost always refers to *economic* development. This contrasts the United Nations definition that favors human, social and environmental factors. Development can and should benefit the collective and not merely the individual or an elite minority.

7.4
McDonalds Cycle Centre, Millennium Park, Chicago, Illinois, USA, 2004
Part of Chicago's 'Bike 2010 Plan', the cycle centre includes lockers, showers, repair, rental, café, and parking for 300 bicycles. The roof's 120 solar panels produce 6.5% of the climate-controlled building's electricity supply.

MCDONAL
CYCLE CEN
MILLENNIUM
PARK

7.4

7.5a
7.5b
Sands Bethworks, SWA, Bethlehem, Pennsylvania, USA, 2008
SWA's 20 acre (8ha) low-maintenance design forms part of a casino, resort, museum and retail development, reusing 23 of 33 existing industrial buildings and salvaging site relics (such as the dramatic ore crane as an entry gateway).

The EPA first enacted a site clean of USA's largest brownfield site (1,800 acres/728ha), transporting 375 tons (340 tonnes) of contaminated soil to landfill before backfilling with clean fill. Vegetation suiting the high levels of soil alkalinity from continuous iron ore extraction now complement gabions of reclaimed materials, tracing geometries of former industrial processes. Phytoremediation through trees, shrubs, and groundcover planting (such as birch and juniper) neutralize soil contaminants, while 25 sunken gravel and vegetated bioswales cleanse stormwater runoff from 11 acres (4.5ha) of land, (assisted by the 30 depressed curbs intentionally slowing infiltration and significantly reducing suspended solids, phosphorus, and nitrogen), recharging local aquifers.

7.6a
7.6b
7.6c

Rio Tinto Naturescape Kings Park, Plan (E), Kings Park & Botanic Gardens, Perth, Australia, 2011

A remnant natural creek system in urban bushland forms a 15 acre (6ha) playspace in Perth's 1,003 acre (406ha) Kings Park. Themed zones referencing specific Swan Coastal Plain bioregion associations aim to reconnect children with nature through fun, discovery and immersion. The highly orchestrated, regulated and expensive design is adeptly and skillfully executed to present an appearance of naturally occurring landscapes dotted with serendipitous informal play opportunities. Climbing towers and tunnels integrate into the Banksia woodland, while design elements inspired by the shape of seeds, leaves and nests (such as shelters, viewing towers and seating pods) deliberately 'intrude' into the 'natural' landscape. The project retained trees and vegetation, accommodating high visitation and environmental maintenance practices.

7.6a

7.6b

7.6c

7.5a

7.5b

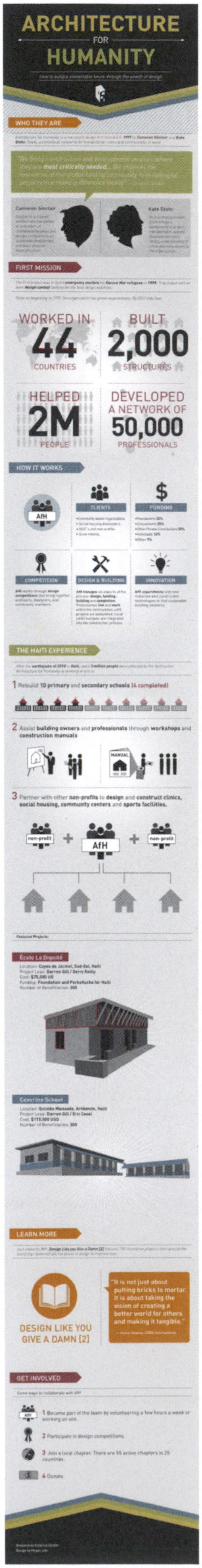
ARCHITECTURE
FOR
HUMANITY
WHO THEY ARE
FIRST MISSION
WORKED IN
44
COUNTRIES
BUILT
2,000
STRUCTURES
HELPED
2M
PEOPLE
DEVELOPED
A NETWORK OF
50,000
PROFESSIONALS
HOW IT WORKS
AfH
CLIENTS
FUNDING
COMPETITION
DESIGN & BUILDING
INNOVATION
THE HAITI EXPERIENCE
AfH
LEARN MORE
DESIGN LIKE YOU GIVE A DAMN [2]
GET INVOLVED

7.7a

"It is helpful to recognize that the present industrial system is, practically speaking, a couch potato."
AMORY LOVINS, HUNTER LOVINS, AND PAUL HAWKEN, NATURAL CAPITALISM (2000)

SOCIAL SUSTAINABILITY

Social sustainability is a broad concept. It encompasses topics such as social equity; livability; health equity; community development; diversity; social capital; social support; human rights; labor rights; quality of life; place-making; social responsibility; social justice; multiculturalism; social cohesion; cultural competence; community resilience; disaster and emergency response; political and economic accountability and human adaptation. Social sustainability is largely at odds with the prevalent thrust of Western society that believes that improved quality of life is primarily achieved through an individualistic pursuit of wealth creation.

7.7b

ONE

7.7c

7.7a
7.7b
7.7c
Design humanitarian organizations, location: worldwide
Environmental and humanitarian ethics are central to non-profit design organizations such as Architecture Sans Frontiéres, Architects Without Borders, Architecture for Humanity (see 7.7a), and Architects Without Frontiers (7.7b and 7.7c shown here undertaking student-assisted projects in Nepal 2010, 2012). These organizations typically provide design, development and construction services to underprivileged and vulnerable communities in response to natural disaster, conflict, crisis, and community need worldwide. They aim to create ecologically sensitive, culturally appropriate projects respecting local identity and enhancing self-reliance exchanging knowledge and skills. Usually staffed by architecture, planning, urban design, and landscape architecture volunteers, securing ongoing funding and participation can be challenging.

"City space, with its human propinquity, distinctive neighbourhoods and humanly scaled politics—like rural space, with its closeness to nature, its high sense of mutual aid and its strong family relationships—is being absorbed by urbanisation, with its smothering traits of anonymity, homogenisation, and institutional gigantism."
MURRAY BOOKCHIN, THE RISE OF URBANIZATION AND THE DECLINE OF CITIZENSHIP (1987)

Social spaces

Social sustainability in more specific relation to planning and landscape architecture encompasses the goal of creating communities and public spaces that are healthy; livable; equitable; diverse; connected; democratic, and provide a good quality of life through hard and soft amenities and infrastructures. Transparent and accountable decision-making processes assist place-making by increasing trust and rapport between municipalities and communities.

7.8

7.9

7.8
Baugruppen
Baugruppen are collectives formed with the intent of building communities and housing that eliminate the developer. Germany is leading baugruppen implementation (Vauban in Freiburg shown here) and urban development policy can be skewed to favor elimination of real-estate speculation (for example, parts of Berlin).

7.9
Bo01, Malmö, Sweden, 1998–2005
Created as part of the 2001 European Housing Expo, the housing development occupies a formerly contaminated island of reclaimed land. Environmental features include: soil remediation coupled with a highly permeable stormwater system; green roofs reducing runoff; aesthetic WSUD; gardens of 50 plant varieties providing habitat (returning mixed results); 50% open space dedication; and favoring walking/cycling. The energy system is designed to provide for 914,930 square feet (85,000m^2) of living space, producing 6,300 MWh heating, 4,450 MWh electricity, and 1,000 MWh cooling (exported off-site). Heating and cooling is extracted by pump from 10 cold and warm wells in a 130–230 foot deep aquifer (40–70m) containing a stable temperature of 10–11°C throughout the year. Solid waste management and solar thermal collectors (15,070 square foot/1,400m^2; 2,150 square foot/200m^2 vacuum collectors) produce additional heat. The electricity system is grid connected to balance supply and demand from its 2MW wind turbine and 1,290 square foot (120m^2) photovoltaic solar panels. The district matches production with consumption, and residents can track their use (higher than anticipated). Sustainability aspirations have not necessarily coincided with occupants' lifestyles, resulting in removal, under-performance, or additional provision (such as the building of a carpark).

"Space is fundamental in any form of communal life; space is fundamental in any exercise of power."
MICHEL FOUCAULT, SPACE, KNOWLEDGE AND POWER (1984)

"My life belongs to the whole community and as long as I live, it is a privilege to do for it whatsoever I can. I want to be thoroughly used up when I die, for the harder I work, the more I live. I rejoice in life for its own sake. Life is no 'brief candle' to me. It is a sort of splendid torch which I have got hold of for the moment; and I want to make it burn as brightly as possible before handing it on to future generations."
GEORGE BERNARD SHAW (1907)

7.10
Acampada en la Puerta del Sol, Madrid (Spain), 2011
Public spaces in democratic cities are the rightful epicenters of dissidence and have for many centuries facilitated the questioning of boundaries of law, order and civil rights. Protest marches in over 50 Spanish cities for political and economic change resulted in Madrid's Puerta del Sol occupation being awarded a special category in the 2012 European Prize for Urban Public Space. United by the slogan "we are not commodities in the hands of politicians and bankers", protesters' concerns included: the highest unemployment in the European Union; housing access; corruption; parliamentary representation and the rescue of banks with public money. Lightweight and improvised structures from discarded materials, ropes, cables, canvas, plastic and adhesive tape, were resourcefully arranged for requirements such as sanitary services and sun/rain protection. Constructions were configured to avoid damage to infrastructure and carefully avoided spaces of public interest, thoroughfares, libraries and crèches. Suppressed by the national media or denounced by as an illegal appropriation of urban space, the Puerta del Sol occupation disappeared a few weeks after its spontaneous appearance. Cleaning brigades organised by the campers left the space as they had found it.

Passive or active social values

Public space's equity, diversity and social justice are determined through local and regional social values, combined with prevalent planning and design ethics, paradigms and trends. These change over time—being contested, lobbied and debated in the public realm. In many developed regions in the mid to late 20th century, the dominant themes of land use centered on visual amenity; leisure; recreation; sport; respite and tourism. These routinely exist within British/European visual and aesthetic styles such as 'picturesque', 'countryside', 'aristocratic' and 'estate', with accompanying 'passive', observational behavioral expectations (with the exception of sporting activities), evident in a range of control mechanisms such as fencing, signage ('keep off the grass', 'no ball games'), restrictive by-laws and ornamental planting palettes. A landscape designed for activities such as walking, promenading and viewing even obviates the need for direct participation or 'getting one's hands dirty' (typically, users look but do not touch or actively participate). Accordingly, the individual can arguably be seen to be subjugated as a passive subordinate rather than a sharer and shaper of public and common land. Furthermore, not all spaces are distributed equally, with cities' cited percentages of green space often inequitably placed, favoring higher socio-economic areas in greater abundance, quality, maintenance, programming and safety, than economically deprived counterparts.

7.10

"Cultures & climates differ all over the world, but people are the same. They'll gather in public if you give them a good place to do it."
JAN GEHL (2005)

"Community is not something you have, like pizza. Nor is it something you can buy. It's a living organism based on a web of interdependencies—which is to say, a local economy. It expresses itself physically as connectedness, as buildings actively relating to each other, and to whatever public space exists, be it the street, or the courthouse or the village green."
JAMES KUNSTLER, THE GEOGRAPHY OF NOWHERE (1993)

7.11a

7.11b

7.11a
7.11b
7.11c
7.11d

Auckland Waterfront, TCL & Wraight + Associates, Auckland, New Zealand, 2011
Urban waterfront redevelopments commonly result in port and harbor activities relocating to large scale industrial and robotic operations (a problem Han Meyer discusses in his book, 'City and Port'). Crediting "a very brave" client "willing to change and see the waterfront still had use", the design team fought to preserve post-industrial structures and retain a working harbor on the 4.4 acre (1.8ha) site. A key design intent was to establish intentional friction between locals, tourists and harbor activities. The project includes WSUD measures such as rain gardens and a bioretention wetland collecting and filtering stormwater from the wider site catchment.

7.11c

7.11d

Social remediation

Industrial landscapes can involve social design initiatives as an integral part of the project. In addition to current practices of cleansing and environmental remediation (Chapter 3), mining and industrial landscapes can facilitate positive social legacies through reuse and repurposing of sites as part of their overall strategy (see Northumberlandia). This multifunctional and multidimensional approach incorporates both pre and post project planning to attempt creation of enduring social legacies and community viability beyond the operational time-frame of the mine or project site.

7.12a
7.12b
Northumberlandia, Charles Jencks, Shotton surface coal mine, Northumberland, UK, 2012
Debates on the merits of this project oscillate within landscape architectural discourse, however discussions usually overlook its planned relationship between mining and the social viability of the local communities post-mining (see Chapters 3 and 7). The 46 acre (18.6ha) land-art project is the world's largest human landform sculpture (of a reclining female figure). A privately funded £3 million (around $4.3 million) outcome of the Shotton open cut coal mine (which can be seen from the highest point), the project aims to enhance social and economic impacts to the surrounding area through creating a regional tourist destination and community park. This is achieved through using the waste mine 'slag' to construct a 100 foot high (30m), quarter of a mile long (402m) sculpture from 1.5 million tons of rock, clay and soil. Free public access to the site gains access to 4 miles (6.4km) of footpaths on and around the landform.

7.12a

7.12b

7.13a

7.13b

7.13c

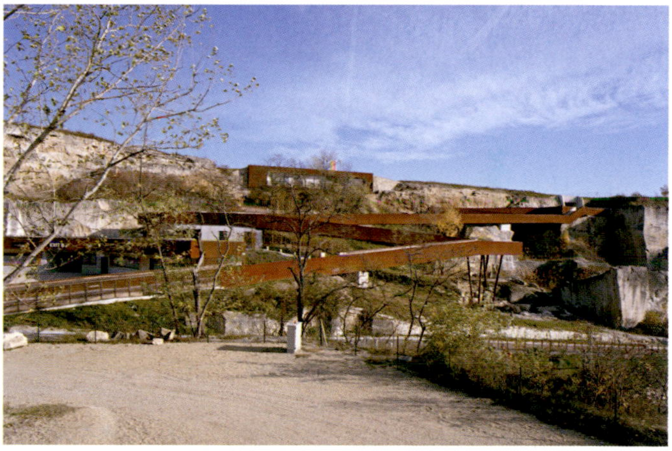

7.13d

7.13a
7.13b
7.13c
7.13d
Open Air Festival Arena, AllesWirdGut Architektur, St Margarethen, Austria, 2005–2008
This repurposed Roman quarry theater and arena creates an immersive experience, with a circulation system woven through the excavated site. Quarries and mine sites can be reused to assist social recovery for industrial areas that have lost their economic functions.

"This ground and this earth
Like brother and mother
We like this earth to sing
Because he is staying forever and ever
We don't want to lose him
We say, Sacred, leave him."
BIG BILL NEIDJIE (1920–2002)

"For if we are to make any headway intellectually and spiritually as we enter the third millennium, the first notion we have to deconstruct is that of progress itself, and the first illusion that of the soaraway future."
ANTHONY O'HEAR, AFTER PROGRESS: FINDING THE OLD WAY FORWARD (1999)

"With deregulation, privatisation, free trade, what we're seeing is yet another enclosure and, if you like, private taking of the commons … wealth is only created when it's owned privately. What would you call clean water, fresh air, a safe environment? Are they not a form of wealth? And why does it only become wealth when some entity puts a fence around it and declares it private property? Well, you know, that's not wealth creation. That's wealth usurpation."
ELAINE BERNARD, DOCUMENTARY: THE CORPORATION (2003)

"Supply without demand. Landscape whose horizon is marked by mountains of butter and hogs, plateaus of cars fresh off the assembly line and imageless television sets. Compulsive overproduction, a growth rate driven to utopian heights by the principle of maximum productivity."
GÜNTER GRASS, ALBRECHT DÜRER AND HIS LEGACY (2002)

ECONOMICS AND LANDSCAPE AS AN ECONOMIC GENERATOR

While many of the works in this book demonstrate catalyzing economic growth and development and increasing property prices through proximity to high quality green spaces (exemplified in The High Line, Chapter 3), very little landscape architecture has explored public landscapes' capacity to generate on-site and ongoing economic returns, employment and social benefits, while operating within a paradigm of common good and social responsibility.

Perpetual growth treadmill

Currently, we operate within a global free-market, capitalist, continuous growth economic system that is not environmentally sustainable, as we consume more natural resources than are regenerated. It is a system requiring continual growth based on exploiting a finite natural resource base. Worse still, these natural resources have not been and are still largely not included in most economic calculations, thereby encouraging the exploitation and destruction of the very thing that sustains us for maximum economic gain.

Economy and environment irreconcilable?

There have been numerous efforts to improve the capitalist model to improve its sustainability and environmental outcomes with limited success. Initiatives such as 'ecologically sustainable development'; attempts at 'natural' and ethical capitalism; a steady state economy; ecological economics; de-growth; smart growth; carbon pricing; and biodiversity offsetting have largely been subsumed by the larger governing system at the continuing expense of the Earth's natural systems.

"Our economy is at war with many forms of life on earth, including human life. What the climate needs to avoid collapse is a contraction in humanity's use of resources; what our economic model demands to avoid collapse is unfettered expansion. Only one of these sets of rules can be changed, and it's not the laws of nature."
NAOMI KLEIN, THIS CHANGES EVERYTHING: CAPITALISM VS THE CLIMATE (2014)

"A country could cut its forests and deplete its fisheries, and this would show only as a positive gain in GDP without registering the corresponding decline in assets (wealth). A number of countries that appeared to have positive growth in net savings (wealth) in 2001 actually experienced a loss in wealth when degradation of natural resources were factored into the accounts."
MILLENNIUM ECOSYSTEM ASSESSMENT (2005)

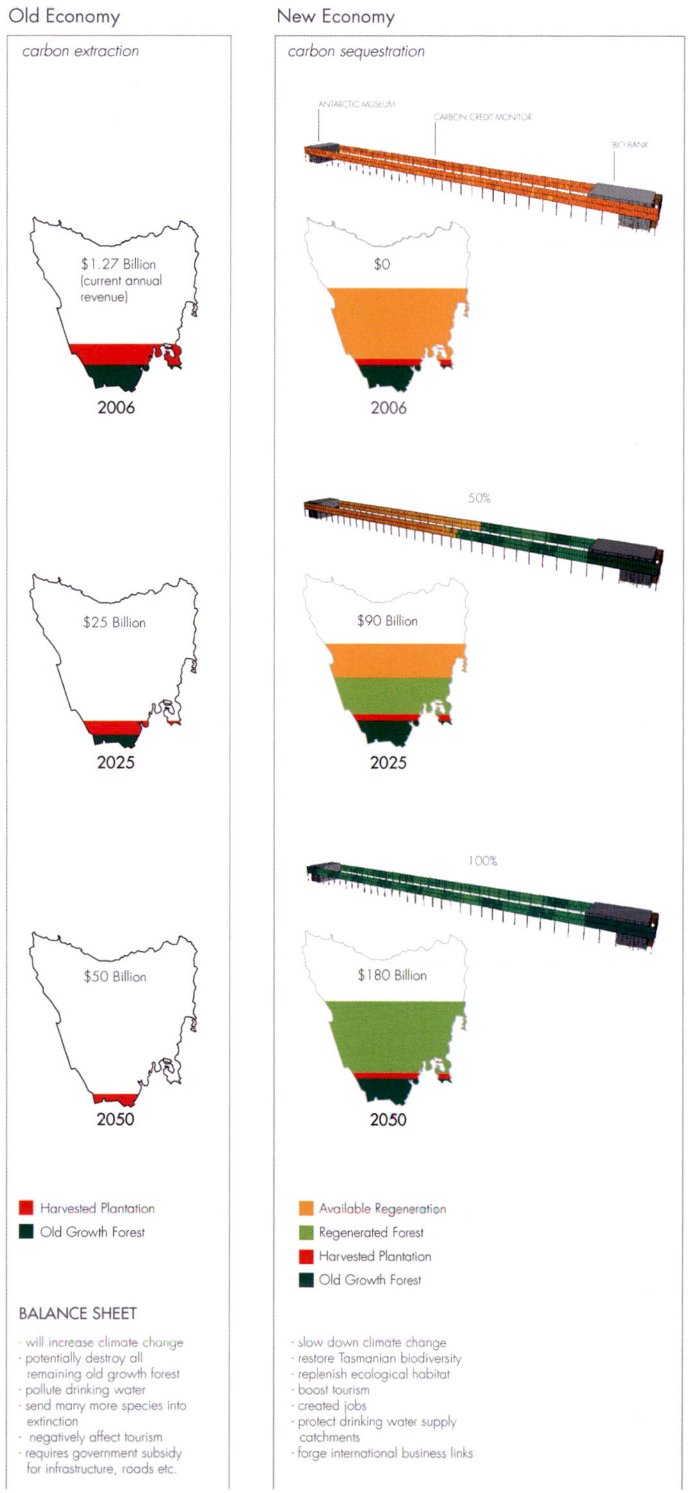

Old Economy
carbon extraction
$1.27 Billion (current annual revenue)
2006
$25 Billion
2025
$50 Billion
2050
Harvested Plantation
Old Growth Forest
BALANCE SHEET
- will increase climate change
- potentially destroy all remaining old growth forest
- pollute drinking water
- send many more species into extinction
- negatively affect tourism
- requires government subsidy for infrastructure, roads etc.
New Economy
carbon sequestration
ANTARCTIC MUSEUM
CARBON CREDIT MONITOR
BIO BANK
$0
2006
50%
$90 Billion
2025
100%
$180 Billion
2050
Available Regeneration
Regenerated Forest
Harvested Plantation
Old Growth Forest
- slow down climate change
- restore Tasmanian biodiversity
- replenish ecological habitat
- boost tourism
- created jobs
- protect drinking water supply catchments
- forge international business links

7.14

7.14
Hobart Waterfront Competition, McGregor Coxall & Ingo Kumic, Hobart, Tasmania, Australia, 2006
The once forest-covered state's environmental resources have always been its major economic source, both industrially and as a tourist destination. As part of their entry for the 2006 Hobart Waterfront Design Competition, the design team proposed redirecting this landscape-based timber economy from logging, forest extraction and wood chipping to forest planting, carbon banking and conservation. By providing its internationally significant old-growth and regenerating forests and large areas suitable for afforestation as carbon credits for international businesses, Hobart could position itself as an influential financial and research leader in the multi-billion dollar global carbon banking economy. If adopted, this frontier opportunity to bio-bank its economic future using green capital could boost business links, with carbon income being used to regenerate Hobart's downtown waterfront, public and cultural facilities, transport systems and city environs for further enhancement and sustainable development.

"Sorry, did I say nature? We don't call it that any more. It is now called natural capital. Ecological processes are called ecosystem services because, of course, they exist only to serve us. Hills, forests, rivers: these are terribly out-dated terms. They are now called green infrastructure. Biodiversity and habitats? Not at all à la mode my dear. We now call them asset classes in an ecosystems market. I am not making any of this up. These are the names we now give to the natural world."
GEORGE MONBIOT, THE PRICING OF EVERYTHING (2014)

"The environment is part of the economy and needs to be properly integrated into it so that growth opportunities will not be missed."
DIETER HELM, THE STATE OF NATURAL CAPITAL (2014)

Natural capital

Some ecologists argue that the environment is increasingly treated as part of the economy, rather than the economy being governed by finite environmental limits (Chapter 7). Infiltration of economic terminology in environmental sustainability language and discourse has recently increased (for example, natural *capital*; ecosystem *services*; green *infrastructure*; natural *assets*). This is both voluntary and involuntary, that is, some environmentalists see this as positive, while others regard it as a threat. Benefits may include updating terms of reference to stay politically influential and socially relevant, or conversely, as George Monbiot argues, we "are effectively pushing the natural world even further into the system that is eating it alive". The resultant risk is that increased economic speculation will translate to further environmental speculation, which is a poor approach to environmental management. Additionally, perpetuation and increased normalization of 'greenwash' may be assisted through the corruptive influence of money and economic lobbying.

Public or common landscapes?

Utilizing public lands for landscape-based commerce and activities 'for the common good' (essentially, reclaiming the (urban) commons), not only deserves further exploration, but may prove to be crucial in bolstering our cities' resilience. Urban and peri-urban open spaces are collective natural and cultural resources and as such, must fulfil society's needs. Public green spaces were initially introduced for the common good (see Birkenhead Park), largely for the urban population's respite from intensive manufacturing and industry. Recreation and passive outdoor activities remain valid uses of land, but will likely diminish when faced with greater concerns of future resource scarcity and climate change. As in the case of Cuba during the Soviet Collapse, or Argentina through economic meltdown, public space becomes appropriated for the urgent need for food production. It is a startling fact that most developed countries have no 'plan B' (certainly not plans that are publicly discussed) for scenarios of economic crisis or collapse. With combinations of vision, planning, scenario testing, interconnected thinking, progressive political leadership and grassroots action, however, urban areas can be made increasingly resilient and successfully repurposed, retrofitted and maximized for resource productivity. If well designed these can provide aesthetic dimensions and beauty (Chapter 6). Encouragingly, sustainable livelihoods, community and social benefits are emerging through urban agriculture, productive landscapes, ecosystem services, green infrastructures and decentralized production (Chapters 2, 3, 4 and 5).

7.15a

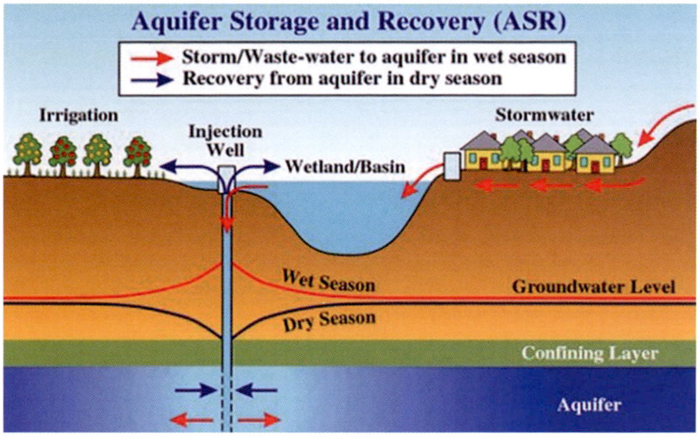

Aquifer Storage and Recovery (ASR)
Storm/Waste-water to aquifer in wet season
Recovery from aquifer in dry season
Irrigation
Injection Well
Wetland/Basin
Stormwater
Wet Season
Groundwater Level
Dry Season
Confining Layer
Aquifer

7.15b

7.16a

7.16b

7.16c

7.15a
7.15b

Parafield Stormwater Harvesting Facility, City of Salisbury, Parafield, Adelaide, Australia, 1999

Australia's largest wool processing company, G. H. Michell & Sons, require 300 million gallons (1,100 million litres) of wool washing water per year, producing large quantities of effluent and sludge. As the company were considering cheaper locations due to water and sewerage costs (potentially resulting in the loss of 700 jobs and local economic activity), the city proposed a A$3.7 million, 27.3 acre (11.2ha) stormwater harvesting and filtration facility. Stormwater is diverted from a 3,953 acre (1,600ha) catchment to a 13 million gallon (50 million litre) capture basin, pumped to a holding unit and flowing to a 4.4 acre (2ha) cleansing reedbed, reducing nutrient and pollutants by up to 90% (with treated water salinity at 150–250 mg/L). The system holds stormwater for around 10 days for optimal treatment efficiency and has a supply capacity of 291 million gallons (1,100 million litres) per year. A two bore Aquifer Storage and Recovery (ASR) system creates continuity when the filtration system has no inflow. The project helped grow both new and established industries, while increasing local employment.

7.16a (During construction)
7.16b
7.16c

Northala Fields, FoRM Associates, Ealing, London, UK, 2007

The 67 acre (27ha) Northala Fields was London's largest new park for a century. It is defined by four substantial conical earth mounds along the A40 roadway built from 65,000 lorry loads of construction waste from projects such as Heathrow Terminal 5, Wembley Stadium and White City. The tallest, 84 foot high (25m) mound provides a 360-degree panoramic view of the characteristically flat region as far as central London and Canary Wharf. The mounds reduce visual and noise pollution, providing a landmark gateway and major 'land art' installation for west London. Importantly, the controlled deposition on site delivered £6 million (around $8.5 million) income, delivering the park at no cost to taxpayers. The project involved two year's consultation with locals, with surrounding communities becoming significant supporters. Ecological enhancement includes wildlife ponds, wetlands, habitat creation of woodland, wildflower meadows and new watercourses.

"... the current political economy has an inappropriate core DNA, since it combines a false belief in the infinity of material resources (pseudo-abundance), with the belief that immaterial resources which are abundant, should be maintained artificially scarce either through legal means (legal repression against the sharing of knowledge) or through outright technological sabotage of the sharing technologies."
MICHEL BAUWENS, COMMONS BASED PEER PRODUCTION (2014)

"Whether we and our politicians know it or not, Nature is party to all our deals and decisions, and she has more votes, a longer memory, and a sterner sense of justice than we do."
WENDELL BERRY, THE DYING OF THE TREES (1997)

DESIGN AS A SERVICE SECTOR

The 'service' (or tertiary) sector is the portion of the economy that produces intangible goods. In developed economies, significant proportions of urban inhabitants are often in service sectors and speculative industries (as opposed to primary industries (raw materials) and secondary (manufacturing)). Design and planning fall into the 'service' sector as they provide knowledge-based outputs and services such as masterplans, guidelines, reports, drawings and management. Service sectors can suffer in times of economic downturn.

The design process

Like many imperceptible services in the tertiary economy, the design process can be a mystery to those outside of the design professions, and thus its economic justification may at times be challenging (especially when design does not result in something physical or built manifesting or a minimal intervention). Depending on cultural contexts, landscape architects are usually not involved in 'hands-on' physical construction itself, rather, providing supervision and input. 'Design and build' is common in some regions and discipline areas, such as garden design, but less common in public domain works (and thus, many landscape architects spend more time indoors than they would like!).

Modes of production

Intellectual property and copyright issues are important for private landscape architectural practices (often small or individual enterprises), providing protection that assists survival. Yet as part of a larger phenomenon of creeping acquisitions and conflating economic monopolies in business, these 'modes of production' can become counterproductive to environmental and social sustainability. Although a very complex topic area and beyond the scope of this chapter, there are various inventions, mechanisms and recent movements that attempt to bypass the standard neoliberal economic models of service, production and consumption. Some of these include creative commons (CC); cooperatives; peer production (mass collaboration); mutualization (a business where employees or customers own a majority of shares); and crowd-sourced funding. The Landscape Architecture Commons™, part of the Digital Commons Network™ is at present, a rare free provider of scholarly work supported by a small number of progressive landscape architecture institutions and academics. Some amateur photographers make their work available through creative commons agreements and several notable industry blogs and websites make use of CC images. All of these initiatives can potentially assist landscape architecture (and its benefits) reach a broader audience.

"Power is always dangerous. Power attracts the worst and corrupts the best."
EDWARD ABBEY (1927–1989)

"In the last decades, the global effort has continued to address the ideal healthy green city. However, many meaningful ideas remain only on paper—so many words, so little action. It is time for the mise en scene of thought to involve all the players; designers, engineers, politicians and citizens."
MARTA POZO GIL, CITIES ALIVE (2014)

GOVERNANCE

Realizing landscape architecture within the public domain is inherently political. It involves local, state and federal governments, politicians, boards and panels, multiple stakeholders, public consultation, the media and public opinion, shifting budgets and timeframes—notwithstanding jostling amongst professional disciplines for leadership, peer design review and anonymous 'trolling' via social media commentary. Construction challenges are multifarious and present additional challenges. Countless factors can thus scuttle years of dedicated work to the realm of an 'unrealized' project. Accordingly, landscape practitioners who realize successful public domain projects are often dedicated and decisive operators and adept mediators who can navigate politicized design and construction processes, while remaining firmly dedicated to the design vision collectively produced through team input. Knowing when to compromise, however, is routinely needed to maintain amiable relations.

Planning for whom?

Most democratic governments have rigorous planning systems that consider and assess multiple factors when granting project approvals. This process can fail under certain systems (such as the UK and Australia) if a Minister for Planning/Government Planning Inspector/Secretary of State ignores or overrides planning decisions and outcomes (even after appeals processes). This compromises environmental and social legislation and the democratic process and is liable to corruption through powerful and well-funded lobbies. Planning processes can be too closely aligned to governments in power and their short-term agendas. The neutral language, tone and writing style found in most government policy, reports and legislation is frequently contradictory to the biases, agendas and strong opinions expressed by some leading politicians (and those who successfully lobby them and donate funds to their political parties). Balanced strategies, planning and scenario testing are therefore too often relegated to unrealized academic or student exercises.

"Turenscape's influence has been on government decision-makers from the ministry level to that of mayors. I send mayors my book *The Road to Urban Landscape* and give lectures at meetings of mayors and city-level decision-makers at least ten times a year ... At the Mayor's Forum in Beijing, I lecture to about fifty mayors at least twice a year. Most of my clients are mayors. As one of two papers about urban planning and design, my lecture 'Building an Ecological City' is included in a must-read textbook published by the National Library for ministry-level Chinese officials."
KONGJIAN YU, TURENSCAPE LANDSCAPE ARCHITECTURE, URBAN DESIGN, ARCHITECTURE, BEIJING (2010)

Short-term governance

Most contemporary governments have a commercial, 'econocentric' approach, seeking job and economic development in their jurisdictions during their short term in power, rather than addressing long-term considerations such as ecological sustainability, likely to be realized beyond their timeframe. Big-picture, far-reaching outcomes and visions are fundamental to sustainable planning and landscape architecture and are challenged by short-term, risk-averse political cycles that restrict innovation. Change in government is often slow and beneficial work can be undone by successive governments or through adversarial political games.

Working from within

Working with governments internally or externally at any level (local, state, national or international) can be simultaneously rewarding and frustrating. The relative regularity of government work can be a savior to landscape practices during times of economic downturn but its scope largely depends on the political, economic and environmental agenda of the political party in power. Despite such challenges, many dedicated sustainability-seeking planners and landscape architects understand the essential role that policy, legislation and guidelines play in determining socially just outcomes and improving environmental conditions. Landscape-based approaches to infrastructure and development can provide economically and environmentally superior solutions to standard proposals (Chapters 3 and ,4), however, these must affect time-poor decision makers and thus be rapidly tangible. Accordingly, clear and effective verbal, written and visual communication skills are crucial.

7.17
Curitiba, Paraná, Brazil
Developed by mayor Jamie Lerner in 1971, this innovative scheme responded to huge population growth where waste and disease accumulated in Paraná's capital city's narrow favelas (slums) inaccessible to garbage trucks. Receiving the United Nations Environment Program's (UNEP) highest environmental award in 1990, Curitiba's huge clean-up and economic resuscitation occurred without loans, raising taxes, wealth distribution or charity. Using their abundant food supply (Chapter 9) and underutilized bus system (Chapter 4), the city introduced 'complementary currencies' of bus tokens (for a bag of pre-sorted garbage) and chits exchangeable for fresh produce (for paper and cartons). Over 70% of households participated, with 62 neighborhoods alone swapping 11,000 tons of garbage for 1,200 tons of food and almost 1 million bus tokens. A school initiative saw 100 schools trade 200 tons of garbage for 1.9 million notebooks in just three years—saving the equivalent of 1,200 trees per day. Curitiba's Gross Domestic Product increased by 75% more than Paraná's and 48% more than Brazil's between 1975 and 1995, financing housing, building restoration and green space creation.

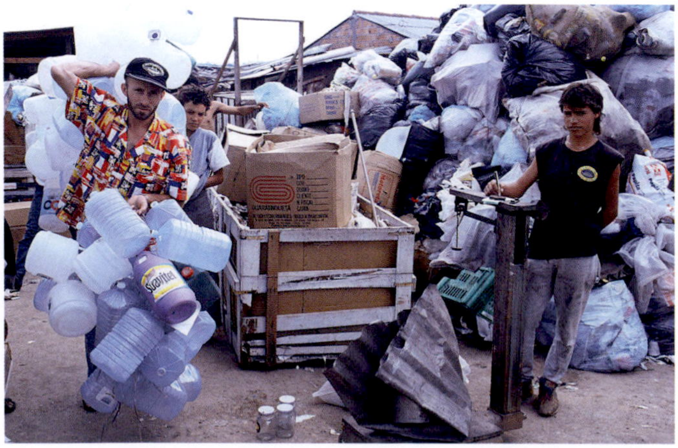

7.17

"We must realise that not only does every area have a limited carrying capacity, but also that this carrying capacity is shrinking and the demand growing. Until this understanding becomes an intrinsic part of our thinking and wields a powerful influence on our formation of national and international policies we are scarcely likely to see in what direction our destiny lies."
WILLIAM VOGT, ROAD TO SURVIVAL (1948)

7.18
Catskill Catchment Protection
This integrative, multi-partner, problem-solving initiative avoided building an expensive filtration plant to purify New York City's (NYC) 1.2 billion gallons daily water use through protecting the Catskill-Delaware watershed from development (and the Marcellus Shale region from hydraulic fracturing for natural gas). NYC historically sourced high quality drinking water from rural catchments. Following the EPA's raising of surface water standards in 1989, the city faced either building a $6 billion filtration plant (at $250 million annual operating cost) or developing an improved strategy for the continued use of natural water ($1–$1.5 billion). Rather than the 'top-down' single-issue response by engineering and public health experts, the commissioner for the Department of Environmental Protection and director of NYC Water and Sewer sought mutually beneficial solutions with initially angry farmers and rural landowners in the watershed. Each farm received 'whole farm planning' through custom design pollution control measures, maximizing effectiveness and minimizing cost.

This ecosystems approach saved billions of dollars, provides 90% of the city's water to approximately 9 million people at no more than 1/8th of the cost of filtration, and preserves 700,000 acres (283,080 ha) of biologically diverse landscape in Catskills Park.

7.18

7.19

7.19
Medellin, Colombia
Since 2004, progressive mayors have dramatically reduced crime and unemployment through innovative urban development that has been inclusive of isolated and deprived areas in what was one of the most dangerous cities in the world. Some initiatives include free cable cars and escalators (used by over 500,000 people per day) and the establishment of green spaces, schools, libraries, and cultural centers.

"No place is a place until things that have happened in it are remembered in history, ballads, yarns, legends, or monuments. Fictions serve as well as facts."
WALLACE STEGNER, THE SENSE OF PLACE (1989)

"A good city is like a good party—people stay longer than really necessary, because they are enjoying themselves."
JAN GEHL (2001)

EDUCATION

Public domain projects frequently have the opportunity to incorporate passive and active, formal and informal educational interventions. Social and learning programs can be built into projects before, during and after completion, leading to increased awareness, activation and project success. Communication and transparency throughout the duration of a project helps to establish trust and engender community ownership, as many communities are resistant to change, distrustful of developers and cynical of governments. Community 'engagement' is more substantial than 'consultation' as it involves collective visioning rather than dictatorial, top-down approaches.

Opportunities
Several possibilities for educational and social planning and programs include:

- creating physical and social infrastructures to enable activities such as community hubs; community gardens; '(men's) sheds'; plant nurseries; courses; workshops; education programs and apprenticeships (see Union Orchard—Chapter 5, Coal Loader, Chicago Museum);
- incorporating volunteers as site guides and for maintenance who also facilitate public interface, information and educational programs;
- establishing relationships with non-government and not-for-profit organizations such as conservation, environment and social groups (see Gary Comer Center, Chapter 5);
- creating partnerships with government and NGO programs related to education, health and the environment (see Eden Project);
- creating partnerships with industry and commercial organizations that publically share results;
- including interpretative facilities and alignment with design and education curricula in schools and universities (see Adelaide Botanic Wetland, Chapter 3);
- arrangements with academic research and organizations to provide detailed and peer-project review (see Landscape Architecture Foundation, Chapter 9).

7.20a

7.20b

7.20a (Before)
7.20b (Before)
7.20c
7.20d
7.20e
7.20f

Coal Loader Centre for Sustainability, North Sydney Council & HASSELL, Waverton, Sydney, Australia, 2005–

This 6.2 acre (2.5ha) Sydney Harbor former coal transfer depot has been transformed into an environmental and community showpiece. A suite of 'sustainability ticks' have been woven skillfully into the site's skeleton, including: retrofitted existing built forms; re-vegetation; on-site wastewater treatment; storm and rainwater harvesting and reuse; passive solar design; solar hot water; solar PV panels; recycled, reclaimed and recyclable materials; community garden and chicken pen; and indigenous plant nursery. Magnificent rock art by the indigenous Cammeraygal people was unearthed from under a dirt road, reconnecting the area to its pre-European history. The centre is well detailed with robust materials such as hardwood timber (decks), galvanized steel (stairs and handrails), concrete (steps and paths) and asphalt, with the added patina of local sandstone and salvaged brick pavements. Given that the local community secured the site from commercial development, it is apt that the site's programming is now based around a successful community center featuring public events, activities and workshops.

7.20c

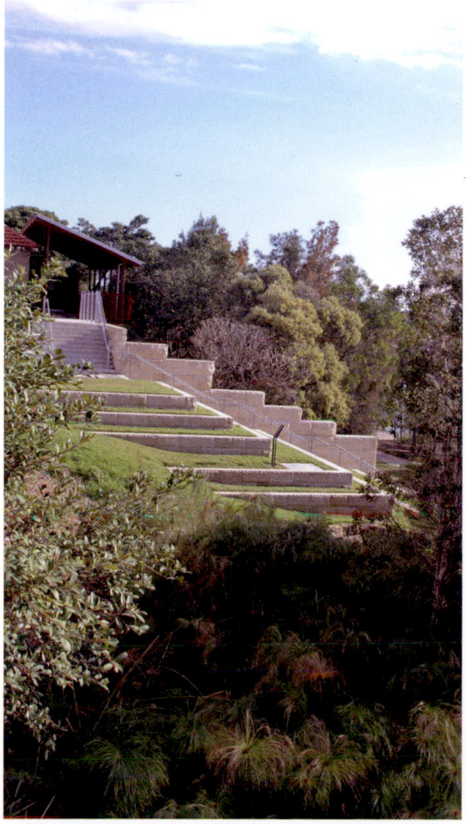
7.20d

7.20e

7.20f

7.21a

7.21b

Cucumber 'Crystal Lemon'

7.21c

7.22

7.22

Chicago Museum of Science and Industry Smart Home, Jacobs/Ryan Associates, 5700 S Lake Shore Drive Chicago, Illinois 60637, USA, 2008

This pre-fabricated modular "home of the future" was intended as a one year display demonstrating integrated green technology, sustainable practices and contemporary design. The public exhibit annually manages 208,000 gallons (787,365l) of stormwater through a permeable pavement system, bioswale and rain garden; provides over 350lb (159kg) of fruit, vegetables and herbs (using on-site composting); and produces 300lb (136kg) of honey. Features include rainwater harvesting, habitat-oriented native planting; and an energy producing green roof. The popular interactive exhibit received 450,000 visitors from 2008–2012. Educational programing has included biodiversity; the gardening–harvesting–composting cycle; children's health; and training and volunteer opportunities for 40–50 Master Gardeners (annually contributed over 5,500 hours between 2008–2010).

7.23

Native Garden, TCL, Adelaide Botanic Garden, Australia, 2010

Intended to inspire sustainable landscape approaches for Adelaide's domestic gardens, this demonstration garden features water-wise, non-invasive native plants and local, recycled materials. A diversity of spaces and garden rooms have been skillfully executed within the constrained site that presented various technical difficulties such as shading and established tree root zones.

7.23

7.21a (Before)
7.21b
7.21c
The Eden Project, St Austell, Cornwall, UK, LUC and multidisciplinary team, 2001
Formally a china clay quarry, the now iconic Eden Project attracts over 850,000 annual visitors to its 74 acre (30ha) gardens and biomes of around 2 million plants, beehives, art works and facilities. Sustainable design features include: green architecture and construction; balancing cut and fill; using root systems rather than engineered solutions to stabilize quarry slopes (less than 5% of pit walls were secured with concrete); soil generation from site sources and mine wastes (83,000 tons at commencement); around two-thirds of water demand supplied by water collected in site drainage and storage systems; green and food waste composting for reuse on-site; natural pest control; and plans for a 3–4 MW geothermal power plant. The educational charity exemplifies genuine passion for initiating, facilitating and demonstrating a wide array of social and technical sustainable practices. Some of the many initiatives are ethical and local purchasing; an education center hosting 40,000+ annual school visitors; global school gardening programs; a degree program in 'hands-on' environmental disciplines; community engagement and employment initiatives; publishing publically accessible sustainability reports and involvement in sustainability certification; and waste recycling and upcycling through art projects.

Communicating process

Beyond direct educational initiatives, there are opportunities to acknowledge landscape architecture itself, effectively creating a two-way public interface. Many landscape architectural projects fail to effectively communicate the significant transformations that regularly take place on a site, which may have resulted from a combination of planning, design, engineering, construction, maintenance and management. Due to the regular lack of interpretative material and the almost non-existent acknowledgement of a project team, visitors to project sites and public places can be unaware or uninformed about rich historical layers, changing site uses, systems in place, sustainability ratings or initiatives, innovative resilience outcomes and the overall design intent. This frequent invisibility is a lost opportunity to communicate how landscape architecture facilitates site design and transformation to the general public and the media (for advocacy and advancement of the profession).

Professional education

While most professional institutes require annual amounts of 'continuing professional development' (CPD or equivalents) for professionals to maintain certification, continuing education could be improved through increased critical discourse, provocation (Chapter 6) and increasing post-completion review of projects to disseminate lessons learnt and ground truths (Chapter 9).

Interpretation

Interpretive design in landscape architecture aims to create installations and interventions that captivate and educate site visitors in an inspiring and entertaining way. Interpretive design typically encompassing signage and wayfinding (such as information displayed on signs) that clarifies site access, facilitating knowledge of circulation, distances and timeframes. Potentially revealing both seen and unseen site layers, values and meanings, possible benefits can also include: revealing the site's history and cultural heritage; highlighting other species' presence; providing geological and environmental history; increasing attachment to local places; and creating an unexpected or explorative journey. These may aid sustainability outcomes through raising awareness of a place's inherent value and helping people to recognize the significance of the locations in which they live and visit. This understanding in turn increases appreciation for the sensitive integration of future additions within a context of cultural, historical and environmental awareness. Interpretive design can thus facilitate attachment to place, which can make people and communities care for the wellbeing of the local environment and lead to action to preserve and enhance sites.

7.24

Legible London, London, UK, 2004–

Previously, there were 32 different wayfinding systems in central London alone. Transport for London's implemented a city-wide pedestrian signage system of 1,300 signs in one consistent visual language (known as *Monoliths, Midiliths, Miniliths* and *Fingerposts*) with continued plans for expansion. Intended to encourage walking assisting Tube decongestion, it is reportedly the world's largest pedestrian wayfinding project. 'Walking circles' display a 15 minute (0.7 miles/1,125 meter) and 5 minute (1/4 mile/375 meter) walk (based on an average pace of 2.8mph/4.5km/h). Maps also show steps, pavement widths and pedestrian crossings.

SOUTH BANK
The London Eye

7.24

Digital engagement

Standard approaches to interpretive material such as signage are yet absent from much work, rendering site change and processes invisible to the visitor. The digital medium (signage, interactive displays and smartphone apps, for example) presents new opportunities for enhanced two-way communication (see Callan Park). This can include revealing natural processes and engagement with real-time data such as volumes of water being filtered, stored and reused on-site, volumes of carbon sequestered, the numbers of vehicles, visitors or species and historic incarnations of a site.

BP
SITE

7.25a

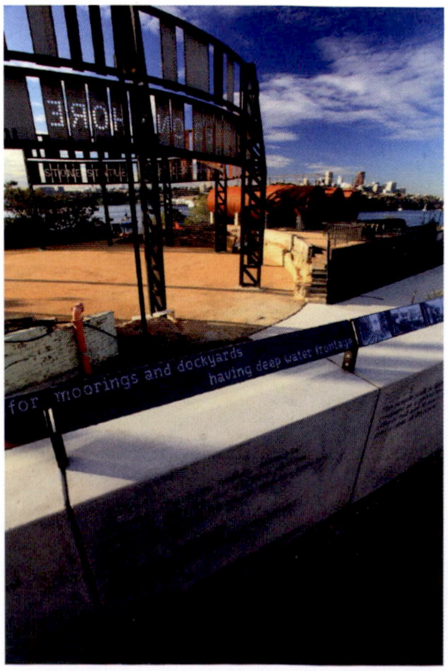
for moorings and dockyards
having deep water frontage

7.25b

7.26
Interpretive Design at Adelaide Botanic Garden Wetland by David Lancashire Design and TCL, Australia
This interpretive design explores stories, science, aspects of biological systems and water conservation. Aligned with local curriculum standards, its various installations provide a non-didactic and experiential educational facility for primary, secondary and tertiary students.

7.26

Acknowledging the profession

Traditionally, many buildings have borne a plaque or identifying feature displaying the name of the architect. Landscape architects' names, and those of built environment professionals in general are, on the other hand, absent in the great majority of built contemporary projects, perhaps contributing to the lack of visibility and appreciation of the profession amongst the general population. Explanation of the site planning and design process—responses, meanings and their reasons—would aid understanding by the general population to the many, often invisible aspects of design in the public realm.

HEALTHY LANDSCAPES

7.25a
7.25b
Former BP Park and Ballast Point Park Signage, Australia
Signage at the Former BP Park (Chapter 3) (McGregor Coxall, Deuce Design and North Sydney Council) and at Ballast Point Park (Chapters 3 and 9) (McGregor Coxall and Deuce Design).

Landscape architecture has always been a transformative agent in human health and wellbeing as health and landscape are inextricably linked. Yet their potential synergies are an oft-unrealized aspect of landscape architectural practice. Landscape planning and design can encourage a healthy and sustainable existence through facilitating activity and exercise, producing clean air and water, providing affordable social services and infrastructures and supplying local food. These can help counteract growing incidences of mental illness (such as depression), physical health issues related to sedentary lifestyles (like obesity), car travel and processed food consumption (for example, diabetes and heart disease) and increased sensitivity to pollutants (such as asthma and allergies). Specific health projects such as healing gardens (Institute for Child Development) and landscapes are frequently associated with hospitals (Khoo Teck, Sky Farm), health care and treatment facilities (Arizona Center) where the direct benefits of convalescence and rehabilitation are notably apparent.

TherapeuticLandscapesNetwork The resource for gardens and landscapes that promote health and well-being
about
resources
designers
gardens
sponsors
support
blog
search
Gardens/Gardens in Healthcare and Related Facilities
Gardens: An Overview
Healthcare Gardens
Other Healing Landscapes
Community Gardens
Gardens in Prisons
Memorial Gardens
Other restorative landscapes
Map: Gardens by Location
a b c d e f g h i j k l m n o p q r s t u v w x y z
Arizona Cancer Center at UMC North. Image courtesy Ten Eyck Landscape Architects

7.27

7.27

The Therapeutic Landscapes Network

This online gathering space for healing gardens, restorative landscapes, and green spaces promotes health and well-being and provides an extensive collection of case-studies and resources.

7.28a

7.28a
7.28b

Institute for Child and Adolescent Development, Reed Hilderbrand, Wellesley, Massachusetts, USA, 1995–1998

Prior to being demolished in 2006 for residential development, the former 1 acre (4,000m^2) clinical psychiatric practice garden was utilized to diagnose and treat children's trauma. The intentionally inward-oriented landscape featured natural dendritic watercourses, with a ribbon of water weaving through spaces mirroring stages of a child's recovery from trauma—a cave-like ravine for the security of home, a woodland for exploration, a mount for climbing, an island and pond for discovery, steep and shallow slopes for challenge, and a large glade for running and playing. The project was an early of articulation of Reed Hilderbrand's belief that gardens can engender emotional wellbeing, helping us to understand our individual place natural and cultural orders.

7.28b

7.29a
7.29b
7.29c

Arizona Cancer Center, Ten Eyck Landscape Architects, Arizona, USA, 2008

Based on healing both body and site, the center provides a variety of garden spaces for patients, their families and hospital staff to connect with the southern Arizona landscape and climate, including a water harvesting arroyo (gully).

7.29a

7.29c

7.29b

7.30a
7.30b

Khoo Teck Puat Hospital, CPG Consultants, Peridian Asia, 90 Yishun Central, Singapore, 2010

This decidedly non-clinical 'Hospital in a Garden' utilizes existing site assets (in particular a large body of water), facilitating ventilation and day lighting. Densely planted terrace, roof, vertical, therapeutic, citrus and edible gardens, focus on a central courtyard designed to soothe and rejuvenate.

7.30a

7.30b

7.31
Sky Farm, Land Collective, HOK, Eskenazi Health Hospital, Indianapolis, Indiana, USA, 2009–2014
Part of the larger 'Commonground' health and wellness project embodying a democratic and participatory landscape philosophy, the 5,000 square foot (465m^2) rooftop garden was created by a community-supported agriculture partnership between Eskenazi Health and non-profit Growing Places. The Outpatient Care Center roof features raised garden beds, with produce served to the plaza's café, while a social program provides education and health coaches.

Preventative health

With health being the largest global financial industry, it is hardly surprising that most health systems are geared towards treating symptoms and not causes. A range of published literature in landscape architecture and health presents peer-reviewed evidence of preventative, healing, physical and mental health benefits through public green spaces, parks, gardens, trees, plants and animals. Yet it is rare to find landscape architectural commissions intended to be preventative from the outset. Similarly, funding and collaborative relationships between health and landscape organizations are surprisingly infrequent, especially at a national scale. Landscape projects (as evident in Chapters 3 and 4) are often implemented as a solution to an already present problem. When applied with foresight, projects can be increasingly initiated to prevent problematic outcomes rather than as occasional treatments for recovery.

Breadth of health

Healthy landscapes support social connection, democratically facilitate social justice (through providing public access and shared spaces); facilitate physical exercise; aid mental restoration; enable safety and wayfinding; assist in avoiding exposure to harmful substances and reduce and avoid light pollution. In the context of environmental sustainability, they extend beyond the direct human-based benefits to include health implications and positive outcomes for other species and ecosystems. At present, the term 'healthy landscapes' primarily refers to the health of people and the places in which they live, work and play, rather than to animals, plants, or indeed the ecosystem as a whole—despite the fact that their health implications extend beyond the immediate site to all associated activities embodied in the design, construction and maintenance processes. Moving from the project or landscape scale to a macro view of the town, city, nation and planet, healthiness can be measured by means such as a 'city health index' that considers a wider spectrum of health factors in context of global and collective resilience.

7.31

"Never doubt that a small group of thoughtful, committed citizens can change the world. Indeed, it is the only thing that ever has."
MARGARET MEAD, CURING NUCLEAR MADNESS (1984)

PUBLIC CONSULTATION, COMMUNITY ENGAGEMENT AND MAINTENANCE

Public consultation and community engagement facilitate connections between governments and citizens on a range of policy, planning, design, program and service issues. It may involve giving, extracting or exchanging information and reaching agreement or compromise in a one-off or an ongoing manner. A plan, strategy or design might be visionary, but if it lacks community support, it may go unrealized or be destined for failure. While effective top-down leadership can result in rapid (be it positive or negative) change, bottom-up (grassroots) community-led support and lobbying can be a more enduring means of project sustainability implementation. Planning and landscape architecture have a long legacy of stakeholder engagement and community consultation through a well-established participatory approach.

Democratic design

Realized projects can facilitate public democratic debate and expression through spatial design, collaborative and inclusive, socially-oriented features (such as the 'Council Ring' by Jens Jensen in Columbus Park, Chicago). The use of innovative technologies to increase input and interaction with sites is increasingly being explored both before the project is designed (see Callan Park) and following completion. Incorporating democratic participation through the consultation, development, design and construction stages additionally allows a more equitable, relevant and responsive process and outcome.

Maintenance

Design has the potential to bring magnificent visions to life but only if successfully managed and maintained. Strategies such as naturalistic design, the mimicking of local conditions, low water planting and xeriscapes can help to reduce maintenance intensity. Meaningful stakeholder engagement during the design process builds and capitalizes on community pride and assists in realizing local desires by engendering stewardship and creating opportunities for community maintenance, ongoing surveillance and input. Many local municipal authorities are actively seeking such outcomes to reduce their often diminishing maintenance and vandalism budgets for public spaces. Such community participation and pride is more feasible in areas that have an emerging, established, stable or active local community.

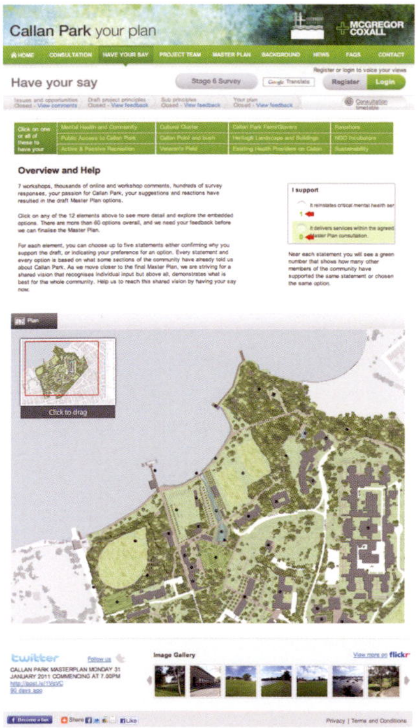
Callan Park your plan
MCGREGOR COXALL
Have your say
Overview and Help
I support
Click to drag
twitter
Image Gallery
flickr

7.32

7.32

Callan Park, McGregor Coxall & Binary, Sydney, Australia, 2010–2011

Built specifically for the project, the design team developed an interactive online consultation website called 'yourplan' (www.callanparkyourplan.com.au), breaking the typical mould of *in situ* physical consultation. After 90,000 page views of 1,600 users' feedback and six months of community meetings and workshops, the team developed the Wellness Sanctuary master plan.

7.33

Vancouver Green Streets volunteer gardening

Believing long-term sustainability depends on community engagement, the City of Vancouver encourages public participation in their conceptualization and development of the Greenways and Streets initiative (see Chapter 4). This includes a volunteer maintenance program, where a neighborhood can elect to take care of a space, building pride and community.

7.33

STUDY/DISCUSSION QUESTIONS

Is corporate sponsorship of public space projects in the public interest? Does this approach call into scrutiny the sponsor's wider activities?

Is corporate sponsorship of public places in highly visible and trafficked urban locations strategic greenwashing or philanthropic outreach?

What is the difference between education and indoctrination?

What is ROTE learning? Is this widespread? Is it problematic? When is it useful?

What aspects of environmental education are important?

Find a good and a bad example of interpretive design in landscape architecture and discuss.

What are ethics? Are ethics important? Do they equate to practice? Give examples.

What are environmental ethics?

What are values?

What are morals?

How do values and morals differ from ethics? Which relates most directly to the profession of landscape architecture?

Does ethical common ground exist in the discipline of landscape architecture? What do you think these ethics are? Are they determined by professional institutes?

What constitutes a healthy landscape? Give some examples of healthy landscapes.

Is the environment quantifiable in economic value? Is it currently given value? Should it be?

Communities regularly oppose change. What strategies can be employed to make them aware of the benefits of a project?

Should the community be engaged in the process of a public project? Why or why not?

What is the difference between consultation and engagement? What are the pros and cons of both approaches?

Should experts (assuming that they have been democratically or independently appointed) or the community (through consultation) have priority in shaping the outcomes of a public project?

Why do governments need to appear impartial (such as neutral language in reports and guidelines)? Does this reflect the reality of governance?

Should governments 'leave it to the market'? What impact can this have on the environment?

Should public landscapes be used to generate economic returns? Can this be done in an environmentally and socially appropriate way? What are some of the potential problems?

Can/do people enjoy 'economically-optimized' landscapes? Can you give examples?

What are the benefits and drawbacks of community maintenance of public landscapes? What considerations need to be factored for this to be successful?

FURTHER READING

Alexander, C., Ishikawa, S. and Silverstein, M. (1977) *A pattern language: towns, buildings, construction*, New York: Oxford University Press.

Clayton, S. (2012) *The Oxford handbook of environmental and conservation psychology*, New York: Oxford University Press.

Cosgrove, D. (1998) *Social Formation and Symbolic Landscape*, Madison: University of Wisconsin.

Daly, H. and Farley, J. (2011) *Ecological economics: principles and applications*, Washington: Island Press.

Deming, M. E. and Swaffield, S. (2011) *Landscape architectural research: inquiry, strategy, design*, Hoboken, NJ: Wiley.

Fox, W. (2006) *A theory of general ethics: human relationships, nature, and the built environment*, Cambridge, Mass: MIT.

Freyfogle, E. (2003) *The land we share: private property and the common good*, WashingtoN DC: Island Press.

Galea, S. and Vlahov, D. (2008) *Handbook of urban health: populations, methods, and practice*, New York: Springer.

Grahame-Shane, D. (2011) *Urban Design Since 1945 – A Global Perspective*, UK: Wiley.

Hansen, A. and Cox, J. (2015) *The Routledge handbook of environment and communication*, London: Routledge.

Harvey, D. (2009) *Social justice and the city*, Athens: The University of Georgia Press.

Hawken, P, Lovins, A. and Lovins, L. (2000) *Natural Capitalism: creating the next industrial revolution*, New York: Little Brown & Company.

Kostof, S. (1992) *The City Assembled*, London: Thames & Hudson.

Kostof, S. (1999) *The City Shaped*, London: Thames & Hudson.

LeGates, R. and Stout, F. (2015) *The city reader*, 6th ed, London: Routledge.

Mäler, K. and Vincent, J. (2005) *Handbook of environmental economics: valuing environmental changes*, Amsterdam: Elsevier.

Meijer, J. and Berg, A. (2010) *Handbook of environmental policy*, New York: Nova Science Publishers.

Millennium Ecosystem Assessment (Program) (2001). *Millennium Ecosystem Assessment*, <http://www.millenniumassessment.org/en/index.html> [accessed 03 April 2006].

Odum, H. (1996) *Environmental accounting: EMERGY and environmental decision making*, New York: Wiley.

Papanek, V. (2009) *Design for the real world: human ecology and social change*, London: Thames and Hudson.

Saul, J. R. (2005) *The collapse of globalism: and the reinvention of the world*, Toronto: Viking Canada.

Schumacher, E. F. (1973) *Small is beautiful; economics as if people mattered*, New York: Harper & Row.

Souter-Brown, G. (2015) *Landscape and urban design for health and well-being: using healing, sensory, therapeutic gardens*, Abingdon, Oxon: Routledge.

Thwaites, K., Mathers, A. and Simkins, I. (2013) *Socially restorative urbanism: the theory, process and practice of experiemics*, New York: Routledge.

You might also like to look for further information on the following projects:

Columbus Park, Jens Jensen, Chicago, Illinois, USA, 1915–1920

West Point Foundry Preserve Signage, C&G Partners & Mathews Nielsen Landscape Architects, Cold Spring, New York, USA

Arkadian Winnenden, Atelier Dreiseitl, Stuttgart, Germany, 2011

The Energy Café, Pilot Publishing, London, UK, 2008–2011

Advocate Lutheran General Hospital Patient Tower, Conservation Design Forum, Park Ridge, Illinois, USA, 2009

INTERVIEW Richard Weller

Professor Richard Weller is the Martin and Margy Meyerson Chair of Urbanism, Professor and Chair of Landscape Architecture at the University of Pennsylvania (Penn). He is also Adjunct Professor at the University of Western Australia and former Director of the Australian Urban Design Research Centre (AUDRC). His multiple award winning consultancy and academic career include international design competition awards, and the Australian National Teaching Award (2012). Professor Weller has published four books, over 80 single-authored papers and is Creative Director of interdisciplinary journal of landscape architecture *LA+*. His research projects have involved scenario planning for cities, megaregions and nations.

Would landscape architecture benefit from more intellectual rigor? If so, why, and what would this provide?

You know, the automatic response is to say yes and the apparent lack of philosophical, scientific, creative and critical rigor in the field is often commented on. But actually, intellectual rigor can also be its own worst enemy if it is overly academic or drifts into sophistry. I don't buy the line that landscape architecture lacks rigor because it has no theoretical canon or that old ruse; the scientific method.

The question really, is does the ecological crisis require intellectual rigor and would intellectual rigor make landscape architecture more powerful as a discipline and a profession? Maybe not. That said, we certainly need enough intelligence to keep both paradisiacal romanticism and utopian fascism at bay. We also need enough intelligence to see through our own rhetoric and be critical of the profession's propensity for self-congratulation and hypocrisy.

Rather than intellectual rigor per se I think we just need more critical and creative designers.

What new ways can landscape architects and environmental designers pursue to solicit work and help to realize their visions?

Firstly you need to have a vision. The problem for landscape architects has been that they tend to think that by just saying 'stewardship' they are automatically visionaries, but then they go to work and do storm-water swales for sprawl or put some more parsley on the pig.

So the vision thing is the first matter. What is it? How does it work? To whom and what does it apply? Why is it visionary? Visions aren't easy.

Assuming the vision survives for a while as an idea then it has to be represented in a compelling manner. Then you just need to push it out there—to the media, to the authorities, to the academy, to the bureaucrats, to whoever is part of the puzzle. The Darwinian world of culture will sort out pretty quickly whether it lives or dies. Australia can be tough like this—it tends to kill ideas before they even take their first breath.

How can we reach a larger audience, beyond the design industry and those already literate in what we can do?

How does anyone in the 21st century get an audience? You can ask for institutional support but I'm a believer in individuals just making things happen.

Should major issues (climate change, food security, biodiversity loss) occupy a primary focus of what we do? How can we increasingly realize and implement these projects as beyond conceptual and student work? What type of clients do we need?

Yes and no. We are now a profession that dominates the design and delivery of the public realm in urban environments but we can't just keep turning first world cities into pop-up playgrounds and outdoor lounges. You don't really need a profession for that.

As the world urbanizes it is important that we design good public space and that we become increasingly concerned and expert in regard to urban ecological performance. But we also need to scale up and reclaim what used to be called landscape planning. We need a deeper structural presence in suburbia both in regard to retrofitting the extant and planning the new. Beyond that the peri-urban is a vast unrealized resource for cities but remains a virtual void in terms of design thinking. Then we need to work at a catchment scale, at a food bowl scale and at a scale commensurate with biodiversity migrations and climate change with a long-term view.

How to move this beyond conceptual or student work is a good question. If you superimpose a map of where all the landscape architecture schools are with a map of landscapes most in crisis they are two different worlds. I am keenly aware that later in the 21st century scholars and students will look back on us now the way we look upon people who were designing beaux-arts gardens in the early 20th century—nice, but irrelevant. On the other hand there is a strong post-landscape urbanism movement that is chasing larger scale systemic and infrastructural issues but so far this has not resulted in anything real. It's all posturing, but important nonetheless.

With that in mind my current research is about global biodiversity and about the peri-urban conditions of cities in the world's biodiversity hotspots. It's called the Atlas for the End of the World. I would call it a guide book of places we should go to work in. As to how we take action on the ground; we could learn a lot from the way in which the global conservation community has gone from a bunch of hippies in the 60s to a major corporate and political force today. Our clients should be Conservation International, The World Bank, the UN, governments, multinationals wanting to clean up their act, even the military.

To what extent should landscape architects accept current, problematic paradigms (such as population and economic growth) versus challenge these doctrines based on ethical concerns and principles? Is there a place for an activist or provocative approach?

Population growth and economic growth are facts and we must relate everything to an expected global peak of circa 10 billion people, many of them poor, many of them in vulnerable environmental circumstances. Of course there is a role for the activist and provocateur but only if they devote their life to it and have skin in the game. I don't think the righteous will save the world, the smart will. We need creative landscape architects muscling into territories of conflict, not sitting around in the salons of New York, Paris and London.

Institutional capacity is also an issue. We need at least one good design school in each of the world's 35 biodiversity hotspots (there are almost none) and the world's existing schools should be running studios on global flashpoints where resource depletion will trigger conflict. We should be all over these places. I realize this is easier said than done but at Penn, we are trying.

I'm convinced that if you airlifted a smart landscape architect into a complex, fraught territory their methods and ways of working would be enormously valuable. IFLA should turn its attention to some practical capacity building program along these lines. You know we all feel distressed, landscape architecture is so weak and pathetic in comparison to its founding McHargian vision.

You have a course that explores different cultures ideas of nature. What is your idea of nature?

The course begins by asking students 'what is nature'? Fifteen years ago I would still receive the birds and bees answer, that is; 'nature as nice, nature as victim and nature as other', but now most students realize it's what we make it. My answer: It is us, we are it. Cities are nature.

But no one ever gets the right answer, which is: It's a word, a very dangerous word.

What key qualities and skills do young landscape architects need to cultivate?

Anger is motivational. Ambition is a necessary curse. Criticality is central. Self-reflexivity is important. Hand-to-mind feedback through drawing and writing is crucial. Lateral thinking is very useful. Recognition of beauty is something. Take risks. The ability to creatively use and control technology instead of just learning the programs and producing the images is going to be very important. And yes, try to get along with the hobbits in the shire, but know when to get out of there.

8.1
Underwood Family Sonoran Landscape Laboratory
This university campus project turned a parking lot into Sonoran Desert contextualized landscape.

8

LESS IS MORE: A LIGHTER TOUCH

Light-touch design aids environmental and social sustainability through minimizing intervention, site disturbance and the embodied processes from project activities and material use. This should include both the immediate design site and wider impacted environments. A sensitive appreciation for 'place' and its corresponding natural and cultural dimensions is a central foundation of landscape architecture. An ethical designer knows where and when to design, including when a site needs little or no enhancement. Sensitivity is relevant to all contexts, not just those we perceive as 'natural' or 'cultural'. Even degraded sites, where the 'natural' environment has been erased, can possess characteristics justifying careful design intervention. This is particularly the case for fragile sites. Effective communication, mediation and respectful leadership across design, construction, and maintenance further assists enduring sustainability.

"Consult the genius of place in all."
ALEXANDER POPE, EPISTLE IV (1731)

"The soul of place is like an invisible net—or a force field—cast up at times from within a house, neighborhood, or landscape to draw us into its labyrinthine folds."
LINDA LAPPIN, THE SOUL OF PLACE (2015)

"Our relationship to the ground is, culturally speaking, paradoxical: for we appreciate it only in so far as it bows down to our will… instantly our engineering instinct is to wipe it out; to lay our foundations on rationally – apprehensible level ground."
PAUL CARTER, THE LIE OF THE LAND (1996)

8.2a
8.2b
8.2c
8.2d
Projects in South Australian National Parks, TCL, South Australia, c. 1995–2003
8.2a Flinders Chase National Park at Kangaroo Island's western edge.
8.2b Flinders Ranges National Park is in the northern central part of South Australia's largest mountain range.
8.2c Innes National Park on Yorke Peninsular's southwest coastal tip.
8.2d Morialta and Blackhill Conservation Parks are close to Adelaide, containing rugged ridges, gullies and seasonal waterfalls.

Working with National Parks and Wildlife South Australia, TCL upgraded hundreds of public facilities throughout the state, informed by detailed analysis of environmental, indigenous and cultural heritage, local materials, and landscape colors and textures. Masterplans, visitor facilities and park infrastructures (including trail networks; paths; lookouts; camping grounds; car parks; toilets and historic homesteads) were designed to ameliorate visual impact, allowing the magnificent landscapes to dominate amongst challenging gradients, steep terrain and fragile ecosystems.

LANDSCAPE SENSITIVITY

Landscape sensitivity requires a mindful, careful design approach. Designers from a range of disciplines routinely impose preconceived styles, regardless of natural and cultural contexts. Whether innate or cultivated, environmental attunement and deep-seated appreciation for historical, cultural, visual, spiritual and four-dimensional landscape is essential to sensitive design. These attributes are further developed through listening, observation, study, intuition, practice and engagement, equating to an inherent understanding of *genius loci*—the sense of place.

Physical site visits

Until the explosion of global travel, commerce and digital communication, landscape practice was more substantially rooted in the local and national context. Several decades ago, undertaking a landscape architecture project without a detailed site visit was almost unthinkable. It is now, unfortunately, more commonplace, increasing the likelihood of non-contextual, homogeneous design responses.

Tabula rasa

Ecologists frequently recommend avoiding practices that disturb land (for example, soils and vegetation) as stability greatly assists inter-species relationships and increased biological diversity. *Tabula rasa* (clearing a site to a 'clean slate' for ease of work and calculations) is still commonly employed in design, engineering and construction, yet is devastating to remnant, precious ecosystems. The geological stability of a continent like Australia, for example, has given rise to complex and biodiverse plant and species relationships, over millions of years of evolution (and in other global biodiversity 'hotspots'). It is therefore imperative to avoid disturbance in sites that have intact soil and vegetative conditions to preserve ecosystem integrity.

8.2a

8.2b

8.2c

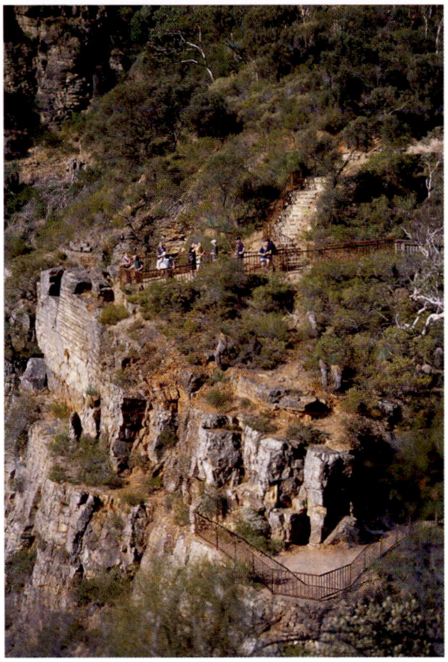

8.2d

Past visualization

It is essential to 'read', analyze and visualize landscape bioregions, sub-regional conditions and immediate sites. Even where indigenous vegetation has been completely removed, the underlying geological, topographical, soil, aspect, hydrological conditions, as well as the climate, present plant species and local historical knowledge and research can draw an indicative 'picture' of the site's pre-existing historical and natural conditions. Such mappings (remnant vegetation communities for example) and the ability to envision past landscapes guides design and planting (see National Gallery, Underwood Laboratory) and ecological restoration (Chapter 2).

"The odd silence of the housing estate, sans birds, sans chatter, sans water running, is a deafness produced by months of dynamiting, drilling, earth moving, earth-stamping, and their hectic offspring, radios blaring to no other end than to mask with their little noise the larger noise of power or 'progress'."
PAUL CARTER, THE LIE OF THE LAND (1996)

"Animals and plants do what they can to survive. If that means taking over a quarry or a dump, so be it. We should not judge this as 'unnatural.' If we are surprised, it only shows that our picture of nature is faulty. We need new ways to explain what we see."
TIM LOW, THE NEW NATURE (2003)

Composing diversity

There are multiple natural and cultural considerations that landscape architects should be conversant with when designing. They should be skilled in assembling, leading, unifying and participating in multidisciplinary teams of experts and consultants with diverse (and often specific) viewpoints: an ecologist might focus on remnant ecosystems, an anthropologist on site excavations, a cultural geographer on indigenous factors, a heritage architect on existing built form, while a developer's concern may be maximum profit. Landscape architects and planners have ranging levels of project and political influence depending on their individual (director or junior) and team (lead or sub consultant) position, the importance of a project (of national public significance or a private garden) and their profile, affiliations and professional contacts. Sensitivity should also be shown to past practitioners who have planned or designed on the site.

Inadequate protection mechanisms

Practitioners seeking a sensitive approach frequently face challenges. The disturbance of site geology and soils and removal of significant vegetation are routinely proposed or result as a matter of standard construction practice. Similarly, planning mechanisms have frequently approved developments in inappropriate locations such as areas of ecological, historical, cultural or scenic value or on floodplains and low-lying sites. Depending on the shifting sands of local, national and international legislation, zoning, protection and guidance mechanisms, these sites can range from fully protected to having none at all. While it might not be feasible to change immediate results, subsequent projects can be improved through lobbying, advocacy, acting for expert assessment panels, and writing submissions and policy in the attempt to change laws and protection mechanisms.

Flexible mind

Landscape sensitivity and a light touch require openness and flexibility. 'Pristine' environments and 'wilderness' have largely been reduced to myths, albeit as compelling notions that have created significant momentum and outcomes for environmental protection (Chapters 1 and 2). Instead, most of the Earth now consists of hybridized nature and novel ecosystems with new and complex species relationships. Sensitivity is therefore not only required where a site has more visible features like remnant indigenous vegetation, fauna or a ruin, but also in degraded locations and wastelands, where plants, animals and features of conservation, intrinsic and sustainability value may exist (see Brick Pit Ring).

8.4a (Before)
8.4b
8.4c
8.4d
Underwood Family Sonoran Landscape Laboratory, Ten Eyck Landscape Architects, Tucson, AZ USA, 2007
This Sonoran Desert project reflectS the region's innate landscape character, even when previously destroyed. Here, a barren 1.2 acre (0.5ha) parking lot has been converted into A balanced composition of culture and nature utilizing local materials, labor and plants. Its notable water strategies include re-directing 250 gallons/day (950l) of university sand filter well backwash (previously discharged into the stormwater system) into a wetland pond supporting fish and vegetation; providing 85% of annual irrigation (280,000 gallons/1,272,905 liters) during the 5 year establishment period from recycled water (243,000 gallons consisting of rainwater 84,000; HVAC condensate 95,000; well blow-off 45,000; grey water 19,000); and eliminating potable water use after the establishment period.

8.3

National Gallery Australia Sculpture Garden, Harry Howard & Associates, Canberra, Australia, 1978
Considered to be one of Australia's most significant landscape architecture design sites, the National Gallery's sculpture garden represented a departure from the Parliamentary triangle's European character. The Australian bush character is divided into four seasonal areas ensuring year round planting interest and features international sculptural works.

8.4a

8.4b

8.4c

8.4d

8.5
Brick Pit Ring, Durbach Block Jaggers Architects, Sydney Olympic Park, Sydney, 2004–2005
Following 100 years of operation (during which it produced 3 billion bricks), Sydney Olympic Park's Brick Pit site closed in 1988 to be colonized by the endangered Green and Golden Bell Frog (*Litoria aurea*). Initially proposed for the Games' tennis facility, organizers shifted venue placement on discovering the frog species. The Brick Pit Ring's subsequent A$6.5 million design features a 61 foot (18.5m) high aerial walkway and outdoor exhibition but excludes ground level access. Frog populations expanded to 700 in 15 freshwater ponds featuring boulder shelters, grasses and reeds.

8.5

Direct and indirect

Sensitive design extends far beyond the reaches of an immediate site. The immense impacts of globalized culture (well articulated through measurement mechanisms like ecological footprinting and embodied energy (Chapters 6 and 9)) can reveal the substantial extent of requirements (such as productive land, water, carbon) from the multitude of processes contained within a project, service or material. This may include sourcing, extracting, processing, and the transportation of materials and project team members.

"In the end, our society will be defined not only by what we create, but by what we refuse to destroy."
JOHN SAWHILL, THE NATURE CONSERVANCY (1936–2000)

RESTRAINT

Restraint involves careful consideration of the existing natural and cultural conditions, the project brief, needs and desires of the community, and conscious interrogation of one's own biases and preconceived design notions. Sensitivity and restraint are undervalued design skills frequently overridden by passion for design or overzealous design ego. The ethical designer does not always need to assert dominance or leave their 'mark'. Some projects may require little design intervention or only subtle enhancement due to pre-existing natural or cultural features, allowing the innate beauty or power of a site to hold center stage (see Uluru Cultural Centre). This light-touch approach of designing only when necessary to minimize site disturbance and built intervention is, however, in stark contrast to a minimalist design style or trend (see National Park projects).

Apparent versus actual

Whether minimalist architecture, interior architecture, product design, art or landscape design, this aesthetic approach seeks a humanistic, near impossible pursuit of perfection and in many cases, a trail of waste to achieve it. Environmental restraint is very different to aesthetic restraint. Aesthetic restraint is usually achieved through a design approach of pared-back material palettes, simplified spatial gestures and highly crafted work. In landscape, minimalist design can require intensive ongoing maintenance to achieve this look, for example, simplified or singular planting palettes (duocultures, monocultures) are more prone to failure and less resilient than diversified planting schemes. Although minimal planting approaches were more common during the reign of modernist landscape architecture (mid 20th century), well-known practitioners from this period continue to yield significant influence (such as Luis Barragán). The profession's more recent increase in ecological literacy is shifting the dominant planting and design approach from modernist and aesthetic restraint to layered compositions encouraging biodiversity (Chapter 2) that generate multiple benefits (Chapters 3, 4 and 7) and reduce intensive maintenance (Chapter 8).

"Kevin and I undertook landscape architecture studies at the same time some 29 years ago under the leadership of Jim Sinatra. Our very first design exercise was to redesign the Victoria Market in Melbourne. I remember scheming, like many others in our class, to knock bits of it over and build instead a hotel or office block. I distinctly remember Kevin by contrast … presenting the Victoria Market essentially as it was. Kevin asked why change a place that provided real experiences and already had a soul? It was a revelation."
PERRY LETHLEAN, A TRIBUTE TO KEVIN TAYLOR (1953–2011)

Communicating values

Clients may not realize the immediate value of a design strategy if it does not involve obvious physical or visible results. Clear verbal and graphic communication throughout the design process and a strong project narrative may help to convince stakeholders of existing and proposed values (see Houston Arboretum). This can be greatly assisted by a rigorous site analysis that provides tangible information demonstrating pre-existing site values. It is important to demonstrate how these have been linked to inform design decisions and proposed outcomes.

8.6
Site analysis
Houston Arboretum's (Chapter 2) site analysis identified issues such as canopy mortality from drought and climate change, investigating possible *in situ* correlations (e.g. micro topography, watercourses and poorly drained silt-clay loam soils). This prompted a more representative design proposal including larger areas of prairie and meadow typologies.

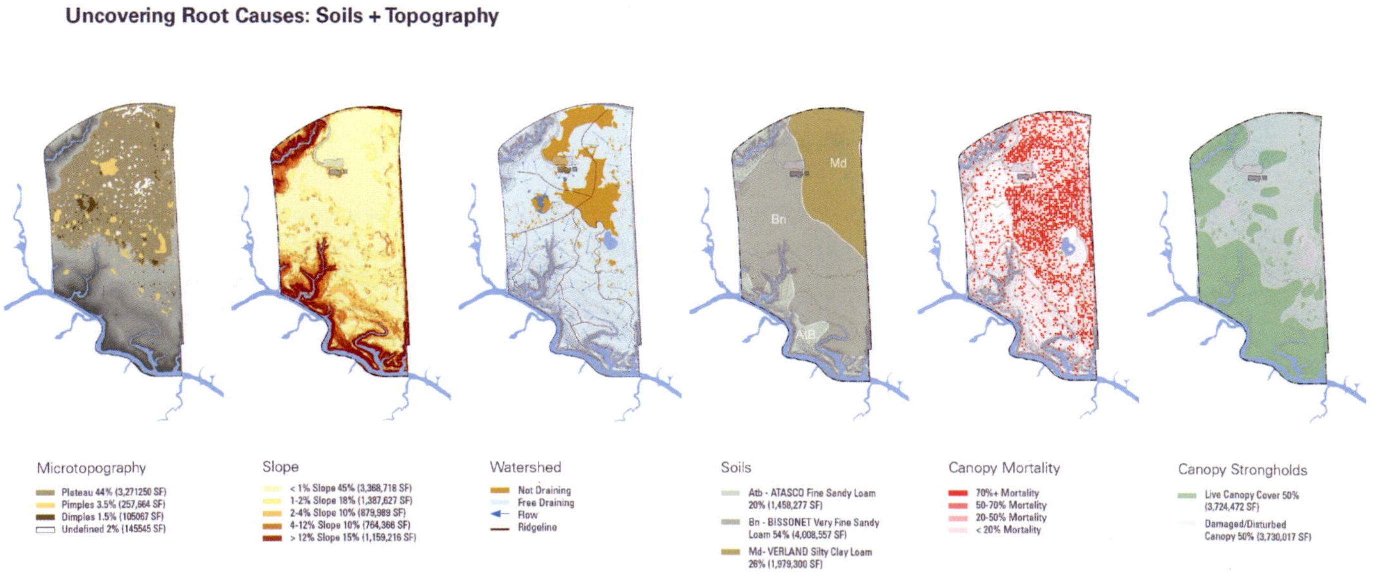
Uncovering Root Causes: Soils + Topography
Md
Bn
AtB
Microtopography
Plateau 44% (3,271250 SF)
Pimples 3.5% (257,664 SF)
Dimples 1.5% (105067 SF)
Undefined 2% (145545 SF)
Slope
< 1% Slope 45% (3,368,718 SF)
1-2% Slope 18% (1,387,627 SF)
2-4% Slope 10% (879,989 SF)
4-12% Slope 10% (764,366 SF)
> 12% Slope 15% (1,159,216 SF)
Watershed
Not Draining
Free Draining
Flow
Ridgeline
Soils
Atb - ATASCO Fine Sandy Loam 20% (1,458,277 SF)
Bn - BISSONET Very Fine Sandy Loam 54% (4,008,557 SF)
Md- VERLAND Silty Clay Loam 26% (1,979,300 SF)
Canopy Mortality
70%+ Mortality
50-70% Mortality
20-50% Mortality
< 20% Mortality
Canopy Strongholds
Live Canopy Cover 50% (3,724,472 SF)
Damaged/Disturbed Canopy 50% (3,730,017 SF)

8.6

8.7a

8.7b

8.7c

8.7d

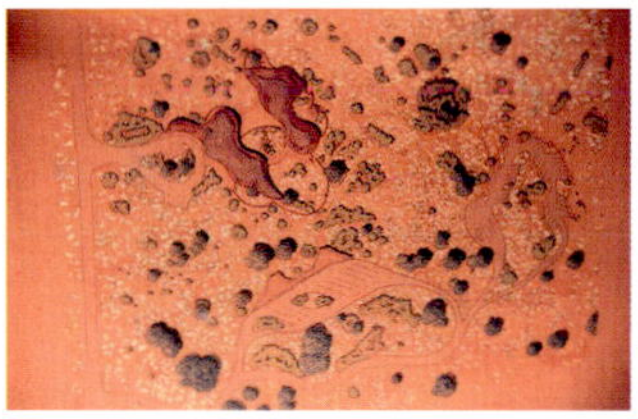

8.7e

8.7a
8.7b
8.7c
8.7d
8.7e

Uluru-Kata Tjuta Aboriginal Cultural Centre, TCL with Gregory Burgess Architects, Uluru, Northern Territory, Australia, 1995

The sacredness of Uluru-Kata Tjuta to its traditional Anangu custodians extends beyond the iconic 'rock' to its surrounding landscape. The 22-acre (9ha) project's design intended to minimize impact and maximize visitors' immersive experience of the desert's beauty and meaning through almost invisible landscape architecture. Located one kilometre from Uluru's base, the Cultural Centre intertwines with the desert sand with fluidity symbolic of the give and take of its joint indigenous and National Parks management and the inner and outer experience of culture. The Anangus' desire for a landscape 'island' around the visitor centre to create a preparatory state through walking and experiencing the landscape before visiting Uluru, took a year of negotiations with tourist and park operators and was effectively realized through a 330 yard (300m) separation from the car park. No trees were removed, gradients changed or planting added to ensure that the site maintained its indigenous integrity. Through careful siting, the sensitive and restrained design invites a profound relationship between the desert landscape and those moving through it, facilitating wider interpretation of its elements and qualities.

"Time is flying never to return."
VIRGIL, GEORGICS (29 BCE)

"Landscape was the original dwelling; the human species evolved among plants and animals, under the sky, upon the earth, near water. Each of us carries that legacy in body and mind."
ANNE WHISTON SPIRN, THE LANGUAGE OF LANDSCAPE (1998)

8.8

8.8
Swamp Garden, West 8 Landscape Architects, Charleston, South Carolina, USA, 1997
For the Spoleto Art Festival theme, 'Art and Landscape in Charleston and the low country', West 8 created a garden design for the cypress swamps, within the diverse regional landscape context of ocean, estuaries, rivers and salt water marshes. A meandering boardwalk leads from solid ground to a secluded area separated by steel poles and wires, hung with ultra-light, wavy walls of Spanish Moss causing constant modulations in atmosphere and lending a meditative quality to the open-air room.

“A dying forest. A nurtured garden.”
SAUL WILLIAMS, SONG: RELEASE PART 2 (2002)

ENVIRONMENTAL MANAGEMENT AND MAINTENANCE

A design may propose a suite of sustainability initiatives but without adequate management and maintenance, environmental systems (which often require increased upkeep) will likely fail. Maintaining landscapes to nurture a design vision to fruition is a continuous challenge. Projects may lack design team input following construction or establishment/maintenance, or may have involved multiple design firms from masterplanning or sketch stage through to construction. Post-completion involvement (Chapter 9) is particularly important in landscape architecture projects. It can take decades for planting to establish and a landscape vision to become realized, thus placing maintenance considerations as critical to long-term landscape sustainability.

Horticultural imperialism

In many developed countries, the legacy of landscape maintenance is rooted in formalist, ornamental horticultural practices based on dominion and control. Colonial-era travel facilitated a new interest in exotic botany, establishing plant collections sourced from regions differing from the local climatic and ground conditions. This has influenced the perception of a dominant landscape aesthetic (see Chapter 2 Interview), where notions of beauty (see Chapter 6, 10) can be detached from place, functionality and traditional horticultural roots (such as in physic, herbal, fruit and vegetable gardens). Edible species—the providers of our sustenance—are experiencing a resurgence (Chapter 5) but still receive minimal focus in the public domain, where they are almost non-existent and still perceived as utilitarian or unattractive (except in some regions such as parts of the Mediterranean). Poorly considered or artificially imposed landscape features from ill-fitting environmental, cultural or historical contexts come at an environmental cost (such as proliferous British and Western European grass lawn use—first in ex-colonial counties and now world-wide—irrespective of unsuitability to weathered soils, harsher sunlight and higher evapotranspiration). This exotic, ornamental heritage embodies practices that fail to be environmentally and sustainably appropriate to time, place and social needs.

8.9a
8.9b
8.9c
Crosby Arboretum, Edward L. Blake, Jr, Andropogon Associates, Picayune, Mississippi, USA, 1979–
The Mississippi State University affiliated Crosby Arboretum contains a 64 acre (26ha) Interpretive Center built on a former pine plantation and disused farmland. Its 700 acres (283ha) of habitat contains over 300 indigenous plants species in seven natural areas. Dedicated to preserving and protecting native plants, management includes prescribed burns of pine savannah.

8.10
Lurie Garden, Piet Oudolf (with Gustafson Guthrie Nichol), Millennium Park, Chicago, USA, 2001–2004
The Lurie Garden is one of Piet Oudolf's many triumphs of low water, perennial and xeriscape planting, where local vegetation species are generally conducive to reducing or eliminating supplementary irrigation.

Perpetual intervention

Mainstream horticulture is largely dependent upon continual human intervention to avert design and landscape collapse; malfunction of an irrigation system may cause planting failure, without continual pruning the spatial design may not function, or minus irrigation, synthetic fertilizers, pesticides and chemicals, lawn will not meet visual expectations. Control techniques may achieve the desired site outcomes (through killing turf beetles or 'weeds', for instance), but pollute soils, waterways and aquifers and create biological accumulation in humans and animals (this approach also correlates with industrialized agriculture (Chapter 5)). The opposite end of the maintenance spectrum is 'wilding' or near-zero maintenance attempting to recreate 'natural' ecosystems (Chapter 2). Not only difficult to achieve, wilding can create its own set of problems, such as urban visual safety considerations, accumulation of woody and/or flammable plant material posing fire risk, and reduced biodiversity from invasive species taking over terrestrial and aquatic areas. Nevertheless, this approach is widely considered more sustainable than intensive, ornamental horticulture.

Community maintenance

Intensive landscape maintenance trends are diminishing in many Western cities due to increased labor costs and low maintenance budgets for public spaces. In developed countries, landscape maintenance has become highly mechanized and dependent on cheap fossil fuels through vehicles and motorized equipment to reduce human labor costs. These high emissions equipment (such as two-stroke machinery trimmers, blowers and mowers) are both unhealthy and environmentally detrimental. Community-interactive maintenance projects and health schemes could help to shift public green spaces from static to active, passive to participatory, and ornamental to productive (Chapter 5). With increased urban density and a corresponding lack of private green spaces in much of the world, public spaces need to deliver positive benefits, active participation and productivity to urban inhabitants with greater sophistication.

8.9a

8.9b

8.9c

8.10

8.11a

8.11b

8.11c

8.11d

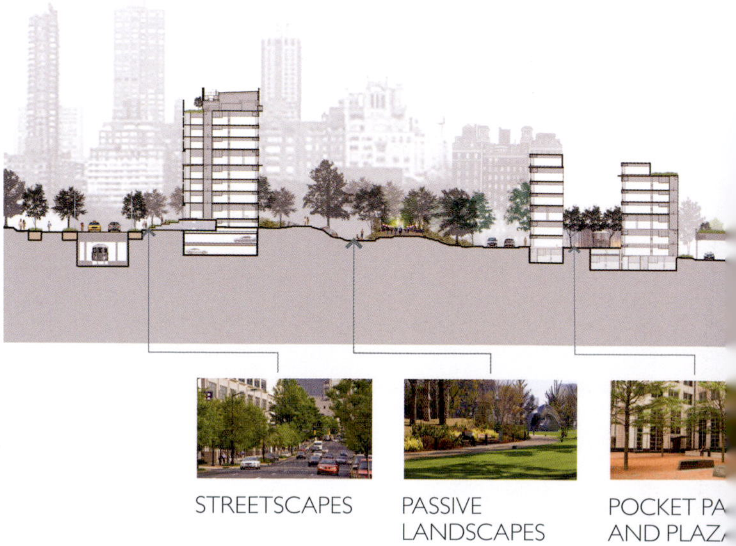
STREETSCAPES
PASSIVE
LANDSCAPES
POCKET PA
AND PLAZ

8.12a

8.11a
8.11b
8.11c
8.11d
General Mills Sculpture Garden, Michael Van Valkenburgh Associates, Minneapolis, Minnesota, USA, 1989–1991 (garden was demolished by the client in 2000)
The design created an entry landscape and sculptures walk amidst native prairie grasses and wildflowers. A balance of expressive ecology and modernist minimalism was achieved to fit the 1957 architecture by Skidmore, Owings, & Merrill. Part of the annual landscape maintenance included burning the meadow to encourage new growth, creating changing multi-seasonal color and texture over the year. While mowing, spraying and other noisy and potentially toxic practices are routine in landscape maintenance and management, burning is less common, especially in urban conditions.

8.12b

8.12a
8.12b
High Performance Landscape Guidelines: 21st Century Parks for NYC, Design Trust & NYC Parks Department, New York City, USA, 2008–2011
It is key that NYC Parks reduce the urban heat island effect, cleaning air, absorbing storm water, providing habitat, and addressing climate change. This online, downloadable park design and construction manual contains a range of diverse case studies and best practices for sustainability outcomes.

COMPOSITE SECTION
SITE TYPES FOR NYC PARKS
New York City's urban landscape includes a complex network of open spaces, characterized by different site conditions, uses and surrounding contexts. High Performance Landscape Guidelines defines nine types of open spaces, highlighted in the composite section below. From waterfronts to playgrounds, active recreation areas to passive landscapes, this section illustrates prominent features, opportunities, and constraints that everyone designing, building and maintaining the city's 21st century parks should understand.

BROWNFIELDS AND RECOVERED SITES
WATERFRONTS
PARKS OVER STRUCTURES
PLAYGROUNDS
ACTIVE RECREATION AREAS
RESTORATION AREAS

"Narratives… intersect with sites, accumulate as layers of history, organize sequences, and inhere in the very materials and processes of the landscape. In various ways, stories 'take place..'"
MATTHEW POTTEIGER AND JAMIE PURINTON, LANDSCAPE NARRATIVES (1998)

COMMUNICATION AND RELATIONSHIPS

Positive relationships are crucial to creating professional trust and an enduring design practice. Strong education programs and leading landscape architects recognize the importance of effective communication, presentation, listening, mediation and leadership skills, as well as cultural sensitivity. This is particularly the case when proposing innovative or working on environmental and cultural projects where issues transcend landscape boundaries, potentially crossing multiple jurisdictions and cultures (see Yawuru Cultural Management Plan). While digital communication has dramatically changed business and education, at present, most commercial dealings in landscape architectural practice result from in-person, human-formed networks and interpersonal communications.

Competing or complimentary interests?

Large-scale projects cross innumerable groups and municipalities (see Mersey Basin). Isolated silos can compete for individual agenda, whether local/state governments; architects/landscape architects; engineers/designers; designers/contractors; designers/maintenance staff; landscape architects/garden designers, adjacent communities and so forth. Interdisciplinary respect and effective leadership are key to achieving sustainability results and harmonious working relationships.

8.13a
8.13b
Yawuru Cultural Management Plan, UDLA with Nyamba Buru Yawuru, Broome, Western Australia, 2010–2011
The Australian Institute of Landscape Architects national awards jury said of the Yawuru Cultural Management Plan (YCMP): "It is more than a conversation, more than a listening and recording, more than walking and seeing the land; it is all of these things, but most importantly, it is none of these, but the land and its people."

The experiential nature of the indigenous Yawuru people's land management was uniquely captured by UDLA. Commissioned by the Yawuru people to design a long-term management plan, it details joint management practices of the Yawuru Conservation Estate and beyond. Produced under Nyamba Buru Yawuru curatorship and endorsed by the Yawuru Registered Native Title Holders Body Corporate (RNTHBC), the plan outlines best-practices in partnership with ranger and country manager teams, the Department of Parks and Wildlife, Shire of Broome, government agencies, and researchers.

YAWURU

8.13a

Yawuru Seasons
Laja
October–November
Man-gala
December–March
Marrul
April–May
Wirralburu
May–June
Barrgana
June–August
Wirlburu
September
Yawuru Six Seasons Wheel.
Source: UDLA /Martha Lee & Maxine Charlie
YCMP
18

8.13b

8.14a

8.14b

8.14a
8.14b

Collingwood Children's Farm, TCL, Abbotsford, Melbourne, Australia, 2001–

This unique 20 acre (8ha) not-for profit community farm is only 2.5 miles (4km) from the city center and seeks to provide both a safe haven for at-risk children and city residents with country experiences. A sensitive masterplan developed in consultation with the farm community designed a range of facilities such as animal pens, paddocks, barn, café, vegetable plots and composting area, which can be viewed from the shared bicycle/ pedestrian path skirting the farm. Frequent social programs are held on-site, such as farmers markets, bonfire nights, children's birthday parties, horse riding for the disabled, and participatory cow-milking.

8.15a

8.15b

8.15a
8.15b
The Mersey Basin Campaign, Northwest England, UK, 1985–2010
The dirtiest river in the world at the time of the 1985 Environmental Regeneration Campaign, the Mersey passes through 29 local authority areas, with 5 million people within its catchment. A unified body brought together a myriad of different organizations and communities, recognizing the relationship between environmental improvement and economic regeneration. A network of 20 'Action Partnerships' were set up to facilitate improvement projects in public, private and voluntary sectors, coordinating volunteers, schools, businesses, regulators, and local authorities.

Construction

Challenges can arise from project inception to post-construction maintenance and management. Highly mechanized, insensitive modern construction techniques easily lead to land damage, clearance and soil erosion (see Half-Mile Line). Leadership, advocacy and vigilance are required at all stages of the project by the design team. Documented designs protecting natural and cultural site assets (as well as design intent) must be communicated to site contractors and monitored by frequent site visits to prevent the site integrity or design vision being compromised (such as through the loss of soil and vegetation). Creating a sound rapport and good working relationship aids this process from the outset.

Inclusiveness

The 20th-century model of architect or master designer dictating, demanding and ordering the terms is shifting to a more inclusive and collaborative approach in contemporary landscape practice. Mutli-disciplinary teams working with respect and in harmony can achieve an improved overall outcome. This is helped if the project lead (ideally a landscape architect!) can act as symphony conductor, orchestrating each discipline's strengths into a cohesive arrangement, providing decisive leadership mediates through a considered, sensitive and contextual design responses.

8.16a

8.16a
8.16b
Half-Mile Line, Reed Hilderbrand, West Stockbridge, Massachusetts, USA, 2003–2012
Originally commissioned by the owner to aid stewardship of the forests covering 70% of the 50 acre (20ha) site, Reed Hilderbrand proposed uniting the property with a circuit trail to the pristine, previously unreachable Berkshires wetland. Following a collaborative nine month design approval process (which included conservation biologists), aerial photography enabled the planning of path alignment that navigated trees, snags, woody thickets, beaver impoundments, perennial stream courses, and wildlife corridors. *In situ* hand construction methods included carpenters assembling the meandering boardwalk in the water (hauling materials and using floats), helical support piles driven into the subsoil with crowbars and debris contained using silt curtains and shovels.

The decking's 5,000 pieces of locally milled hemlock were chosen for the rustic, raised grain and ease of cutting. The varied and dynamic Half-Mile Line is a series of contrasting intimate, woody thickets, marsh grasslands, and large areas of open and running water. The path arrives at two observatory platforms set in open waters revealing the surrounding forest and the Berkshires.

8.16b

8.17a

8.17a
8.17b
8.17c
8.17d

Clark Art Institute, Reed Hilderbrand, Tadao Ando Associates, Gensler, Annabelle Selldorf, ARCADIS, Williamstown, Massachusetts, USA, 2002–2014

This 140 acre (57ha) Art Institute campus of forest, meadows, streams, ponds and lawn includes a museum collection focusing on artists' relationships with nature. Enhancement of the site combined environmental performance with minimalist aesthetics, exemplified by its 1 acre tiered reflecting pool that is forms the center of the campus' storm water management system.

8.17b

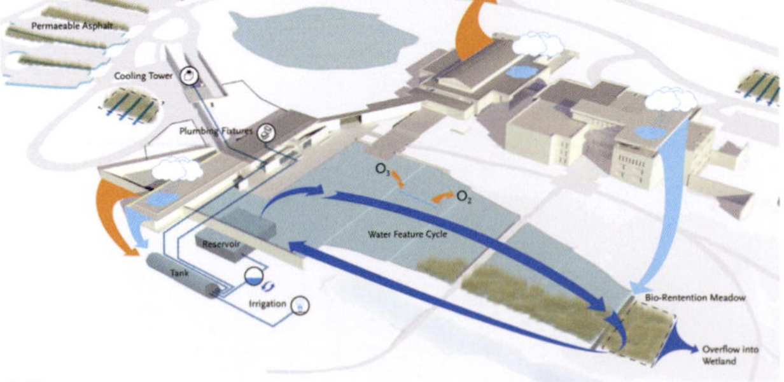
Permaeable Asphalt
Cooling Tower
Plumbing Fixtures
O_3
O_2
Water Feature Cycle
Reservoir
Tank
Irrigation
Bio-Rentention Meadow
Overflow into Wetland

8.17c

8.17d

STUDY/DISCUSSION QUESTIONS

Is sensitivity an important attribute in landscape architecture? Does this differ from keen observation?

What do you think 'reading' landscapes entails? Apply the exercise of 'reading' a local landscape and discuss your observations. How does cultural conditioning and upbringing affect this?

Is communing with nature important in order to create a connection between humankind and the environment?

Is sensitivity to nature an important attribute where remnant and natural ecosystems have been destroyed and lost?

Is restraint important in environmental design? Can you give any examples?

Do you think a sensitive approach to environmental design can help to rebalance our relationship with the natural world?

Can 'light-touch' and sensitive approaches be heard and make a difference in the face of the 'noise' of the day-to-day world?

FURTHER READING

Carter, P. (1996) *The lie of the land*, London: Faber and Faber.

Casey, E. (1993) *Getting back into place: toward a renewed understanding of the place-world*, Bloomington: Indiana University Press.

Hough, M. (1990) *Out of Place: Restoring identity to the regional landscape*, New Haven: Yale University Press.

Huggan, G. and Tiffin, H. (2015) *Postcolonial ecocriticism: literature, animals, environment*, Oxon, UK: Routledge.

Jackson, J. B. (1984) *Discovering the Vernacular Landscape*, New Haven: Yale University Press.

Johnston, R. (1991) *A question of place: exploring the practice of human geography*, Oxford, UK: Blackwell.

Kunstler, J. (1993) *The Geography of Nowhere: The Rise and Decline of America's Man-Made Landscape*, New York: Simon & Schuster.

LaGro, J. (2008) *Site analysis: a contextual approach to sustainable land planning and site design*, Hoboken, NJ: John Wiley & Sons.

Larice, M. and Macdonald, E. (2013) *The urban design reader*, London: Routledge. (See Part 3 and Norberg-Schulz, pp. 741–775).

Lippard, L. (1997) *The lure of the local: senses of place in a multicentered society*, New York: New Press.

Potteiger, M. and Purinton, J. (1998) *Landscape Narratives: design practices for telling stories*, New York: J. Wiley.

Seddon, G. (1998) *Landprints: reflections on place and landscape*, Cambridge UK: Cambridge University Press.

Spirn, A. (1998) *The Language of Landscape*, New Haven: Yale University Press.

Starke, B. and Simonds, J. (2013) *Landscape Architecture: A Manual of Site Planning and Design*, 5th Edition, London: McGraw-Hill.

Tuan, Yi-Fu. (1990) *Topophilia: A study of environmental perception, attitudes, and values*, New York: Columbia University Press.

ADDITIONAL PROJECTS

You might also like to look for further information on the following projects:

Columbus Park, Jens Jensen, Chicago, Illinois, USA, 1915–1920

Kaurna Seasonal Calendar, Scott Heyes, Adelaide Plains, 1999

West Point Foundry Preserve, Mathews Nielsen Landscape Architects, Cold Spring, New York, USA

Swaner Ecocenter, Park City, Utah, USA

Blue Hole Regional Park, Wimberley, Texas, USA

Horseshoe Farm Nature Preserve, Raleigh, North Carolina, USA

Hempstead Plains Interpretive Center, Garden City, New York, USA

Manor Fields Park, Sheffield, UK

INTERVIEW Douglas Reed and Gary Hilderbrand, Reed Hilderbrand

Douglas Reed is partner and co-founder of Reed Hilderbrand Landscape Architecture, and an American Society of Landscape Architects Fellow. In 2011 he was recognized as a Resident of the American Academy in Rome. He lectures widely and participates as a critic on reviews for design schools nationwide. As a founding board member of the Cultural Landscape Foundation and as board co-chair for 13 years, he has consistently shaped a platform that delivers knowledge about design heritage and how it matters in people's everyday lives.

Professor Gary Hilderbrand is partner and co-founder of Reed Hilderbrand Landscape Architecture and Professor in Practice at the Harvard Graduate School of Design, where he has taught since 1990. His honors include Harvard University's Charles Eliot Traveling Fellowship, the Rome Prize in Landscape Architecture, the Architectural League's Emerging Voices Award with Douglas Reed, and the 2013 ASLA Firm of the Year award. Professor Hilderbrand's essays have been featured in *Landscape Architecture, Topos, Harvard Design Magazine, Architecture Boston, Clark Art Journal, Arnoldia, New England Journal of Garden History*, and *Land Forum*.

Why is (or isn't) sensitivity an important quality for environmental design and landscape architecture?

We value human attributes of sensitivity in most things. But sensitivity to landscape on its own does not necessarily help generate coherent and meaningful design. We read sites through empathetic responses, astute observation, and an objective knowledge of the systems that define character. Out of this we define foundational values for conceptualizing a project, rooted in environmental and cultural significances. Our landscape architecture strives to make those values visible.

What conditions or factors do you think help to cultivate landscape sensitivity?
a. Do you think interaction and communing with nature engenders landscape sensitivity?
b. If so, should we be concerned by a lack of opportunities in many urban regions across the globe and in places where 'nature' has largely been destroyed?

We often assert, as Lewis Mumford did in his writings about urbanization, that 'nature' is a human construct. It's as possible to engage deeply with nature in the city as it is in the country. Nature can be destroyed; it can also be rebuilt. Our project for Long Dock Park in Beacon, New York (see Chapter 9), a prominent site on the Hudson River, had always served an industrial purpose. We rebuilt the site as a popular open space and working landscape. It now embraces and responds to the hardship of destructive ice floes and debris at this point in the Hudson. Where 'nature' is absent or apparently destroyed, we see an opportunity to imagine a new future.

To be sure, though, the experience of nature and its living systems is crucial to human wellbeing and understanding one's place in the world. This was brought home to us powerfully in our early project for the Institute for Child and Adolescent Development (see Chapter 7), a garden designed to help in the diagnosis and treatment of emotional trauma. It coincided with the startling evidence of the deficit in authentic interaction with nature among today's children.

Is there a difference between cultural and environmental sensitivity? For example, in your 'Half-Mile Line' project (in this chapter), do you see any conflict between the negatives of allowing access as opposed to the positive relationships and stewardship that this can create?

Our clients for Half-Mile Line knew their property possessed an extensive and vital wetland network. But they had little understanding of the potential spatial experience of this resource. Our project revealed this to them—a source of ongoing discovery for them. Accessibility to the wetland reinforces their commitment to stewardship. So environmental and cultural sensitivity can be complementary. The tension—not conflict—you observe originates in regulation and regulatory conventions. There are areas of the country where protections are too lax. There are also areas where any human contact with habitats of high ecological value is prohibited. Reed Hilderbrand and many of our peers seek to set examples of innovation in responsible and appropriate ways that also protect resources and precious species.

Notwithstanding that each site is unique, are there certain qualities or attributes that you prioritize, seek to reveal, or highlight? I.e, what are your values or ethics? What qualities are you seeking to emphasize and what responses do you aim to evoke?

We love this question, and it gets to the heart of the matter about building a body of work with consistent values and a recognizable identity. Values of history, culture, ecology, program and philosophy are present on every site. We work as editors, calling some forward, obscuring or suppressing others. It is inherently discretionary—the judgment we exercise underlies the art of what we do. The way we see it, landscape architecture succeeds when it expands the human stories of a place while also strengthening its ecologies, its biophysical exchange. It must also cohere and appeal to human perception—we aspire to beauty and performance.

In the face of complex experiential, historic, technical and environmental factors, what is your approach to achieving legible design outcomes?

We always seek to weave a site's heritage, its new uses, and highly technical demands into a total experience. We find that a site's legibility requires clarity of intent, and in the process of our work we invest in the rigor it takes to attain that clarity. A project like the Clark Art Institute (in this chapter), a museum that traditionally focused on pastoral traditions of landscape painting, now engages the visitor in a comprehensive and coherent narrative about the historical and ecological development of the property. This transformation amplifies the mission of the museum, deepening the Clark's stake in its own place and its public.

What techniques and approaches do you employ to mediate your design aims with the practicalities and challenges of maintenance and the ability of both construction and maintenance staff to understand, respect and seek ongoing realization of your vision and intent?

Your question is a reminder that our discipline's defining feature might be its temporal dimension—we work with a dynamic, living medium. For a designed landscape to endure as originally conceived requires extraordinary commitment from stewards and designers alike. In one sense, the design itself must inspire that commitment. It must also meet realities of skilled labor and budgets. We try to stay involved well after the project is "substantially complete", and when that happens, we can manage the transition well with its owners and caretakers. Each year we visit our project at Central Wharf Plaza (see Chapter 4) on the Boston waterfront to review the condition of a grove of mixed oak species supported by a precise and particular infrastructure of soils, stormwater management, and irrigation. We have continued to attend to the site and the trees have flourished, growing into one of our city's iconic landscapes.

Is part of environmental sensitivity understanding that adaptive approaches are ultimately more effective than controlling approaches, or is control an inevitable part of human habitation?

We favor both. As designers, we want to control everything, but we recognize that the work must be adaptive and resilient. So this tension is where the work gets interesting:

We create specific spatial forms and aim for certain effects in a landscape. But systems of nature that we work with are cyclical, entropic, spontaneous, and thus inherently unpredictable. Out of this, though, come the many phenomena that surprise and delight us in a landscape. At the Houston Arboretum and Nature Center (see Chapter 2), catastrophic loss of the tree canopy from drought and the impact of hurricanes has required a pervasive restarting of the ecology by employing historic eco-zones endemic to the region. Our plan largely encourages adaptation while our maintenance/management regime is precise and rigorous over many years. Even where our plan is prescriptive, we expect continuous adaptation.

Is sensitivity paradoxical to the need for widespread change for environmental sustainability? Do you think landscape architects need to be more forthright or assertive?

Once again, it's both. Awareness and sensitivity are about education and knowledge. Landscape architects do have a responsibility to lead their clients and the public, to advance an agenda that expands environmental sustainability. Rather than pursue activism on paraprofessional issues, our contribution on this front comes through excellence in built works. As we have described in our individual projects, we are committed to long-term progress achieved incrementally, involving everything we do.

SITES v2 Scorecard Summary

ES	?	NO			
0	0	0	**1: SITE CONTEXT**	**Possible Points:**	**13**
Y			**CONTEXT P1.1**	Limit development on farmland	
Y			**CONTEXT P1.2**	Protect floodplain functions	
Y			**CONTEXT P1.3**	Conserve aquatic ecosystems	
Y			**CONTEXT P1.4**	Conserve habitats for threatened and endangered species	
			CONTEXT C1.5	Redevelop degraded sites	**3 to 6**
			CONTEXT C1.6	Locate projects within existing developed areas	**4**
			CONTEXT C1.7	Connect to multi-modal transit networks	**2 to 3**
0	0	0	**2: PRE-DESIGN ASSESSMENT + PLANNING**	**Possible Points:**	**3**
Y			**PRE-DESIGN P2.1**	Use an integrative design process	
Y			**PRE-DESIGN P2.2**	Conduct a pre-design site assessment	
Y			**PRE-DESIGN P2.3**	Designate and communicate VSPZs	
			PRE-DESIGN C2.4	Engage users and stakeholders	**3**
0	0	0	**3: SITE DESIGN - WATER**	**Possible Points:**	**23**
Y			**WATER P3.1**	Manage precipitation on site	
Y			**WATER P3.2**	Reduce water use for landscape irrigation	
			WATER C3.3	Manage precipitation beyond baseline	**4 to 6**
			WATER C3.4	Reduce outdoor water use	**4 to 6**
			WATER C3.5	Design functional stormwater features as amenities	**4 to 5**
			WATER C3.6	Restore aquatic ecosystems	**4 to 6**
0	0	0	**4: SITE DESIGN - SOIL + VEGETATION**	**Possible Points:**	**40**
Y			**SOIL+VEG P4.1**	Create and communicate a soil management plan	
Y			**SOIL+VEG P4.2**	Control and manage invasive plants	
Y			**SOIL+VEG P4.3**	Use appropriate plants	
			SOIL+VEG C4.4	Conserve healthy soils and appropriate vegetation	**4 to 6**
			SOIL+VEG C4.5	Conserve special status vegetation	**4**
			SOIL+VEG C4.6	Conserve and use native plants	**3 to 6**
			SOIL+VEG C4.7	Conserve and restore native plant communities	**4 to 6**
			SOIL+VEG C4.8	Optimize biomass	**1 to 6**
			SOIL+VEG C4.9	Reduce urban heat island effects	**4**
			SOIL+VEG C4.10	Use vegetation to minimize building energy use	**1 to 4**
			SOIL+VEG C4.11	Reduce the risk of catastrophic wildfire	**4**
0	0	0	**5: SITE DESIGN - MATERIALS SELECTION**	**Possible Points:**	**41**
Y			**MATERIALS P5.1**	Eliminate the use of wood from threatened tree species	
			MATERIALS C5.2	Maintain on-site structures and paving	**2 to 4**
			MATERIALS C5.3	Design for adaptability and disassembly	**3 to 4**
			MATERIALS C5.4	Use salvaged materials and plants	**3 to 4**
			MATERIALS C5.5	Use recycled content materials	**3 to 4**
			MATERIALS C5.6	Use regional materials	**3 to 5**

9.1
Sustainable Sites Initiative
SITES™ is landscape's primary rating tool to facilitate more sustainable development and projects.

YES	?	NO			
0	0	0	**6: SITE DESIGN - HUMAN HEALTH + WELL-BEING**	**Possible Points:**	**30**
			HHWB C6.1	Protect and maintain cultural and historic places	**2 to 3**
			HHWB C6.2	Provide optimum site accessibility, safety, and wayfinding	**2**
			HHWB C6.3	Promote equitable site use	**2**
			HHWB C6.4	Support mental restoration	**2**
			HHWB C6.5	Support physical activity	**2**
			HHWB C6.6	Support social connection	**2**
			HHWB C6.7	Provide on-site food production	**3 to 4**
			HHWB C6.8	Reduce light pollution	**4**
			HHWB C6.9	Encourage fuel efficient and multi-modal transportation	**4**
			HHWB C6.10	Minimize exposure to environmental tobacco smoke	**1 to 2**
			HHWB C6.11	Support local economy	**3**
0	0	0	**7: CONSTRUCTION**	**Possible Points:**	**17**
Y			**CONSTRUCTION P7.1**	Communicate and verify sustainable construction practices	
Y			**CONSTRUCTION P7.2**	Control and retain construction pollutants	
Y			**CONSTRUCTION P7.3**	Restore soils disturbed during construction	
			CONSTRUCTION C7.4	Restore soils disturbed by previous development	**3 to 5**
			CONSTRUCTION C7.5	Divert construction and demolition materials from disposal	**3 to 4**
			CONSTRUCTION C7.6	Divert reusable vegetation, rocks, and soil from disposal	**3 to 4**
			CONSTRUCTION C7.7	Protect air quality during construction	**2 to 4**
0	0	0	8. OPERATIONS + MAINTENANCE	Possible Points:	**22**
Y			O+M P8.1	Plan for sustainable site maintenance	
Y			O+M P8.2	[illegible]	
			O+M C8.3	Recycle organic matter	**3 to 5**
			O+M C8.4	Minimize pesticide and fertilizer use	**4 to 5**
			O+M C8.5	Reduce outdoor energy consumption	**2 to 4**
			[illegible]	[illegible]	**3 to 4**
			[illegible]	[illegible]	**2 to 4**
0	0	0	9. EDUCATION + PERFORMANCE MONITORING	Possible Points:	**11**
			EDUCATION C9.1	Promote sustainability awareness and education	**3 to 4**
			EDUCATION C9.2	Develop and communicate a case study	**3**
			[illegible]	[illegible]	**4**
0	0	0	10. INNOVATION OR EXEMPLARY PERFORMANCE	Bonus Points:	**9**
			INNOVATION C10.1	Innovation or exemplary performance	**3 to 9**
YES	?	NO			
0	0	0	TOTAL ESTIMATED POINTS	Total Possible Points:	**200**
KEY				**SITES Certification levels**	Points

9
LANDSCAPE AND PERFORMANCE

Progressive landscape architectural measurement and rating tools assess and demonstrate the landscape medium's productive capacity to generate ecosystem services, rather than merely minimizing negative impacts. These mechanisms are steadily increasing, especially in the USA, with the industry benchmark SITES™ rating tool and the Landscape Performance Series analysis and measurement of crucial post-construction outcomes. These provide a consistent means of measurement and comparison, helping to reduce greenwashing. Selecting, arranging and considering future reuse of construction materials involves factors such as embodied energy, material life cycles, sustainable and ethical material selection, the use of salvaged and waste materials, upcycling, downcyling and material hybridity. These can all mitigate the considerable impact of built environment material cycles on global ecosystems.

PERFORMANCE AND RATINGS

Environmental discourse stresses the need to reduce consumption and energy intensive, inefficient practices. Accordingly, it is increasingly a requirement for development to closely examine the performance of both entire projects and individual materials. An abundance of guidelines, protocols, frameworks and other documents exist in most municipalities' planning and urban design processes. These can be generalist and not facilitate a specific means of rating environmental performance (although can provide useful references and case studies). Construction and design codes and standards (such as ISO/ASTM/ICC and local equivalents (ANSI/ANS (USA) British/Australian/NZ Standard) often guide or stipulate minimum requirements to comply with national/state/local legal regulations, but are not oriented towards environmental sustainability. Built environment sustainability performance rating tools have increasingly emerged in recent decades (BREEAM was released in 1990) and although usually voluntary, are inherently incentivizing, making improvements and outcomes clear and tangible.

Existing tools

A well-established architectural and building-centric range of performance tools already exists (for example BREEAM (UK), LEED, Living Building Challenge, Green Globes, WELL Building Standard (USA), Green Star, NABERS, BASIX, EER (Australia), CASBEE (Japan) and Estidama (Abu Dhabi)). Assessment of sustainability performance has been slower to emerge in landscape architecture. Various attempts at creating landscape-centric performance and rating tools failed to establish as platforms for benchmarking and assessment until development of the SITES tool (USA, 2009). Some site planning tools (such as LEED Neighborhood, STAR and GBCA 'Communities') have also expanded from the previously cursory consideration given to landscape dimensions.

Landscape versus building rating

Factoring site context is crucial to landscape design and performance. Many architectural tools are internally focused, treating a building as an 'object in space', effectively sealed from its environment (measuring, for example, quantifiable energy water, waste, indoor light and air quality). Buildings' capacity to generate ecosystem services is limited to generating partial energy requirements, capturing water or growing produce on rooftop gardens. Landscapes, on the other hand, can sustainably output ecosystem services through working with natural processes (such as phytoremediation of toxins in soil and water (Chapter 3); carbon

"If nature adhered to the human model of efficiency, there would be fewer cherry blossoms, and fewer nutrients. Fewer trees, less oxygen, and less clean water. Fewer songbirds. Less diversity, less creativity and delight. The idea of nature being more efficient, dematerializing, or even not 'littering' (imagine zero waste or zero emissions for nature!) is preposterous. The marvelous thing about effective systems is that one wants more of them, not less."
WILLIAM MCDONOUGH & MICHAEL BRAUNGART, CRADLE TO CRADLE (2002)

"An artist must have his measuring tools not in the hand, but in the eye."
MICHELANGELO (1475–1564)

"A great building must … begin with the unmeasurable, must go through measurable in the process of design, but must again in the end be unmeasurable … it must evoke unmeasurable qualities."
LOUIS KAHN, THE VALUE AND AIM IN SKETCHING (1930)

"If I were a young architect today looking at supposed eco-architecture, I wouldn't want to do it; it's a one-liner. When ecology becomes the major issue, you're left with a scientific box that does nothing for the spirit. I cannot separate the idea of the poetic and the rational. If there's not a junction, we've got merchandise, not architecture."
GLENN MURCUTT, ARCHITECTURE: PRITZKER PRIZE (2002)

"In this age of recession, one could argue that green building and green infrastructure, commonly reduced to checklists and engineering-based techniques, have been some of the few areas of growth … it's the distillation of ecologically sensitive planning and design into a checklist and set of easily understood techniques that is the problem. It can be seen as an oversimplification of the design process."
M. MARGARET BRYANT, AND IT BEGAN WITH ARCOSANTI (2012).

sequestration through soil and trees; water cleansing wider catchment areas and on-site storage for reuse (Chapter 3); air filtration through planting; food and material production (Chapter 5); habitat provision (Chapter 2); as well as health and psychological benefits (Chapter 7). Their measurable material use (like lighting, water, and paving, aggregates, concrete, topsoil, fertilizer) can therefore be offset by their larger productive capacity. This can be both difficult and intensive to capture and is most evident post construction and plant establishment (and therefore challenging and potentially inaccurate with current rating system's focus on the design stage).

Criticism

Measurement and rating tools can be divisive within design discourse, criticized for being prescriptive and automating the design process through check box inclusions. 'Capital D' Design purists argue that tools can reduce the conscious element of design, including its artistic, poetic, aesthetic and spatial dimensions. Rating tools can also be geared to merely minimize commercial development harm. As they are usually implemented before construction and based on projected outcomes, developers can exploit high projected project ratings as a means to generate increased profits (through higher sales or rents), without meeting anticipated ratings. Quantified factual results by researchers, academics and organizations (see Landscape Performance Series) are crucial to measuring post-completion performance (such as electricity consumption/production). Regular updates help to mitigate these issues, facilitating current best practices and improving outcomes.

9.2a
9.2b
The Sustainable Sites Initiative (SITES™), Green Business Certification Inc, developed by American Society of Landscape Architects, Lady Bird Johnson Wildflower Center at University of Texas at Austin, and the United States Botanic Garden, USA, pilot launched 2009, v2 launched June 2014
SITES is currently the most comprehensive established rating tool system for landscape development projects, used by landscape architects, architects, engineers, developers and policy makers. Originally modelled on the US Green Building Council's LEED rating system, it was developed through study of peer-reviewed literature and case studies, and interdisciplinary collaboration of over 70 contributors (including technical advisers, practitioners and educational organizations). The two year pilot program encompassed 100 projects informing the current, second edition. Sections cover site context; pre-design assessment and planning; water; soil and vegetation; materials selection; human health and wellbeing; construction; operations and maintenance; education and performance modelling and innovation or exemplary performance. There are 18 required baseline prerequisites, such as conducting a site assessment prior to design, with points awarded from 1–6 for implementing initiatives. The prerequisites and 48 credits total 200 points resulting in four certification levels—one to four star, or 'certified' (70), 'silver' (80), 'gold' (100), and 'platinum' (135).

9.2a

Sustainable
SITES
Initiative

9.2b

Embodied bias

Advocates for performance rating can be aligned with scientific and technical quantification and people who understand that many decision makers require 'scientific' and data-based evidence (empirical, quantitative) to perceive tangible value and/or 'solid' evidence for a project. Although rating tools are presented as quantitative, empirical and impartial, it is important to maintain conscious critique of any inherent biases. Do they assume every building is sealed/air conditioned? Are native plants appropriate in the given context? Have they been commercially funded? Many tools have been developed through peer-input, consultation, review and feedback processes, which significantly reduce bias. Measurement mechanisms and rating tools are only as good at the minds behind them, the breadth of their capture, the sophistication of measurement, the rigor of the science used for quantification, and the inbuilt ability to encourage and facilitate innovation.

Benefits

Notwithstanding shortcomings, rating tools provide a rigorous audit process and quality assurance for design, helping to ensure consideration and incorporation of a breadth of sustainability initiatives. Rating tools are highly beneficial in contexts where clients, developers and communities lack comprehension of landscape's value. They can somewhat de-mystify the design process, or at least, make beneficial outcomes more explicit. Furthermore, the clear and measured summarization of (projected) outcomes provides benchmarks for comparison and security for clients, developers, municipalities, governments, and media.

9.3a
9.3b
9.3c

Center for Sustainable Landscapes, Andropogon Associates, Phipps Conservatory and Botanical Gardens, Pittsburgh, Pennsylvania, 2012

This 2.9 acre (1.2 ha) $15 million brownfield now supports a 24,350 square foot (2,262m^2) education and research building and 1.5 acres (0.6ha) of green space, including tropical forest conservatory and terrestrial biome and achieves zero net energy and water use. It was the first in the world to achieve LEED Platinum, SITES four-star certification, and the Living Building Challenge and the highest rated project during the SITES pilot stage. Following nine months of charrettes with local community, the multidisciplinary team tackled degraded, contaminated and compacted soils, leaking underground storage tanks and complex underground infrastructure networks. The design manages and treats 100% of its stormwater, wastewater and a 1:10-year storm event on site (3.3 inches (84mm) in 24 hours). All greywater and blackwater is treated using passive systems and UV filters, before reuse as toilet flushing water (required to be tested bi-quarterly by an EPA-certified lab). As rainwater reuse does not meet local health codes' potable water standards, the project is forced to use municipal water supply (and sought exception from the Living Building Challenge in this aspect). The 12,000 square foot (1,115m^2) conservatory roof supplies rainwater to a 4,000 square foot (372m^2) stormwater lagoon, while an estimated 500,000 gallons (1,893kl) of annual runoff is reused for the conservatory's irrigation. The center generates 100% of the building's energy on-site (99% through on-site solar photovoltaics and 1% from a single wind turbine). Geothermal wells significantly offset the building's HVAC energy requirements. The project features responsibly sourced materials, accounting for distances from origins, and has successfully reintroduced 150 native plant species. Project performance is being closely analyzed via several research arrangements.

"The central message of the Sustainable Sites Initiative program is that any landscape—whether the site of a large subdivision, a shopping mall, a park, an abandoned rail yard, or even one home—holds the potential both to improve and to regenerate the natural benefits and services provided by ecosystems in their undeveloped state … Our built landscapes can be modelled after healthy systems, thereby continually increasing the benefits they provide post-development."
SUSTAINABLE SITES INITIATIVE, GUIDELINES AND PERFORMANCE BENCHMARKS (2008)

"The SITES system better allows us to bring forward landscape related project benefits in more measurable terms."
CHRISTIAN GABRIEL, CLIENTS MAKE THE CASE (2015)

"The SITES certification process is especially valuable to organizations with little or no experience with constructing or conserving sustainable landscapes. SITES foundational guidance provided a holistic, iterative, and integrated process to follow."
MICHELLE SLOVENSKY, CLIENTS MAKE THE CASE (2015)

"What [SITES] provides is a logical and structured methodology to accomplish a rich diversity of improvements that can be shared with clients and the community. The more thorough a team is with embracing the credits the better the project can be for the public or private users. The structure allows us as designers to do a better job explaining the complexity of what it is we do and the certification allows the team and client to celebrate good work."
HUNTER BECKHAM, LANDSCAPE ARCHITECTS MAKE THE CASE (2015)

9.3a

9.3b

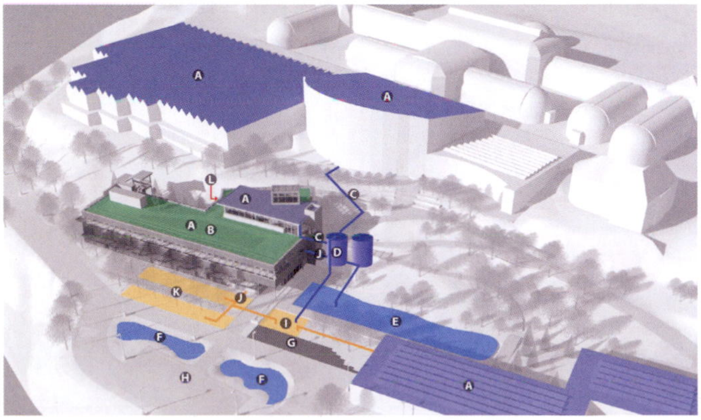

9.3c

9.4a (Before)
9.4b
9.4c
9.4d
9.4e

Long Dock Park, Reed Hilderbrand, Beacon, New York USA, 2004–2014

Achieving three out of four stars in the initial SITES pilot group, this former railroad siding and hazardous brownfield dumping site on reclaimed land is now a 14 acre (5.7ha) public riverfront park featuring environmental artwork, recreation, and education facilities. The park returned access to the river, remediated contaminated soils, restored degraded wetlands, reused *in situ* materials and increased ecological diversity.

1914
1957

9.4a

SITE FORMATION
INDUSTRIALIZATION
DEGRADATION
RECOVERY AND RENEWAL
1800
1890
1914
1960
1999
2001
2009
2011
2014
2017
ECOLOGY AND IN SITU REMEDIATION

9.4b

9.4c

9.4d

9.4e

Wider measurement

Beyond measurement and rating for landscape architectural projects, sustainability indexes and 'green' ratings also exist for cities (for example, Arcadis and Siemens Indices) as well as countries (for example, CASBEE for Cities, Arcadis and Siemens Indices). Measurement metrics require close examination and interrogation: Dubai, for example (not renowned for its sustainability) is ranked #33 in Arcadis (2015), while the OECD only ranks member countries. 'Ecological footprinting' is a measurement approach that can meaningfully measure individual or collective living and consumption patterns against the Earth's capacity to sustain them (such as the Global Footprint Network). Measurement occurs against the entire human population and the biocapacity of the Earth (see Ecological Footprint, Chapter 6).

"The construction industry is responsible for the consumption of 40% of global resources, 12% of potable water reserves, 55% of wood products, 45–65% of produced waste, 40% of raw materials, and the emission of 48% of harmful greenhouse gases, which leads to air and water pollution, threat of depletion of natural resources, and global warming."
OZGE SUZER, A COMPARATIVE REVIEW OF ENVIRONMENTAL CONCERN PRIORITIZATION (2015)

"The built environment is responsible for significant use of final energy (62%) and is a major source of greenhouse gas emissions (55%) ... The industry sector, which includes embodied material impacts among other sources, is responsible for 27% of final energy consumption and generates 24% of greenhouse gas emissions. Within the industry sector, cement and steel alone are responsible for around 5% and 6–7% of global CO emissions respectively. The built environment is consequently the dominant driver of global energy consumption and greenhouse gas emissions."
JOHN ANDERSON, GEBHARD WULFHORST & WERNER LANG, ENERGY ANALYSIS OF THE BUILT ENVIRONMENT (2015)

EMBODIED ENERGY AND MATERIAL LIFE CYCLES

The measurement of materials or processes' embodied energy is the sum of all the energy required to produce associated goods or services, expressed as energy incorporated or 'embodied' in the product or service itself. It can encompass natural resources' extraction and mining, processing, manufacturing, transportation, final product delivery. Broad-scale embodied energy accounts for a life-cycle assessment that may also factor assembly, installation, disassembly, deconstruction as well as human labor and secondary resources. Different methodological approaches take varying scales and scopes of embodied processes into account, such as 'embodied carbon', which is focused on carbon emissions and may not factor a wider range of measurable factors. When examining worldwide statistical evidence regarding the impact of the built environment and construction sectors, the need for mandated sustainability rating tools for both projects and materials is convincing (see Quotes).

Transportation

Embodied energy calculations are specific to individual localities and it is important to be mindful of where calculations are produced. Fossil fuel based transport significantly contributes to embodied energy (especially air and road). Data from the USA used in New Zealand, for example, is likely to disregard the immense transport distances between the two locations (the same is true for the USA's West to East coasts). Construction process measurement (such as volumes of materials brought on and off site and the sourcing locations) is sometimes available to the design team or public, allowing for analysis, quantification and communication of environmental performance.

Considerations beyond energy

It is important for designers to remain impartial of sustainability bias when selecting materials if aiming to reduce embodied energy and life-cycle costs: locally quarried stone for an Australian project, for example, may be processed in Vietnam or China, doubling the embodied energy in transportation than if Vietnamese/Chinese stone were used. Beyond purely embodied energy use, the *genius loci* expression of 'place' and integrity towards local geological and contextual conditions are important considerations for selecting materials (see Chapter 8). Additionally, certification and assurances of human and worker rights, child labor issues and health and safety conditions are not always assured, available or credible in the material selection process. Certification of products, such as some timber, attempt to provide quality, environmental and/or ethical assurances. Certification standards can vary and some have been brought into question by environment groups for effectively endorsing products from questionable practices such as illegal logging and old-growth timber harvesting or woodchipping.

9.5
Dutch Kills Green concrete recycling
The 32,145 square feet (803 tons) of salvaged concrete used for median 'no-go' barriers avoided the use of 214 tons of new concrete (which would have cost over $135,000 and generated over 30 tons of CO_2 emissions). The barriers direct pedestrians and cyclists through new crosswalk/bike path systems while facilitating stormwater infiltration.

9.6
Material considerations
The selection of materials can be an overwhelming process within the full spectrum of economic, social and environmental considerations. While materials' embodied energy is often accounted for within the built environment disciplines, ethical social sourcing information and certifications like 'fairtrade' (for food) are less developed. Cheaper construction materials are often imported from countries with poor working conditions and not subject to rigoros ethical and environmental standards.

9.5

9.6

"Our desire for beauty detached from utility is weakening, and it should be. In our new world, survival is at stake. Wastefulness becomes viscerally unattractive, if not immoral. But there is plenty of opportunity for joyful pleasure in useful things."
KONGJIAN YU, BEAUTIFUL BIG FEET: TOWARD A NEW LANDSCAPE AESTHETIC (2010)

RESPONSIBLE MATERIALS

'Closing the loop' is a well used concept in the built environment to facilitate the necessary shift from a linear 'input-use-waste' industrial system to 'cradle to cradle' and 'zero-waste' approaches. Closed-loop systems were more commonplace before the Industrial Revolution and the widespread transportation of materials across the globe (as seen in practices like the local reuse of animal manures on agricultural fields before the use of synthetic fertilizers). In recent decades, many forms of 'waste' have increasingly been seen as resources and opportunities rather than as problems. Considering 'waste as a resource' presents opportunities for hydrology (for example, wastewater and stormwater, Chapter 3); energy (such as waste heat and waste byproducts like coal slag used as an aggregate in concrete, Chapter 4); landfill (methane energy generation, Chapters 3 and 4); manures (for biofermentation, Chapter 5); and waste material use (reuse of demolition and salvaged building materials, see Potemkin, Ballast Point, and Brooklyn Bridge Park).

Composites

Over the past century, construction materials, much like food, have transitioned from natural to highly processed. Many contemporary materials are composites containing significant numbers of chemical additives and undergoing complex manufacturing processes. While these materials may be more durable with respect to their intended use, they can cause problems once that use expires. Selection, use and application of materials, their components, the ongoing management and life cycles are crucial considerations to avoid potentially toxic and dangerous manufacturing and construction processes and unhealthy finished outcomes. Some companies provide information and verification on the materials' ingredients' pollution, and toxicity content but this is not always available.

9.7
Potemkin – Post Industrial Meditation Park, Casagrande & Rintala, Kuramata village by the Kamagawa River, Echigo-Tsumari, Japan, 2003
This post industrial 'temple' encourages meditation on our connection with nature. As part of the 2003 Echigo-Tsumari Contemporary Art Triennial, the 14,000 square foot (1,300m^2) park is founded on an illegal garbage dump and exists as a cultivated junk yard between ancient rice fields, a river and Shinto temple. Recycled urban and industrial waste includes concrete, asphalt, glass and pottery, which are combined with local steel, river bed stones, white gravel and oak, while site grading reflects the idea of human artefacts returning to nature.

9.7

Recycled and salvaged materials

Demolition, construction and waste materials can be diverted from disposal for salvage and reuse, yet can also be toxic when reused. This may be exacerbated if recycled materials are crushed or machined, releasing toxic chemicals, adhesives and treatments used both in manufacture and during their lifecycle (such as lead paint, mineral stain treatments and formaldehydes). Recycled railway sleepers, for example, that have been treated with creosote and other preservatives are restricted for reuse in the European Community in certain areas (playgrounds, in human contact such as picnic tables and internal use) due to present toxins. Despite the potential risks of recycled materials, issues of virgin materials such as child labor and worker exploitation, embodied energy from long-distance transport, lack of relationship to place and toxicity of composites are factors that can strengthen the use of salvaged and waste materials. These issues also reinforce the case for using natural and non-toxic materials.

9.8
Brooklyn Bridge Park, Michael Van Valkenburgh Associates, Brooklyn, New York, USA, 2003–
Brooklyn's post-industrial waterfront retains and reinvents raw elements and existing structures as well as utilizing on-site and off-site recycled materials like marine timbers, stone and pavements, lighting fixtures and fill. Salvaging materials requires extensive work, including sourcing, stock-taking and measurement, design incorporation, and extra construction labor.

9.8

9.9a
9.9b
9.9c
9.9d
9.9e
9.9f

Recycled materials and salvaged structures at Ballast Point Park

The strong environmental philosophy of the design sought to not degrade other sites in the construction of the new park. Use of salvaged and recycled materials is a key strategy in seeking this philosophy and retention and adaptive reuse of existing structures assisted this approach. The diagram quantifies the project's environmental initiatives (such as 1,450 tons of recycled rubble used in gabion wall systems to retain the former oil storage tanks' excavations).

9.9a

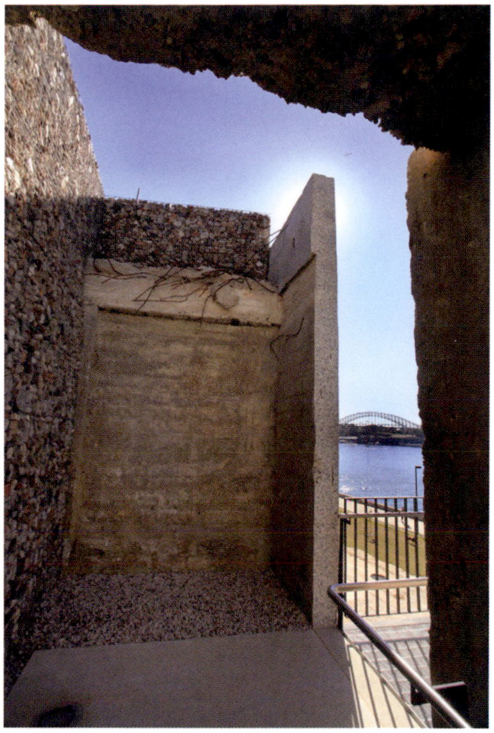

9.9b

Ballast Point Park Cradle to Cradle
Components
Environmental Outcome
40%
20%
20%
528t
100%
100%
100%
19,450m³
100%
9,333m
98%
95%
350t Co2
100%
100%
2,600m³
25%
100%
8kW

9.9c

9.9d

9.9e

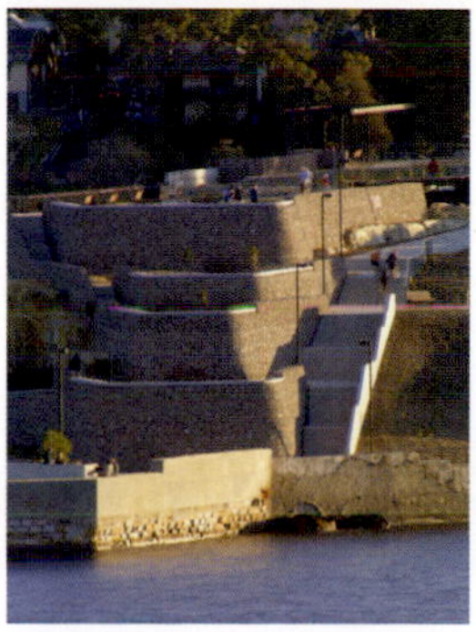

9.9f

According to some accounts, more than 90% of materials extracted to make durable goods in the United States becomes waste almost immediately.
WILLIAM MCDONOUGH & MICHAEL BRAUNGART, CRADLE TO CRADLE (2002)

9.10
Design for disassembly
At the initial design stage, the composition and arrangement of materials should consider the ability for future disassembly, relocation and reuse, for example, does metal need to be welded or can joints be bolted?

9.11
Cambio Verde (Green Change) Curitiba, Brazil
Curitiba's Cambio Verde (Green Change) program allowed citizens to exchange sorted recyclable materials in exchange for fresh food from local farms (Chapter 7). Mexico City's District Federal Government Environment Agency based their 2012 Mercado de Trueque (Barter Market) on Curitiba's program.

Challenges of waste materials

Landscape projects are more frequently using waste materials in well-executed, aesthetic compositions to reverse perceptions of waste as ugly or undesirable. Carefully composing discarded materials and expressing their character and qualities is gaining favor, and imported or virgin materials perceived as unnecessary, unethical or unsustainable. Specification and reuse of waste materials (and ad hoc waste products) can, however, be challenging. Many recycled and salvaged materials are not in standard sizes, lengths and volumes, inconsistent supplies require complex incorporation into detailed design and specification, or materials specified within construction documents may no longer be available. Recycled materials may be restricted or prohibited through building codes and standards. Data certifying strength and durability assurances are often unavailable, testing may be prohibitively expensive or engineers may not want to risk giving structural approval. Challenges are also presented through the digital mechanization of drawing production and CAD-based software that bias standardized and regular geometries.

9.10

IDEROL

9.11

9.12
Waternet Green Urine, Amsterdam, the Netherlands
Urine has the ideal NPK ratio (nitrogen/phosphorus/potassium) required for fertilizer. Water utility World Waternet's campaign 'Urinating for a Greener Amsterdam', placed public urinals on the Beursplein, then extracted phosphates for a hectare of city 'living roofs'. Amsterdam's public utility integrates water cycle management with its Waste to Energy Plant (Chapter 4) for increased efficiency, using water treatment waste products in the production of electricity, gas and heat.

Upcycling, downcycling and zero waste

Many contemporary construction materials and products are 'monstrous hybrids', a term coined by Michael Braungart and William McDonough for products, components and materials that cannot be easily separated, thereby rendering them unsuitable for recycling and reuse. This is related to the concept of 'designing for disassembly' and creating products that can be reused in their original state (upcycling).

Upcycling is a production aspiration whereby reuse of discarded objects or materials can create products of higher quality or value than the original.

Downcycling essentially involves converting materials and products into materials of lesser quality (a common example is that of hardscape materials (bricks, concrete etc) being crushed and reused as aggregates).

The concept of 'zero waste' (Chapter 4) reflects the ideal that everything can be useful. When applied to landscape architecture, it is important to think about the life cycle of materials beyond their intended use. Can they be readily reused, disassembled and transported or do they require intensive processes like cutting or crushing? While some sustainability advocates have called for increased producer responsibility at the point of production, most current manufacturing and political systems do not require cradle to cradle and life-cycle accountability. Producer and user responsibility also applies at the landscape scale, such as a company being responsible for cleaning a site that they have polluted. Mandating and incentivizing industry obligation would greatly assist the reduction of negative environmental and social outcomes.

GREEN URINE

9.12

"A society grows great when old men plant trees whose shade they know they shall never sit in."
GREEK PROVERB

POST-COMPLETION REVIEW

Planning and design can often only anticipate a project's actual outcomes, when there is routinely little involvement from the design team following construction. This has implications for not only the design integrity but for continuing environmental performance. Ongoing maintenance commonly alters original design intent without consultation with the lead designer. Post-completion review involves reflecting, researching and documenting outcomes (and possibly beyond maintenance periods, typically ranging from six months to two and sometimes five years). The most valuable project lessons often become evident through ongoing involvement, though this is not always possible. The WELL Building Standard®, for example, emphasizes actual rather than projected outcomes by focusing on habitation and health during occupancy, indicating increased emphasis on actual rather than projected outcomes. Landscapes take considerable time to form, mature, and develop through slow growth of trees and (re)establishment of vegetation and ecosystems. Complex large-scale projects can take decades to complete various stages and construction (see Fresh Kills, Chapter 3) and a realized design vision may take generations to establish.

Candid self-appraisal

Analysis of failures demands more professional attention if environmental and social sustainability are to be seriously addressed. Honest, candid review of completed and established projects and/or access to failed works by researchers is currently uncommon (the Landscape Performance Series is a notable exception). This is perhaps indicative of a range of factors, including a general deficiency in advocating fees for ongoing management (Chapter 8) and a need to acknowledge and share constructive discourse and learn from mistakes.

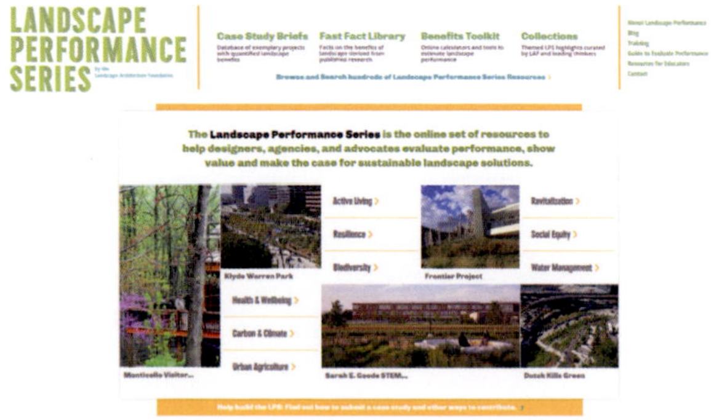
LANDSCAPE PERFORMANCE SERIES
Case Study Briefs
Fast Fact Library
Benefits Toolkit
Collections
The Landscape Performance Series is the online set of resources to help designers, agencies, and advocates evaluate performance, show value and make the case for sustainable landscape solutions.
Active Living
Resilience
Biodiversity
Revitalization
Social Equity
Water Management
Klyde Warren Park
Frontier Project
Health & Wellbeing
Carbon & Climate
Urban Agriculture
Monticello Visitor...
Sarah E. Goode STEM...
Dutch Kills Green

9.13

9.13
Landscape Architecture Foundation: Landscape Performance Series, 2010–
The Landscape Performance Series measures actual project outcomes and shares this information and other sustainability resources on their online portal (LandscapePerformance.org). This includes innovative research from industry and academia and over 100 case studies, 120 'fast facts', and various 'benefits toolkit' calculators. A range of precedents demonstrates the value of sustainable landscape solutions, metrics and methods quantify environmental, social, and economic outcomes, and teaching materials help integrate landscape performance into design curricula.

STUDY/DISCUSSION QUESTIONS

Should landscape architecture projects be measured and rated? Why or why not? In what situations?

What are the pros and cons of 'checkbox' sustainability?

Do artistic arguments hold less influence than scientific in landscape architecture?

Are the scientific and the artistic opposites? Why? Give examples.

What are typical life cycles of public domain projects? Is this determined by durability or by trends? Give examples and discuss.

Should materials selection prioritize factors such as local supply and 'sense of place' over technical considerations? Why/why not?

Are there any examples of upcycling in landscape?

Do you have a favorite reuse or execution of salvaged/waste/recycled materials in a landscape/urban project?

FURTHER READING

Addis, W. (2007) *Building with reclaimed components and materials: A design handbook for reuse and recycling*, London: Earthscan.

Calkins, M. (2009) *Materials for sustainable sites: a complete guide to the evaluation, selection, and use of sustainable construction materials*, Hoboken, NJ: Wiley.

Calkins, M. (2011) *The sustainable sites handbook*, Hoboken, NJ: Wiley.

Klanten, R. (2008) *Data flow: visualising information in graphic design*, Berlin: Gestalten.

McDonough, W. and Braungart, M. (2002) *Cradle to Cradle*, NY: North Point Press.

Thompson, W. and Sorvig, K. (2008) *Sustainable Landscape Construction*, Washington: Island Press.

Tufte, E. (1992) *The visual display of quantitative information*, Cheshire (Connecticut): Graphics Press.

Ware, C., Culbertson, K., Squadrito, P. and Urban, J. (2016) *Landscape architecture documentation standards: principles, guidelines, and best practices*, New Jersey: John Wiley & Sons.

Windhager S., Simmons M., Steiner F. and Heymann D. (2010) 'Toward ecosystem services as a basis for design', *Landscape Journal* (29): 107–123.

Zimmermann, A. (2009) *Constructing landscape: materials, techniques, structural components*, Basel: Birkhäuser.

ADDITIONAL PROJECTS

You might also like to look for further information on the following projects:

Hunts Point Landing, Bronx, New York, USA

Washington Canal Park, Washington DC, USA

George 'Doc' Cavalliere Park, Scottsdale, Arizona, USA

Burbank Water and Power – Ecocampus, Burbank, California, USA

The Woodland Discovery Playground at Shelby Farms, Memphis, Tennessee, USA

Grand Valley State University (GVSU) Student Recreation Fields, Allendale, Michigan, USA

Tonsley, Oxigen, Adelaide, Australia

INTERVIEW Steve Windhager

Dr Steve Windhager was the first Director of the Sustainable Sites Initiative (SITES). Dr Windhager holds two degrees in Philosophy and a PhD in Environmental Science focusing on restoration ecology. He has worked on multiple design, landscape and engineering projects to rebuild damaged ecosystems. As Executive Director of the Santa Barbara Botanic Garden, Dr Windhager continues to extend his theoretical and technical expertise to solving problems in the designed landscape through native plants.

What is the central purpose of landscape measurement tools and what are their key benefits?

At their base, the intention behind measurement tools is a recognition that we can go well beyond reducing resource use in the built environment. We have to move to a design process where we use the built environment to reinforce or regenerate the landscape's capacity to provide ecosystem services such as clean air and water, pollination services, wildlife habitat, carbon sequestration, heat island mitigation, and so forth. Landscapes can provide all these services if they are intentionally designed to do so. Unfortunately, when not explicit, these goals are forgotten or ignored, particularly when they increase construction or design costs. By participating in a rating system like LEED or SITES, the design team and client are forced to surpass current regulatory minimum standards and move toward actual performance standards in the landscape.

Is landscape able to be quantified or are there important qualities that cannot be measured?

Most ecosystem services can be quantified in the landscape but require a significant financial commitment in monitoring and documentation that can generally only occur after construction and operation for some period of time. Unlike a building, which will typically function most efficiently when it is initially completed, living systems take time to mature before they can perform at their peak capacity. Because of this lag time, the cost of monitoring, and the desire to be certified when the project 'opens', the technical committees on SITES have developed ways to qualify for credit based on calculations that can be undertaken during the design process. We hope that these surrogates will provide a lower-cost indication of landscape performance, but we will only know for sure after we assess a range of completed projects to confirm their actual performance. I am sure that there will be further modification to the SITES program, as there has been to LEED over time, which will enhance its effectiveness.

What are some of the primary challenges faced when measuring a living medium compared to say, a building?

Machines and buildings typically function most efficiently with highest performance levels shortly after construction. This is the opposite of living systems, which require a period of maturation before they operate at peak performance levels. This means that measuring initial performance may not be indicative of future performance—which we would hope would improve, but if not well designed, could actually deteriorate further if the designed system fails to thrive.

To what extent are these quantification tools geared towards:

- **providing a means of justification for decision makers to produce 'hard evidence' to support their agendas;**
- **preventing landscape architecture from exclusion from a built environment culture increasingly oriented towards measurement and justification;**
- **reducing or eliminating greenwash?**

Rating systems are indeed intended to address all three of these issues, though none are the primary goals for the SITES program (at least in my opinion). We do want to be able to demonstrate the landscape's potential to provide goods and services that provide value for our communities in ways that include, but go beyond, beauty. The current SITES rating system will produce a limited amount of hard evidence to support the potential of the landscape, but it will be future research on these and other landscapes that provide the actual data that I believe that decision makers will need to support an agenda which incentivizes ecosystem services into our design goals. These standards are a first step to the measurement of building performance, but alone, they do not provide for a full assessment of landscape performance. They are, however, the best system we have to date, and a large step in the correct direction. I believe that they will help to reduce unintentional greenwashing. There are many practices that are common in the design of the built environment that seem like they should provide environmental value, but in the end require more resources than they produce. Green roofs are a great example of this. In many locations around the world green roofs can be a valuable addition to a design project, providing storm-water mitigation, wildlife habitat, heat island reduction and access to green space in urban centers. But in other locations or in cases of poor design, green roofs can require significant potable water inputs, necessitate high levels of maintenance resources (both in terms of labor and amendments), and actually degrade storm-water quality. But the public cannot tell the difference between these types of green roofs, and therefore might even consider poorly designed green roofs a sustainable element on any building. By looking at the resources required to maintain these systems, measurement tools will be a check against installing sustainable practices in unsustainable ways.

Do measurement tools pose any risk to reducing design (over time) to an overly pragmatic, predetermined process rather than an imaginative, creative one?

There is no risk of this at all. Great art is about overcoming limitations and obstacles and seeing things differently. Great landscape design will always be able to provide for specific project needs (client desires, the protection of the health, safety and welfare, and provisioning of ecosystem services) in innovative and creative ways. That said, there are many building and landscapes, whether certified by a rating system or not, which are examples of unimaginative design. That is the fault and limitation of the designer, not the rating system.

Why did landscape tools take longer to develop than architectural tools?

Architectural rating systems, such as LEED, started earlier, as building performance in terms of energy use was much easier to quantify and gains in resource conservation were more obvious. SITES actually used the LEED model in the development of the landscape tool, and took a similar amount of time to create the tool that is currently available for open enrolment.

Is it feasible to retrospectively incorporate measurements after project completion (such as gallons of water filtered/stored/reused and pounds of produce grown), or do rating tools only apply to new developments?

Like LEED, whose initial tool only applied to new construction, quantification tools are really most appropriately applied to the design and installation of a new landscape. I anticipate that future versions of SITES will be developed for optimizing landscape performance in existing landscapes (similar to the LEED tool 'Existing Buildings, Operations and Management') but that tool has not yet been developed.

Why have materials, much like food, become so highly processed? Why don't we use natural, 'healthy' and 'pure' materials?

This is difficult to answer briefly but landscapes in particular rely on natural materials. We are increasingly seeing the use of engineered materials in urban projects to meet project design needs in extraordinary conditions (such as root, water and air penetration under sidewalks while meeting a specific design load). These are not natural conditions and developing an engineered media can provide replicable results. In some cases, these designed media are composed of all 'natural' materials, but put together in a recipe that has been studied and provides consistent performance. In other cases these can be a mixture of synthetic and 'natural' materials, but the goal is the same.

Can landscape projects' capacity as generators/providers of ecosystem services and productivity be incorporated into rating tools (more than merely conserving and reducing)?

Absolutely. Increasingly we are finding ways to assess the production of ecosystem services at a more reasonable cost. As we sharpen our ability to monitor or understand the surrogate measures which are correlated to landscape performance in the production of ecosystem services, these will be incorporated. But as with LEED, which has progressively become a greater challenge to achieve and attain through its various versions, we did not want to make the initial version of SITES so difficult to participate in that we could not engage the market in thinking about the potential of the landscape to help achieve their sustainability goals. As rating tools become an accepted part of the design process, I expect we will see the requirements to achieve certification increase as well.

10.1
Urban Utopia: The woven city
Luc Schuiten's conceptual 'archiborescence' biomimetic architecture city features a vegetal mesh of strangler fig roots. The stable and resistant fig dwellings' outer walls are made from semi-transparent biotextiles comparable to silkworm cocoons or spider webs, capturing solar power to supply the energy required for heating and electricity. Footbridges overhang the uncultivated plain, allowing natural processes to continue. Organic waste decomposition nourishes and irrigates host trees.

10
SCENARIOS, CHALLENGES AND REFRAMING LAND(SCAPE)

This final chapter poses questions and future key disciplinary sustainability foci centered on generative, productive landscape architecture and stewardship. When implemented through the multidimensional, ingenuitive approaches demonstrated by the previously featured projects, the relatively young discipline of landscape architecture can provide well-considered, sustainable solutions to social and environmental challenges.

"We must not see the Anthropocene as a crisis, but as the beginning of a new geological epoch ripe with human-directed opportunity."
ERLE ELLIS, THE PLANET OF NO RETURN (2012)

"It is not just the 'environment' that needs to be fixed, but humans ourselves—the environmental crisis is the product of gross human ecological dysfunction (or if you prefer, of humanities spectacular evolutionary success)."
WILLIAM REES, NATURE (27 FEBRUARY 2003)

"Environmental problems may seem overwhelming and insurmountable. But landscape architects offer solutions to improve our roofs, our blocks, our neighborhoods, a nearby waterway, or the city at large. If that sounds patronizing, it's not meant to be. In the absence of aggressive federal (let alone global) environmental action to address the myriad of challenges we face, these interventions take on a critical, if piecemeal, significance."
ALAN G. BRAKE, LANDSCAPE ARCHITECTURE'S ASCENDANCE (2012)

NEW APPROACHES

(Land)scape lost or territory (re)gained?

Mass urbanization has led to an over-emphasis of cities' significance as the central place for landscape practice, if we are merely 'playing the fiddle as Rome burns'. While the city might be where most of us reside, it should not occupy our central focus. The city is part of a far greater organism, fed by a network of expansive territories sustained through intensive, unsustainable resource consumption. The traditional urban/rural binary ignores current vast urban footprints and consumptive patterns shaping rural practices, rendering visually oriented 20th-century concerns outdated. In the Anthropocene (the age of survival), the peri-urban and rural context must be recalibrated through the strategic, the spatial and the social, not merely in order for cities to thrive, but for the greater landscapes that sustains the city to survive.

Keep perspective

Unless they can be radically up-scaled, exponentially replicated and rapidly deployed, small urban landscapes possess less potential to meaningfully contribute increased sustainability modes than significant land areas. This is not to say that we should neglect them. It is more so a call, as a small professional discipline, to keep perspective, focusing on the challenges in most need of attention and optimization (Chapter 7—Interview). Do small areas of private, inaccessible and disconnected green roofs and walls deserve so much focus when peri-urban and rural open spaces lie fallow, degraded, eroded and saline, needing radical recovery strategies? How can we adaptively reuse and retrofit our cities to reclaim streets from the incessant traffic onslaught for safe pedestrian and cycle passage; utilize green spaces to grow more food; produce renewable energy; collect, filter and reuse water; and mobilize and empower local communities?

"We must be the change we want to see in the world."
MAHATMA GANDHI (1869–1948)

"We are drowning in information, while starving for wisdom. The world henceforth will be run by synthesizers, people able to put together the right information at the right time, think critically about it, and make important choices wisely."
E. O. WILSON, CONSILIENCE: THE UNITY OF KNOWLEDGE (1998)

10.2
Salisbury Wetlands: City of Salisbury

10.2

10.3
Dutch Kills Green: WRT, Margie Ruddick Landscape, Marpillero Pollak Architects, Michael Singer Studio

10.3

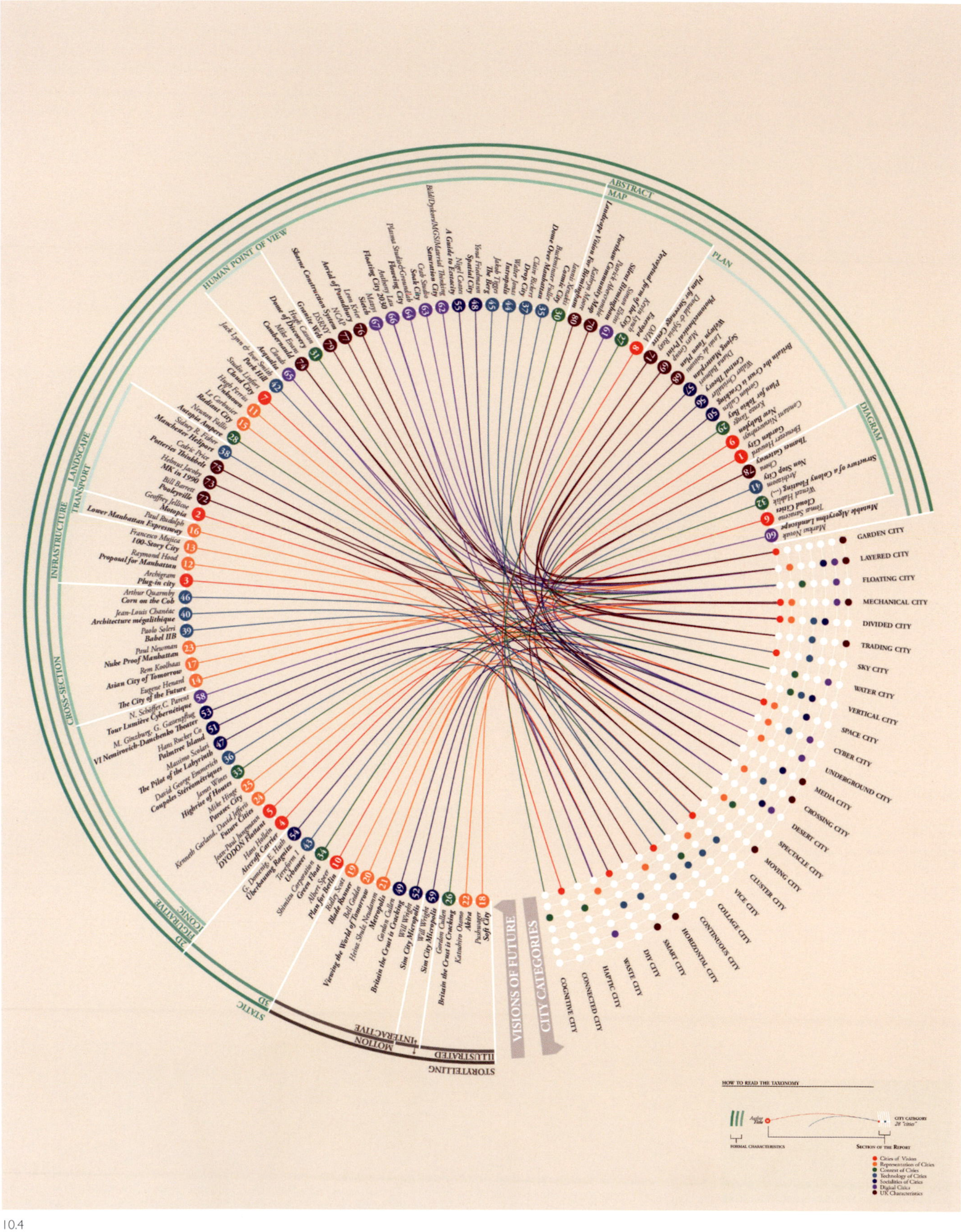
ABSTRACT
MAP
PLAN
DIAGRAM
HUMAN POINT OF VIEW
LANDSCAPE
TRANSPORT
INFRASTRUCTURE
CROSS-SECTION
ICONIC
FIGURATIVE
2D
3D
STATIC
MOTION
INTERACTIVE
ILLUSTRATED
STORYTELLING
VISIONS OF FUTURE
CITY CATEGORIES
GARDEN CITY
LAYERED CITY
FLOATING CITY
MECHANICAL CITY
DIVIDED CITY
TRADING CITY
SKY CITY
WATER CITY
VERTICAL CITY
SPACE CITY
CYBER CITY
UNDERGROUND CITY
MEDIA CITY
CROSSING CITY
DESERT CITY
SPECTACLE CITY
MOVING CITY
CLUSTER CITY
VICE CITY
COLLAGE CITY
CONTINUOUS CITY
HORIZONTAL CITY
SMART CITY
DIY CITY
WASTE CITY
HAPTIC CITY
CONNECTED CITY
COGNITIVE CITY
HOW TO READ THE TAXONOMY
Author Title
CITY CATEGORY 28 "cities"
FORMAL CHARACTERISTICS
SECTION OF THE REPORT
Cities of Vision
Representation of Cities
Context of Cities
Technology of Cities
Socialities of Cities
Digital Cities
UK Characteristics

10.4

10.4
Taxonomy for visualisation of future cities, Prof. Nick Dunn, Dr Paul Cureton & Serena Pollastri, 2014
'A Visual History of the Future' collects, analyses and displays over 90 images from a wide range of designers and artists to imagine the future. The concluding taxonometric infographic communicates the complexity of their relationships through identifying thematic patterns and modes of representation (landscape; infrastructure; transport; storytelling; static; abstract).

"City form, in other words, is not some autonomous organic growth, nor is it dictated by ineluctable economic laws. It is in fact an artefact—an artefact of a curious kind, compounded of willed and random events, imperfectly controlled. If it is related to physiology at all, it is more like a dream than anything else."
JOSEPH RYKWERT, SEDUCTION OF PLACE (2000)

"No one is interested in changing our current behavior."
JAMES KUNSTLER, WHERE WE'RE AT (2008)

"Where all think alike, no one thinks very much."
WALTER LIPPMANN, STAKES OF DIPLOMACY (1915)

"When written in Chinese, the word crisis is composed of two characters – one represents danger, and the other represents opportunity."
TED NORDHAUS AND MICHAEL SHELLENBERGER, THE DEATH OF ENVIRONMENTALISM (2004)

Think big

With minor exceptions, we have shown unwillingness to relinquish our resource-intensive lifestyles required for 'one planet living'. Overpopulation is the elephant in the room carving a vast destructive chasm in the landscape. Strategies and incentives to tackle overpopulation are needed on a global scale. How can we decouple from capitalist economic growth but still live worthwhile and dignifying lives based on useful and productive activities? How can society become more equitable? These are big questions that can only be addressed with big-picture thinking.

10.5
Future Scenarios
Permaculture co-originator David Holmgren presents four possible future scenarios for peak oil and climate change challenges ('Techno Fantasy, Green-Tech Stability, Earth Stewardship and Collapse') (2009). Holmgren predicts a 'collapse' or 'atlantis' scenario if 'business as usual' continues unabated.

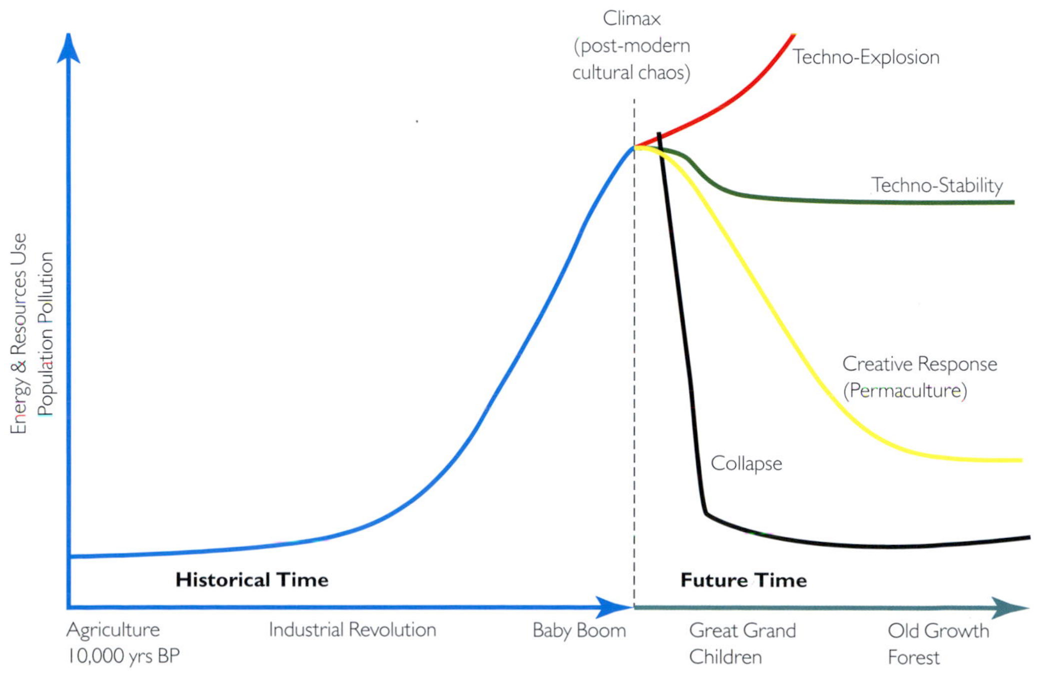

Climax (post-modern cultural chaos)
Techno-Explosion
Techno-Stability
Creative Response (Permaculture)
Collapse
Energy & Resources Use
Population Pollution
Historical Time
Future Time
Agriculture 10,000 yrs BP
Industrial Revolution
Baby Boom
Great Grand Children
Old Growth Forest

10.5

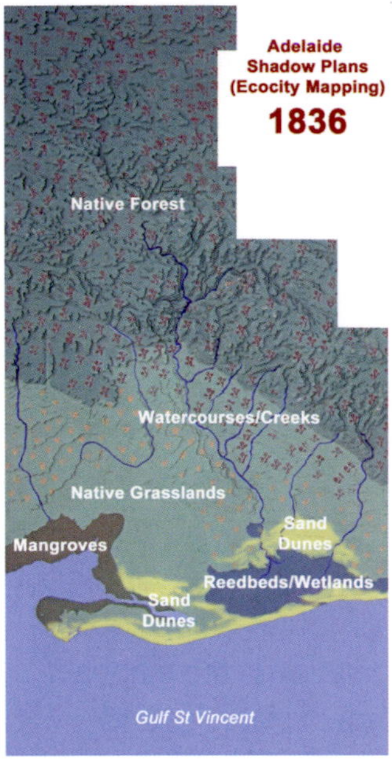
Adelaide
Shadow Plans
(Ecocity Mapping)
1836
Native Forest
Watercourses/Creeks
Native Grasslands
Mangroves
Sand
Dunes
Reedbeds/Wetlands
Sand
Dunes
Gulf St Vincent

10.6a

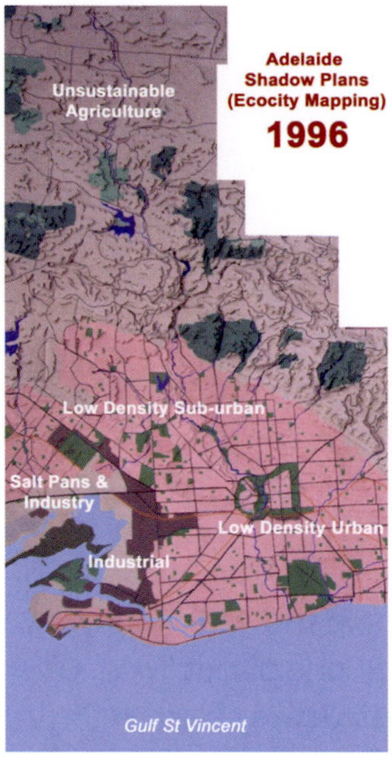
Adelaide
Shadow Plans
(Ecocity Mapping)
1996
Unsustainable
Agriculture
Low Density Sub-urban
Salt Pans &
Industry
Industrial
Low Density Urban
Gulf St Vincent

10.6b

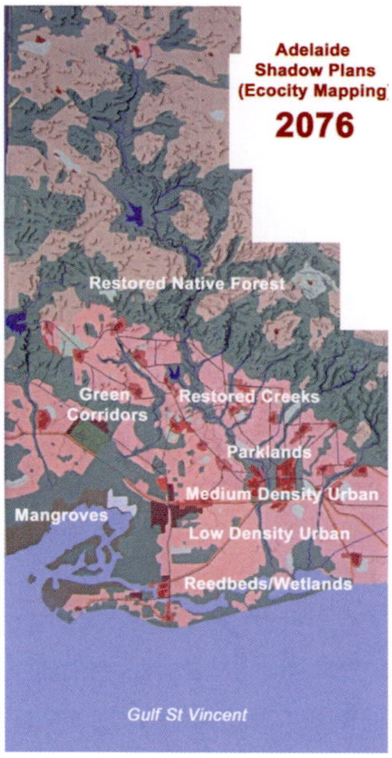
Adelaide
Shadow Plans
(Ecocity Mapping)
2076
Restored Native Forest
Green
Corridors
Restored Creeks
Parklands
Medium Density Urban
Mangroves
Low Density Urban
Reedbeds/Wetlands
Gulf St Vincent

10.6c

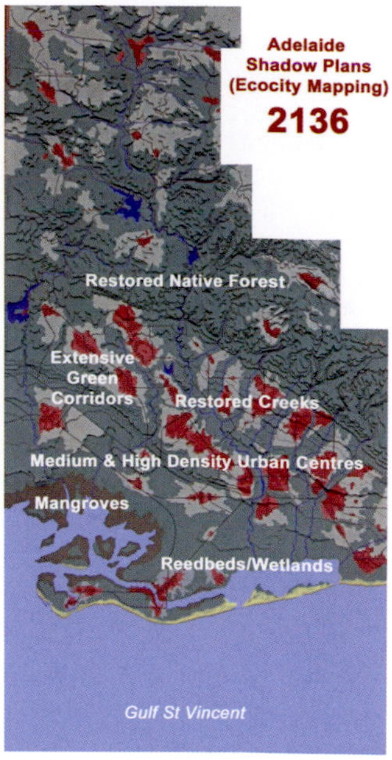
Adelaide
Shadow Plans
(Ecocity Mapping)
2136
Restored Native Forest
Extensive
Green
Corridors
Restored Creeks
Medium & High Density Urban Centres
Mangroves
Reedbeds/Wetlands
Gulf St Vincent

10.6d

Transition Network.org

10.7a

10.7b

Transition Network.org
About Transition Network | Contact us
About
Training
News
Resources
Community
Support
Home » Transition Initiatives Map
Transition Initiatives Map
If you cannot see your initiative on this map it is because we do not have accurate location data for you. Initiatives can add their own simply. Please let your core team know and contact us.
Map
Satellite
ASIA
AFRICA
ASIA
AFRICA
SOUTH AMER
Atlantic Ocean
Pacific Ocean
Indian Ocean
Indian Ocean
Google
Terms of Use
Report a map error
Key
Official initiative
Mulling initiative

10.7c

10.7a
10.7b
10.7c
Transition Towns and Transition Network

Rob Hopkins began the Transition Towns movement in 2005 in Kinsale, Ireland, to "support community-led responses to peak oil and climate change, building resilience and happiness". The subsequently formed charity 'Transition Network' aims to inspire, encourage, connect, support and train communities, and like permaculture, focus on self-organized adaptation to peak oil and climate change. Now spread worldwide, the Network's '21 stories for COP21' produced for the 2015 Paris climate change talks feature inspiring outcomes and community-led actions.

10.6a
10.6b
10.6c
10.6d
Shadow Plans
Dr Paul Downton @ University of South Australia, Adelaide, Australia, 1996

The 'City as an Organism' university studio utilized Richard Register's shadow planning process (US founder of Urban Ecology, 1975), challenging students to re-envision the City of Adelaide's future within its Tandanya bioregion. Like countless cities (but in a shorter timescale than most), Adelaide has cleared indigenous vegetation; levelled sand dunes; drained wetlands; concreted and undergrounded hydrological systems; and covered agricultural lands with low-density housing. The plans show the city at European settlement in 1836, then 150 years later in 1986 (with red tones representing hard surfaces of buildings and roads) and finally in 2136 as a vision of how the city could remodel itself. The future plan proposes increased density satellite settlements linked by sustainable public transport systems. Rivers, creeks and the marine environment are restored and adapted to sea level rise, land re-vegetated and rehabilitated, native animal and bird populations recovered, and food grown closer to the city. Unfortunately, such macro-timescale planning exercises are rarely done—even within academia, yet alone by governments and planning authorities.

10.8a
10.8b
Biocity Studio: University Studios, McGregor Coxall (R&D arm)
The Biocity Studio's four university courses from 2007–2010 required researching a city region's 'system' in a present or future peak oil and climate change crisis scenario, developing interconnected, holistic solutions. City systems encompassed biodiversity; built form; culture/education; economy; pollution/chemicals; energy; food; governance; human health; transport; and waste and water. Students' lateral solutions to complex issues developed in a short time frame were favorably met by jurors, who included notable politicians; scientists; developers; planners; landscape architects; and engineers.

The Sydney Morning Herald

Tuesday November 15, 2005 First published 1831 No. 52,469 $1.20 (inc GST)

FOOD WAR ESCALATES IN EUROPE

2035: The Sartor Famine

Level 1 food rations in place

Economic depression not seen since 1929 depression and the 1980s stockmarket crash

It all started when Frank Sartor's 2005 Metro Strategy for Sydney failed to recognise or secure the food source for city's own population. Over the next 10 years, Sydney's vegetable crisper was swallowed up to make way for 1.2 million new residents in the north-west and south west sectors.

While this growth was happening, the government, in their infinite wisdom, forgot to secure agricultural land to feed the exploded population. Meanwhile, New South Wales' agriculturally unproductive centre, where it is four times less efficient as its Sydney Basin counterpart, was given the responsibility of trying to produce enough food for the city.

As droughts hit with accelerating severity and frequency, food prices soared, exacerbated by rapidly diminishing oil supplies. The economy suffered, as our major exports of beef and wheat were culled to preserve our own oil reserves. Ax the farmer's producing our food gradually went belly-up under economic pressure, Sydney found itself in the grips of a debilitating food crises.

The Government has stepped, by instating food rations to stabilise food prices, but once again, their short sightedness has resulted in a band-aid solution that does not solve the scarcity of food for Sydneysiders.

Sent ad te doluptat nulluptat amcor sisl ut nonsequis at. Nit utat. Tet, qui ea commolendre magnim iriusti ncilisci tisit, conse digna feuisl ullandre diat, quis eugait ut lobor aci bla conullummy nullan hent nim il er sed deliquis nim vent utet lore et loreet iure tat vent la augait volum ipit, conum in vel in heniat verit delit aute molor sum nullummy nis nim do odiam nonsequat. Oluptatie magna feuipis do del utate dunt lore dolor susto con etummy nibh ex ex eugiatis deliquate vel ut iurem vulla feum quat. Ut alisim at augner am inim alit ullummy nosto enisi ex et ipsum zzrit loreetum iurem veliquis alismolore doluptat irit aut dolore del do odiat lobortio odiam iriliquis nit dolorerat. Ut nulla feugue etum vel utpat irilis essit velesent iure tate magna facil incillute velisim alit aut utpat dolor iliquis cidunt wisnodDo, quon sum si ingul vilicer ratusa demur. Internum peciptis ca; etiu si sil cles es re est quidicae faciondaci strum aperce nirtesilica nocumus consul habeffreo ublincusa nulatifecrum praris venam oecid idica; in de defenam tabusat quodicies num. Dem publis simus; etiampe ropubli in Itamuncerfir labulii sessolum tem noste hora? Natusci enimantra et paris; nostrae furo in sena verei ia? Simant.

Bonfiris. Valer ant andi sensu quod con sum publica perfecest pra? Pala reditis? Na, pris coriam furorus adductum conon sid sis andem, nonvert eritia aperi issupio, dii pri simum id mandius, qua L. At publiam res condicaed ini fachum P. Et pulost es cam hachuiu intem tilin Itam in vagil tastrum et; nimover ibustem at.

Catiem dictus egilinihin abenam patioris crenimenam inclut nihil verum atqua consunt, sus? Tum dienate, sedena, quam poendi publin venihi, porbis hocta publin Itat, vertimu ntilicae a octor quam, consus. Nam oc, prorum is An dum nequam acionem ad reciver ibemus; est videsi ineque nocchilin dumus, non virmandius ad Caturo tam aure iam etres perbem. Graret, ignonsil viderfitem linguloccio ac moludam ora conculos confent erissenari publium cont. Ifentrae nox senatum host dem pertem or hos ortam ala inte fac terum, sena, omnim escis. Idii in horae aucid nis, Casdam, Caturni cioraela omnorum hoc, cludees ina, tudetorben publiss essenterem egitastrit; hos hostrum, cierficut creviri prius et ancienam, dit, duamaniquod Casdam.

Orebatora? P. Istiam vidium fuit L. Dectod inatuus, qui issente, caestrorum commit iam te desseret vidi publicomnit

10.8a

one
:cease the release of agricultural land for development
10.8b

Flux

Landscape, environmental planning and design usually involve long timeframes (several years or even decades) to attempt to realize design visions and strategies. This can be at odds with short-term political cycles and the instability of our hyper-accelerated world. Landscape architects forecast and anticipate future scenarios: political, economic, social, and environmental. Project sequencing and phasing should be accordingly arranged. Fixed designs and static masterplans are becoming increasingly outdated modes of output. Climate change and associated impacts of sea level rise, plant selection and threats to sedentary settlements and infrastructures increase the complexity of design processes, highlighting the need for both collaboration with scientists and requirements for ongoing adaptive management and maintenance. Projects need to be multidimensional and address a range of issues from a range of perspectives, exploratory beyond political agendas and commercial restrictions, collaboratively multidisciplinary to eliminate siloed-thinking, and yet tangible and rapidly implementable.

10.9

Houston Arboretum and Nature Center, Reed Hilderbrand

This evolutionary implementation strategy includes ongoing adaptation to climate change, nutrient recycling, volunteer site restoration, long-term management,and community education.

Implementing and Managing Resilient Ecologies
REMOVE
Clearing dead trees + debris
Hazard evaluation
RE-PURPOSE
Forestry mulching + chipping
Biomass recycling
Erosion control
PROPOGATE
On-site nurseries
Local genetic strains
Volunteer collaboration
INSTALL
Volunteer collaboration
Education opportunity
ESTABLISH
Temporary irrigation
Fertilization
MANAGE
Thinning + pruning
Invasive species removal
Controlled burns
EVALUATE
Species diversity
Ecosystem health
Woodland to Savannah
Woodland Restoration
Ravine Restoration

10.9

Why design?

Landscape architecture's big picture perspective, combined with a democratic and inclusive design process, synthesizes science with art and the technical with the intangible. Design thinking and the design process encourages unconventional, creative, and lateral problem solving that can bypass restrictions and methodically formulate effective processes, solutions and outcomes. Strategies and interventions are thus rooted in place (Chapters 2 and 8), enhancing culture and social sustainability (Chapters 6, 7) and sustained through optimization and management of environmental systems (Chapters 3, 4, 5, 8 and 9).

Earth as a landscape

Due to the interconnected, interdependent and interaction between natural and cultural environments worldwide, the Earth itself can be viewed as a landscape requiring our ongoing care and management. This necessity of stewardship transcends borders, beliefs and backgrounds. The key concepts pervading landscape discourse continue to be somewhat artificially separated into categories such as 'natural landscapes' (frequented by the disciplines of ecology and environmentalism) and 'cultural landscapes' (the realm of history, archaeology, and social science).

10.10

Shenyang Architectural University Campus: Turenscape

10.11

Orongo Station Conservation Masterplan: Nelson Bird Woltz

"Any intelligent fool can make things bigger, more complex, and more violent. It takes a touch of genius—and a lot of courage to move in the opposite direction."
E. F. SCHUMACHER, THE RADICAL HUMANIST (1973)

"We are the children of our landscape; it dictates behavior and even thought in the measure to which we are responsive to it."
LAWRENCE DURRELL, JUSTINE (1957)

"The most important issue of the 21st century will be the condition of the global environment."
IAN MCHARG (1920–2001)

"The biggest challenge we face is shifting human consciousness, not saving the planet. The planet doesn't need saving, we do."
XIUHTEZCATL ROSKE-MARTINEZ (2015)

10.10

10.11

10.12

10.12
Minghu Wetland Park: Turenscape

Evolution from 'scape'

Is landscape architecture outgrowing its name (or rediscovering its past) as it evolves further beyond predominantly visual design concerns? '*Landscaping*' art and trends are well served by a highly skillful garden design industry (especially so in the UK, where garden design is significantly established and practiced). *Land planning* and *land architecture*, on the other hand, transcend decorative surface treatments to address deeper issues and pressing contemporary concerns. Such practice, focused on survival, is embedded in a productive land ethic geared to achieving structural influence on systems and processes—whether environmental, social, political or more likely, a combination. Can this be the evolution of the Olmstedian and McHargian traditions that have provided a backbone of substance, purpose and inspiration for the profession?

LA?

Land Architecture is uniquely positioned as restorer of living systems; harnesser of land's productive capacity; healer of degraded sites; and role model of ethical stewardship governed by a flexible, creative and rigorous design process free from a myopic obsession for creating object, artefact or monument. Generative without being destructive, land architecture can play a vital role in optimizing humanity's ongoing positive relationship and dependence on the Earth.

What system?

Can (and indeed, should) design play a role in reconfiguring increasingly bureaucratic, market-driven, risk-adverse, change-skeptical government and institutional systems? What can replace our current political economy and how will it operate? Do we need a complete redesign of a defunct system, or can and should the current model be salvaged or tweaked? What incarnations can

"... it has been argued ... that landscape tends to be repressed by architects and planners, or appropriated only to the extent that it frames and enhances the primacy of urban form. Landscape is employed here as a bourgeois aesthetic, or naturalized veil."
JAMES CORNER, TERRA FLUXUS (2006)

"To build a sustainable society for our children and future generations—the great challenge of our time—we need to fundamentally redesign many of our technologies and social institutions so as to bridge the wide gap between human design and the ecologically sustainable systems of nature."
FRITJOF CAPRA, THE HIDDEN CONNECTIONS (2002)

"A political economy approach provides the sort of understanding of power and structure that is absent in much of the conventional theorizing about transitions and green transformations ... A more explicitly political and historical analysis allows us to move beyond glib statements about 'green growth' and 'win-win solutions' to reveal the conflicts, trade-offs and compromises that are implied by a fundamental restructuring of the economy and the relations of power which will determine which pathway is chosen. The 'incumbent' regime of existing actors and interests that benefit from ongoing reliance on a fossil fuel economy ... will not give up their position easily."
PETER NEWELL, GREEN TRANSFORMATIONS IN CAPITALISM (2015)

social survival take (Chapter 7)? Just as the world needs to de-couple economic growth from environmental degradation, can design de-couple from destructive development?

Key thoughts for design

If the built environment professions are to mature, it is crucial to expand their reach and impact. As designers, we must ask how design can:

- bypass or negotiate the neoliberal, continual economic growth model that places financial growth for the few above the environment's capacity to sustain the entire human population;
- reformulate, retool and situate design to overcome reliance on clients solely concerned with economic development;
- convince potential and new clients of the multiple benefits design can generate to justify commissions;
- secure commissions and funding from ethical organizations;
- self-generate economic returns and sustainable livelihoods through and in landscape for the public good;
- act in the public interest but avoid risk adverse, business-as-usual approaches;
- contribute to building ethically oriented societies based less on the individual and more on collective good, practicing accountability and transparency.

10.13
Baugruppen

10.13

10.14
Evergreen Brick Works: Claude Cormier + associés

10.15
Duisburg-Nord Landscape Park: Latz & Partner

10.16a (Before)
10.16b
Restauració del Paratge de Tudela-Culip (Club Med Restoration): EMF Estudi Martí Franch

This book does not intend to conclude by summarizing the impressive, innovative work and ideas by the designers featured herein. While landscape architecture's achievements warrant celebration (and it is essential to do so both for our own inspiration and guidance but also for the profession's wider recognition and impact) we as a discipline must keep the horizon in view and use such work to stimulate, illuminate, and edge further forward—continually expanding and improving current best practice. Far from resting on our laurels, the relatively boutique, often misunderstood profession deserves to rapidly expand its realm of influence, exponentially increase its generation of outcomes and broadcast its benefits from the rooftops.

10.14

"Of all the paths you take in life, make sure a few of them are dirt."
UNKNOWN

"Time goes forward because energy itself is always moving from an available to an unavailable state. Our consciousness is continually recording the entropy change in the world around us. We watch our friends get old and die. We sit next to a fire and watch its red-hot embers turn slowly into cold white ashes. We experience the world always changing around us, and that experience is the unfolding of the second law. It is the irreversible process of dissipation of energy in the world. What does it mean to say, 'The world is running out of time'? Simply this: we experience the passage of time by the succession of one event after another. And every time an event occurs anywhere in this world energy is expended and the overall entropy is increased. To say the world is running out of time then, to say the world is running out of usable energy. In the words of Sir Arthur Eddington, 'Entropy is time's arrow'."
JEREMY RIFKIN, ENTROPY (1980)

10.15

10.16a

10.16b

INTERVIEW Kongjian Yu

Professor Kongjian Yu is a celebrated world leader in ecological planning and design. He is the founder of Turenscape, founder and Dean of the College of Architecture and Landscape at Peking University and Visiting Professor of Landscape Architecture and Urban Planning and Design, Harvard University. Selected awards include: 8 ASLA Design and Planning Awards, 5 Human Habitat Awards, 2 World's Best Landscape Awards, 3 Excellence on the Waterfront Awards, the World Architecture Award, ULI Global Award for Excellence, 2 Commended for the Emerging Architectural Awards, and the National Gold Medal of Fine Arts. Professor Yu has published 25 books, over 250 papers and is Chief Editor of *LA China*. He is one of Landscape Architecture's most inspirational and influential thinkers and practitioners.

*Please note this is an interview excerpt – the full interview is available at www.bloomsbury.com/zeunert-landscape-architecture

You speak of beauty in the productive, working and everyday (rural) landscape, yet in urban areas we typically have a preference for ornamental and consumptive landscapes and reductive, 'doing less ill' approaches. Landscape architecture has a close association with ornamental, high-culture, 'capital D' Design, complicit with pleasure-seeking that largely fails to address pressing issues of sustainability and survival (such as water, energy, food, productivity systems and social justice). Should the profession (or a branch of it) break away from this legacy to shift our focus to these issues?

Yes, I strongly believe landscape architecture needs a redirection, a revolutionary redefinition. People are inclined to see landscape architecture as an evolution from gardening and ornamental horticulture, because it is where all the history books traced our profession and most influential programs of landscape architecture worldwide evolved. However, it is heavily biased and largely the interest of high-culture class inside the intellectual ivory tower. There are two tiers of Chinese culture. This high culture belongs to the class of literati and aristocracy who think more aesthetically and visually about landscape architecture and less about the issues of working and production, leading to wasteful behavior. Facing the challenges of today's urgent environmental and social problems, if we keep on this track, we are doomed. We need to promote the wisdom of the low culture that is evolved for survival. This revolutionary way of thinking about the profession of landscape architecture is to redefine it as an art of survival, an art of working and functioning. It is the art derived from low culture, but the wisdom and skills in field making, irrigation, agricultural planning under the circumstance of flood and drought, selecting sites for cities to avoid natural disasters, selecting sites and orientating houses for people to make best use of natural conditions are exactly those we need for today's challenges. If the profession can follow this track, making landscape productive, making our cities resilient and buildings in the right position and making ourselves feel connected to the land, the community and past, the landscape is deemed to be safe, healthy, productive, and beautiful. We have to promote the art of survival, the living vernacular culture, not the dead culture of the imperial, aristocracy and literati. The legacy of ornamental and consumptive landscape should be only considered dead 'world heritage', and landscape architects today have a far more important role to play, dealing with the issue of survival.

Do we need to exert more influence in urban and regional planning?

It is important to recognize that the conventional approach to urban development planning, based on population projections, grey infrastructure and architectural objects is unable to meet the challenges and needs of an ecological and sustainable urban form. The alternative urbanity that we advocate is the planning and design of ecological infrastructure, which is better to be laid out before urban and regional development planning. Ecological infrastructure (EI) is the necessary structure of a sustainable landscape in which the output of goods and services is maintained and the capacity of the system to deliver those same goods and services to future generations is not undermined. The four categories of services are: provision, related to the production of food and clean water; regulating, related to the control of climate and disease, and the mediation of flood and drought; supporting, related to nutrient cycles and providing habitat for wild plant and animal species; and cultural, related to spiritual and recreational benefits. For the sake of ecological service and cultural integrity of the land, ecological infrastructure needs to be safeguarded across multiple scales, landscape needs to be considered as the holistic totality of land, and landscape architecture as the planning, design and management of the holistic system of land and arrangement of elements on the land, including architectures, rivers, and cities and so on. It is the 'Negative Planning' that I have stressed to mayors, to firstly demarcate large-scale 'non-buildable areas' for EI, or where not to urbanize, to eliminate the possibility of big mistakes in development and construction. In the past 18 years, Turenscape and Peking University has promoted these ideas in over 200 cities across China at multiple scales. 'Negative Planning' is an advanced version of McHarg's 'design with nature' idea, and that of Patrick Geddes, trying solve the contemporary problems in China – rapid urbanism, fragile environment and unregulated environment, but this also has universal significance.

You have stated that the dominant desire for beauty detached from utility is weakening. Even though your realized landscapes demonstrate that productivity and beauty are not mutually exclusive, why is the merger of productivity and aesthetics (such as your work at Shenyang Architectural Campus) not more prevalent?

Simply put, productive landscapes often do not meet public visual expectations under current pervasive aesthetics. In the west, people have internalized the idea that a controlled, maintained and clean environment is a prerequisite to beauty. Similarly, contemporary Chinese cities have a predominant taste for either Chinese traditional gardens or the high costs and maintenance of ornamental horticulture. The aesthetics of uselessness, leisure, and adornment have taken over in China as part of a larger overwhelming urge to appear modern and sophisticated. Everyday, vernacular scenes like reeds, crops, terraces and other features are related to low culture and disregarded by mainstream aesthetics.

The reasons behind these predominant aesthetics include our professional education and orientation of public values. Our education in landscape design does little to advance aesthetics of students and gives practically no mention of the practice and wisdom of landscape shaping for human survival. As a result, urban planning or design professionals seem to be weak and incapable in the face of the strong 'City Beautiful Movement' and even add fuel to its fire. Their theoretical and practical levels are also greatly limited due to their lack of international experience. Mostly, they are reduced to simulating photos taken home from abroad by mayors.

Secondly, both modern agricultural and industrial practices boast exploiting natural resources and controlling natural process through technological advancement as being civilized and see those adapted to natural forces as primitive. Policy makers favor showy and outrageously expensive architecture such as the CCTV tower and the Bird's Nest, despite their 10 times cost respective to an ordinary building in China that functions the same. All of these have exerted influence on public's aesthetics. In post-modern times we need to call upon a new aesthetics that matches contemporary environmental ethics and the principle of sustainability. Designers, government and public must all adapt to this new aesthetic. I call this 'Big feet revolution'.

How can we engage clients and landscape architects in productive landscapes of agriculture, energy, water, and raw materials?

Firstly, we have to change the idea of decision makers towards productive and functional landscape. As I mentioned, in China it is actually the mayors that determine city planning, thus we seek to transform decision makers' values and aesthetics through discourse. I've given lectures to more than 1,000 mayors and CPC secretaries, and also distributed the book '*The Road to Urban Landscape: Talks to Mayors*', with over 20,000 copies in circulation. During this process they are informed of the lessons of western urbanization, the destructive consequence and cause of China's city beautiful movement, a new aesthetics and road of establishing Ecological Infrastructure—which is our well-defined solution. I also wrote a letter to Prime Minister Wen Jiabao. The prime minister responded to my letter quickly, followed by the Ministry of Environmental Protection, which sponsored our national ecological security pattern research and this is of great strategic significance. In addition, the 'Sponge City', which we initiated and promoted for over a decade, eventually picked up by President Xi Jinping, has now become a national campaign.

Secondly, we need to restructure educational programs to make younger generations well prepared for the challenges of survival. As the Dean of the College of Architecture and Landscape at Peking University, landscape architecture education is positioned at producing designers who understand contemporary environmental ethics, master modern science and technology and a keenness for negotiating the relationship of humans and nature. I'm optimistic about their ability to play leading roles in addressing big environmental and survival issues.

Thirdly, mass media, both traditional and new, have powerful influence on the general public. They can play an important role in drawing people's attention to pressing social and environmental problems as well as productive and functional landscape as a solution.

In addition, our successfully realized projects are essential for increasing the confidence of collaborating mayors and media, since applying the principle of sustainability, ecological and functional landscapes is relatively new. Also, public spaces such as parks and riverbanks have immeasurable impact on the formation of cultural values. The places that Turenscape have designed are full of educational meanings to the common people. Gradually, the public could internalize the aesthetics, become able to do their own interpretation and then educate others.

Do you think the term sustainability has been corrupted and a term such as survival is more appropriate?

First of all, I do not reject the concept of 'sustainability', but I believe sustainability and survival are twin concepts. The former is 'Think like A King'; the latter is to 'Act Like A peasant'. We need both of course!

At the action level, I think survival is a more accurate word to describe our situation and a more powerful and practical word to lead action. First of all, sustainability is defined as meeting the needs of the present generation without compromising the ability of future generations to meet their own needs. But how can we talk about sustainability when the survival of the present generation is threatened? For example, in China 70% of surface water and more than half of urban ground water is thought to be polluted, 10 million hectares of arable land are contaminated by heavy metals and pesticide residues, more than 20% of fresh water wetlands and 50% of coastal wetlands have been lost in the past 50 years, hundred of species of plans and animals are threatened. On global level, climate change has brought additional floods, storms, droughts and diseases. 'Sustainability' is an ideal vision but somehow vague and empty, and we are born with a tendency of wasting, with no concern for saving. 'Survival', on the other hand, gives a pressing sense to arouse people's instinct through the history, story and images that they are familiar with, and at least gives a rough idea about how to act. People tend to regard sustainability as largely depending on strategic plans of governments or professionals, yet survival will help them realize that it should be the efforts of everyone. In short, it is more likely to draw individual's attention and inspire actions.

In addition, all around the world, our ancestors of different civilizations have accumulated survival experience and wisdom to tell and share, including dealing with floods, droughts, soil erosion, field making and food production under various circumstances. They are the active energy essential to people's survival and development. This can form a global thinktank that stores lessons and best practices that are ready for us to draw upon in the face of contemporary challenges. When they are actively valued, shared and practiced, they may eventually lead us to achieve the goal of sustainability.

What key strategies and lessons would you encourage and share?

(1) Influence influential persons. In China's case, they are referred to the political leaders. In each specific case efforts should be made to analyze and identify the influential persons and seek effective ways to communicate your concept.

(2) Do what you mean. You need to accomplish examples to support your theory and advocacy. During this process, it's key to refine your techniques in applying ecological principals to real projects.

(3) Make your productive attractive: In order to convey new aesthetics into the conventional notion of beauty, we should make productive landscape beautiful so that people will be touched by their sensual experience and then value, desire and nurture it.

(4) Perseverance. It will be a way full of challenges but we have to hold onto it. In my 2002 Zhongshan Shipyard Park project, my proposal of keeping remnant rusty docks and machinery and planting weeds were turned down by 99 of the 100 expert panel. It was our dogged persuasion to make it realized. It was the same painful negotiation process with, for example, water resource departments to persuade governments to cease channelizing rivers through straightening and embankments with concrete and replace with a riparian wetland system or natural bank, considering our strategy in part contradicted the legally defined engineering code. However, we shall believe that government, landscape architects and the public must adapt to this new aesthetic and value. My promotion for 'Spongy City' idea has been turned down many times by decisionmakers as well as 'experts' for decades, until picked by China's president, and now we are riding the tide and harvesting the returns. It's advancing.

Chen, W.Y. (2012) *Handbook of climate change mitigation*, New York: Springer.

Dryzek, J., Norgaard, R. and Schlosberg, D. (2011) *Oxford handbook of climate change and society*, Oxford, UK: Oxford University Press.

Handmer, J., Dovers, S. and Handmer, J. (2013) *Handbook of disaster policies and institutions: improving emergency management and climate change adaptation*, Abingdon, Oxon, UK: Routledge/Earthscan.

Heinberg, R. and Lerch, D. (eds) (2010) *The Post Carbon Reader: Managing the 21st Century's Sustainability Crises*, California: Watershed Media.

Holmgren, D. (2009) *Future Scenarios: How Communities Can Adapt to Peak Oil and Climate Change*, Canada: Chelsea Green.

Hopkins, R. (2008) *The Transition Handbook*, VT: Chelsea Green.

Leal Filho, W. (2015) *Handbook of climate change adaptation*, Heidelberg: Springer Reference.

Saunders, W. (2012) *Designed ecologies the landscape architecture of Kongjian Yu*, Basel: Birkhäuser.

Scoones, I., Leach, M. and Newell, P. (2015). *The politics of green transformations*, Oxon, UK: Routledge.

Waldheim, C. (ed.) (2006) *The Landscape Urbanismfurther Reader*, New York: Princeton Architectural Press.

Yu, K. & Padua, M. (2006) *The art of survival: recovering landscape architecture*, Victoria: The Images Publishing Group.

GLOSSARY

This glossary clarifies terms, concepts and abbreviations/acronyms used within this publication. Some definitions are specific to terminology and meanings in environmental design, planning practices and industry issues.

Access. 1. A point of entry to a site or building. 2. To approach or enter.
Adaptive reuse. The process of reusing an existing structure for a different purpose than what it was built or designed for.
Aesthetic. 1. A set of principles or philosophical theory that governs the idea of beauty at a given time and place. 2. The art and science of perception.
Agricultural Revolution. See Neolithic Revolution.
Agrobiodiversity. Agricultural biological diversity, the diversity of agriculture.
AMD (Acid Mine Drainage). The outflow of acidic water from mines.
Anthropocene. A geological era whereby human activities are responsible for reshaping the Earth's ecosystems, as opposed to other geologic epochs where natural processes and non-human events have shaped outcomes.
Anthropocentric. Human centeredness. The philosophy that holds humans as the most important entity in the universe, superior to and separate from other life forms and the environment.
Anthropogenic. Caused or influenced by human activity, often used in relation to environmental and climatic impacts.
ASR (Aquifer Storage and Recovery). Also known as Managed Aquifer Recharge (MAR), it is the injection of water into an aquifer for recovery and reuse.
Biodiversity. Biological diversity, the diversity of all life forms.
Biomimicry. The design and production of materials, structures, and systems that are modeled on biological entities and processes. In design, this can be applied superficially, such as in visual terms, or it can be applied more substantially through mimicking processes such as nutrient cycles, such as 'closing the loop'.
Biophilia. An innate and genetic affinity of humans with the natural world.
Bioregion. A region that constitutes a natural ecological community defined by characteristics of the natural environment rather than by human-made divisions.
Biotope. Synonymous with habitat. The region associated with a specific ecological community.
BMP (Best Management Practice). A term used in the United States and Canada to describe a technique of water pollution control, for example in industrial wastewater, municipal sewage and stormwater control and wetland management.
Brief. An initial description of a project problem that defines the parameters within which the designer will work. Usually issued by a client but it is sometimes necessary to be written by the designer as a return brief in the absence of a client brief.
Brownfield. Land previously used for industrial purposes or commercial uses that is contaminated or polluted (or likely to be).
Built environment. The human-made material, spatial and cultural environment in which people live, work, and recreate on a day-to-day basis. Built environment professions include and are not limited to: landscape architecture, planning, urban design, architecture, interior architecture, and many related disciplines in engineering, construction, and project management, infrastructure, law, policy, health, and environmental sustainability.
CAD. Computer-Aided Design. The use of computer systems and software to assist in the creation, modification, analysis, optimization and presentation of a design, particularly for technical drawing and construction.
CAFO (Concentrated Animal Feeding Operation). An animal production process that concentrates large numbers in confined arrangements, utilizing infrastructures (such as feeding, temperature control and manure management) as opposed to land and labor.

Carrying Capacity. Also known as Ecological Limits. The maximum population size of the species that the environment or planet can sustain indefinitely, given the food, habitat, water and other resources available in the environment.
Catchment. Also known as a watershed. An entire region that drains into a river or body of water.
Circulation. The movement of people and vehicles through and around a site.
Climate change. Usually refers to human induced climate change, the process whereby collective human activities are responsible for altering the Earth's naturally occurring and average climatic patterns. This is predominantly through the use and subsequent pollution from fossil fuels like coal, gas and oil. The great majority (around 97%) of peer-reviewed scientific literature confirms the phenomenon of human induced climate change.
Climate change adaption. The process of anticipating, designing, planning, adapting, and increasing resilience to climatic change and weather events.
Climate change mitigation. The process and activities associated with halting and reversing the causes of climate change, such as carbon sequestration through tree planting and increasing soil carbon.
Closing the loop. The continuous life cycle and process from production, consumption, recycling and or reuse that ultimately returns to production.
Commission. 1. The authority given to perform planning or design. 2. To award a job to a chosen and willing firm. 3. A group entrusted by an official body.
Community. 1. A group with interests or conditions in common. 2. An inhabited area populated with people who have interests in common, at least due to geographic proximity to each other.
Composition. The arrangement of design elements in relation to each other, resulting in a pleasing unity.
Concept. An idea. A notion that serves to underpin or to communicate a design proposal or process.
Conservation. The action of conserving or preserving something, such as natural and cultural resources.
Contour. A representative line on a drawing that traces a single elevation on the surface of the land to indicate topography (see Topography).
Corridor. An area of land or linear landscape feature linking two areas.
Cradle to Cradle. An approach to the design of products and systems that models human industry on nature's processes viewing materials as nutrients circulating in healthy, safe metabolisms. See Biomimicry.
Cradle to Grave. Occurring or persisting from beginning to end, such as taking responsibility for the disposal of goods but not necessarily putting products' constituent components back into service.
Cultural landscape. A distinctive landscape that is the combined works of nature and of humans.
Degradation. The condition or process of degrading, being degraded and in decline.
Density. A measure of the intensity of the occupation of a site or area by humans, animals, buildings, and the like, such as population per square mile.
Design thinking. A term referencing the cognitive activities specific to the process of designing, in contrast to scientific thinking.
Eco pragmatism. Also known as eco-modernism and modernist greens who affirm that humanity needs to shrink its impacts on the environment but embrace intensive 'green' technologies to achieve this, such as nuclear power, geoengineering, and bioengineering.
Ecological footprint. The area of productive land and water ecosystems required to produce the resources that the population or individuals consume and require to assimilate waste production. This is often measured in acres, hectares or the number of 'planet earths' required.
Ecology. The study of relations between organisms and their physical surroundings. A branch of the movement concerned with protection of the environment.
Ecoregion. See Bioregion.
Ecosystem services. Ecosystem services are the beneficial outcomes provided by ecosystems and the processes by which the environment produces resources utilized by humans such as clean air, water, food and materials. There are four categories: provisioning, regulating, supporting, and cultural.
EIA (Environmental Impact Assessment). The process of assessing the environmental consequences of a proposed project prior to the decision to move ahead. Can also refer to a proposed plan, policy or program and this may be termed as a 'strategic' environmental impact assessment. Measures may or may not be proposed to avoid or minimize adverse impacts, however, the EIA process does not facilitate an environmental veto.
EIS (Environmental Impact Statement). The report or document produced in the process of Environmental Impact Assessment.
Elevation. 1. The distance of a specific point on the land above or below a fixed reference point, usually sea level. 2. An orthographic drawing that is a flat representation view from one side, such as a façade of a building.
Environment. 1. The totality of the overall systems of land, water, vegetation, wildlife etc. that comprise the setting for life on earth. 2. A setting or milieu for something or someone.
Fossil Fuel. A finite, combustible organic material such as oil, coal and gas, which has been formed in the geological past from the remains of living organisms.
GAIA. The idea of the Earth as an integrated whole and a living being. From the primal Greek goddess personifying the Earth, the Greek concept of 'Mother Nature' and Earth Mother.
Generative. Capable and geared to production.
Genius loci. Latin. The unique qualities or spirit of a place, both human and natural, that should ideally be understood and valued.
GIS (Geographic Information System). A computerized data management system used to capture, store, manage, retrieve, analyze, and display spatial information, such as maps. In digital form, GIS maps are usually configured as a series of layers that can be turned on or off.
Geopolitics. The effects of human and physical geography on international politics and international relations.
GPS (Global Positioning System). A computer and satellite system designed to assist global navigation and cartography that links satellites and handheld receivers to calculate coordinates on the Earth's surface.
Green Infrastructure. An interconnected network of green open spaces that provide multiple ecosystem services and benefits to assist improvement of urban and climatic conditions and challenges.
Green Revolution. The shift in agricultural practices from the 1940s–1960s that led to large increases in crop production in developing countries, achieved through the use of artificial fertilizers, pesticides, high-yield crop varieties and large-scale mechanization.
Greenfield. Peri-urban or rural undeveloped land (except for agricultural use) considered for urban, commercial or industrial development.
Greenwash. Making unsubstantiated or misleading claims that attempt to pass off products, designs, services, technologies, or practices as environmentally sustainable or having environmental benefits.
Habitat. The natural home or environment of an animal, plant, or other organism and groups of these.
Historic conservation. The work of designing for and protecting landscapes and environments of historic and/or archaeological significance.

Horizontal hostility. A term (originating from feminism in the 1970s) to describe infighting, or factionalism.
Industrial Revolution. A period of rapid development of fossil fuel powered machinery and resultant industry that took place during the late 1700s and early 1800s, beginning in Great Britain and quickly spreading throughout the world.
Infrastructure. The physical and organizational structures and facilities such as buildings, roads, power supplies, communications, water and wastewater for the effective operation of a society or enterprise.
Land management. The process of managing the use and development in urban and rural settings of land resources for a variety of purposes such as agriculture, forestry, water resource management and ecotourism.
Landscape character. The overall and distinct attributes of a region that result in its unique appearance and environment.
Landscape management. The intended and ongoing strategic, maintenance and care activities for designed landscapes.
Landscape planning. The study, practice and development of policies and strategies for landscapes that assess past, current, and future capabilities to support different land use activities that account for environmental, economic, and social health and wellbeing.
Landscape science. The study and administration of processes, complexes and systems, both physical and natural, in geography, ecology and the environment.
Land use. The activity or zoning in a given area, such as 'commercial', 'industrial', 'residential', or 'green open space'. Rarely, however, is any area singular in its use and 'mixed use' is common.
Land use planning. Land use planning is akin to urban planning, regional planning, community planning, and any other planning exercise that plays a role in defining how land is used.
Landscape Urbanism. A theory and movement that posits that landscape disciplines and the medium of landscape, rather than architecture and the medium of buildings, should be basis for design of urban regions and cities.
LCA (Life Cycle Assessment/Analysis). A systematic evaluation technique to assess environmental impacts associated with all the stages of a product or service's life cycle.
LID (Low Impact Development). See WSUD.
LVIA (Landscape and Visual Impact Assessment) or Visual Impact Assessment (VIA). Processes that use perspective views and other cartographic and orthographic tools to estimate and assess a proposal's visual effects and the degree of change for scenic landscape and/or visual quality.
Master plan. A plan, development proposal or strategy for a site area, often a large site. Usually composed of a package of drawings, written and visual documents that outline how the master plan will be executed.
Meanwhile Space. Temporary use of vacant land (or buildings) for social or economic gain until they are brought back into commercial use.
Microclimate. The climatic conditions in a specific area, such as a site area or specific areas within the site itself, such as a valley, top of a hill, or under trees. Microclimates exist within climatic regions, but are also site-specific and thus not necessarily consistent with regional climatic data.
Nativist. 1. A psychology or policy of favoring native inhabitants, plants and animals as opposed to immigrants or exotic plants and animals. 2. The revival or perpetuation of indigenous culture, plants and animals in opposition to acculturation.
Natural capital. An anthropocentric, economic concept that values the stock of natural ecosystems to measure a possible yield of ecosystem goods or services. It is the extension of the economic notion of capital (the manufactured means of production) to goods and services provided by the environment.
Natural landscape. A landscape that is unaffected by human activity. While many scholars posit that these landscapes no longer exist, however, there is no place on earth that cannot return to natural landscape if abandoned by human culture.
Neoliberalism. A capitalist, *laissez faire* economic approach beginning in the 1970s and 1980s, which advocates extensive economic liberalization, free trade, privatization, open markets, deregulation and reductions in government and public sector spending, activities and intervention in order to enhance the role of the private and corporate sector in the economy.
Neolithic Revolution. Also known as the Agricultural Revolution, this was the transition of many human cultures from hunting and gathering to agriculture and settlement, giving humans the ability to support an increasingly large population.
New Urbanism. An urban design movement based on the resurrection of European urban principles that promote diverse, walkable, local and place-based neighborhoods containing a range of housing, land use and job types.
Orthographic projection. A means of representing a three-dimensional object in two dimensions. It is usually a drawing, to scale, based on geometry as parallel projection, where all the lines are orthogonal to the projection plane. Plan and section drawings are orthographic projections.
Paradigm. A cognitive framework containing basic assumptions, ways of thinking, and a methodology that is commonly accepted by members of a discipline, community or group.
Peak Oil. The point in time when the global extraction and production of oil reached its maximum rate, after which production enters terminal decline.
Peasant. Herein used in reference to family and artisanal agriculture, as opposed to a pejorative or political/social meaning.
Permaculture. Permanent agriculture. A concept, design system and practice developed in Australia by Bill Mollison and David Holmgren in the 1970s. Permaculture is a branch of ecological design, ecological engineering, environmental design, construction and integrated water resources management that develops sustainable, regenerative and self-maintained agricultural and living systems modeled on natural ecosystems and indigenous practices.
Perspective. A drawing that represents three-dimensional images on a two-dimensional picture plane. Perspective drawings are constructed with lines that converge to horizon 'vanishing points' and these provide the image with depth and a horizon, whereby the size of objects seems to diminish according to distance.
Photomontage. A technique similar to collage that compiles existing and intended elements together into an image that represents a desired outcome. May also be referred to as an 'artist's impression'.
Place. A space within the landscape that has acquired human meaning through human inhabitation.
Plan. An orthographic, two-dimensional scaled drawing that places the viewer in an imaginary position above the site or object looking straight down at it without any distortion or perspective.
Planning. 1. The process of making plans, strategies and a systematic arrangement for something. 2. A term that encompasses the disciplines of urban, regional, spatial, environmental and land use planning.
Plant community. A collection of plant species within a designated geographical area that forms a relatively uniform and distinguishable patch, distinct from neighboring patches of different types. Also known as vegetation and plant associations.
Planting palette. A selection of plants specified by a designer or horticulturalist.

Precautionary Principle. Includes several meanings depending on context including: shifting the obligation of proof to the proponents of an activity; taking preventive action in the face of uncertainty; extensively exploration of alternatives to possibly harmful activities; enacting strong protective measures if there is doubt about an animal's or plant's conservation status; and increasing public participation in decision making.
Preservation. The intent or action of preserving something, such as a remnant ecosystem.
Program. The interrelationship of elements, uses, activities and human and environmental processes that provide the parameters for a site's design that balances the needs and requirements of the site, client and users.
Propinquity. In social psychology, refers to physical or psychological proximity between people that can lead to interpersonal attraction.
Public realm. Any space that is free and accessible for the use of all people, usually in reference to an urban context.
Public space. Any space that is free and accessible for the use of all people.
Representation. 1. An image that represents and expresses an idea, concept, or elements of the physical world. 2. The creation of such imagery.
Resilient. The ability to withstand or recover quickly from difficult conditions or disturbance.
Restoration. The intent or action of restoring something, such as past ecosystems.
Retrofitting. The adding or repurposing of something that was not part of the original design or construction.
Scale. The process through which it is possible to create orthographic projections at a specific fraction of the full-size dimensions of a site or object. Scale is expressed as a fraction or a ratio in imperial or metric conventions. Scale facilitates measurements and thus construction of designs and objects.
Section. A two-dimensional orthographic drawing showing the heights, widths and scales sizes of objects. Sections are created through taking a vertical slice—usually a straight line—through the objects as indicated on a plan drawing.
Site. An area nominated and marked for human activity, planning or design.
Site analysis. The process of researching and investigating site characteristics and determining implications for planning, design, or strategic undertakings.
Site inventory. The process of gathering, compiling and recording site information and characteristics.
Site survey. An accurate record of a site's surface, boundaries and features, usually completed by a surveyor using survey equipment to output drawings.
Social justice. Relates to justice within a society in terms of distribution of wealth, opportunities, and privileges.
Spatial. How objects and elements are composed and fit together in space.
Stewardship. An ethical approach to planning and management of global and local resources, across a broad range of factors such as the environment, economics, health, and heritage.
Sublime. The grandest and most terrifying aspects of nature, with greatness beyond all possibility of calculation, measurement, or imitation. The concept has differing applications and meanings depending on the discipline/context.
Succession. The act or process of following in order or sequence. In ecology, it is the progressive replacement of one dominant type of species or community by another in an ecosystem.
SuDS Sustainable urban drainage system. See WSUD.
Sustainability. The ability to meet the needs of the present without compromising the ability of future generations to meet their own needs. The practice of ensuring that design, construction, and occupation of a site or region are in balance with their context, including environmental, social, cultural, and economic factors. Offering possibility of balance and permanence.
Swale. A low tract of land, either a natural feature or human-created, which is often moist or marshy. Used for drainage in landscape design to direct water. May or may not be planted.
Synthesis. The process of bringing analysis, concepts, design and strategic material together to create solutions for the problems posed by the brief.
Systems thinking. A holistic approach that concerns an understanding of a system by examining the linkages and interactions between the elements that compose the entirety of the system, over time and within the context of larger systems.
Tabula rasa. Latin. In a design context denotes a blank or empty state, or the process of achieving this through wiping clean and complete removal.
Topography. The rise and fall of the land's natural and artificial features created by natural and built elements such as water, soil, geology and buildings. Topography communicates the shape of the land on maps or plans through contour lines that follow a specific height above (or below) sea level.
Topophila. Love of a place or an affective bond with one's environment.
Transit-oriented development (TOD). Usually a mixed-use, medium or high-density residential and commercial area designed to maximize walkability and accessibility to high quality public transport systems.
Triple bottom line. A business and development framework of three components, financial, social and environmental (or ecological). These are also referred to as the three P's: people, planet and profit.
Urban design. The inter and multidisciplinary processes of shaping the physical spaces of human settlement in cities, towns and villages.
Urban planning. The technical and political process involving the use and protection of land, the environment, and the public, including natural and infrastructure networks within and beyond urban areas.
Urbanism. The study and design of the various forces that shape urban spaces and activities.
W2E (Waste to energy). A waste management facility that combusts wastes to produce electricity.
Watershed. See Catchment.
Wayfinding. A form of spatial problem solving that provides means to locate one's physical position in an environment, showing where the desired location is, and knowing how to get there from the present location.
Weed. A wild plant growing where it is not desired, in competition with cultivated plants.
Wilderness. An uncultivated, uninhabited, and inhospitable region thought to be unaffected by human activities, with either a negative or a romantic connotation depending on the viewpoint of the observer.
WSUD (Water sensitive urban design). A land planning, landscape and engineering design approach that integrates the water cycle and water infrastructure, such as stormwater, groundwater and wastewater management and water supply, into urban design to minimize environmental degradation, improve water quality and aesthetic and amenity appeal.
Xeriscape. A landscape approach that requires little or no irrigation for planting and minimal other maintenance, often in dry and arid regions.

Please visit www.bloomsbury.com/zeunert-landscape-architecture for landscape and sustainability resources including:

General information; international organizations; European organizations; professional organizations by country; professional journals; and environmental, social and NGO organizations and resources.

General Information

The following websites provide information to those who are interested to learn more about landscape architecture, urbanism and planning:

APA Sustaining Places http://blogs.planning.org/sustainability
Be a Landscape Architect http://bealandscapearchitect.com
Become a Landscape Architect www.asla.org/become.aspx
The Center for Land Use Interpretation http://clui.org
The Cultural Landscape Foundation www.tclf.org
The Dirt http://dirt.asla.org
Garden Visit www.gardenvisit.com
Global Planners Network www.globalplannersnetwork.org
I Want to be a Landscape Architect https://www.youtube.com/watch?v=zbx3FDDNeQM
Land8Lounge www.land8lounge.com
Landscape Architects Network www.landarchs.com
Landscape + Urbanism www.landscapeandurbanism.com
LANDZINE www.landezine.com
Pinterest https://www.pinterest.com/explore/landscape-architecture
Project for Public Spaces www.pps.org
World Landscape Architecture www.worldlandscapearchitect.com

International Organizations

There are many international organizations that are directly or indirectly concerned with landscape, urbanism and the environment, and following are a small selection of the more significant:

CELA Council of Educators in Landscape Architecture www.thecela.org
COP Commonwealth Association of Planners www.commonwealth-planners.org
EDRA Environmental Design Research Association www.edra.org
GPN Global Planner Network www.globalplannersnetwork.org
IALE International Association for Landscape Ecology www.landscape-ecology.org
ICLEI Local Governments for Sustainability www.iclei.org
ICMA International City/County Management http://icma.org
ICOMOS International Council on Monuments and Sites www.icomos.org
IFHP International Federation for Housing and Planning www.ifhp.org
IFLA International Federation of Landscape Architects http://iflaonline.org
IFLA Americas http://iflaonline.org/about/ifla-regions/ifla-americas
IFLA Asia-Pacific http://iflaapr.org
ISOCARP International Society of City and Regional Planners www.isocarp.org
IUCN International Union for the Conservation of Nature www.iucn.org
Metropolis World Association of the Major Metropolises www.metropolis.org
SER Society for Ecological Restoration www.ser.org
UNEP United Nations Environment Program www.unep.org
UN Habitat United Nations Human Settlement Program www.unhabitat.org

European Organizations

Europe's networks and associations for both for professionals and students are numerous:

AESOP The Association of European Schools of Planning www.aesop-planning.eu
CEU Council for European Urbanism www.ceunet.org
ECLAS European Council of Landscape Architecture Schools www.eclas.org
ECTP European Council of Spatial Planners www.ectp-ceu.eu
ELASA European Landscape Architecture Student Association www.elasa.org
IEEP Institute for European Environmental Policy www.ieep.org.uk
IFLA Europe (International Federation of Landscape Architects) http://iflaeurope.eu
International Biennial of Landscape Architecture (Barcelona) www.facebook.com/Barcelonalandscapebiennial/
Landscape Europe www.landscape-europe.net
Le:Notre Thematic Network in Landscape Architecture www.le-notre.org
UDG Urban Design Group www.udg.org.uk
Uniscape European Network of Universities for the Implementation of the European Landscape Convention www.uniscape.eu

Professional Organizations by Country

For information about studying, practicing and certification of landscape architecture and other built environment professions, the central point of contact is the national professional organization. Some country national organizations are listed below. Others may be listed at the International Federation of Landscape Architects (IFLA) website: http://iflaonline.org.

Australia
AILA Australian Institute of Landscape Architects www.aila.org.au
Planning Institute of Australia www.planning.org.au
Canada
Canadian Institute of Planners https://www.cip-icu.ca
CSLA-AAPC The Canadian Society of Landscape Architects (L'Association des architectes paysagistes du Canada) www.csla-aapc.ca
China
CHSLA Chinese Society of Landscape Architecture www.chsla.org.cn
IACP International Association for China Planning www.chinaplanning.org
France
FFP Fédération Française du Paysage www.f-f-p.org
SFU French Society of Urban Planners www.urbanistes.com
Germany
BDLA Bund Deutscher Landschaftsarchitekten Bundesgeschaeftsstelle www.bdla.de
DiFu German Institute of Urban Affairs www.difu.de
Hong Kong
HKILA Hong Kong Institute of Landscape Architects www.hkila.com
Hong Kong Institute of Planners www.hkip.org.hk
Hong Kong Institute of Urban Design www.hkiud.org
Hungary
Hungarian Association of Landscape Architects www.tajepiteszek.hu
India
The Institute of Town Planners www.itpi.org.in
ISOLA Indian Society of Landscape Architects www.isola.org.in
Ireland
Irish Landscape Institute www.irishlandscapeinstitute.com
Irish Planning Institute www.ipi.ie
Israel
IPA Israel Planners Association www.aepi.org.il
Italy
CeNSU National Centre for Town Planning Studies www.censu.it
Japan
City Planning Institute of Japan www.cpij.or.jp
IFLA Japan www.ifla-japan.net
The Japanese Institute of Landscape Architecture www.jila-zouen.org

Malaysia
ILAM Institute of Landscape Architects Malaysia www.ilamalaysia.org
Malaysian Institute of Planners www.mip.org.my
The Netherlands
NVTL Nederlandse Vereniging voor Tuin en Landschapsarchitektuur www.nvtl.nl
New Zealand
New Zealand Institute of Landscape Architects www.nzila.co.nz
New Zealand Planning Institute https://www.planning.org.nz/
Singapore
Singapore Institute of Landscape Architects www.sila.org.sg/website
South Korea
KILA Korean Institute of Landscape Architecture www.kila.or.kr
South Africa
ILASA Institute for Landscape Architecture in South Africa www.ilasa.co.za
SACLAP South African Council for the Landscape Architectural Profession www.saclap.org.za
South African Planning Institute www.sapi.org.za
Sweden
Swedish Society for Town and Country Planning www.planering.org
Turkey
TCLA Turkish Chamber of Landscape Architects www.peyzajmimoda.org.tr
United Kingdom
LI The Landscape Institute www.landscapeinstitute.org
Royal Town Planning Institute www.rtpi.org.uk
United States of America
AICP – American Institute of Certified Planners (American Planning Association) https://www.planning.org/aicp
American Planning Association https://www.planning.org
ASLA American Society of Landscape Architects www.asla.org

Professional Journals

The breadth of the field of landscape architecture means that there are thousands of relevant journals. Some journals focus on practice, some are scholarly (peer-reviewed), scientific, design-centric or theoretical. The list below is focused on landscape architectural practice. Many environmental publications are scientific and do not accommodate planning and design concerns.

a+u Architecture and Urbanism (Japan) www.japan-architect.co.jp
a+t (Spain) http://aplust.net/tienda/revistas
Anthos (Switzerland) www.anthos.ch
Ark (Finland) www.ark.fi
Arkitektur (Sweden) www.arkitektur.se
Arquitetura & Urbanismo (Brazil) www.piniweb.com.br
aU (Brazil) www.au.pini.com.br
Australasian Journal of Environmental Management http://www.tandfonline.com/toc/tjem20/current
Blauwe Kamer (Netherlands) www.blauwekamer.nl
Chinese Landscape Architecture www.jchla.com
Formes (Canada) www.formes.ca
Garden Design Magazine www.gardendesign.com
Garten + Landschaft (Germany) www.garten-landschaft.de
Harvard Design Magazine www.gsd.harvard.edu/research/publications/hdm
International Journal of Landscape Architecture www.journalnetwork.org/journals/international-journal-of-landscape-architecture
JOLA (Europe) http://www.jola-lab.eu/
Journal of Landscape Architecture (India) www.lajournal.in
Journal of Urban Design (UK) www.tandf.co.uk/journals/carfax/13574809.html
Journal of Urbanism (UK) www.tandf.co.uk/journals/titles/17549175.asp
Kerb: The Journal of Landscape Architecture (Australia) www.kerbjournal.com
LA+ (USA) http://laplusjournal.com
LAD Journal (Russia)
LAM – Landscape Architecture Magazine www.landscapearchitecturemagazine.org
Landscape and Urban Planning (USA) www.journals.elsevier.com/landscape-and-urban-planning
Landscape Architecture Australia www.aila.org.au/landscapeaustralia
Landscape Architecture New Zealand architecturenow.co.nz/magazines/landscape-architecture-new-zealand
Landscape Journal (USA) www.wisc.edu/wisconsinpress/journals/journals/lj.html
Landscape Management www.landscapemanagement.net
Landscape Research (UK) www.tandf.co.uk/journals/carfax/01426397.html
Landscape Review (NZ) http://journals.lincoln.ac.nz/index.php/lr
Landscape: The Journal of the Landscape Institute www.landscapethejournal.org
Landscapes/Paysages (Canada) www.csla-aapc.ca/landscapes-paysages-0
Landskab (Denmark) www.arkfo.dk
Metropolis www.metropolismag.com
Paisea (Spain) www.paisea.com
Places Journal https://placesjournal.org
Project Russia (Russia) www.prorus.ru
Quaderns (Catalonia) www.coac.net/quaderns
Scapegoat Architecture/Landscape/Political Economy www.scapegoatjournal.org
Site/Lines www.foundationforlandscapestudies.org/sitelines
Tasarim (Turkey) www.tasarimgroup.com.tr
Terrain.org: A Journal of Built and Natural Environments www.terrain.org
Topos: The International Review of Landscape Architecture and Urban Design www.topos.de
Urban Design Journal www.udg.org.uk/publications/journal
URBAN DESIGN International www.palgrave-journals.com/udi/index.html
World Landscape Architecture worldlandscapearchitect.com.

Events

Professional organizations hold annual or biannual awards that showcase the best projects from the region or country as judged by a body of peers. Refer to the websites of professional organizations for details as many of these provide online catalogues and award profiles. These website usually publish lists of other events, activities and conferences.

Environmental, Social and NGO Organizations and Resources

There are many active organizations that work to create a socially just and environmentally sustainable world:

Amnesty International https://www.amnesty.org
Architects Without Frontiers www.architectswithoutfrontiers.com.au
Architecture Sans Frontières www.asfint.org
ASLA, Sustainable ASLA https://www.asla.org/sustainableasla.aspx https://www.asla.org/sustainablelandscapes/index.html
Avaaz https://www.avaaz.org
Ethical Corporation www.ethicalcorp.com
IPCC Intergovernmental Panel on Climate Change www.www.ipcc.ch
Millennium Ecosystem Assessment www.millenniumassessment.org
RUAF www.ruaf.org
SumofUs http://sumofus.org

I would like to thank everyone that I have neglected in the exhaustive, multi-year process of completing this book! My grateful thanks goes to my wife, Alys Daroy, for her patience, persistence, and huge support and skill in proofing and editing the manuscript.

This book resulted from the generosity of Tim Waterman, who shared his publishing contacts and networks and my thanks extend to Tim for being a supportive colleague and friend.

I give my gratitude to all Bloomsbury staff involved in the commissioning, editing, production and promotion of this book, in particular, to Leafy Cummins for her dedicated and supportive editorial management. Thanks also to Louise Baird-Smith and Kate Duffy for their editorial management and to Brendan O'Connell for picture organization. Thanks to Gillian Haggart for copyediting and to Dave at Saxon Graphics and Adam at Hoop Design.

My gratefulness is given to the Peer Reviewers of the manuscript (and proposal).

A special thanks is extended to all contributors of project images, drawings and information. There are too many people to thank individually during this (exhausting!) process but please know your efforts are highly valued. Without your generous contributions, this book would be reduced to words.

I would like to thank the interviewees for sharing their perspectives (and time)—I know that the readership will greatly value your insights.

I would like to thank my parents Heather and Jack, my family and friends for their ongoing support and perspective.

I give my gratitude to supportive and collegial colleagues—past and present—at Deakin University, particularly Prof. David Jones and Dr Beau Beza, Writtle School of Design and the University of Adelaide.

My intellectual thanks are too wide to acknowledge but I would like to thank my mentors, role models and students in academia, professional practice and the wider world, who have influenced, inspired, and shaped my education, perspectives, and professional experiences.

I would like to gratefully acknowledge the creators of the projects, visions, quotes and literature featured in this book. My intention was to scaffold, assemble and feature this notable collection of work to a greater audience for a worthy cause. I hope I have done this justice.

Joshua Zeunert
29 February 2016

IMAGE CREDITS

1.1a United States Department of Agriculture (public domain)
1.1b US Forest Service (public domain)
1.2 US Geological Survey, designed by Joseph Graham, William Newman, and John Stacy (public domain)
1.5 Darren Newbery/Alamy Stock Photo
1.7 Reproduction from The Yorck Project (used under GNU license)
1.8 Benjamin Franklin (public domain)
1.9a and 1.9b © State of Victoria, Department of Environment Land Water and Planning 2015 www.delwp.vic.gov.au. Reproduced with permission
1.10 Iconotec/Alamy
1.11 Richard Woldendorp
1.12 redrawn from several sources
1.13 Public domain
1.15a–c NASA
1.16 NASA/Goddard Space Flight Center
1.17 NASA/Goddard Space Flight Center
1.18 NASA/Goddard Space Flight Center
1.19 ©Alex MacLean
1.20 © Edward Burtynsky, courtesy Nicholas Metivier Gallery, Toronto/Admira, Milano
1.21 Aerial Archives/Alamy
1.22a-b NASA Photo/Alamy
1.22c Deco/Alamy
1.23a NASA/GSFC/METI/Japan Space Systems and US/Japan ASTER Science Team
1.23b JOEL SAGET/AFP/Getty Images
1.24 Jochen Tack/Getty
2.1 Courtesy Bill Rowland
2.2a–b Courtesy Bill Rowland
2.3a–b Agriculture, Fisheries and Conservation Department, Hong Kong SAR Government
2.4a Bruce Leander, Lady Bird Johnson Wildflower Center, The University of Texas at Austin
2.4b Philip Hawkins, Lady Bird Johnson Wildflower Center, The University of Texas at Austin
2.5 Michael Van Valkenburgh Associates Inc.
2.6a–d Martí Franch, Pau Ardèvol and EMF
2.7a–g © OLIN/Sahar Coston-Hardy
2.8a–b Randall L. Scheiber, Randall Lee Scheiber Photography
2.9 National Park Service (public domain)
2.10 Graphic by Pete Guest
2.11 Larry Geddis/Alamy
2.12 Lencer (Creative Commons)
2.13a–b Courtesy of Wildlands Network. Photo credit: Kristen Caldon
2.14 Smaack (Creative Commons)
2.15a © Goois Natuurreservaat
2.15b–c ©Alterra/E.A. van der Grift
2.16 Courtesy of UWA Publishing
2.17a–b Tom Fox/SWA
2.18a–c LOLA Landscape Architects
2.19a–d Image courtesy of Reed Hilderbrand
2.20a–f © City of Salisbury
2.21a–d Nelson Byrd Woltz Landscape Architects
3.1 Turenscape
3.2a Seattle Municipal Archives (Public Domain)
3.2b Photo by Liesl Matthies (Creative Commons)
3.3a–e Emschergenossenschaft
3.4a © Latz + Partner
3.4b © Michael Latz
3.4c Barrett Doherty
3.4d–g © Latz + Partner
3.5a–c Turenscape
3.6a–b SmithGroupJJR

3.7a Christine Ten Eyck © Ten Eyck Landscape Architects, Inc.
3.7b–c Bill Timmerman © Ten Eyck Landscape Architects, Inc.
3.8a Author unknown (public domain)
3.8b–c Roland zh (Creative Commons)
3.9a–e Guillaume Paradis
3.10a–c Copyright Morgan Gillham, Image Courtesy of Josh Byrne & Associates
3.11a–b Photo courtesy of Friends of the High Line
3.12a–f Courtesy of D.I.R.T. studio
3.13a–g PWP Landscape Architecture
3.14a–c Olympic Delivery Authority
3.14d Hargreaves Associates
3.14e–f LDA Design, photo credit Claire Borley
3.14g LDA Design
3.15 Mary Margaret Jones
3.16a–b © Peter Cook
3.17a–b John Gollings Photography
3.17c RiverCity Company
3.18a–c Michael Van Valkenburgh Associates, Inc.
3.19a–h © James Corner Field Operations
3.20a–d McGregor Coxall
3.21a, 3.21b and 3.21d McGregor Coxall
3.21c and 3.21e Mark Syke
3.22a–e Turenscape
3.23a–d Batlle I Roig, Eva Serrats, Jordi Surroca and Joan Batlle
3.24 © Lorna Jordan
3.25 Josh Zeunert
3.26b Photo by Roman Piro
3.27 Bruel-Delmar
3.28a–b Tom Fox/SWA
3.29a–b Bruel-Delmar
3.30a © Craig Kuhner
3.30b Courtesy of Sasaki Associates
3.30c © Eric Taylor
3.30d © Craig Kuhner
3.31a–b Photographer: John Gollings
3.32 Photographer: Michael Nicholson
3.33a–b Jeff Amram Photography
3.34a–b Turenscape
3.35a–d Turenscape
3.36a–b Turenscape
3.37a–e Turenscape
3.38a–h Turenscape
4.1 STOSS Landscape Urbanism
4.2a–g Detroit Future City. Copyright STOSS Landscape Urbanism
4.3 Scott Williams (Creative Commons)
4.4 © J.A. Brennan Associates
4.5 City of Hamburg
4.6 imageBROKER/Alamy
4.7a Photograph by Luuk Kramer
4.7b–c Images by Dutch Dialogues – H+N+S Landscape Architects
4.8 Image by Dutch Dialogues – H+N+S Landscape Architects
4.9a–c Kimberly Garza and Sarah Thomas Karle proposed a speculative climate adaptation project, "Dedamming the Dutch Delta" for the Netherlands Delta region. The project was part of the "Depoldering Dordrecht" studio, co-taught by Pierre Bélanger and Nina-Marie Lister at the Harvard Graduate School of Design in 2009.
4.10 LDA Design Seaford
4.11 Paul Street/Alamy Stock Photo
4.12 Richard Nowitz/Getty
4.13a–b Courtesy of the Design Trust for Public Space
4.14 Marcelo Rudini/Alamy Stock Photo
4.15 Alain Le Bot/Getty
4.16a–d Land Systems, courtesy of Damien Mugavin
4.17a CHOI JAE-KU/Getty
4.17b © ROUSSEL IMAGES/Alamy Stock Photo
4.18a–d Reed Hilderbrand
4.19 Heini Kettunen/Alamy Stock Photo
4.20 RWL /Getty
4.21a–h © Municipality Madrid
4.21i–j © Municipality Madrid
4.21k © West 8
4.22 CORBIS
4.23 © ICLEI – Local Governments for Sustainability, 2013
4.24a J Bewley/Sustrans
4.24b–c www.sustrans.org.uk
4.25a–b Photographer Ben Wrigley
4.26 All Canada Photos/Alamy Stock Photo
4.27a–d SEA
4.28 Joshua Zeunert
4.29a–b Bruel-Delmar
4.30 AFP/Getty
4.31 Photographer: John Gollings
4.32a Staff, Margie Ruddick Landscape
4.32b–d Sam Oberter
4.33a–d © Pacific Hydro Pty Ltd
4.34 © Agencja Fotograficzna Caro/Alamy Stock Photo
4.35 LDA Design Swansea Bay Tidal Lagoon – Lagoon Wall visualisation
4.36a–c BIG Architects
5.1 Hirz/Getty Images
5.2 Reproduced from *Leberecht Migge, Die Wachsende Siedlung* (Stuttgart: Frankh'sche Verlagshandlung, 1932), 23
5.3 National Geographic Creative/Alamy
5.4 www.3000acres.org
5.5 Imagno/Getty
5.6a–d Turenscape
5.7 Keystone View Company/FPG/Archive Photos/Getty
5.8 MVRDV
5.9 TCL
5.10a–c Tom Fox/SWA
5.11a–b Btlle I Roig
5.12 Valery Rizzo/Alamy
5.13 Public Domain
5.14 Dan Mihai Pitea (Creative Commons)
5.15 JSquish (GNU Licence)
5.16 Antione Gyori/Sygma/Corbis
5.17 Rick Strange/Alamy
5.18 Photograph by Estelle Brown
5.19a–b © Municipality Madrid
5.19c © West 8
5.20a Photograph by Hedrich Blessing. Courtesy of John Ronan
5.20b Photograph by Jasmin Shah. Courtesy of John Ronan
5.21 Photographer Robert Frith of Acorn Photography. Image Courtesy of Josh Byrne & Associates
5.22a–c Hagenbuch Weikal Landscape Architecture
5.23a–b Designed and produced by Wayward. Photos © Mike Massaro.
6.1 Armin Walcher
6.2 Paul Klee (Public Domain)
6.3 Rebar
6.4 John McGrail/The LIFE Images Collection/Getty
6.5a Ian Hobbs
6.5b Adelaide Biennale
6.6a–b Images courtesy of the artist and Tolarno Galleries, Melbourne
6.7 Armin Walcher
6.8a–b © West 8

6.9 © West 8
6.10a–b McGregor Coxall
6.11 Martha Schwartz Partners
6.12 UWA Publishing
6.13 Photograph by Simon Wood
6.14 Asher Durand (Public Domain)
6.15a TCL
6.15b–c John Gollings
6.15d Peter Hyatt
6.15e John Gollings
7.1 Courtesy of Studiofink
7.2 jardinimages/Alamy
7.3a–e © James Corner Field Operations with FABRICations
7.4 Torsodog (Creative Commons)
7.5a–b Tom Fox/SWA
7.6a Richard Gale, Gale Force Photography
7.6b Jody D'Arcy
7.6c PLAN E
7.7a © Megan Jett/meganjett.com/@mmjett
7.7b–c Photographs by Beau Beza
7.8 imageBROKER/Alamy
7.9 LOOK Die Bildagentur der Fotografen GmbH/Alamy
7.10 Alberto Paredes/Alamy
7.11a Jonney Davis
7.11b–d Simon Devitt
7.12a Graeme Peacock/Alamy
7.12b S.Forster/Alamy
7.13a–d Hertha Hurnaus
7.14 McGregor Coxall
7.15a–b © City of Salisbury
7.16 Courtesy of Studiofink
7.17 GETTY
7.18 ALAMY
7.19 Xinhua/Alamy
7.20c–f Image courtesy of North Sydney Heritage Centre, Stanton Library. Photographer: Cameron Sparks
7.19b Image courtesy of Noel Mannering, Stanton Library
7.19c–f Image courtesy of North Sydney Council. Photographer: Nathaneal Hughes
7.21a–b The Eden Project
7.21c Emily Whitfield-Wicks/The Eden Project
7.22 Photo by Bernard Jacobs, FASLA
7.23 Emily Hughes
7.24 Justin Kase zsixz/Alamy
7.25a Dianna Snape
7.25b Christian Borchert
7.26 John Gollings
7.27 The Therapeutic Landscapes Network
7.28a–b Image courtesy of Reed Hilderbrand
7.29a–b Image courtesy of Bill Timmerman
7.30a–b Images courtesy of CPG Consultants
7.31 © 2014 Land Collective/William Belcher
7.32 McGregor Coxall
7.33 City of Vancouver
8.1 Bill Timmerman
8.2a, 8.2b and 8.d TCL
8.2c Emily Taylor
8.3 Joshua Zeunert
8.4a, 8.4d Christine Tem Eyck
8.4b, 8.4c Bill Timmerman
8.5 Guy Wilkinson
8.6 Reed Hilderbrand
8.7a–e TCL
8.8 © West 8
8.9a–c The Crosby Arboretum/Lynn Crosby Gammill
8.10 Peter Titmuss/Getty
8.11a–d MVVA
8.12a–b Courtesy of the Design Trust for Public Space
8.13a Sarah Yu
8.13b Yawuru Registered Native Title Body Corporate
8.14a–b Ben Wrigley
8.15a–b Mersey Basin Campaign
8.16a–b Reed Hilderbrand
8.17a Alex MacLean
8.17b Charles Mayer
8.17c Reed Hilderbrand
8.17d James Ewing
9.1 USGBC, US Green Building Council, used with permission
9.2a USGBC, US Green Building Council, used with permission
9.2c USGBC, US Green Building Council, used with permission
9.3a © Paul G. Wiegman
9.3b © Annie O'Neill
9.3c Phipps Conservatory and Botanical Gardens
9.4a, 9.4b, 9.4e Reed Hilderbrand
9.4c, 9.4d James Ewing
9.5 Sam Oberter
9.6 Gerhard Joren/Getty
9.7 Dean Carman/Casagrande Laboratory
9.8 Prsima Bildagentur AG/Alamy
9.9a Brett Boardman
9.9b McGregor Coxall
9.9c Christian Borchert
9.9d McGregor Coxall
9.9e McGregor Coxall
9.9f Christan Borchert
9.9 ALAMY
9.10 PATRIK STOLLARZ/AFP/Getty
9.11 Marion Kaplan/Alamy
9.12 wareham.nl (Algemene Nieuws)/Alamy
10.1 Luc Schuiten (www.vegetalcity.net)
10.2 © City of Salisbury
10.3 Sam Orberter
10.4 © Nick Dunn, Paul Cureton & Serena Pollastri, 2014
10.5 based on David Holmgren, Future Scenarios
10.6a–d Prepared under the direction of Paul Downton ©
10.7a © Transition Network/www.transitionnetwork.org
10.7b © Transition Network/Artist Jennifer Johnson/www.transitionnetwork.org
10.7c © Transition Network/www.transitionnetwork.org
10.8a–b McGregor Coxall
10.9 Reed Hilderbrand
10.10 Turenscape
10.11 NBWLA/David Lepage
10.12 Turenscape
10.13 imageBROKER/Alamy
10.14 Guillaume Paradis
10.15 Photographer Jens Sundheim
10.16 Martí Franch and Pau Ardèvol, EMF.